THE COMPLETE WORKS OF ROBERT BROWNING, VOLUME XV

This volume is dedicated to the memory of Paul D. L. Turner (1917–2005).

Portrait of Robert Browning by Robert Wiedemann Barrett Browning, 1882.
Courtesy of Armstrong Browning Library.

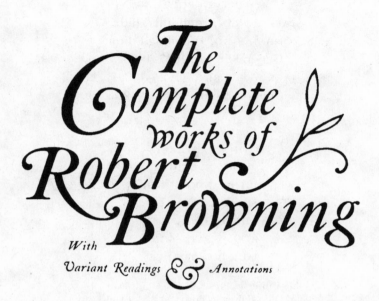

The Complete works of Robert Browning

With Variant Readings & Annotations

Volume XV

EDITED BY

ALLAN C. DOOLEY
DAVID EWBANK

OHIO UNIVERSITY PRESS
ATHENS, OHIO
BAYLOR UNIVERSITY
WACO, TEXAS
2007

THE COMPLETE WORKS OF ROBERT BROWNING

Editorial Board

ALLAN C. DOOLEY, General Editor

SUSAN CROWL

PARK HONAN, Founding Editor

ROMA A. KING, Founding Editor
General Editor, 1967–1985

JACK W. HERRING (1925–1999)
General Editor, 1985–1999

Contributing Editors

JOHN C. BERKEY

MICHAEL BRIGHT

ASHBY BLAND CROWDER

SUSAN E. DOOLEY

DAVID EWBANK

RITA S. PATTESON

PAUL D.L. TURNER

Ohio University Press, Athens, Ohio 45701
© 2007 by Ohio University Press and Baylor University
Printed in the United States of America
All rights reserved

14 13 12 11 10 09 08 07   5 4 3 2 1

Ohio University Press books are printed on acid-free paper ∞™

Portrait of Robert Browning in 1882 by his son, Robert Wiedemann Barrett Browning.
Courtesy of the Armstrong Browning Library.

Library of Congress Cataloging-in-Publication data

Browning, Robert, 1812–1889.
The complete works of Robert Browning, with variant readings & annotations.

Vol. 15 edited by Allan C. Dooley
and David Ewbank.
Includes bibliographical references and indexes.
I. King, Roma A., 1914–   , ed.
II. Title.
PR4201.K5 1969 821'.8   68-18389
ISBN-10 0-8214-1727-4 (v. 15)
ISBN-13 978-0-8214-1727-0 (v. 15)

CONTENTS

Contents

I CONTENTS

This edition of the works of Robert Browning is intended to be complete. It will comprise at least seventeen volumes and will contain:

1. The entire contents of the first editions of Browning's works, arranged in their chronological order of publication. (The poems included in *Dramatic Lyrics, Dramatic Romances and Lyrics,* and *Men and Women,* for example, appear in the order of their first publication rather than in the order in which Browning rearranged them for later publication.)

2. All prefaces and dedications which Browning is known to have written for his own works and for those of Elizabeth Barrett Browning.

3. The two prose essays that Browning is known to have published: the review of a book on Tasso, generally referred to as the "Essay on Chatterton," and the preface for a collection of letters supposed to have been written by Percy Bysshe Shelley, generally referred to as the "Essay on Shelley."

4. The front matter and the table of contents of each of the collected editions (1849, 1863, 1865, 1868 [70, 75], 1888-1889) which Browning himself saw through the press.

5. Poems published during Browning's lifetime but not collected by him.

6. Poems not published during Browning's lifetime which have come to light since his death.

7. John Forster's *Thomas Wentworth, Earl of Strafford,* to which Browning contributed significantly, though the precise extent of his contribution has not been determined.

8. Variants appearing in primary and secondary materials as defined in Section II below.

9. Textual emendations.

10. Informational and explanatory notes for each work.

II PRIMARY AND SECONDARY MATERIALS

Aside from a handful of uncollected short works, all of Browning's works but *Asolando* (1889) went through two or more editions during his lifetime. Except for *Pauline* (1833), *Strafford* (1837), and *Sordello*

(1840), all the works published before 1849 were revised and corrected for the 1849 collection. *Strafford* and *Sordello* were revised and corrected for the collection of 1863, as were all the other works in that edition. Though no further poems were added in the collection of 1865, all the works were once again corrected and revised. The 1868 collection added a revised *Pauline* and *Dramatis Personae* (1864) to the other works, which were themselves again revised and corrected. A new edition of this collection in 1870 contained further revisions, and Browning corrected his text again for an 1875 reimpression. The printing of the last edition of the *Poetical Works* over which Browning exercised control began in 1888, and the first eight volumes are dated thus on their title-pages. Volumes 9 through 16 of this first impression are dated 1889, and we have designated them 1889a to distinguish them from the second impression of all 16 volumes, which was begun and completed in 1889. Some of the earlier volumes of the first impression sold out almost immediately, and in preparation for a second impression, Browning revised and corrected the first ten volumes before he left for Italy in late August,1889. The second impression, in which all sixteen volumes bear the date 1889 on their title-pages, consisted of a revised and corrected second impression of volumes 1-10, plus a second impression of volumes 11-16 altered by Browning in one instance. This impression we term 1889 (see section III below).

Existing manuscripts and editions are classified as either primary or secondary material. The primary materials include the following:

1. The manuscript of a work when such is known to exist.

2. Proof sheets, when known to exist, that contain authorial corrections and revisions.

3. The first and subsequent editions of a work that preserve evidence of Browning's intentions and were under his control.

4. The collected editions over which Browning exercised control:

1849—*Poems.* Two Volumes. London: Chapman and Hall.

1863—*The Poetical Works.* Three Volumes. London: Chapman and Hall.

1865—*The Poetical Works.* Three Volumes. London: Chapman and Hall.

1868—*The Poetical Works.* Six Volumes. London: Smith, Elder and Company.

1870—*The Poetical Works.* Six Volumes. London: Smith, Elder and Company. This resetting constituted a new edition, which was stereotyped and reimpressed several times; the 1875 impression contains revisions by Browning.

1888-1889—*The Poetical Works.* Sixteen Volumes. London: Smith,

Elder and Company. Exists in numerous stereotype impressions, of which two are primary material:

1888-1889a—The first impression, in which volumes 1-8 are dated 1888 and volumes 9-16 are dated 1889.

1889—The corrected second impression of volumes 1-10 and a second impression of volumes 11-16 altered by Browning only as stated in section III below; all dated 1889 on the title pages.

5. The corrections in Browning's hand in the Dykes Campbell copy of 1888-1889a, and the manuscript list of corrections to that impression in the Brown University Library (see section III below).

Other materials (including some in the poet's handwriting) that affected the text are secondary. Examples are: the copy of the first edition of *Pauline* which contains annotations by Browning and John Stuart Mill; the copies of the first edition of *Paracelsus* which contain corrections in Browning's hand; a very early manuscript of *A Blot in the 'Scutcheon* which Browning presented to William Macready, but not the one from which the first edition was printed; informal lists of corrections that Browning included in letters to friends, such as the corrections to *Men and Women* he sent to D. G. Rossetti; verbal and punctuational changes Browning essayed in presentation copies of his works or in his own copies, if not used by his printers; Elizabeth Barrett's suggestions for revisions in *A Soul's Tragedy* and certain poems in *Dramatic Romances and Lyrics;* and the edition of *Strafford* by Emily Hickey for which Browning made suggestions.

The text and variant readings of this edition derive from collation of primary materials as defined above. Secondary materials are occasionally discussed in the notes and sometimes play a part when emendation is required.

III COPY-TEXT

The copy-text for this edition is Browning's final text: the first ten volumes of 1889 and the last six volumes of 1888-1889a, as described above. For this choice we offer the following explanation.

Manuscripts used as printer's copy for twenty of Browning's thirty-four book publications are known to exist; others may yet become available. These manuscripts, or, in their absence, the first editions of the works, might be considered as the most desirable copy-text. And this would be the case for an author who exercised little control over his text after the manuscript or first edition stage, or whose text clearly became corrupted in a succession of editions. To preserve the intention of such an author, one would have to choose an early text and emend it as evidence and judgment demanded.

With Browning, however, the situation is different, and our copy-text choice results from that difference. Throughout his life Browning continually revised his poetry. He did more than correct printer's errors and clarify previously intended meanings; his texts themselves remained fluid, subject to continuous alteration. As the manuscript which he submitted to his publisher was no doubt already a product of revision, so each subsequent edition under his control reflects the results of an ongoing process of creating, revising, and correcting. If we were to choose the manuscript (where extant) or first edition as copytext, preserving Browning's intention would require extensive emendation to capture the additions, revisions, and alterations which Browning demonstrably made in later editions. By selecting Browning's final corrected text as our copy-text, emending it only to eliminate errors and the consequences of changing house-styling, we present his works in the form closest to that which he intended after years of revision and polishing.

But this is true only if Browning in fact exercised extensive control over the printing of his various editions. That he intended and attempted to do so is apparent in his comments and his practice. In 1855, demanding accuracy from the printers, he pointed out to his publisher Chapman, "I attach importance to the mere stops . . ." (DeVane and Knickerbocker, p. 83). There is evidence of his desire to control the details of his text as early as 1835, in the case of *Paracelsus*. The *Paracelsus* manuscript, now in the Forster and Dyce collection in the Victoria and Albert Museum Library, demonstrates a highly unconventional system of punctuation. Of particular note is Browning's unrestrained use of dashes, often in strings of two or three, instead of more precise or orthodox punctuation marks. It appears that this was done for its rhetorical effect. One sheet of Part 1 of the manuscript and all but the first and last sheets of Part 3 have had punctuation revised in pencil by someone other than Browning, perhaps J. Riggs, whose name appears three times in the margins of Part 3. In addition to these revisions, there are analogous punctuation revisions (in both pencil and ink) which appear to be in Browning's hand, and a few verbal alterations obviously in the poet's script.

A collation of the first edition (1835) with the manuscript reveals that a major restyling of punctuation was carried out before *Paracelsus* was published. However, the revisions incorporated into the first edition by no means slavishly follow the example set by the pencilled revisions of Parts 1 and 3 of the manuscript. Apparently the surviving manuscript was not used as printer's copy for the first edition. Browning may have submitted a second manuscript, or he may have revised extensively in proof. The printers may have carried out the revisions to punctuation, with or without the poet's point by point involvement. With the present evidence, we cannot be conclusive about the extent of Browning's control over the first edition of *Paracelsus.* It can be stated, however, in the light of the incompleteness of the pencilled revisions and the frequent lack or correspondence between the pencilled revisions and the lines as printed in 1835, that Browning himself may have been responsible for the punctuation of the first edition of *Paracelsus.* Certainly he was responsible for the frequent instances in the first and subsequent editions where the punctuation defies conventional rules, as in the following examples:

> What though
> It be so?—if indeed the strong desire
> Eclipse the aim in me—if splendour break
> (Part I, ll. 329-331)

> I surely loved them—that last night, at least,
> When we . . . gone! gone! the better: I am saved
> (Part II, ll. 132-133)

> Of the body, even,)—what God is, what we are,
> (Part V, l. 642, 1849 reading)

The manuscripts of *Colombe's Birthday* (1844) and *Christmas-Eve and Easter-Day* (1850) were followed very carefully in the printing of the first editions. There are slight indications of minor house-styling, such as the spellings *colour* and *honour* for the manuscripts' *color* and *honor.* But the unorthodox punctuation, used to indicate elocutionary and rhetorical subtleties as well as syntactical relationships, is carried over almost unaltered from the manuscripts to the first editions. Similar evidence of Browning's painstaking attention to the smallest details in the printing of his poems can be seen in the manuscript and proof sheets of *The Ring and the Book* (1868-69). These materials reveal an interesting and significant pattern. It appears that Browning wrote swiftly, giving primary attention to wording and less to punctuation, being satisfied to use dashes to indicate almost any break in thought, syntax, or rhythm. Later, in the proof sheets for Books 1-6 of the poem and in the manuscript itself for Books 7-12, he changed the dashes to more specific and purposeful punctuation marks. The revised punctuation is what was printed, for the most part, in the first edition of *The Ring and the Book*; what further revisions there are conform to Browning's practice, though hardly to standard rules. Clearly Browning was in control of nearly every aspect of the published form of his works, even to the "mere stops."

Of still greater importance in our choice of copy-text is the substantial evidence that Browning took similar care with his collected editions. Though he characterized his changes for later editions as trivial and few in number, collations reveal thousands of revisions and corrections in each successive text. *Paracelsus,* for example, was extensively revised for the 1849 *Poems;* it was again reworked for the *Poetical Works* of 1863. *Sordello,* omitted in 1849, reappeared in 1863 with 181 new lines and short marginal glosses; Browning admitted only that it was "corrected *throughout*" (DeVane and Knickerbocker, p. 157). The poems of *Men and Women* (1855) were altered in numerous small but meaningful ways for both the 1863 and 1865 editions of the *Poetical Works* (see Allan C. Dooley, "The Textual Significance of Robert Browning's 1865 *Poetical Works,*" *PBSA* 71 [1977], 212-18). Michael Hancher cites evidence of the poet's close supervision of the 1868 collected edition ("Browning and the *Poetical Works* of 1888-1889," *Browning Newsletter,* Spring, 1971, 25-27), and Michael Meredith has traced Browning's attentions to his text in the 1870 edition and an 1875 reimpression of it ("Learning's Crabbed Text," *SBHC* 13 [1985], 97-107); another perspective is offered in Allan C. Dooley's *Author and Printer in Victorian England* (1992), Ch. 4-5. Mrs. Orr, writing of the same period in Browning's life, reports his resentment of those who garbled his text by misplacing his stops (*Life,* pp. 357-58).

There is plentiful and irrefutable evidence that Browning controlled, in the same meticulous way, the text of his last collected edition, that which we term 1888-1889. Hancher has summarized the relevant information:

The evidence is clear that Browning undertook the 1888-1889 edition of his *Poetical Works* intent on controlling even the smallest minutiae of the text. Though he at one time considered supplying biographical and explanatory notes to the poems, he finally decided against such a scheme, concluding, in his letter to Smith of 12 November 1887, "I am correcting them carefully, and *that* must suffice." On 13 January 1888, he wrote, regarding the six-volume edition of his collected works published in 1868 which was to serve as the printer's copy for the final edition: "I have thoroughly corrected the six volumes of the Works, and can let you have them at once." . . . Browning evidently kept a sharp eye on the production of all sixteen of the volumes, including those later volumes. . . . Browning returned proof for Volume 3 on 6 May 1888, commenting, "I have had, as usual, to congratulate myself on the scrupulous accuracy of the Printers"; on 31 December he returned proofs of Volume 11, "corrected carefully"; and he returned "the corrected Proofs of Vol. XV" on 1 May 1889.

Throughout his long career, then, Browning continuously revised and corrected his works. Furthermore, his publishers took care to follow his directions exactly, accepting his changes and incorporating them into each successive edition. This is not to say that no one else had any effect whatsoever on Browning's text: Elizabeth Barrett made suggestions for revisions to *A Soul's Tragedy* and *Dramatic Romances and Lyrics*. Browning accepted some suggestions and rejected others, and those which he accepted we regard as his own. Mrs. Orr reports that Browning sent proof sheets to Joseph Milsand, a friend in France, for corrections (*Life*, p. 183), and that Browning accepted suggestions from friends and readers for the corrections of errors in his printed works. In some of the editions, there are slight evidences of minor housestyling in capitalization and the indication of quotations. But the evidence of Browning's own careful attention to revisions and corrections in both his manuscripts and proof sheets assures us that other persons played only a very minor role in the development of his text. We conclude that the vast majority of the alterations in the texts listed above as Primary Materials are Browning's own, and that only Browning's final corrected text, the result of years of careful work by the poet himself, reflects his full intentions.

The first impression of Browning's final collected edition (i.e., 1888-1889a) is not in and of itself the poet's final corrected text. By the spring of 1889 some of the early volumes of the first impression were already sold out, and by mid-August it was evident that a new one would be required. About this time James Dykes Campbell, Honorary Secretary of the London Browning Society, was informed by Browning that he was making further corrections to be incorporated into the new impression. According to Dykes Campbell, Browning had corrected the first ten volumes and offered to transcribe the corrections into Dykes Campbell's copy of 1888-1889a before leaving for Italy. The volumes altered in Browning's hand are now in the British Library and contain on the flyleaf of Volume I Dykes Campbell's note explaining precisely what happened. Of course, Dykes Campbell's copy was not the one used by the printer for the second impression. Nevertheless, these changes are indisputably Browning's and are those which, according to his own statement, he proposed to make in the new impression. This set of corrections carries, therefore, great authority.

Equally authoritative is a second set of corrections, also in Browning's hand, for part of 1888-1889a. In the poet's possession at the time of his death, this handwritten list was included in lot 179 of Sotheby, Wilkinson, and Hodge's auction of Browning materials in 1913; it is today located in the Brown University Library. The list contains corrections only to Volumes 4-10 of 1888-1889a. We know that Browning, on 26 July 1889, had completed and sent to Smith "the corrections for Vol. III in readiness for whenever you need them." By the latter part of August, according to Dykes Campbell, the poet had finished corrections for Volumes 1-10. Browning left for Italy on 29 August. The condition of the Brown University list does not indicate that it was ever used by the printer. Thus we surmise that the Brown list (completing the corrections through volume 10) may be the poet's copy of another list sent to his publisher. Whatever the case, the actual documents used by the printers—a set of marked volumes or handwritten lists—are not known to exist. A possible exception is a marked copy of *Red Cotton Night-Cap Country* (now in the Berg Collection of the New York Public Library) which seems to have been used by printers. Further materials used in preparing Browning's final edition may yet appear.

The matter is complicated further because neither set of corrections of 1888-1889a corresponds exactly to each other nor to the 1889 second impression. Each set contains corrections the other omits, and in a few cases the sets present alternative corrections of the same error. Our study of the Dykes Campbell copy of 1888-1889a reveals fifteen discrepancies between its corrections and the 1889 second impression. The Brown University list, which contains far fewer corrections, varies from the second impression in thirteen instances. Though neither of these sets of corrections was used by the printers, both are authoritative; we consider them legitimate textual variants, and record them as such. The lists are, of course, useful when emendation of the copy-text is required.

The value of the Dykes Campbell copy of 1888-1889a and the Brown University list is not that they render Browning's text perfect. The corrections to 1888-1889a must have existed in at least one other, still more authoritative form: the documents which Browning sent to his publisher. That this is so is indicated by the presence of required corrections in the second impression which neither the Dykes Campbell copy nor the Brown University list calls for. The significance of the existing sets of corrections is that they clearly indicate two important points: Browning's direct and active interest in the preparation of a corrected second impression of his final collected edition; and, given the high degree of correspondence between the two sets of corrections and the affected lines of the second impression, the concern of the printers to follow the poet's directives.

The second impression of 1888-1889 incorporated most of Browning's corrections to the first ten volumes of the first impression. There is no evidence whatever that any corrections beyond those which Browning sent to his publisher in the summer of 1889 were ever made. We choose, therefore, the 1889 corrected second impression of volumes 1-10 as copy-text for the works in those volumes. Corrections to the first impression were achieved by cutting the affected letters or punctuation out of the stereotype plates and pressing or soldering in the correct pieces of type. The corrected plates were then used for many copies, without changing the date on the title pages (except, of course, in volumes 17 [*Asolando*] and 18 [*New Poems*], added to the set by the publishers in 1894 and 1914 respectively). External evidence from publishers' catalogues and the advertisements bound into some volumes of 1889 indicate that copies of this impression were produced as late as 1913, although the dates on the title pages of volumes 1-16 remained 1889. Extensive plate deterioration is characteristic of the later copies, and use of the Hinman collator on early and late examples of 1889 reveals that the inserted corrections were somewhat fragile, some of them having decayed or disappeared entirely as the plates aged. (See Allan C. Dooley, "Browning's *Poetical Works* of 1888-1889," *SBHC* 7:1 [1978], 43-69.)

We do not use as copy-text volumes 11-16 of 1889, because there is no present evidence indicating that Browning exercised substantial control over this part of the second impression of 1888-1889. We do know that he made one correction, which he requested in a letter to Smith quoted by Hancher:

> I have just had pointed out to [me] that an error, I supposed corrected, still is to be found in the 13th Volume—(Aristophanes' Apology) page 143, line 9, where the word should be Opora—without an i. I should like it altered, if that may be possible.

This correction was indeed made in the second impression. Our collations of copies of volumes 11-16 of 1889a and 1889 show no other intentional changes. The later copies do show, however, extensive type batter, numerous scratches, and irregular inking. Therefore our copy-text for the works in the last six volumes of 1888-1889 is volumes 11-16 of 1888-1889a.

IV VARIANTS

In this edition we record, with a very few exceptions discussed below, all variants from the copy-text appearing in the manuscripts and in the editions under Browning's control. Our purpose in doing this is two-fold.

1. We enable the reader to reconstruct the text of a work as it stood at the various stages of its development.

2. We provide the materials necessary to an understanding of how Browning's growth and development as an artist are reflected in his successive revisions to his works.

As a consequence of this policy our variant listings inevitably contain some variants that were not created by Browning; printer's errors and readings that may result from house-styling will appear occasionally. But the evidence that Browning assumed responsibility for what was printed, and that he considered and used unorthodox punctuation as part of his meaning, is so persuasive that we must record even the smallest and oddest variants. The following examples, characteristic of Browning's revisions, illustrate the point:

> *Pauline,* l. 700:
>> 1833: I am prepared—I have made life my own—
>> 1868: I am prepared: I have made life my own.
> "Evelyn Hope," l. 41:
>> 1855: I have lived, I shall say, so much since then,
>> 1865: I have lived (I shall say) so much since then,
> "Bishop Blougram's Apology," l. 267:
>> 1855: That's the first cabin-comfort I secure—
>> 1865: That's the first-cabin comfort I secure:
> *The Ring and the Book,* Book 11 ("Guido"), l. 1064:
>> 1869: What if you give up boys' and girls' fools'-play
>> 1872: What if you give up boy and girl fools'-play
>> 1889a: What if you give up boy-and-girl-fools' play

We have concluded that Browning himself is nearly always responsible for such changes. But even if he only accepted these changes (rather than originating them), their effect on syntax, rhythm, and meaning is so significant that they must be recorded in our variant listings.

The only variants we do not record are those which strongly appear to result from systematic house-styling. For example, Browning nowhere indicated that he wished to use typography to influence meaning, and our inference is that any changes in line-spacing, depth of paragraph indentation, and the like, were the responsibility of the printers of the various editions, not the poet himself. House-styling was also very probably the cause of certain variants in the apparatus of Browning's plays, including variants in stage directions which involve a change only in manner of statement, such as *Enter Hampden* instead of

Hampden enters; variants in the printing of stage directions, such as *Aside* instead of *aside,* or [*Aside.*] instead of [*Aside*], or [*Strafford.*] instead of [*Strafford*]; variants in character designations, such as *Lady Carlisle* instead of *Car* or *Carlisle.* Browning also accepted current convention for indicating quotations (see section V below). Neither do we list changes in type face (except when used for emphasis), nor the presence or absence of a period at the end of the title of a work.

V ALTERATIONS TO THE COPY-TEXT

We have rearranged the sequence of works in the copy-text, so that they appear in the order of their first publication. This process involves the restoration to the original order of the poems included in *Dramatic Lyrics, Dramatic Romances and Lyrics,* and *Men and Women.* We realize, of course, that Browning himself was responsible for the rearrangement of these poems in the various collected editions; in his prefatory note for the 1888-1889 edition, however, he indicates that he desired a chronological presentation:

> The poems that follow are again, as before, printed in chronological order; but only so far as proves compatible with the prescribed size of each volume, which necessitates an occasional change in the distribution of its contents.

We would like both to indicate Browning's stated intentions about the placement of his poems and to present the poems in the order which suggests Browning's development as a poet. We have chosen, therefore, to present the poems in order of their first publication, with an indication in the notes as to their respective subsequent placement. We also include the tables of contents of the editions listed as Primary Materials above.

We have regularized or modernized the copy-text in the following minor ways:

1. We do not place a period at the end of the title of a work, though the copy-text does.

2. In some of Browning's editions, including the copy-text, the first word of each work is printed in capital letters. We have used the modern practice of capitalizing only the first letter.

3. The inconsistent use of both an ampersand and the word *and* has been regularized to the use of *and.*

4. We have eliminated the space between the two parts of a contraction; thus the copy-text's *it 's* is printed as *it's,* for example.

5. We uniformly place periods and commas within closing quotation marks.

6. We have employed throughout the modern practice of indicating quoted passages with quotation marks only at the beginning and end of the quotation. Throughout Browning's career, no matter which publisher or printer was handling his works, this matter was treated very inconsistently. In some of the poet's manuscripts and in most of his first editions, quotations are indicated by quotation marks only at the beginning and end. In the collected editions of 1863 and 1865, issued by Chapman and Hall, some quoted passages have quotation marks at the beginning of each line of the quotation, while others follow modern practice. In Smith, Elder's collected editions of 1868 and 1888-1889, quotation marks usually appear at the beginning of each line of a quotation. We have regularized and modernized what seems a matter of house-styling in both copy-text and variants.

The remaining way in which the copy-text is altered is by emendation. Our policy is to emend the copy-text to eliminate apparent errors of either Browning or his printers. It is evident that Browning did make errors and overlook mistakes, as shown by the following example from "One Word More," the last poem in *Men and Women*. Stanza sixteen of the copy-text opens with the following lines:

> What, there's nothing in the moon noteworthy?
> Nay: for if that moon could love a mortal,
> Use, to charm him (so to fit a fancy,
> All her magic ('tis the old sweet mythos)
> She . . .

Clearly the end punctuation in the third line is incorrect. A study of the various texts is illuminating. Following are the readings of the line in each of the editions for which Browning was responsible:

MS:	fancy)	1855:	fancy)	1865:	fancy)	1888:	fancy
P:	fancy)	1863:	fancy)	1868:	fancy)	1889:	fancy,

The omission of one parenthesis in 1888 was almost certainly a printer's error. Browning, in the Dykes Campbell copy corrections to 1888-1889a, missed or ignored the error. However, in the Brown University list of corrections, he indicated that *fancy* should be followed by a comma. This is the way the line appears in the corrected second impression of Volume 4, but the correction at best satisfies the demands of syntax only partially. Browning might have written the line:

> Use, to charm him, so to fit a fancy,

or, to maintain parallelism between the third and fourth lines:

> Use, to charm him (so to fit a fancy),

or he might simply have restored the earlier reading. Oversights of this nature demand emendation, and our choice would be to restore the punctuation of the manuscript through 1868. All of our emendations will be based, as far as possible, on the historical collation of the passage involved, the grammatical demands of the passage in context, and the poet's treatment of other similar passages. Fortunately, the multiple editions of most of the works provide the editor with ample textual evidence to make an informed and useful emendation.

All emendations to the copy-text are listed at the beginning of the Editorial Notes for each work. The variant listings for the copy-text also incorporate the emendations, which are preceded and followed there by the symbol indicating an editor's note.

VI APPARATUS

1. *Variants.* In presenting the variants from the copy-text, we list at the bottom of each page readings from the known manuscripts, proof sheets of the editions when we have located them, and the first and subsequent editions.

A variant is generally preceded and followed by a pickup and a drop word (example a). No note terminates with a punctuation mark unless the punctuation mark comes at the end of the line; if a variant drops or adds a punctuation mark, the next word is added (example b). If the normal pickup word has appeared previously in the same line, the note begins with the word preceding it. If the normal drop word appears subsequently in the line, the next word is added (example c). If a capitalized pickup word occurs within the line, it is accompanied by the preceding word (example d). No pickup or drop words, however, are used for any variant consisting of an internal change, for example a hyphen in a compounded word, an apostrophe, a tense change or a spelling change (example e). A change in capitalization within a line of poetry will be preceded by a pickup word, for which, within an entry containing other variants, the < > is suitable (example f). No drop word is used when the variant comes at the end of a line (example g).

a.   [611]| *1840:*but that appeared   *1863:*but this appeared

b.   variant at end of line: [109]| *1840:*intrigue:"   *1863:*intrigue.
variant within line: [82]| *1840:*forests like   *1863:*forests, like

c.   [132]| *1840:*too sleeps; but   *1863:*too sleeps: but   [77]| *1840:*that night
by   *1863:*that, night by night,   *1888:*by night

d.   [295]| *1840:*at Padua to repulse the   *1863:*at Padua who repulsed the

e.   [284]| *1840:*are   *1863:*were
[344]| *1840:*dying-day,   *1863:*dying day,

f.   capitalization change with no other variants: [741]| *1840:*
retaining Will,   *1863:*will,
with other variants: [843]| *1840:*Was < > Him back! Why   *1863:*Is
< > back!" Why   *1865:*him

g.   [427]| *1840:*dregs: *1863:*dregs.

Each recorded variant will be assumed to be incorporated in the next edition if there is no indication otherwise. This rule applies even in cases where the only change occurs in 1888-1889, although it means that the variant note duplicates the copy-text. A variant listing, then, traces the history of a line and brings it forward to the point where it matches the copy-text.

With regard to manuscript readings, our emphasis is on the textual development and sequence of revisions; visual details of the manuscripts are kept to a minimum. For economy of space, we use formulae such as §crossed out and replaced above by§, but these often cannot report fine details such as whether, when two words were crossed out, the accompanying punctuation was precisely cancelled also. Our MS entries provide enough information to reconstruct with reasonable accuracy B's initial and revised manuscript readings, but they cannot substitute for direct scrutiny of the documents themselves.

It should be noted that we omit drop words in manuscript entries where the final reading is identical to the printed editions—thus

MS:Silence, and all that ghastly §crossed out and replaced above by§ tinted pageant, base

Printed editions: Silence, and all that tinted pageant, base

is entered as

MS:that ghastly §crossed out and replaced above by§ tinted

in our variant listings.

An editor's note always refers to the single word or mark of punctuation immediately preceding or following the comment, unless otherwise specified.

In Browning's plays, all character designations which happen to occur in variant listings are standardized to the copy-text reading. In listing variants in the plays, we ignore character designations unless the designation comes within a numbered line. In such a case, the character designation is treated as any other word, and can be used as a pickup or drop word. When a character designation is used as a pickup word, however, the rule excluding capitalized pickup words (except at the beginning of a line) does not apply, and we do not revert to the next earliest uncapitalized pickup word.

2. *Line numbers.* Poetic lines are numbered in the traditional manner, taking one complete poetic line as one unit of counting. In prose passages the unit of counting is the type line of this edition.

3. *Table of signs in variant listings.* We have avoided all symbols and signs used by Browning himself. The following is a table of the signs used in the variant notes:

§ . . . §	Editor's note
< >	Words omitted
/	Line break
/ / , / / / , . . .	Line break plus one or more lines without internal variants

4 *Annotations.* In general principle, we have annotated proper names, phrases that function as proper names, and words or groups of words the full meaning of which requires factual, historical, or literary background. Thus we have attempted to hold interpretation to a minimum, although we realize that the act of selection itself is to some extent interpretive.

Notes, particularly on historical figures and events, tend to fullness and even to the tangential and unessential. As a result, some of the information provided may seem unnecessary to the scholar. On the other hand, it is not possible to assume that all who use this edition are fully equipped to assimilate unaided all of Browning's copious literary, historical, and mythological allusions. Thus we have directed our efforts toward a diverse audience.

TABLES

1. *Manuscripts.* We have located manuscripts for the following of Browning's works; the list is chronological.

Preface

Paracelsus
    Forster and Dyce Collection,
    Victoria and Albert Museum, London
Colombe's Birthday
    New York Public Library
Christmas-Eve and Easter-Day
    Forster and Dyce Collection,
    Victoria and Albert Museum, London
"Love Among the Ruins"
    Lowell Collection,
    Houghton Library, Harvard University
"The Twins"
    Pierpont Morgan Library, New York
"One Word More"
    Pierpont Morgan Library, New York
"James Lee's Wife," ll. 244-69
    Armstrong Browning Library, Baylor University
"May and Death"
    Armstrong Browning Library, Baylor University
"A Face"
    Armstrong Browning Library, Baylor University
Dramatis Personae
    Pierpont Morgan Library, New York
The Ring and the Book
    British Library, London
Balaustion's Adventure
    Balliol College Library, Oxford
Prince Hohenstiel-Schwangau
    Balliol College Library, Oxford
Fifine at the Fair
    Balliol College Library, Oxford
Red Cotton Night-Cap Country
    Balliol College Library, Oxford
Aristophanes' Apology
    Balliol College Library, Oxford
The Inn Album
    Balliol College Library, Oxford
Of Pacchiarotto, and How He Worked in Distemper
    Balliol College Library, Oxford
"Hervé Riel"
    Pierpont Morgan Library, New York

The Agamemnon of Aeschylus
 Balliol College Library, Oxford
La Saisiaz and The Two Poets of Croisic
 Balliol College Library, Oxford
Dramatic Idylls
 Balliol College Library, Oxford
Dramatic Idylls, Second Series
 Balliol College Library, Oxford
Jocoseria
 Balliol College Library, Oxford
Ferishtah's Fancies
 Balliol College Library, Oxford
Parleyings With Certain People of Importance in Their Day
 Balliol College Library, Oxford
Asolando
 Pierpont Morgan Library, New York

We have been unable to locate manuscripts for the following works, and request that persons with information about any of them communicate with us.

Pauline	*The Return of the Druses*
Strafford	*A Blot in the 'Scutcheon*
Sordello	*Dramatic Romances and Lyrics*
Pippa Passes	*Luria*
King Victor and King Charles	*A Soul's Tragedy*
"Essay on Chatterton"	"Essay on Shelley"
Dramatic Lyrics	*Men and Women*

 2. *Editions referred to in Volume XV.* The following editions have been used in preparing the text and variants presented in this volume. The dates given below are used as symbols in the variant listings at the foot of each page.

  1880 *Dramatic Idyls, Second Series.*
      London: Smith, Elder and Company.

  1883 *Jocoseria.*
      First edition. London: Smith, Elder and Company.

  1883a *Jocoseria.*
      Second edition. London: Smith, Elder and Company.
      (second impression of 1883)

1884	*Ferishtah's Fancies.* First edition. London: Smith, Elder and Company.
1885	*Ferishtah's Fancies.* Second edition. London: Smith, Elder and Company. (corrected impression of 1884)
1885a	*Ferishtah's Fancies.* Third edition. London: Smith, Elder and Company. (corrected impression of 1885)
1889a	*The Poetical Works.* Volumes 9-16. London: Smith, Elder and Company.

3. *Short titles and abbreviations.* The following short forms of reference have been used in the Editorial Notes:

ABL	Armstrong Browning Library, Baylor University, Waco, TX
B	Browning
Broughton	L. N. Broughton, C. S. Northup, and R. Pearsall. *Robert Browning: A Bibliography, 1830-1950.* Ithaca, NY, 1953.
Curle	*Robert Browning and Julia Wedgewood,* ed. Richard Curle. New York, 1937.
Hebraism	Judith Berlin-Lieberman. *Robert Browning and Hebraism.* Jerusalem, 1934
DeVane and Knickerbocker	*New Letters of Robert Browning,* ed. W. C. DeVane and K. L. Knickerbocker. New Haven, CT, 1950.
Correspondence	*The Brownings' Correspondence,* ed. P. Kelley, R. Hudson, S. Lewis, and E. Hagen. Winfield, KS, 1984-.
DeVane, *Hbk.*	W. C. DeVane. *A Browning Handbook,* 2nd ed. New York, 1955.
EBB	Elizabeth Barrett Browning
Hood	*Letters of Robert Browning Collected by Thomas J. Wise,* ed. T. L. Hood. New Haven, CT, 1933.
Irvine and Honan	William Irvine and Park Honan. *The Book, the Ring, and the Poet.* New York, 1974.

Letters of EBB	*The Letters of Elizabeth Barrett Browning*, ed. F. G. Kenyon. New York, 1897.
Litzinger and Smalley	*Browning: the Critical Heritage*, ed. B. Litzinger and D. Smalley. London, 1970.
McAleer, *DI*	*Dearest Isa: Robert Browning's Letters to Isabella Blagden*, ed. E. C. McAleer. Austin, TX, 1951.
McAleer, *LL*	*Learned Lady: Letters from Robert Browning to Mrs. Thomas FitzGerald 1876-1889*, ed. E. C. McAleer. Cambridge, MA, 1966.
Meredith and Patteson	*More Than Friend: the Letters of Robert Browning to Katharine deKay Bronson*, ed. M. Meredith and R. Patteson. Winfield, KS, 1985.
OED	*The Oxford English Dictionary*, 2nd ed. Oxford, 1989.
Orr, *Hbk.*	Mrs. Sutherland Orr. *A Handbook to the Works of Robert Browning*. 6th ed. London, 1892.
Orr, *Life*	Mrs. Sutherland Orr. *Life and Letters of Robert Browning*. 2nd ed. London, 1891.
Peterson	*Browning's Trumpeter: the Correspondence of Robert Browning and Frederick J. Furnivall, 1872-1889*, ed. W. S. Peterson. Washington, D. C., 1979.
Reconstruction	*The Browning Collections, a Reconstruction, with Other Memorabilia*, comp. P. Kelley and B. A. Coley. Waco, TX; New York; Winfield, KS, and London, 1984.
Zimmern	Helen Zimmern. *The Epic of Kings: Stories Retold from Firdusi*. London, 1882.

Citations and quotations from the Bible refer to the King James Version unless otherwise specified.

Citations and quotations from Shakespeare refer to *The Riverside Shakespeare*, 2nd ed., ed. G. B. Evans, et al., Boston, 1997.

ACKNOWLEDGMENTS

For making available to us materials under their care we thank the Armstrong Browning Library and its Browning Database at Baylor University; the Balliol College Library, the Bodleian Library, and Sackler Library, all of Oxford University; the Carl H. Pforzheimer Library of the New York Public Library; Texas Christian University Library; the Widener Library of Harvard University.

For assistance in preparing this volume, we particularly thank the following: James Binns, Penelope Bulloch, John Day, Wadaa Fahel, Penny Herring Flood, Greg Grotyohann, Jacky Turner, and the staff of the Dare County Public Library.

DRAMATIC IDYLS, SECOND SERIES

Edited by David Ewbank

JOCOSERIA

Edited by Allan C. Dooley

FERISHTAH'S FANCIES

Edited by Allan C. Dooley

DRAMATIC IDYLS, SECOND SERIES

Edited by David Ewbank

DRAMATIC IDYLS, SECOND SERIES

"You are sick, that's sure"—they say:
    "Sick of what?"—they disagree.
" 'Tis the brain"—thinks Doctor A;
    " 'Tis the heart"—holds Doctor B;
⁵ "The liver—my life I'd lay!"
    "The lungs!" "The lights!"
                     Ah me!
    So ignorant of man's whole
Of bodily organs plain to see—
So sage and certain, frank and free,
¹⁰ About what's under lock and key—
    Man's soul!

"YOU ARE SICK"   ²| MS:disagree: *P1880:*disagree.   ³| MS:thinks Doctor A.,
*1889a:*thinks Doctor A.;   ⁴| MS:holds Doctor B.,   *1889a:*holds Doctor B;
⁶| MS:lights"! *P1880:*lights!"

DRAMATIC IDYLS, SECOND SERIES

1877

ECHETLOS

Here is a story shall stir you! Stand up, Greeks dead and gone,
Who breasted, beat Barbarians, stemmed Persia rolling on,
Did the deed and saved the world, for the day was Marathon!

No man but did his manliest, kept rank and fought away
5   In his tribe and file: up, back, out, down—was the spear-arm play:
Like a wind-whipt branchy wood, all spear-arms a-swing that day!

But one man kept no rank and his sole arm plied no spear,
As a flashing came and went, and a form i' the van, the rear,
Brightened the battle up, for he blazed now there, now here.

10   Nor helmed nor shielded, he! but, a goat-skin all his wear,
Like a tiller of the soil, with a clown's limbs broad and bare,
Went he ploughing on and on: he pushed with a ploughman's share.

Did the weak mid-line give way, as tunnies on whom the shark
Precipitates his bulk? Did the right-wing halt when, stark
15   On his heap of slain lay stretched Kallimachos Polemarch?

Did the steady phalanx falter? To the rescue, at the need,
The clown was ploughing Persia, clearing Greek earth of weed,
As he routed through the Sakian and rooted up the Mede.

DRAMATIC IDYLS,   SECOND SERIES   §MS in Balliol College Library, Oxford. Ed.
P1880, CP1880, 1880, 1889a. See Editorial Notes and Table of Editions§
ECHETLOS   ¹| MS:Here §over Hear§ is §inserted above§ a story, that §crossed out§
*1889a:*story shall   ³| MS:deed that §crossed out and replaced above by§ and < > world,
since the   *1889a:*world, for the   ⁷| MS:and a §crossed out and replaced above by§ his
¹⁶| MS:faulter   *1889a:*falter   ¹⁸| MS:he rooted up §last two words replaced by two words§
routed through < > and routed through §last two words replaced by two words§ rooted up

But the deed done, battle won,—nowhere to be descried
On the meadow, by the stream, at the marsh,—look far and wide
From the foot of the mountain, no, to the last blood-plashed
    seaside,—

Not anywhere on view blazed the large limbs thonged and brown,
Shearing and clearing still with the share before which—down
To the dust went Persia's pomp, as he ploughed for Greece, that
    clown!

How spake the Oracle? "Care for no name at all!
Say but just this: 'We praise one helpful whom we call
The Holder of the Ploughshare.' The great deed ne'er grows small."

Not the great name! Sing—woe for the great name Míltiadés
And its end at Paros isle! Woe for Themistokles
—Satrap in Sardis court! Name not the clown like these!

---

¹⁹| MS:the day §crossed out and replaced above by§ deed   ²¹| MS:sea-side,—
1889a: seaside,—   ²³| MS:Clearing and shearing §marked for transpositioon to§
Shearing and clearing   ²⁴| MS:went Persia's weed §crossed out and
replaced above by§ pomp   ²⁶| MS:this: We   *1889a:* this: 'We
²⁷| MS:the Ploughshare. The   *1889a:* the Ploughshare.' The

CLIVE

I and Clive were friends—and why not? Friends! I think you laugh, my
    lad.
Clive it was gave England India, while your father gives—egad,
England nothing but the graceless boy who lures him on to speak
"Well, Sir, you and Clive were comrades—" with a tongue thrust in
    your cheek!
5   Very true: in my eyes, your eyes, all the world's eyes, Clive was man,
I was, am and ever shall be—mouse, nay, mouse of all its clan
Sorriest sample, if you take the kitchen's estimate for fame;
While the man Clive—he fought Plassy, spoiled the clever foreign
    game,
Conquered and annexed and Englished!

                           Never mind! As o'er my punch
10   (You away) I sit of evenings,—silence, save for biscuit-crunch,
Black, unbroken,—thought grows busy, thrids each pathway of old
    years,
Notes this forthright, that meander, till the long-past life appears
Like an outspread map of country plodded through, each mile and
    rood,
Once, and well remembered still: I'm startled in my solitude
15   Ever and anon by—what's the sudden mocking light that breaks
On me as I slap the table till no rummer-glass but shakes
While I ask—aloud, I do believe, God help me!—"Was it thus?
Can it be that so I faltered, stopped when just one step for us—"
(Us,—you were not born, I grant, but surely some day born would be)
20   "—One bold step had gained a province" (figurative talk, you see)
"Got no end of wealth and honour,—yet I stood stock still no less?"
—"For I was not Clive," you comment: but it needs no Clive to guess
Wealth were handy, honour ticklish, did no writing on the wall

---

CLIVE   ⁷| MS:kitchen <> fame,   *P1880:*kitchen's <> fame;   ⁹| MS:annexed
and Englished! §¶ no line space§ Never   *1889a:*annexed and Englished! §¶ line space
added§ Never   ¹⁰| *P1880:*biscuit crunch   *1889a:*biscuit-crunch
¹⁴| MS:Once and   *P1880:*Once, and   ¹⁸| MS:faultered   *1889a:*faltered
²⁰| MS:—One   *P1880:*"—One   ²¹| MS:Got <> honor <> stock-still
P1880:"Got   *1880:*stock still   *1889a:*honour   ²²| MS:—For <> not Clive, you
P1880:—"For <> not Clive," you   ²³| MS:honor   *1889a:*honour

Warn me "Trespasser, 'ware man-traps!" Him who braves that
    notice—call

25   Hero! none of such heroics suit myself who read plain words,
Doff my hat, and leap no barrier. Scripture says the land's the Lord's:
Louts then—what avail the thousand, noisy in a smock-frocked ring,
All-agog to have me trespass, clear the fence, be Clive their king?
Higher warrant must you show me ere I set one foot before

30   T'other in that dark direction, though I stand for evermore
Poor as Job and meek as Moses. Evermore? No! By-and-by
Job grows rich and Moses valiant, Clive turns out less wise than I.
Don't object "Why call him friend, then?" Power is power, my boy, and
    still

Marks a man,—God's gift magnific, exercised for good or ill.

35   You've your boot now on my hearth-rug, tread what was a tiger's skin:
Rarely such a royal monster as I lodged the bullet in!
True, he murdered half a village, so his own death came to pass;
Still, for size and beauty, cunning, courage—ah, the brute he was!
Why, that Clive,—that youth, that greenhorn, that quill-driving clerk,
    in fine,—

40   He sustained a siege in Arcot . . . But the world knows! Pass the wine.

Where did I break off at? How bring Clive in? Oh, you mentioned
    "fear"!

Just so: and, said I, that minds me of a story you shall hear.

We were friends then, Clive and I: so, when the clouds, about the orb
Late supreme, encroaching slowly, surely, threatened to absorb

45   Ray by ray its noontide brilliance,—friendship might, with steadier eye
Drawing near, bear what had burned else, now no blaze—all majesty.
Too much bee's-wing floats my figure? Well, suppose a castle's new:
None presume to climb its ramparts, none find foothold sure for shoe

---

25| MS:Hero—none   *P1880:*Hero! none   26| *P1880:*says, the land's   *1889a:*says the
land's   27| MS:smock frocked   *P1880:*smock-frocked   28| MS:be Clive and king?
*P1880:*be Clive their king?   31| MS:as Moses. Evermore? No,—bye and bye
*P1880:*as Moses. Evermore? No! Bye   *1889a:*as Moses. Evermore? No! By-and-by
32| MS:Job may grow rich, Moses   *P1880:*Job grows rich and Moses
36| MS:lodged my bullet   *P1880:*lodged the bullet   40| MS:in Arcot . . But
*P1880:*in Arcot . . . But   45| MS:brilliance, friendship   *CP1880:*brilliance, §caret
inserted and dash added in margin§ —friendship   46| MS:blaze all   *1889a:*blaze—all

'Twixt those squares and squares of granite plating the impervious
　　　pile
50　As his scale-mail's warty iron cuirasses a crocodile.
Reels that castle thunder-smitten, storm-dismantled? From without
Scrambling up by crack and crevice, every cockney prates about
Towers—the heap he kicks now! turrets—just the measure of his
　　　cane!
Will that do? Observe moreover—(same similitude again)—
55　Such a castle seldom crumbles by sheer stress of cannonade:
'Tis when foes are foiled and fighting's finished that vile rains invade,
Grass o'ergrows, o'ergrows till night-birds congregating find no holes
Fit to build in like the topmost sockets made for banner-poles.
So Clive crumbled slow in London—crashed at last.

　　　　　　　　　　　　　　　　　　　　A week before,
60　Dining with him,—after trying churchyard-chat of days of yore,—
Both of us stopped, tired as tombstones, head-piece, foot-piece, when
　　　they lean
Each to other, drowsed in fog-smoke, o'er a coffined Past between.
As I saw his head sink heavy, guessed the soul's extinguishment
By the glazing eyeball, noticed how the furtive fingers went
65　Where a drug-box skulked behind the honest liquor,—"One more
　　　throw
Try for Clive!" thought I: "Let's venture some good rattling question!"
　　　So—
"Come, Clive, tell us"—out I blurted—"what to tell in turn, years
　　　hence,
When my boy—suppose I have one—asks me on what evidence
I maintain my friend of Plassy proved a warrior every whit
70　Worth your Alexanders, Cæsars, Marlboroughs and—what said Pitt?—
Frederick the Fierce himself! Clive told me once"—I want to say—

48|　MS:ramparts, find a foothold　*P1880:* ramparts, none find foothold
49|　MS:Twixt　*P1880:* 'Twixt　　　53|　MS:now, turrets—see, the　*P1880:* now! turrets—just
the　　　54|　MS:again)　*P1880:* again)—　　　55|　MS:crumbles down by honest §crossed
out and replaced above by two words§ stress of　*P1880:* crumbles by sheer stress
56|　MS:that slow rains　*P1880:* that vile rains　　　57|　MS:o'ergrows, and so till
P1880: o'ergrows, o'ergrows till　　　59|　MS:crumbled down in　*P1880:* crumbled slow in
60|　MS:churchyard talk §crossed out and replaced above by§ chat < > yore,
P1880: churchyard-chat < > yore,—　　　61|　MS:head and foot piece　*P1880:* head-piece
foot-piece　　　64|　MS:noticed where §crossed out and replaced above by§ how

13

"Which feat out of all those famous doings bore the bell away
—In his own calm estimation, mark you, not the mob's rough guess—
Which stood foremost as evincing what Clive called courageousness!
75   Come! what moment of the minute, what speck-centre in the wide
Circle of the action saw your mortal fairly deified?
(Let alone that filthy sleep-stuff, swallow bold this wholesome Port!)
If a friend has leave to question,—when were you most brave, in
    short?"

Up he arched his brows o' the instant—formidably Clive again.
80   "When was I most brave? I'd answer, were the instance half as plain
As another instance that's a brain-lodged crystal—curse it!—here
Freezing when my memory touches—ugh!—the time I felt most fear.
Ugh! I cannot say for certain if I showed fear—anyhow,
Fear I felt, and, very likely, shuddered, since I shiver now."

85   "Fear!" smiled I. "Well, that's the rarer: that's a specimen to seek,
Ticket up in one's museum, *Mind-Freaks, Lord Clive's Fear, Unique!*"
Down his brows dropped. On the table painfully he pored as though
Tracing, in the stains and streaks there, thoughts encrusted long ago.
When he spoke 'twas like a lawyer reading word by word some will,
90   Some blind jungle of a statement,—beating on and on until
Out there leaps fierce life to fight with.

                                            "This fell in my factor-days.
Desk-drudge, slaving at St. David's, one must game, or drink, or craze.
I chose gaming: and,—because your high-flown gamesters hardly take
Umbrage at a factor's elbow if the factor pays his stake,—
95   I was winked at in a circle where the company was choice,
Captain This and Major That, men high of colour, loud of voice,
Yet indulgent, condescending to the modest juvenile
Who not merely risked but lost his hard-earned guineas with a smile.

76| MS:saw the mortal   *P1880:*saw your mortal   77| MS:swallow me this   *P1880:*swallow
bold this   82| MS:touches but the   *P1880:*touches—ugh—the   *1889a:*ugh!—the
84| MS:felt, so, very   *P1880:*felt, and, very   85| MS:smiled I, "Why, that's
*P1880:*smiled I, "Well, that's   88| MS:thoughts entrusted long   *P1880:*thoughts encrusted
long   96| MS:colour, bold of   *P1880:*bold §crossed out and replaced by§ loud
98-99| MS:guinea <> smile. / §no¶§ Down   *P1880:*guineas   *1889a:*smile. / §¶§ "Down

"Down I sat to cards, one evening,—had for my antagonist
Somebody whose name's a secret—you'll know why—so, if you list,
Call him Cock o' the Walk, my scarlet son of Mars from head to heel!
Play commenced: and, whether Cocky fancied that a clerk must feel
Quite sufficient honour came of bending over one green baize,
I the scribe with him the warrior,—guessed no penman dared to raise
Shadow of objection should the honour stay but playing end
More or less abruptly,—whether disinclined he grew to spend
Practice strictly scientific on a booby born to stare
At—not ask of—lace-and-ruffles if the hand they hide plays fair,—
Anyhow, I marked a movement when he bade me 'Cut!'

"I rose.

'Such the new manœuvre, Captain? I'm a novice: knowledge grows.
What, you force a card, you cheat, Sir?'

"Never did a thunder-clap
Cause emotion, startle Thyrsis locked with Chloe in his lap,
As my word and gesture (down I flung my cards to join the pack)
Fired the man of arms, whose visage, simply red before, turned black.

When he found his voice, he stammered 'That expression once
  again!'
"'Well, you forced a card and cheated!'

"'Possibly a factor's brain,
Busied with his all-important balance of accounts, may deem
Weighing words superfluous trouble: *cheat* to clerkly ears may seem
Just the joke for friends to venture: but we are not friends, you see!

101| MS:heel.   *P1880:*heel!   102| MS:and whether   *P1880:*and, whether
103| MS:baize   *P1880:*baize,   104| MS:the clerk §crossed out and replaced above by§
scribe <> penman like to   *P1880:*warrior, guessed no penman dared to   *1889a:*warrior,—
guessed   106| MS:Somewhat more abruptly   *P1880:*More or less abruptly
108| MS:At—nor question lace-and-ruffles   *P1880:*At—not ask of—lace-and-ruffles
109| MS:me "Cut!" §¶§ I   *P1880:*me 'Cut!' §¶§ "I   110| MS:Such   *P1880:*'Such
111| MS:cheat, Sir? §¶§ Never   *P1880:*cheat, Sir?' §¶§ "Never   115| MS:stammered
"That <> again!"   *P1880:*stammered 'That <> again!'   116| MS:"Well <> cheated!"
§¶§ "Possibly   *P1880:*"'Well <> cheated!' §¶§ "'Possibly   118| MS:trouble: 'cheat' to
*P1880:*trouble: *cheat* to   119| MS:for friend   *P1880:*for friends

120 When a gentleman is joked with,—if he's good at repartee,
He rejoins, as do I—Sirrah, on your knees, withdraw in full!
Beg my pardon, or be sure a kindly bullet through your skull
Lets in light and teaches manners to what brain it finds! Choose
quick—
Have your life snuffed out or, kneeling, pray me trim yon candle-
wick!'

125 "'Well, you cheated!'
"Then outbroke a howl from all the friends around.
To his feet sprang each in fury, fists were clenched and teeth were
ground.
'End it! no time like the present! Captain, yours were our disgrace!
No delay, begin and finish! Stand back, leave the pair a space!
Let civilians be instructed: henceforth simply ply the pen,
130 Fly the sword! This clerk's no swordsman? Suit him with a pistol, then!
Even odds! A dozen paces 'twixt the most and least expert
Make a dwarf a giant's equal: nay, the dwarf, if he's alert,
Likelier hits the broader target!'

"Up we stood accordingly.
As they handed me the weapon, such was my soul's thirst to try
135 Then and there conclusions with this bully, tread on and stamp out
Every spark of his existence, that,—crept close to, curled about
By that toying, tempting teasing fool-forefinger's middle joint,
Don't you guess?—the trigger yielded. Gone my chance! and at the
point
Of such prime success moreover: scarce an inch above his head
140 Went my ball to hit the wainscot. He was living, I was dead.

"Up he marched in flaming triumph—'twas his right, mind!—up,
within

123| MS:finds. Choose   *P1880:*finds! Choose   124| MS:candle-wick!"   *P1880:*candle-
wick!'   125| MS:"Well < > cheated!" §¶§ Then   *P1880:*"'Well < > cheated!' §¶§ "Then
127| MS:"End   *P1880:*'End   *1889a:*End §emended to§ 'End §see Editorial Notes§
129| MS:simply §inserted above§   133| MS:target!" §¶§ Up   *P1880:*target!' §¶§ "Up
137| MS:teazing rash forefinger's   *P1880:*teazing fool-forefinger's   138| MS:you
know?—the trigger   *P1880:*you guess?—the trigger   141| MS:Up   *P1880:*"Up

16

Just an arm's length. 'Now, my clerkling,' chuckled Cocky with a grin
As the levelled piece quite touched me, 'Now, Sir Counting-House,
   repeat
That expression which I told you proved bad manners! Did I cheat?'

145   " 'Cheat you did, you knew you cheated, and, this moment, know as
   well.
As for me, my homely breeding bids you—fire and go to Hell!'

"Twice the muzzle touched my forehead. Heavy barrel, flurried wrist,
Either spoils a steady lifting. Thrice: then, 'Laugh at Hell who list,
I can't! God's no fable either. Did this boy's eye wink once? No!
150   There's no standing him and Hell and God all three against me,—so,
I did cheat!'

        "And down he threw the pistol, out rushed—by the door
Possibly, but, as for knowledge if by chimney, roof or floor,
He effected disappearance—I'll engage no glance was sent
That way by a single starer, such a blank astonishment
155   Swallowed up their senses: as for speaking—mute they stood as mice.

"Mute not long, though! Such reaction, such a hubbub in a trice!
'Rogue and rascal! Who'd have thought it? What's to be expected
   next,
When His Majesty's Commission serves a sharper as pretext
For . . . But where's the need of wasting time now? Nought requires
   delay:
160   Punishment the Service cries for: let disgrace be wiped away
Publicly, in good broad daylight! Resignation? No, indeed!

142| MS:length. "Now, my clerkling," chuckled he with such a   *P1880:*length. 'Now, my
clerkling,' chuckled Cocky with a   143| MS:me, "Now   *P1880:*me, 'Now
144| MS:proved ill §crossed out and replaced above by§ bad <> cheat?
*P1880:*cheat?'   145| MS:"Cheat   *P1880:* " 'Cheat   146| MS:to Hell!"
*P1880:*to Hell!'   147| MS:Twice <> ball, flurried   *P1880:* "Twice <> barrel, flurried
148| MS:then, "Laugh   *P1880:*then, 'Laugh   151| MS:cheat!" §¶§ And   *P1880:*cheat!'
§¶§ "And   155-56| MS:mice. §bracket in margin and letters N.P. indicating new
paragraph§ Mute   157| MS:"Rogue   *P1880:* 'Rogue   159| MS:For . . But
*P1880:*For . . . But   161| MS:good §inserted above§ <> indeed!
*1889a:*indeed §emended to§ indeed! §see Editorial Notes§

Drum and fife must play the Rogue's-March, rank and file be free to
    speed
Tardy marching on the rogue's part by appliance in, the rear
—Kicks administered shall right this wronged civilian,—never fear,
165   Mister Clive, for—though a clerk—you bore yourself—suppose we
    say—
Just as would beseem a soldier!'

                "'Gentlemen, attention—pray!
First, one word!'

          "I passed each speaker severally in review.
When I had precise their number, names and styles, and fully knew
Over whom my supervision thenceforth must extend,—why, then—

170   "'Some five minutes since, my life lay—as you all saw, gentlemen—
At the mercy of your friend there. Not a single voice was raised
In arrest of judgment, not one tongue—before my powder blazed—
Ventured "Can it be the youngster blundered, really seemed to mark
Some irregular proceeding? We conjecture in the dark,
175   Guess at random,—still, for sake of fair play—what if for a freak,
In a fit of absence,—such things have been!—if our friend proved
    weak
—What's the phrase?—corrected fortune! Look into the case, at
    least!"
Who dared interpose between the altar's victim and the priest?
Yet he spared me! You eleven! Whosoever, all or each,
180   To the disadvantage of the man who spared me, utters speech
—To his face, behind his back,—that speaker has to do with me:
Me who promise, if positions change and mine the chance should be,

---

162| MS:the Rogue's-March   *1889a:*the Rogue's March §emended to§ Rogue's-March §see
Editorial Notes§   165| MS:say   *CP1880:*say—   166| MS:soldier!" §¶§ "Gentlemen
*P1880:*soldier!' §¶§ "'Gentlemen   167| MS:word!" §¶§ I   *P1880:*word!' §¶"I
170| MS:"Some   *P1880:*"'Some   171| MS:there; not   *P1880:*there. Not
173| MS:the poor clerk §two words crossed out and replaced above by§ youngster
174| MS:proceeding? I conjecture   *P1880:*proceeding? We conjecture
180| MS:Utters—to <> me—speech   *1889a:*To <> me, utters speech
182| MS:And I §two words crossed out and replaced above by two words§ Me who

Not to imitate your friend and waive advantage!'

                                                    "Twenty-five
Years ago this matter happened: and 'tis certain," added Clive,
185 "Never, to my knowledge, did Sir Cocky have a single breath
Breathed against him: lips were closed throughout his life, or since his
     death,
For if he be dead or living I can tell no more than you.
All I know is—Cocky had one chance more; how he used it,—grew
Out of such unlucky habits, or relapsed, and back again
190 Brought the late-ejected devil with a score more in his train,—
That's for you to judge. Reprieval I procured, at any rate.
Ugh—the memory of that minute's fear makes gooseflesh rise! Why
     prate
Longer? You've my story, there's your instance: fear I did, you see!"

"Well"—I hardly kept from laughing—"if I see it, thanks must be
195 Wholly to your Lordship's candour. Not that—in a common case—
When a bully caught at cheating thrusts a pistol in one's face,
I should underrate, believe me, such a trial to the nerve!
'Tis no joke, at one-and-twenty, for a youth to stand nor swerve.
Fear I naturally look for—unless, of all men alive,
200 I am forced to make exception when I come to Robert Clive.
Since at Arcot, Plassy, elsewhere, he and death—the whole world
     knows—
Came to somewhat closer quarters."

                                        Quarters? Had we come to blows,
Clive and I, you had not wondered—up he sprang so: out he rapped

---

183| MS:advantage!" §¶§ "Twenty-five   *P1880:*advantage!' §¶§ "Twenty-five
184| MS:certain" added Clive   *P1880:*certain," added Clive,   185| MS:Never
P1880:"Never   186| MS:life—or   *P1880:*life, or   187| MS:you: *P1880:*you.
190| MS:Came the   *CP1880:*Came §crossed out and replaced by§ Brought
191| MS:procured at   *P1880:*procured, at   192| MS:goose-flesh   *1889a:*gooseflesh
194| MS:"Well,—"I   *P1880:*"Well"—I   195| MS:your Lordship's   *1889a:*your Lordships
§emended to§ your Lordship's §see Editorial Notes§   196| MS:in your face,
*P1880:*in one's face,   197| MS:under-rate   *1889a:*underrate
200| MS:come to Robert Clive—   *P1880:*come to Robert Clive.   202| MS:to even closer
quarters . . " §¶§ Quarters   *P1880:*to somewhat closer quarters." §¶§ Quarters

Such a round of oaths—no matter! I'll endeavour to adapt
205   To our modern usage words he—well, 'twas friendly licence—flung
At me like so many fire-balls, fast as he could wag his tongue.

"You—a soldier? You—at Plassy? Yours the faculty to nick
Instantaneously occasion when your foe, if lightning-quick,
—At his mercy, at his malice,—has you, through some stupid inch
210   Undefended in your bulwark? Thus laid open,—not to flinch
—That needs courage, you'll concede me. Then, look here! Suppose
      the man,
Checking his advance, his weapon still extended, not a span
Distant from my temple,—curse him!—quietly had bade me 'There!
Keep your life, calumniator!—worthless life I freely spare:
215   Mine you freely would have taken—murdered me and my good fame
Both at once—and all the better! Go, and thank your own bad aim
Which permits me to forgive you! What if, with such words as these,
He had cast away his weapon? How should I have borne me, please?
Nay, I'll spare you pains and tell you. This, and only this, remained—
220   Pick his weapon up and use it on myself. I so had gained
Sleep the earlier, leaving England probably to pay on still
Rent and taxes for half India, tenant at the Frenchman's will."

"Such the turn," said I, "the matter takes with you? Then I abate
—No, by not one jot nor tittle,—of your act my estimate.
225   Fear—I wish I could detect there: courage fronts me, plain enough—
Call it desperation, madness—never mind! for here's in rough
Why, had mine been such a trial, fear had overcome disgrace.
True, disgrace were hard to bear: but such a rush against God's face
—None of that for me, Lord Plassy, since I go to church at times,
230   Say the creed my mother taught me! Many years in foreign climes
Rub some marks away—not all, though! We poor sinners reach life's
      brink,
Overlook what rolls beneath it, recklessly enough, but think

205| MS:he,—well <> licence!—flung   *CP1880:*he, §comma crossed out§ <> licence—flung
208| MS:Instantaneously the instant when   *P1880:*Instantaneously occasion when
219| MS:this remained—   *P1880:*this, remained—   223| MS:turn" said I "the
*CP1880:*turn, §comma crossed out§ <> I, §comma crossed out§   *1889a:*turn," said I, "the
228| MS:Ay, disgrace <> bear, but   *P1880:*True, disgrace <> bear: but
232| MS:it recklessly   *P1880:*it, recklessly

There's advantage in what's left us—ground to stand on, time to call
'Lord, have mercy!' ere we topple over—do not leap, that's all!"

²³⁵ Oh, he made no answer,—re-absorbed into his cloud. I caught
Something like "Yes—courage: only fools will call it fear."

                                                          If aught

Comfort you, my great unhappy hero Clive, in that I heard,
Next week, how your own hand dealt you doom, and uttered just the
    word
"Fearfully courageous!"—this, be sure, and nothing else I groaned.
²⁴⁰ I'm no Clive, nor parson either: Clive's worst deed—we'll hope
    condoned.

MULÉYKEH

If a stranger passed the tent of Hóseyn, he cried "A churl's!"
Or haply "God help the man who has neither salt nor bread!"
—"Nay," would a friend exclaim, "he needs nor pity nor scorn
More than who spends small thought on the shore-sand, picking
    pearls,
5   —Holds but in light esteem the seed-sort, bears instead
On his breast a moon-like prize, some orb which of night makes
    morn.

"What if no flocks and herds enrich the son of Sinán?
They went when his tribe was mulct, ten thousand camels the due,
Blood-value paid perforce for a murder done of old.
10   'God gave them, let them go! But never since time began,
Muléykeh, peerless mare, owned master the match of you,
And you are my prize, my Pearl: I laugh at men's land and gold!"

"So in the pride of his soul laughs Hóseyn—and right, I say.
Do the ten steeds run a race of glory? Outstripping all,
15   Ever Muléykeh stands first steed at the victor's staff
Who started, the owner's hope, gets shamed and named, that day.
'Silence,' or, last but one, is 'The Cuffed,' as we use to call
Whom the paddock's lord thrusts forth. Right, Hóseyn, I say, to laugh!"

"Boasts he Muléykeh the Pearl?" the stranger replies: "Be sure
20   On him I waste nor scorn nor pity, but lavish both
On Duhl the son of Sheybán, who withers away in heart
For envy of Hóseyn's luck. Such sickness admits no cure.
A certain poet has sung, and sealed the same with an oath,
'For the vulgar—flocks and herds! The Pearl is a prize apart.'"

MULÉYKEH   [1]| MS:of Hoseyn *P1880:*of Hóseyn   [2]| MS:help this man
*P1880:*help the man   [3]| MS:exclaim "he *P1880:*exclaim, "he
[5]| MS:Holds *P1880:*—Holds   [8]| MS:mulct, a thousand *P1880:*mulct, ten thousand
[13]| MS:laughs Hoseyn *P1880:*laughs Hóseyn   [16]| MS:day, *1889a:*day.
[18]| MS:forth. Right, Hoseyn <> laugh." *P1880:*forth. Right, Hóseyn *1889a:*laugh!"
[20]| MS:I <> pity on him but lavish them both *P1880:*On him I <> pity, but <> them both
*CP1880:*lavish them §crossed out§   [21]| MS:of Sheybán who *P1880:*of Sheybán, who
[22]| MS:of Hoseyn's *P1880:*of Hóseyn's   [24]| MS:For *P1880:*'For

25 Lo, Duhl the son of Sheybán comes riding to Hóseyn's tent,
    And he casts his saddle down, and enters and "Peace!" bids he.
    "You are poor, I know the cause: my plenty shall mend the wrong.
    'Tis said of your Pearl—the price of a hundred camels spent
    In her purchase were scarce ill paid: such prudence is far from me
30 Who proffer a thousand. Speak! Long parley may last too long."

    Said Hóseyn "You feed young beasts a many, of famous breed,
    Slit-eared, unblemished, fat, true offspring of Múzennem:
    There stumbles no weak-eyed she in the line as it climbs the hill.
    But I love Muléykeh's face: her forefront whitens indeed
35 Like a yellowish wave's cream-crest. Your camels—go gaze on them!
    Her fetlock is foam-splashed too. Myself am the richer still."

    A year goes by: lo, back to the tent again rides Duhl.
    "You are open-hearted, ay—moist-handed, a very prince.
    Why should I speak of sale? Be the mare your simple gift!
40 My son is pined to death for her beauty: my wife prompts 'Fool,
    Beg for his sake the Pearl! Be God the rewarder, since
    God pays debts seven for one: who squanders on Him shows thrift.' "

    Said Hóseyn "God gives each man one life, like a lamp, then gives
    That lamp due measure of oil: lamp lighted—hold high, wave wide
45 Its comfort for others to share! once quench it, what help is left?
    The oil of your lamp is your son: I shine while Muléykeh lives.
    Would I beg your son to cheer my dark if Muléykeh died?
    It is life against life: what good avails to the life-bereft?"

    Another year, and—hist! What craft is it Duhl designs?
50 He alights not at the door of the tent as he did last time,
    But, creeping behind, he gropes his stealthy way by the trench
    Half-round till he finds the flap in the folding, for night combines
    With the robber—and such is he: Duhl, covetous up to crime,
    Must wring from Hóseyn's grasp the Pearl, by whatever the wrench.

25| MS:to Hoseyn's   *P1880:*to Hóseyn's   26| MS:enters and "Peace" bids   *1889a:*enters
and "Peace!" bids   31| MS:Said Hoseyn   *P1880:*Said Hóseyn   32| MS:of Muzennem:
*P1880:*of Múzennem: 37| MS:by, lo back   *P1880:*by: lo, back   38| MS:prince!
*P1880:*prince.   43| MS:Said Hoseyn   *P1880:*Said Hóseyn   46| MS:while Muleykeh
*P1880:*while Muléykeh   47| MS:if Muleykeh   *P1880:*if Muléykeh

55 "He was hunger-bitten, I heard: I tempted with half my store,
And a gibe was all my thanks. Is he generous like Spring dew?
Account the fault to me who chaffered with such an one!
He has killed, to feast chance comers, the creature he rode: nay,
    more—
For a couple of singing-girls his robe has he torn in two:
60 I will beg! Yet I nowise gained by the tale of my wife and son.

"I swear by the Holy House, my head will I never wash
Till I filch his Pearl away. Fair dealing I tried, then guile,
And now I resort to force. He said we must live or die:
Let him die, then,—let me live! Be bold—but not too rash!
65 I have found me a peeping-place: breast, bury your breathing while
I explore for myself! Now, breathe! He deceived me not, the spy!

"As he said—there lies in peace Hóseyn—how happy! Beside
Stands tethered the Pearl: thrice winds her headstall about his wrist:
'Tis therefore he sleeps so sound—the moon through the roof
    reveals.
70 And, loose on his left, stands too that other, known far and wide,
Buhéyseh, her sister born: fleet is she yet ever missed
The winning tail's fire-flash a-stream past the thunderous heels.

"No less she stands saddled and bridled, this second, in case some
    thief
Should enter and seize and fly with the first, as I mean to do.
75 What then? The Pearl is the Pearl: once mount her we both escape."
Through the skirt-fold in glides Duhl,—so a serpent disturbs no leaf
In a bush as he parts the twigs entwining a nest: clean through,
He is noiselessly at his work: as he planned, he performs the rape.

54| MS:from Hoseyn's   *P1880:*from Hóseyn's   61| MS:the Holy House my
*P1880:*the Holy House, my   66| MS:myself. Now   *P1880:*myself! Now
67| MS:peace Hoseyn <> beside   *P1880:*peace Hóseyn <> Beside
68| MS:wrist,   *P1880:*wrist: 69| MS:sound, the moon   *P1880:*sound—the moon
72| MS:thundrous   *P1880:*thunderous   74| MS:sieze   *P1880:*seize
75| MS:her, we   *P1880:*her we   76| MS:glides Duhl,—like §crossed out
and replaced above by§ so a serpent, §comma crossed out§

24

He has set the tent-door wide, has buckled the girth, has clipped
80   The headstall away from the wrist he leaves thrice bound as before,
He springs on the Pearl, is launched on the desert like bolt from bow.
Up starts our plundered man: from his breast though the heart be
          ripped,
Yet his mind has the mastery: behold, in a minute more,
He is out and off and away on Buhéyseh, whose worth we know!

85   And Hóseyn—his blood turns flame, he has learned long since to
          ride,
And Buhéyseh does her part,—they gain—they are gaining fast
On the fugitive pair, and Duhl has Ed-Dárraj to cross and quit,
And to reach the ridge El-Sabán,—no safety till that be spied!
And Buhéyseh is, bound by bound, but a horse-length off at last,
90   For the Pearl has missed the tap of the heel, the touch of the bit.

She shortens her stride, she chafes at her rider the strange and queer:
Buhéyseh is mad with hope—beat sister she shall and must
Though Duhl, of the hand and heel so clumsy, she has to thank.
She is near now, nose by tail—they are neck by croup—joy! fear!
95   What folly makes Hóseyn shout "Dog Duhl, Damned son of the Dust,
Touch the right ear and press with your foot my Pearl's left flank!"

And Duhl was wise at the word, and Muléykeh as prompt perceived
Who was urging redoubled pace, and to hear him was to obey,
And a leap indeed gave she, and evanished for evermore.
100   And Hóseyn looked one long last look as who, all bereaved,
Looks, fain to follow the dead so far as the living may:
Then he turned Buhéyseh's neck slow homeward, weeping sore.

---

⁷⁹| MS:girths *P1880:*girth   ⁸⁴| MS:know. *P1880:*know!   ⁸⁵| MS:And Hoseyn
<> flame and he knows full well §last three words crossed out and replaced above by three
words§ learned long since *P1880:*And Hóseyn <> flame, he has learned
⁹⁰| MS:of the spur, the touch *P1880:*of the heel, the touch
⁹¹| MS:stride—she <> queer,— *P1880:*stride, she <> queer: ⁹²| MS:with joy
§crossed out and replaced above by§ hope   ⁹³| *P1880:*thank *1880:*thank.
⁹⁵| MS:makes Hoseyn *P1880:*makes Hóseyn   ⁹⁹| MS:she and <> more: *P1880:*she,
and <> more.   ¹⁰⁰| MS:And Hoseyn *P1880:*And Hóseyn

And, lo, in the sunrise, still sat Hóseyn upon the ground
Weeping: and neighbours came, the tribesmen of Bénu-Asád
105 In the vale of green Er-Rass, and they questioned him of his grief;
And he told from first to last how, serpent-like, Duhl had wound
His way to the nest, and how Duhl rode like an ape, so bad!
And how Buhéyseh did wonders, yet Pearl remained with the thief

And they jeered him, one and all: "Poor Hóseyn is crazed past hope!
110 How else had he wrought himself his ruin, in fortune's spite?
To have simply held the tongue were a task for a boy or girl,
And here were Muléykeh again, the eyed like an antelope,
The child of his heart by day, the wife of his breast by night!"—
"And the beaten in speed!" wept Hóseyn: "You never have loved my
     Pearl."

103| MS:sat Hoseyn *P1880:* sat Hóseyn   104| MS:of Benu-Asád *P1880:* of Bénu-Asád
105| MS:er-Rass §altered to§ green Er-Rass <> grief, *P1880:* grief;
107| MS:bad!— *P1880:* bad!   109| MS:all: "Poor Hoseyn *P1880:* all: "Poor Hóseyn
112| MS:were his §crossed out§   114| MS:in race!" said Hoseyn
P1880: in speed!" wept Hoseyn   *1880:* wept Hóseyn

PIETRO OF ABANO

Petrus Aponensis—there was a magician!
When that strange adventure happened, which I mean to tell my
 hearers,
Nearly had he tried all trades—beside physician,
Architect, astronomer, astrologer,—or worse:
5 How else, as the old books warrant, was he able,
All at once, through all the world, to prove the promptest of
 appearers
Where was prince to cure, tower to build as high as Babel,
Star to name or sky-sign read,—yet pouch, for pains, a curse?

—Curse: for when a vagrant,—foot-sore, travel-tattered,
10 Now a young man, now an old man, Turk or Arab, Jew or Gipsy,—
Proffered folk in passing—O for pay, what mattered?—
"I'll be doctor, I'll play builder, star I'll name—sign read!"
Soon as prince was cured, tower built, and fate predicted,
"Who may you be?" came the question; when he answered "*Petrus
 ipse*,"
15 Just as we divined!" cried folk—"A wretch convicted
Long ago of dealing with the devil—you indeed!"

So, they cursed him roundly, all his labour's payment,
Motioned him—the convalescent prince would—to vacate the
 presence:
Babylonians plucked his beard and tore his raiment,
20 Drove him from that tower he built: while, had he peered at stars,
Town howled "Stone the quack who styles our Dog-star—Sirius!"

PIETRO OF ABANO   ¹| MS:Petrus ille de Apono §last three words crossed out and
replaced above by§ Aponensis *P1880: Petrus Aponensis—* ²| MS:which §crossed out
and replaced above by§ now *CP1880:*now §crossed out and replaced in margin by§ which
⁸| MS:sky-sign §inserted above§ read aright §crossed out§ ¹⁰| MS:young and §crossed
out and replaced above by one word and comma§ man, now ¹²| MS:name and
§crossed out and replaced above by dash and one word§ —sign ¹⁴| MS:question; when
he answered "Petrus ipse," *CP1880:*answered "Petrus ipse," §last two words underlined and
the word *Italic* in margin§ *1889a:*question, when §emended to§ question; when §see
Editorial Notes§ ¹⁵| MS:folks—"The §crossed out and replaced above by§ A
*1889a:*folk ¹⁷| MS:roundly, for his < > payment *P1880:*roundly, all his < > payment,
¹⁸| MS:presence *P1880:*presence: ²¹| MS:our Dogstar *P1880:*our Dog-star

Country yelled "Aroint the churl who prophesies we take no pleasance
Under vine and fig-tree, since the year's delirious,
Bears no crop of any kind,—all through the planet Mars!"

25 Straightway would the whilom youngster grow a grisard,
Or, as case might hap, the hoary eld drop off and show a stripling.
Town and country groaned—indebted to a wizard!
"Curse—nay, kick and cuff him—fit requital of his pains!
Gratitude in word or deed were wasted truly!
30 Rather make the Church amends by crying out on, cramping,
        crippling
One who, on pretence of serving man, serves duly
Man's arch foe: not ours, be sure, but Satan's—his the gains!"

Peter grinned and bore it, such disgraceful usage:
Somehow, cuffs and kicks and curses seem ordained his like to suffer:
35 Prophet's pay with Christians, now as in the Jews'age,
Still is—stoning: so, he meekly took his wage and went,
—Safe again was found ensconced in those old quarters,
Padua's blackest blindest by-street,—none the worse, nay, somewhat
        tougher:
"Calculating," quoth he, "soon I join the martyrs,
40 Since, who magnify my lore on burning me are bent."*

> * "Studiando le mie cifre col compasso,
>   Rilevo che sarò presto sotterra,
>   Perchè del mio saper si fa gran chiasso,
>   E gl' ignoranti m' hanno mosso guerra."
> 5 Said to have been found in a well at Abano in the last century. They were extemporane-
> ously Englished thus: not as Father Prout chose to prefer them :—
>   Studying my ciphers with the compass,
>   I reckon—I soon shall be below-ground;
>   Because of my lore folk make great rumpus,
> 10   And war on myself makes each dull rogue round.

22| MS:prophecies *P1880:*prophesies   23| MS:fig-tree since   *P1880:*fig-tree, since
32| *1880:*gains! *1889a:*gains!"   33| MS:it, this disgraceful   *P1880:*it, such disgraceful
38| MS:byestreet <> worse—nay *P1880:*worse, nay   *1889a:*by-street
39| MS:"Calculating—"quoth he—"soon   *P1880:*"Calculating" quoth he "soon
1889a:"Calculating," quoth he, "soon   40| MS:bent." §large star and marginal note:
"Insert Note at foot of page"§   *P1880:*bent." §followed by superscript number one§
*1889a:*bent." §followed by a superscript star§

Footnote   1| MS:Studiando   *P1880:*"Studiando   4| *1880:*gl'iguoranti   *1889a:*gl'ignoranti
6| MS:them.   *P1880:*them: *1889a:*them:—   9| MS:Because, of <> folks
*1889a:*Because of <> folk

Therefore, on a certain evening, to his alley
Peter slunk, all bruised and broken, sore in body, sick in spirit,
Just escaped from Cairo where he launched a galley
45   Needing neither sails nor oars nor help of wind or tide,
—Needing but the fume of fire to set a-flying
Wheels like mad which whirled you quick—North, South, where'er
    you pleased require it,—
That is—would have done so had not priests come prying,
Broke his engine up and bastinadoed him beside.

As he reached his lodging, stopped there unmolested,
50   (Neighbours feared him, urchins fled him, few were bold enough to
    follow)
While his fumbling fingers tried the lock and tested
Once again the queer key's virtue, oped the sullen door,—
Someone plucked his sleeve, cried "Master, pray your pardon!
Grant a word to me who patient wait you in your archway's hollow!
55   Hard on you men's hearts are: be not your heart hard on
Me who kiss your garment's hem, O Lord of magic lore!

"Mage—say I, who no less, scorning tittle-tattle,
To the vulgar give no credence when they prate of Peter's magic,
Deem his art brews tempest, hurts the crops and cattle,
60   Hinders fowls from laying eggs and worms from spinning silk,
Rides upon a he-goat, mounts at need a broomstick:
While the price he pays for this (so turns to comic what was tragic)
Is—he may not drink—dreads like the Day of Doom's tick—
One poor drop of sustenance ordained mere men—that's milk!

65   "Tell such tales to Padua! Think me no such dullard!
Not from these benighted parts did I derive my breath and being!
I am from a land whose cloudless skies are coloured
Livelier, suns orb largelier, airs seem incense,—while, on earth—
What, instead of grass, our fingers and our thumbs cull,

41| MS:Now as, on   *1889a:*Therefore, on   45| MS:—Needing—why, the   *P1880:*—
Needing but the   48| MS:beside:—   *1889a:*beside.   50| MS:him, none
§crossed out and replaced above by§ few   57| MS:"Mage—I say, who   *P1880:*"Mage—
say I, who   58| MS:Give no credence to the vulgar §transposed to§
To the vulgar Give no credence <> magic   *P1880:*give <> magic,

70 Proves true moly! sounds and sights there help the body's hearing,
    seeing,
Till the soul grows godlike: brief,—you front no numbscull
Shaming by ineptitude the Greece that gave him birth!

"Mark within my eye its iris mystic-lettered—
That's my name! and note my ear—its swan-shaped cavity, my
    emblem!
75 Mine's the swan-like nature born to fly unfettered
Over land and sea in search of knowledge—food for song.
Art denied the vulgar! Geese grow fat on barley,
Swans require ethereal provend, undesirous to resemble 'em—
Soar to seek Apollo,—favoured with a parley
80 Such as, Master, you grant me—who will not hold you long.

"Leave to learn to sing—for that your swan petitions:
Master, who possess the secret, say not nay to such a suitor!
All I ask is—bless mine, purest of ambitions!
Grant me leave to make my kind wise, free, and happy! How?
85 Just by making me—as you are mine—their model!
Geese have goose-thoughts: make a swan their teacher first, then co-
    adjutor,—
Let him introduce swan-notions to each noddle,—
Geese will soon grow swans, and men become what I am now!

"That's the only magic—had but fools discernment,
90 Could they probe and pass into the solid through the soft and
    seeming!
Teach me such true magic—now and no adjournment!
Teach your art of making fools subserve the man of mind!
Magic is the power we men of mind should practise,

61| MS:upon a broomstick §crossed out and replaced above by§ he-goat,—mounts < >
broomstick,— *P1880:*he-goat, mounts < > broomstick: 73| MS:Mark   *P1880:*"Mark
76| MS:song—   *P1880:*song.   *1880:*song   *1889a:*song.   77| MS:vulgar: geese
*P1880:*vulgar! Geese   78| MS:ætherial   *1889a:*etherial   81| MS:Leave
P1880:"Leave   83| MS:mine—purest   *P1880:*mine, purest
89| MS:That's   *P1880:*"That's   91| MS:Teach such magic to me—now
*P1880:*Teach me such true magic—now   92| MS:Teach the art
*P1880:*Teach your art   93| MS:practice   *P1880:*practise,

Draw fools to become our drudges, docile henceforth, never
    dreaming—
95   While they do our hests for fancied gain—the fact is
What they toil and moil to get proves falsehood: truth's behind!

"See now! you conceive some fabric—say, a mansion
Meet for monarch's pride and pleasure: this is truth—a thought has
    fired you,
Made you fain to give some cramped concept expansion,
100 Put your faculty to proof, fulfil your nature's task.
First you fascinate the monarch's self: he fancies
He it was devised the scheme you execute as he inspired you:
He in turn sets slaving insignificances
Toiling, moiling till your structure stands there—all you ask!

105 "Soon the monarch's known for what he was—a ninny:
Soon the rabble-rout leave labour, take their work-day wage and
    vanish:
Soon the late puffed bladder, pricked, shows lank and skinny—
'Who was its inflator?' ask we, 'whose the giant lungs?'
Petri en pulmones! What though men prove ingrates?
110 Let them—so they stop at crucifixion—buffet, ban and banish!
Peter's power's apparent: human praise—its din grates
Harsh as blame on ear unused to aught save angels' tongues.

"Ay, there have been always, since our world existed,
Mages who possessed the secret—needed but to stand still, fix eye
115 On the foolish mortal: straight was he enlisted
Soldier, scholar, servant, slave—no matter for the style!
Only through illusion; ever what seemed profit—
Love or lucre—justified obedience to the *Ipse dixi:*
Work done—palace reared from pavement up to soffit—
120 Was it strange if builders smelt out cheating all the while?

94| MS:drudges—docile   *1889a:*drudges, docile   96| MS:get is—falsehood   *P1880:*get
proves falsehood   97| MS:See *P1880:*"See   98| MS:you *P1880:*you,
102| MS:inspired you—   *P1880:*inspired you: 105| MS:Soon *P1880:*"Soon
108| MS:we—'whose *P1880:*we 'whose   *1889a:*we, 'whose   113| MS:Ay *P1880:*"Ay
115| MS:mortal—straight *P1880:*mortal: straight

"Let them pelt and pound, bruise, bray you in a mortar!
What's the odds to you who seek reward of quite another nature?
You've enrolled your name where sages of your sort are,
—Michael of Constantinople, Hans of Halberstadt!
125 Nay and were you nameless, still you've your conviction
You it was and only you—what signifies the nomenclature?
Ruled the world in fact, though how you ruled be fiction
Fit for fools: true wisdom's magic you—if e'er man—had 't!

"But perhaps you ask me 'Since each ignoramus
130 While he profits by such magic persecutes the benefactor,
What should I expect but—once I render famous
You as Michael, Hans and Peter—just one ingrate more?
If the vulgar prove thus, whatsoe'er the pelf be,
Pouched through my beneficence—and doom me dungeoned,
        chained, or racked, or
135 Fairly burned outright—how grateful will yourself be
When, his secret gained, you match your—master just before?'

"That's where I await you! Please, revert a little!
What do folk report about you if not this—which, though chimeric,
Still, as figurative, suits you to a tittle—
140 That,—although the elements obey your nod and wink,
Fades or flowers the herb you chance to smile or sigh at,
While your frown bids earth quake palled by obscuration
        atmospheric,—
Brief, although through nature nought resists your *fiat*,
There's yet one poor substance mocks you—milk you may not drink!

145 "Figurative language! Take my explanation
Fame with fear, and hate with homage, these your art procures in
        plenty.
All's but daily dry bread: what makes moist the ration?

121| MS:Let *P1880:* "Let   123| MS:are *P1880:*are,   129| MS:But *P1880:* "But
131| MS:'What *P1880:*What   133| MS:be *P1880:*be,   134| MS:—Pouched
*P1880:*Pouched   136| MS:gained you *P1880:*gained, you   137| MS:That's
CP1880: "That's   140| MS:nod or wink *P1880:*or §crossed out and replaced in margin
by§ and   145| MS:Figurative *P1880:* "Figurative   147| MS:ration— *P1880:*ration?

Love, the milk that sweetens man his meal—alas, you lack:
I am he who, since he fears you not, can love you.
150 Love is born of heart not mind, *de corde natus haud de mente*;
Touch my heart and love's yours, sure as shines above you
Sun by day and star by night though earth should go to wrack!

"Stage by stage you lift me—kiss by kiss I hallow
Whose but your dear hand my helper, punctual as at each new
    impulse
155 I approach my aim? Shell chipped, the eaglet callow
Needs a parent's pinion-push to quit the eyrie's edge:
But once fairly launched forth, denizen of æther,
While each effort sunward bids the blood more freely through each
    limb pulse,
Sure the parent feels, as gay they soar together,
160 Fully are all pains repaid when love redeems its pledge!"

Then did Peter's tristful visage lighten somewhat,
Vent a watery smile as though inveterate mistrust were thawing.
"Well, who knows?" he slow broke silence. "Mortals—come what
Come there may—are still the dupes of hope there's luck in store.
165 Many scholars seek me, promise mounts and marvels:
Here stand I to witness how they step 'twixt me and clapperclawing!
Dry bread,—that I've gained me: truly I should starve else:
But of milk, no drop was mine! Well, shuffle cards once more!"

At the word of promise thus implied, our stranger—
170 What can he but cast his arms, in rapture of embrace, round Peter?
"Hold! I choke!" the mage grunts. "Shall I in the manger
Any longer play the dog? Approach, my calf, and feed!

148| MS:lack! *1889a:*lack: 149| MS:who, once he   *P1880:*who, since he
150| MS:*mente, P1880: mente;*   153| MS:Stage   *P1880:* "Stage   155| MS:eaglet's
callow,   *P1880:*eaglet callow   163| MS:silence "Mortals   *P1880:* silence: "Mortals
*CP1880:*silence: §altered to§ silence. "Mortals   165| MS:marvels—   *P1880:*marvels:
167| MS:gained, yes, §comma, one word, and comma crossed out and replaced above by one
word and colon§ me: 168| MS:drop—too true! §dash, last two words, and exclamation
point crossed out and replaced above by two words and exclamation point§ was mine! < >
throw for luck §last three words crossed out and replaced above by two words§ shuffle cards
169| MS:stranger   *P1880:*stranger—   171| MS:grunts "Shall   *P1880:*grunts. "Shall

Bene . . . won't you wait for grace?" But sudden incense
Wool-white, serpent-solid, curled up—perfume growing sweet and
    sweeter
175   Till it reached the young man's nose and seemed to win sense
Soul and all from out his brain through nostril: yes, indeed!

Presently the young man rubbed his eyes. "Where am I?
Too much bother over books! Some reverie has proved amusing.
What did Peter prate of? 'Faith, my brow is clammy!
180   How my head throbs, how my heart thumps! Can it be I swooned?
Oh, I spoke my speech out—cribbed from Plato's tractate,
Dosed him with 'the Fair and Good,' swore—Dog of Egypt—I was
    choosing
Plato's way to serve men! What's the hour? Exact eight!
Home now, and to-morrow never mind how Plato mooned!

185   "Peter has the secret! Fair and Good are products
(So he said) of Foul and Evil: one must bring to pass the other.
Just as poisons grow drugs, steal through sundry odd ducts
Doctors name, and ultimately issue safe and changed.
You'd abolish poisons, treat disease with dainties
190   Such as suit the sound and sane? With all such kickshaws vain you
    pother!
Arsenic's the stuff puts force into the faint eyes,
Opium sets the brain to rights—by cark and care deranged.

"What, he's safe within door?—would escape—no question—
Thanks, since thanks and more I owe, and mean to pay in time
    befitting.
195   What most presses now is—after night's digestion,
Peter, of thy precepts!—promptest practice of the same.
Let me see! The wise man, first of all, scorns riches:
But to scorn them must obtain them: none believes in his permitting

---

173| MS:for §crossed out and replaced above by§ But   177| MS:eyes "Where
*P1880:*eyes. "Where   182| MS:and Good—' swore *P1880:*and Good,' swore
184| MS:now and *P1880:*now, and   185| MS:Peter *P1880:*"Peter
190| MS:vain the §crossed out§   193| MS:What < > doors *P1880:*"What < > door
194| MS:Thanks—since < > owe and *P1880:*Thanks, since < > owe, and
198| MS:scorn them §inserted above§ must first §crossed out§

Gold to lie ungathered: who picks up, then pitches
200   Gold away—philosophizes; none disputes his claim.

"So with worldly honours: 'tis by abdicating,
Incontestably he proves he could have kept the crown discarded.
Sulla cuts a figure, leaving off dictating:
Simpletons laud private life? 'The grapes are sour,' laugh we.
205   So, again—but why continue? All's tumultuous
Here: my head's a-whirl with knowledge. Speedily shall be rewarded
He who taught me! Greeks prove ingrates? So insult you us?
When your teaching bears its first-fruits, Peter—wait and see !"

As the word, the deed proved; ere a brief year's passage,
210   Fop—that fool he made the jokes on—now he made the jokes for,
        gratis:
Hunks—that hoarder, long left lonely in his crass age—
Found now one appreciative deferential friend:
Powder-paint-and-patch, Hag Jezebel—recovered,
Strange to say, the power to please, got courtship till she cried *Jam
        satis!*
215   Fop be-flattered, Hunks be-friended, Hag be-lovered—
Nobody o'erlooked, save God—he soon attained his end.
As he lounged at ease one morning in his villa,
(Hag's the dowry) estimated (Hunks' bequest) his coin in coffer,
Mused on how a fool's good word (Fop's word) could fill a
220   Social circle with his praise, promote him man of mark,—
All at once—"An old friend fain would see your Highness!"
There stood Peter, skeleton and scarecrow, plain writ *Phi-lo-so-pher*
In the woe-worn face—for yellowness and dryness,
Parchment—with a pair of eyes—one hope their feeble spark.

200| MS:philosophizes,—none *P1880:*philosophizes: none   201| MS:So <> abdicating
P1880:"So <> abdicating,   204| MS:Simpleton lauds *P1880:*Simpletons laud
206| MS:Here—my *P1880:*Here: my   213| MS:recovered *1889a:*recovered,
216| MS:end *P1880:*end.   218| MS:coins *P1880:*coin   220| MS:mark—
*P1880:*mark,—   221| MS:old man §crossed out and replaced above by§ friend
224| MS:eyes, one *P1880:*eyes—one

225   "Did I counsel rightly? Have you, in accordance,
     Prospered greatly, dear my pupil? Sure, at just the stage I find you,
     When your hand may draw me forth from the mad war-dance
     Savages are leading round your master—down, not dead.
     Padua wants to burn me: baulk them, let me linger
230   Life out—rueful though its remnant—hid in some safe hole behind
        you!
     Prostrate here I lie: quick, help with but a finger
     Lest I house in safety's self—a tombstone o'er my head!

     "Lodging, bite and sup, with—now and then—a copper
     —Alms for any poorer still,—if such there be,—is all my asking.
235   Take me for your bedesman,—nay, if you think proper,
     Menial merely,—such my perfect passion for repose!
     Yes, from out your plenty Peter craves a pittance
     —Leave to thaw his frozen hands before the fire whereat you're
        basking!
     Double though your debt were, grant this boon—remittance
240   He proclaims of obligation: 'tis himself that owes!"

     "Venerated Master—can it be, such treatment
     Learning meets with, magic fails to guard you from, by all appearance?
     Strange! for, as you entered,—what the famous feat meant,
     I was full of,—why you reared that fabric, Padua's boast.
245   Nowise for man's pride, man's pleasure, did you slyly
     Raise it, but man's seat of rule whereby the world should soon have
        clearance
     (Happy world) from such a rout as now so vilely
     Handles you—and hampers me, for which I grieve the most.

     "Since if it got wind you now were my familiar,
250   How could I protect you—nay, defend myself against the rabble?
     Wait until the mob, now masters, willy-nilly are

226| MS:pupil? Sure at <> you   *P1880:*pupil? Sure, at   *1889a:*you,
233| MS:Lodging   *P1880:* "Lodging   237| MS:craves this §crossed out and replaced above by§ a   239| MS:debt be, grant   *P1880:*debt were, grant
242| MS:with—magic   *P1880:*with, magic   244| MS:boast: *P1880:*boast.
245| MS:pleasure did   *P1880:*pleasure, did   248| MS:me—for   *P1880:*me, for
249| MS:Since   *P1880:* "Since   250| MS:nay defend   *P1880:*nay, defend

Servants as they should be: then has gratitude full play!
Surely this experience shows how unbefitting
'Tis that minds like mine should rot in ease and plenty. Geese may
    gabble,
255   Gorge, and keep the ground: but swans are soon for quitting
Earthly fare—as fain would I, your swan, if taught the way.

"Teach me, then, to rule men, have them at my pleasure!
Solely for their good, of course,—impart a secret worth rewarding,
Since the proper life's-prize! Tantalus's treasure
260   Aught beside proves, vanishes and leaves no trace at all.
Wait awhile, nor press for payment prematurely!
Over-haste defrauds you. Thanks! since,—even while I speak,—
    discarding
Sloth and vain delights, I learn how—swiftly, surely—
Magic sways the sceptre, wears the crown and wields the ball!

265   "Gone again—what, is he? 'Faith, he's soon disposed of!
Peter's precepts work already, put within my lump their leaven!
Ay, we needs must don glove would we pluck the rose—doff
Silken garment would we climb the tree and take its fruit.
Why sharp thorn, rough rind? To keep unviolated
270   Either prize! We garland us, we mount from earth to feast in heaven,
Just because exist what once we estimated
Hindrances which, better taught, as helps we now compute.

"Foolishly I turned disgusted from my fellows!
Pits of ignorance—to fill, and heaps of prejudice—to level—
275   Multitudes in motley, whites and blacks and yellows—

252| MS:they ought to §two words crossed out and replaced above by§ should <> has
§inserted above§   256| MS:fare as *P1880:*fare—as   257| MS:Teach me then to
<> pleasure, *P1880:*"Teach me, then, to <> pleasure!   258| MS:rewarding
*P1880:*rewarding,   260| MS:All §crossed out and replaced above by§ Aught <> proves—
vanishes *P1880:*proves, vanishes   264| MS:wields *1889a:*wield §emended to§ wields
§see Editorial Notes§   266| MS:already,—put *P1880:*already, put
267| MS:rose,—doff *P1880:*rose—doff   270| MS:prize: we <> climb
§crossed out and replaced above by§ mount §crossed out but marked for
reinstatement§ <> feast in §last two words inserted above§ *P1880:*prize! We
271| MS:Just because because §crossed out§   272| MS:which, thanks §crossed out and
replaced above by§ better   273| MS:Foolishly *P1880:*"Foolishly

37

What a hopeless task it seemed to discipline the host!
Now I see my error. Vices act like virtues
—Not alone because they guard—sharp thoms—the rose we first
    dishevel,
Not because they scrape, scratch—rough rind—through the dirt-shoes
280   Bare feet cling to bole with, while the half-mooned boot we boast.

"No, my aim is nobler, more disinterested!
Man shall keep what seemed to thwart him, since it proves his true
    assistance,
Leads to ascertaining which head is the best head,
Would he crown his body, rule its members—lawless else.
285   Ignorant the horse stares, by deficient vision
Takes a man to be a monster, lets him mount, then, twice the distance
Horse could trot unridden, gallops—dream Elysian!—
Dreaming that his dwarfish guide's a giant,—jockeys tell 's."

Brief, so worked the spell, he promptly had a riddance:
290   Heart and brain no longer felt the pricks which passed for conscience-
    scruples:
Free henceforth his feet,—*Per Bacco,* how they did dance
Merrily through lets and checks that stopped the way before!
Politics the prize now,—such adroit adviser,
Opportune suggester, with the tact that triples and quadruples
295   Merit in each measure,—never did the Kaiser
Boast a subject such a statesman, friend, and something more!

276| MS:the crew §crossed out and replaced above by§ host!   277| MS:like §over illegible word§   278| MS:we thereby first   *P1880:*we first   280| MS:Barefoot §altered to two words§ Bare feet climbers §crossed out§ < > boast—   *P1880:*boast.   281| MS:No,—my aim is §crossed out and replaced by§ be nobler, all disinterested!   *P1880:* "No, my aim is nobler, more disinterested!   283| MS:best head—   *P1880:*best head,   285| MS:stares—by   *P1880:*stares, by   286| MS:giant §crossed out and replaced above by§ monster < > mount and, twice   *P1880:*mount, then, twice   287| MS:He could   *CP1880:*He §last letter crossed out and replaced in margin by four letters§ orse   289| MS:riddance—   *P1880:*riddance: 290| MS:pricks he took §two words crossed out and replaced above by two words§ which passed   291| MS:feet,—what wonder if they   *CP1880:*feet,—what wonder if §three words crossed out and replaced in margin by three words§ *Per Bacco,* how   292| MS:before?   *P1880:*before? §question mark crossed out and replaced in margin by exclamation mark§ before!   294| MS:suggester,—with   *P1880:*suggester, with   296| MS:statesman—friend and   *P1880:*statesman, friend, and

As he, up and down, one noonday, paced his closet
—Council o'er, each spark (his hint) blown flame, by colleagues'
    breath applauded,
Strokes of statecraft hailed with *"Salomo si nôsset!"*
300 (His the nostrum)—every throw for luck come double-six,—
As he, pacing, hugged himself in satisfaction,
Thump—the door went. "What, the Kaiser? By none else were I
    defrauded
Thus of well-earned solace. Since 'tis fate's exaction,—
Enter, Liege my Lord! Ha, Peter, you here? *Teneor vix!"*

305 "Ah, Sir, none the less, contain you, nor wax irate!
You so lofty, I so lowly,—vast the space which yawns between us!
Still, methinks, you—more than ever—at a high rate
Needs must prize poor Peter's secret since it lifts you thus.
Grant me now the boon whereat before you boggled!
310 Ten long years your march has moved—one triumph—(though *e* 's
    short)—*hacte¯nus,*
While I down and down disastrously have joggled
Till I pitch against Death's door, the true *Nec Ultra Plus.*

"Years ago—some ten 'tis—since I sought for shelter,
Craved in your whole house a closet, out of all your means a comfort.
315 Now you soar above these: as is gold to spelter
So is power—you urged with reason—paramount to wealth.
Power you boast in plenty: let it grant me refuge!
Houseroom now is out of question: find for me some stronghold—
    some fort—
Privacy wherein, immured, shall this blind deaf huge
320 Monster of a mob let stay the soul I'd save by stealth!

299| MS:Stroke   *P1880:*Strokes   300| MS:the hazard)—every <> double-six—
*CP1880:*the hazard §crossed out and replaced in margin by§ nostrum <> double-six §comma
inserted between word and dash§ double-six,—   301| MS:As §crossed out and replaced
in margin by§ While   *CP1880:*While §crossed out and replaced in margin by§ As
305| MS:"Ah but, none <> contained be, nor   *P1880:*"Ah, Sir, none <> contain you, nor
306| MS:lowly,—while I know §three words crossed out and replaced above by§ vast <> which
yawns §two words inserted above§   309| MS:boggled—   *P1880:*boggled!
310| MS:hactēnus,   *P1880:*hactēnus,   312| MS:door—the   *P1880:*door, the
313| MS:Years   *P1880:*"Years   315| MS:these: just as gold   *P1880:*these: as is gold
320| MS:mob release the   *P1880:*mob let stay the   321| MS:Ay   *P1880:*"Ay

"Ay, for all too much with magic have I tampered!
—Lost the world, and gained, I fear, a certain place I'm to describe loth!
Still, if prayer and fasting tame the pride long pampered,
Mercy may be mine: amendment never comes too late.
325　How can I amend beset by cursers, kickers?
Pluck this brand from out the burning! Once away, I take my Bible-oath,
Never more—so long as life's weak lamp-flame flickers—
No, not once I'll tease you, but in silence bear my fate!"

"Gently, good my Genius, Oracle unerring!
330　Strange now! can you guess on what—as in you peeped—it was I
　　　pondered?
You and I are both of one mind in preferring
Power to wealth, but—here's the point—what sort of power, I ask?
Ruling men is vulgar, easy and ignoble:
Rid yourself of conscience, quick you have at beck and call the fond
　　　herd.
335　But who wields the crozier, down may fling the crow-bill:
That's the power I covet now; soul's sway o'er souls—my task!

"'Well but,' you object, 'you have it, who by glamour
Dress up lies to look like truths, mask folly in the garb of reason:
Your soul acts on theirs, sure, when the people clamour
340　Hold their peace, now fight now fondle,—earwigged through the
　　　brains.'
Possibly! but still the operation's mundane,
Grosser than a taste demands which—craving manna—kecks at
　　　peason—
Power o'er men by wants material: why should one deign
Rule by sordid hopes and fears—a grunt for all one's pains?

322| MS:gained I fear a　*P1880:*gained, I fear, a　　324| MS:Mercy waits §crossed out§
325| MS:But can　*P1880:*How can　　326| MS:my Bible-oath　*CP1880:*my Bible-oath,
328| MS:you but　*P1880:*you, but　　329| MS:oracle
*P1880:*my Genius, Oracle　　334| MS:conscience quick　*P1880:*conscience, quick
335| MS:crow-bill;　*P1880:*crow-bill:　　336| MS:now,—the §crossed out and replaced
above by§ soul's <> souls my　*P1880:*now; soul's <> 　souls—my　　337| MS:'Well but,—
' you object 'you　*P1880:* "'Well but,' you object, 'you　　338| MS:truths, and §crossed out
and replaced above by§ mask　　342| MS:which looked for §last two words crossed out and
replaced above by§ craving <> lights on §two words crossed out and replaced above by two
words§ kecks at　*P1880:*which—craving　　344| MS:all his pains?　*P1880:*all one's pains?

345 "No, if men must praise me, let them praise to purpose!
Would we move the world, not earth but heaven must be our
    fulcrum—*pou sto!*
Thus I seek to move it: Master, why intérpose—
Baulk my climbing close on what's the ladder's topmost round?
Statecraft 'tis I step from: when by priestcraft hoisted
350 Up to where my foot may touch the highest rung which fate allows
    toe,
Then indeed ask favour! On you shall be foisted
No excuse: I'll pay my debt, each penny of the pound!

"Ho, my knaves without there! Lead this worthy downstairs!
No farewell, good Paul—nay, Peter—what's your name remembered
    rightly?
355 Come, he's humble: out another would have flounced—airs
Suitors often give themselves when our sort bow them forth.
Did I touch his rags? He surely kept his distance:
Yet, there somehow passed to me from him—where'er the virtue
    might lie—
Something that inspires my soul—Oh, by assistance
360 Doubtlessly of Peter!—still, he's worth just what he's worth!

"'Tis my own soul soars now : soaring—how? By crawling!
I'll to Rome, before Rome's feet the temporal-supreme lay prostrate!
'Hands' (I'll say) 'proficient once in pulling, hauling
This and that way men as I was minded—feet now clasp!'

345| MS:No *P1880:* "No   346| MS:When I §two words crossed out and replaced above
by two words§ Would we <> world not <> must §crossed out and replaced above by§ should
§crossed out and original reading restored§ must be my §crossed out and replaced above by§
our—*pou sto*—fulcrum §transposed to§ our—fulcrum—*pou sto!* *P1880:* world, not <> our
fulcrum   347| MS:Thus about §crossed out and replaced above by two words§ I seek <>
it—Master, §word and comma inserted above§ why need you §last two words crossed out§
P1880: it: Master   348| MS:Stop §crossed out and replaced above by§ Stay §crossed out
and replaced by§ Baulk   349| MS:from,—when by Priestcraft *P1880:* from: when by
priestcraft   350| MS:toe,— *P1880:* toe,   352| MS:excuse—I'll *P1880:* excuse: I'll
353| MS:Ho <> this person downstairs! *P1880:* "Ho <> this worthy downstairs!
354| MS:farewell—good *P1880:* farewell, good   360| MS:of Peter,—still
P1880: of Peter!—still   361| MS:'Tis *P1880:* "'Tis   362| MS:to Rome: before <>
temporal supreme lay prostrate. *P1880:* to Rome, before <> temporal-supreme
lay prostrate!   363| MS:'Hands *1889a:* Hands §emended to§ 'Hands §see Editorial
Notes§   364| MS:feet they clasp! *P1880:* feet now clasp!'

365 Ay, the Kaiser's self has wrung them in his fervour!
    Now—they only sue to slave for Rome, nor at one doit the cost rate.
    Rome's adopted child—no bone, no muscle, nerve or
    Sinew of me but I'll strain, though out my life I gasp!"

    As he stood one evening proudly—(he had traversed
370 Rome on horseback—peerless pageant!—claimed the Lateran as new
        Pope)—
    Thinking "All's attained now! Pontiff! Who could have erst
    Dreamed of my advance so far when, some ten years ago,
    I embraced devotion, grew from priest to bishop,
    Gained the Purple, bribed the Conclave, got the Two-thirds, saw my
        coop ope,
375 Came out—what Rome hails me! O were there a wish-shop,
    Not one wish more would I purchase—lord of all below!

    "Ha!—who dares intrude now—puts aside the arras?
    What, old Peter, here again, at such a time, in such a presence?
    Satan sends this plague back merely to embarrass
380 Me who enter on my office—little needing you!
    'Faith, I'm touched myself by age, but you look Tithon!
    Were it vain to seek of you the sole prize left—re-juvenescence?
    Well, since flesh is grass which Time must lay his scythe on,
    Say your say and so depart and make no more ado!"

366| MS:Now they <> for Rome nor <> rate: *P1880:*Now—they <> for Rome, nor <>
rate.   368| MS:but shall §crossed out and replaced above by§ I'll strain though, straining
§crossed out and replaced above by two words§ out my, life I gasp!   *P1880:*strain, though out
my life I gasp!"   371| MS:now: Pontiff   *P1880:*now! Pontiff   373| MS:devotion,
from a priest grew bishop,   *P1880:*devotion, grew from priest to bishop,
374| MS:purple <> conclave <> two-thirds   *P1880:*the Purple, bribed the Conclave, got the
Two-thirds   375| MS:me? O <> wish-shop   *P1880:*me! O <> wish-shop,
377| MS:Ha—who   *P1880:*"Ha   *1889a:*"Ha!—who   378| MS:old Peter, back again
*P1880:*old Peter, here again   379| MS:plague now merely to embarrass   *P1880:*plague
back merely to embarrass   381| MS:"Faith <> look Tithon,—   *P1880:*'Faith <> look
Tithon!   382| MS:Vain it were to <> thing wanted §two words crossed out and replaced
above by two words and dash§ prize left—re-juvenescence: *P1880:*Were it vain to <>
re-juvenescence?   384| MS:and then depart <> ado!   *P1880:*and so depart <> ado!"

385 Peter faltered—coughing first by way of prologue—
"Holiness, your help comes late: a death at ninety little matters.
Padua, build poor Peter's pyre now, on log roll log,
Burn away—I've lived my day! Yet here's the sting in death—
I've an author's pride: I want my Book's survival:
390 See, I've hid it in my breast to warm me mid the rags and tatters!
Save it—tell next age your Master had no rival!
Scholar's debt discharged in full, be 'Thanks' my latest breath!"

"Faugh, the frowsy bundle—scribblings harum-scarum
Scattered o'er a dozen sheepskins! What's the name of this farrago?
395 Ha—'*Conciliator Differentiarum*'—
Man and book may burn together, cause the world no loss!
Stop—what else? A tractate—eh, '*De Speciebus*
Ceremonialis Ma-gi-æ?' I dream sure! Hence, away, go,
Wizard,—quick avoid me! Vain you clasp my knee, buss
400 Hand that bears the Fisher's ring or foot that boasts the Cross!

"Help! The old magician clings like an octopus!
Ah, you rise now—fuming, fretting, frowning, if I read your features!
Frown, who cares? We're Pope—once Pope, you can't unpope us!
Good—you muster up a smile: that's better! Still so brisk?
405 All at once grown youthful? But the case is plain! Ass—
Here I dally with the fiend, yet know the Word—compels all creatures
Earthly, heavenly, hellish. *Apage, Sathanas!*
Dicam verbum Salomonis—" "—*dicite!*" When—whisk!—

What was changed? The stranger gave his eyes a rubbing:
410 There smiled Peter's face turned back a moment at him o'er the shoulder,
As the black door shut, bang! "So he 'scapes a drubbing!"

386| MS:Holiness <> late: one's death   *P1880:*"Holiness <> late: a death
388| MS:day,—yet   *P1880:*day! Yet   390| MS:Here I've <> tatters: *P1880:*See, I've <>
tatters!   391| MS:it,—tell   *P1880:*it—tell   392| MS:be 'Thanks!' my <> breath.
*P1880:*be 'Thanks' my <> breath!"   395| MS:Ha—'Conciliator Differentiarum'—
*P1880:*Ha—'*Conciliator Differentiarum*'—   397| MS:eh, 'De Speciebus   *P1880:*eh, *De Speciebus*
398| MS:Ceremonialis Ma-gi-æ.' I   *P1880: Ceremonialis Ma-gi-æ?*' I   401| MS:Help
P1880:"Help   403| MS:once Pope you   *P1880:*once Pope, you   407| MS:hellish.
Apage, Sathanas!   *1889a:*hellish. *Apage, Sathanas* §emended to§ hellish. *Apage, Sathanas!* §see
Editorial Notes§   408| MS:when   *CP1880: dicite!*" When   410| MS:face §inserted
above§   411| MS:the house-door shut   *P1880:*the black-door shut   *1889a:*black door

(Quoth a boy who, unespied, had stopped to hear the talk).
"That's the way to thank these wizards when they bid men
Benedicite! What ails you? You, a man, and yet no bolder?

415 Foreign Sir, you look but foolish!" *"Idmen, idmen!"*
Groaned the Greek. "O Peter, cheese at last I know from chalk!"

Peter lived his life out, menaced yet no martyr,
Knew himself the mighty man he was—such knowledge all his
    guerdon,
Left the world a big book—people but in part err

420 When they style a true *Scientiæ Com-pen-di-um:*
"Admirationem incutit" they sourly
Smile, as fast they shut the folio which myself was somehow spurred
    on
Once to ope: but love—life's milk which daily, hourly,
Blockheads lap—O Peter, still thy taste of love's to come!

425 Greek, was your ambition likewise doomed to failure?
True, I find no record you wore purple, walked with axe and fasces,
Played some antipope's part: still, friend, don't turn tail, you're
Certain, with but these two gifts, to gain earth's prize in time!
Cleverness uncurbed by conscience—if you ransacked

430 Peter's book you'd find no potent spell like these to rule the masses;
Nor should want example, had I not to transact
Other business. Go your ways, you'll thrive! So ends my rhyme.

———————————

414| MS:*Benedicte,*—as then he bade you §last five words crossed out and replaced above by
three words and question mark§ what ails you?   —you, a §last two words crossed out then
restored§   *P1880:Benedicite!* What <> you? You   415| MS:Why §crossed out and
replaced above by three words§   Do you know §three words crossed out and replaced in
margin by two words§ Learned Sir <> foolish? §altered to§ foolish! <> *idmen*—"
P1880:idmen!"   *CP1880:* Learned §crossed out and replaced in margin by§ Foreign
416| MS:the Greek, "O Peter—cheese I now do §last three words crossed out and replaced
above by three words§ at last I   *P1880:*the Greek. "O Peter, cheese   416-17| MS:R.B.
Jan. 20. L.D.I.E. §inserted below line 416 and crossed out§   422| MS:Smile as <> folio—
I myself   *P1880:*Smile, as <> folio which myself   424| MS:lap—Oh   *P1880:*lap—O
427| MS:part,—still   *P1880:*part: still   428| MS:Certain with but those two gifts to
*P1880:*Certain, with but those §altered to§ these two gifts, to   430| MS:like this to
*P1880:*this §altered to§ these   432| MS:thrive!—so   *P1880:*thrive! So

When these parts Tiberius,—not yet Cæsar,—travelled,
Passing Padua, he consulted Padua's Oracle of Geryon
435 (God three-headed, thrice wise) just to get unravelled
Certain tangles of his future. "Fling at Abano
Golden dice," it answered: "dropt within the fount there,
Note what sum the pips present!" And still we see each die, the very
      one,
Turn up, through the crystal,—read the whole account there
440 Where 'tis told by Suetonius,—each its highest throw.

Scarce the sportive fancy-dice I fling show "Venus:"
Still—for love of that dear land which I so oft in dreams revisit—
I have—oh, not sung! but lilted (as—between us—
Grows my lazy custom) this its legend. What the lilt?

437| MS:answered—"dropt *CP1880:*answered— §altered to§ answered: "dropt
440-41| MS:throw./ §¶§ Scarce <> show "Venus": *P1880:*throw./ §no¶§ Scarce <> show
"Venus:" *CP1880:*show "Venus:" §brackets around line 441, star in margin, and note at
bottom of page reading "Leave a space—this being a new stanza."§
442| MS:which I so oft §last three words inserted above§ in my §crossed out§
dreams I oft §last two words crossed out§   443| MS:have—Oh *1889a:*oh
444| MS:Gets §crossed out and replaced above by§ Grows

DOCTOR ——

A Rabbi told me: On the day allowed
Satan for carping at God's rule, he came,
Fresh from our earth, to brave the angel-crowd.

"What is the fault now?" "This I find to blame:
5   Many and various are the tongues below,
Yet all agree in one speech, all proclaim

"'Hell has no might to match what earth can show:
Death is the strongest-born of Hell, and yet
Stronger than Death is a Bad Wife, we know.'

10   "Is it a wonder if I fume and fret—
Robbed of my rights, since Death am I, and mine
The style of Strongest? Men pay Nature's debt

"Because they must at my demand; decline
To pay it henceforth surely men will please,
15   Provided husbands with bad wives combine

"To baffle Death. Judge between me and these!"
"Thyself shalt judge. Descend to earth in shape
Of mortal, marry, drain from froth to lees

"The bitter draught, then see if thou escape
20   Concluding, with men sorrowful and sage,
A Bad Wife's strength Death's self in vain would ape!"

How Satan entered on his pilgrimage,
Conformed himself to earthly ordinance,
Wived and played husband well from youth to age

DOCTOR ——   ³| MS:Black §crossed out and replaced above by§ Freshly < > to show
§crossed out§ *P1880:*Fresh from   ⁷| *CP1880:*show §colon added in margin§ show:
¹²| MS:style Ear §crossed out and replaced above by two words and question mark§ of
Strongest?   ¹⁹| *1880:*'The   *1889a:*"The   ²⁴| and was §crossed out and replaced
above by§ played < > here §crossed out and replaced above by§ well

25   Intrepidly—I leave untold, advance
    Through many a married year until I reach
    A day when—of his father's countenance

    The very image, like him too in speech
    As well as thought and deed,—the union's fruit
30   Attained maturity. "I needs must teach

    "My son a trade: but trade, such son to suit,
    Needs seeking after. He a man of war?
    Too cowardly! A lawyer wins repute—

    "Having to toil and moil, though—both which are
35   Beyond this sluggard. There's Divinity:
    No, that's my own bread-winner—that be far

    "From my poor offspring! Physic? Ha, we'll try
    If this be practicable. Where's my wit?
    Asleep?—since, now I come to think. . . . Ay, ay!

40   "Hither, my son! Exactly have I hit
    On a profession for thee. *Medicus*—
    Behold, thou art appointed! Yea, I spit

27] MS:The §crossed out and replaced above by§ A   29] MS:Thought §crossed out and
replaced above by two words§ As well   32] MS:Requires some §last two words crossed
out and replaced above by§ Needs < > after. §word and period inserted above§ He
36] MS:No, he's §crossed out and replaced above by§ that's my flesh and blood: my fate §last
five words crossed out and replaced above by three words§ own bread-winner—that
37] MS:my sole §crossed out and replaced above by§ poor offspring's §altered to§ offspring!
Medicine? §last word and question mark crossed out and replaced above by one word and
question mark§ Physic? Ha §inserted above§ We'll   *P1880:*offspring! Physic? Ha, we'll
1880:'From   *1889a:*"From   38] MS:If that be < > wit   *P1880:*If this be   *1889a:*wit?
39] MS:think . . Ay   *P1880:*think . . . Ay   40] MS:son! Was never trade so fit §last five
words crossed out and replaced above by four words§ Exactly have I hit
41] MS:As that which I design thee! §last six words and exclamation point crossed out and
replaced above by five words and period§ On the profession for thee. *Medicus*—
*P1880:*On a profession   42] MS:appointed: yea   *P1880:*appointed! Yea
43] MS:eyes, impart §crossed out and replaced above by§ bestow

"Upon thine eyes, bestow a virtue thus
That henceforth not this human form I wear
45 Shalt thou perceive alone, but—one of us

"By privilege—thy fleshly sight shall bear
Me in my spirit-person as I walk
The world and take my prey appointed there.

"Doctor once dubbed—what ignorance shall baulk
50 Thy march triumphant? Diagnose the gout
As cholic, and prescribe it cheese for chalk—

"No matter! All's one: cure shall come about
And win thee wealth—fees paid with such a roar
Of thanks and praise alike from lord and lout

55 "As never stunned man's ears on earth before.
'How may this be?' Why, that's my sceptic! Soon
Truth will corrupt thee, soon thou doubt'st no more!

"Why is it I bestow on thee the boon
Of recognizing me the while I go
60 Invisibly among men, morning, noon

"And night, from house to house, and—quick or slow—
Take my appointed prey? They summon thee
For help, suppose: obey the summons! so!

47| MS:spirit person *P1880:*spirit-person   51| MS:cholic and *P1880:*cholic, and
52| MS:matter! All. as §crossed out and replaced above by apostrophe and §§ All.'s < > cure
§last word inserted above§ *P1880:*matter! All's one   55| MS:stunned the ears
*P1880:*stunned man's ears   57| MS:corrupt. §period crossed out§ thee, §word inserted
above§ too §crossed out§   58| MS:"But why? §last two words and question mark crossed
out and replaced above by three words§ Why is it I have §crossed out§ bestowed §last two
letters crossed out§ *P1880:*'Why *1880:* "Why   60| MS:men,—morning
*P1880:*men, morning   63| MS:help, thou dost §last two words crossed out and replaced
above by one word and colon§ suppose: < > summons: so! *P1880:*summons! so!

"Enter, look round! Where's Death? Know—I am he,
65   Satan who work all evil: I who bring
Pain to the patient in whate'er degree.

"I, then, am there: first glance thine eye shall fling
Will find me—whether distant or at hand,
As I am free to do my spiriting.

70   "At such mere first glance thou shalt understand
Wherefore I reach no higher up the room
Than door or window, when my form is scanned.

"Howe'er friends' faces please to gather gloom,
Bent o'er the sick,—howe'er himself desponds,—
75   In such case Death is not the sufferer's doom.

"Contrariwise, do friends rejoice my bonds
Are broken, does the captive in his turn
Crow 'Life shall conquer'? Nip these foolish fronds

"Of hope a-sprout, if haply thou discern
80   Me at the head—my victim's head, be sure!
Forth now! This taught thee, little else to learn!

And forth he went. Folk heard him ask demure
"How do you style this ailment? (There he peeps,
My father, through the arras!) Sirs, the cure

64| MS:round: where's *P1880:*round! Where's   65| MS:works §last letter crossed out§
all evil: I 'tis, bring *1889a:*evil: I who bring   67| MS:"I, §comma probably added when
following words were replaced§ shall be §two words crossed out and replaced above by two
words§ then, am   69| *1880:*spiriting. *1889a:*spiriting.   70| MS:such a §crossed
out and replaced above by§ mere   74| MS:sick, §comma probably added when following
words were replaced§ man, or §last two words crossed out and replaced above by§ howe'er
*P1880:*sick,—howe'er   78| MS:Crow 'I §crossed out and replaced above by§ Life
*P1880:*conquer?' Nip *1889a:*conquer'? Nip   80| MS:head—my §crossed out and
replaced above by§ a *P1880:*head—my victims   82| MS:went. You heard
*P1880:*went. Folks heard *1889a:*went. Folk   83| MS:do they style *P1880:*do you style

85   "Is plain as A. B. C.! Experience steeps
      Blossoms of pennyroyal half an hour
      In sherris. *Sumat!*—Lo, how sound he sleeps—

      "The subject you presumed was past the power
      Of Galen to relieve!" Or else "How's this?
90   Why call for help so tardily? Clouds lour

      "Portentously indeed, Sirs! (Nought's amiss:
      He's at the bed-foot merely.) Still, the storm
      May pass averted—not by quacks, I wis

      "Like you, my masters! You, forsooth, perform
95   A miracle? Stand, sciolists, aside!
      Blood, ne'er so cold, at ignorance grows warm!"

      Which boasting by result was justified,
      Big as might words be: whether drugged or left
      Drugless, the patient always lived, not died.

100   Great the heir's gratitude, so nigh bereft
      Of all he prized in this world: sweet the smile
      Of disconcerted rivals: "Cure?—say, theft

      "From Nature in despite of Art—so style
      This off-hand kill-or-cure work! You did much,
105   I had done more: folk cannot wait awhile!"

      But did the case change? was it—"Scarcely such
      The symptoms as to warrant our recourse
      To your skill, Doctor! Yet since just a touch

87| MS:lo *P1880:*sherris. *Sumat!*—Lo   92| MS:merely) Still *P1880:*merely.) Still
93| MS:wis, *P1880:*wis   96| MS:At ignorance blood, <> cold, grows *1889a:*Blood,
<> cold, at ignorance grows   97| MS:And boasting *P1880:*Which boasting
101| MS:world: sour the *P1880:*world: sweet the   104| MS:Such §crossed out and
replaced above by§ This   105| MS:more, would §crossed out§ folks but §crossed out and
replaced above by§ cannot *P1880:*more: folks *1889a:*folk   106| MS:But §added in
margin§ Did §altered to§ did <> change? §question mark probably added when following two
words and mark of punctuation were replaced§ on entry? §last two words and question mark
crossed out and replaced above by two words and dash§ was it—   108| MS:skill, Doctor—

"Of pulse, a taste of breath, has all the force
110   With you of long investigation claimed
By others,—tracks an ailment to its source

"Intuitively,—may we ask unblamed
What from this pimple you prognosticate?"
"Death!" was the answer, as he saw and named

115   The coucher by the sick man's head. "Too late
You send for my assistance. I am bold
Only by Nature's leave, and bow to Fate!

"Besides, you have my rivals: lavish gold!
How comfortably quick shall life depart
120   Cosseted by attentions manifold!

"One day, one hour ago, perchance my art
Had done some service. Since you have yourselves
Chosen—before the horse—to put the cart,

"Why, Sirs, the sooner that the sexton delves
125   Your patient's grave, the better! How you stare
—Shallow, for all the deep books on your shelves!

"Fare you well, fumblers!" Do I need declare
What name and fame, what riches recompensed
The Doctor's practice? Never anywhere

130   Such an adept as daily evidenced
Each new vaticination! Oh, not he
Like dolts who dallied with their scruples, fenced

---

yet   *P1880:*skill, Doctor! Yet   114| MS:"Death" was the answer—as   *P1880:* "Death!" was
the answer, as   118| MS:Summon §crossed out and replaced above by quotation marks and
three words§ "Besides, you have my rivals: rather §crossed out§   122| MS:done some
§crossed out§ good service §inserted above§ §illegible punctuation mark, possibly a colon,
crossed out§ but §crossed out§ since §altered to§ Since   *P1880:*done some service. Since
125| MS:His worthy's §two words crossed out and replaced above by two words§ Your patient's
grave—the < > they §crossed out and replaced above by§ you   *P1880:*grave, the   126| MS:on
their §crossed out and replaced above by§ your   129| MS:practise   *P1880:*practice
130| MS:adept was daily   *P1880:*adept as daily   131| MS:By new   *P1880:*Each new

With subterfuge, nor gave out frank and free
Something decisive! If he said "I save
135   The patient," saved he was: if "Death will be

"His portion," you might count him dead. Thus brave,
Behold our worthy, sans competitor
Throughout the country, on the architrave

Of Glory's temple golden-lettered for
140   Machaon *redivivus!* So, it fell
That, of a sudden, when the Emperor

Was smit by sore disease, I need not tell
If any other Doctor's aid was sought
To come and forthwith make the sick Prince well.

145   "He will reward thee as a monarch ought.
Not much imports the malady; but then,
He clings to life and cries like one distraught

"For thee—who, from a simple citizen,
Mayst look to rise in rank,—nay, haply wear
150   A medal with his portrait,—always when

"Recovery is quite accomplished. There!
Pass to the presence!" Hardly has he crossed
The chamber's threshold when he halts, aware

---

[134] MS:decisive. If   *P1880:*decisive! If   [135] MS:patient" saved   *P1880:*patient," saved
[136] MS:portion—" you   *P1880:*portion," you   [137]   MS:our sole sage §two words
crossed out and replaced above by one word and comma§ worthy,—no competitor
*P1880:*worthy, sans competitor   [138] MS:country—on   *P1880:*country, on
[142] MS:smitten §last three letters crossed out§ by sore §inserted above§   [143]   MS:other
aid than his was   *P1880:*other Doctor's aid was   [144]   MS:come to Court §last two words
crossed out§ and forthwith §inserted above§   [148] MS:For   *P1880:*"For
[149]   MS:May'st < > rank—who knows? §last two words and question mark crossed out§ —and
haply §inserted above§   *P1880:*rank,—nay, haply   *1889a:*Mayst   [150] MS:portrait—
always   *P1880:*portrait,—always   [151] MS:Recovery   *P1880:*"Recovery

Of who stands sentry by the head. All's lost.
155 "Sire, nought avails my art: you near the goal
And end the race by giving up the ghost."

"How?" cried the monarch: "Names upon your roll
Of half my subjects rescued by your skill—
Old and young, rich and poor—crowd cheek by jowl

160 "And yet no room for mine? Be saved I will!
Why else am I earth's foremost potentate?
Add me to these and take as fee your fill

"Of gold—that point admits of no debate
Between us: save me, as you can and must,—
165 Gold, till your gown's pouch cracks beneath the weight!"

This touched the Doctor. "Truly a home-thrust,
Parent, you will not parry! Have I dared
Entreat that you forego the meal of dust

"—Man that is snake's meat—when I saw prepared
170 Your daily portion? Never! Just this once,
Go from his head, then,—let his life be spared!

Whisper met whisper in the gruff response
"Fool, I must have my prey: no inch I budge
From where thou see'st me thus myself ensconce."

175 "Ah," moaned the sufferer, "by thy look I judge
Wealth fails to tempt thee: what if honours prove
More efficacious? Nought to him I grudge

157| MS:monarch "Names are §crossed out and replaced above by§ up on §last two words
connected to form one word§   *P1880:*monarch: "Names   158| MS:skill,—
*P1880:*skill—   159| MS:poor crowd <> jowl,—   *P1880:*poor—crowd <> jowl,
*1880:*jowl   160| MS:will—   *P1880:*will!   162| MS:take for fee   *P1880:*take as fee
164| MS:you shall §crossed out and replaced above by§ can   167| MS:you will §crossed
out and replaced above by§ must §crossed out and original reading restored§ will
169| MS:snake's-meat   *P1880:*snake's meat   175| MS:sufferer "by
*P1880:*sufferer, "by   176| MS:honors   *1880:*what i honors   *1889a:*what if honours
177| MS:nought   *P1880:*efficacious? Nought

"Who saves me. Only keep my head above
The cloud that's creeping round it—I'll divide
180 My empire with thee! No? What's left but—love?

"Does love allure thee? Well then, take as bride
My only daughter, fair beyond belief!
Save me—to-morrow shall the knot be tied!"

"Father, you hear him! Respite ne'er so brief
185 Is all I beg: go now and come again
Next day, for aught I care: respect the grief

"Mine will be if thy first-born sues in vain!"
"Fool, I must have my prey!" was all he got
In answer. But a fancy crossed his brain.

190 "I have it! Sire, methinks a meteor shot
Just now across the heavens and neutralized
Jove's salutary influence: 'neath the blot

"Plumb are you placed now: well that I surmised
The cause of failure! Knaves, reverse the bed!"
195 "Stay!" groaned the monarch, "I shall be capsized—

"Jolt—jolt—my heels uplift where late my head
Was lying—sure I'm turned right round at last!
What do you say now, Doctor?" Nought he said:

For why? With one brisk leap the Antic passed
200 From couch-foot back to pillow,—as before,
Lord of the situation. Long aghast

180| MS:thee! No? §last word and question mark inserted above§ What's §apostrophe and last letter probably added when following word was replaced§ remains §crossed out and replaced above by§ left   186| MS:day for   *P1880:* day, for   187| MS:thy §over /§
192| MS:Sat's §crossed out and replaced in margin by§ Jove's   195| MS:monarch "I
P1880: monarch, "I   196| MS:heels are now §last two words crossed out and replaced above by§ uplift   197| MS:last   *P1880:* last!   198| *P1880:* said.   *1880:* said
1889a: said: 199| MS:antic   *P1880:* the Antic   200| MS:bed-foot §first three letters crossed out and replaced above by§ couch <> pillow, as   *P1880:* pillow,—as

The Doctor gazed, then "Yet one trial more
Is left me" inwardly he uttered. "Shame
Upon thy flinty heart! Do I implore

205 "This trifling favour in the idle name
Of mercy to the moribund? I plead
The cause of all thou dost affect: my aim

"Befits my author! Why would I succeed?
Simply that by success I may promote
210 The growth of thy pet virtues—pride and greed.

"But keep thy favours!—curse thee! I devote
Henceforth my service to the other side.
No time to lose: the rattle's in his throat.

"So,—not to leave one last resource untried,—
215 Run to my house with all haste, somebody!
Bring me that knobstick thence, so often plied

"With profit by the astrologer—shall I
Disdain its help, the mystic Jacob's-Staff?
Sire, do but have the courage not to die

220 "Till this arrive! Let none of you dare laugh!
Though rugged its exterior, I have seen
That implement work wonders, send the chaff

202| MS:gazed, till §crossed out and replaced above by§ then   203| MS:uttered.
"Shame   *1889a:*uttered "Shame §emended to§ uttered. "Shame §see Editorial Notes§
204| MS:thy, §over *thee*§ parent mine §comma and two words crossed out and replaced above
by two words and exclamation mark§ flinty heart! ! Did §crossed out and replaced above by§
Do   *P1880:*heart! Do   206| MS:moribund— §altered to§ moribund? or §crossed out
and replaced above by§ I   207| MS:affect? §altered to§ affect: My   209| MS:success
I should §crossed out and replaced above by§ might §crossed out and replaced by§ may
210| MS:thy §over *thine*§ own §crossed out and replaced above by§ pet
211| MS:thy station §crossed out and replaced above by§ favors—curse   *P1880:*favors!—
curse *1889a:*favours   220| MS:arrive! What varlet vents a §last four words crossed out
and replaced above by five words§ Let none of you dare laugh? §altered to§ laugh!

"Quick and thick flying from the wheat—I mean,
By metaphor, a human sheaf it thrashed
225   Flail-like. Go fetch it! Or—a word between

"Just you and me, friend!—go bid, unabashed,
My mother, whom you'll find there, bring the stick
Herself—herself, mind!" Out the lackey dashed

Zealous upon the errand. Craft and trick
230   Are meat and drink to Satan: and he grinned
—How else?—at an excuse so politic

For failure: scarce would Jacob's-Staff rescind
Fate's firm decree! And ever as he neared
The agonizing one, his breath like wind

235   Froze to the marrow, while his eye-flash seared
Sense in the brain up: closelier and more close
Pressing his prey, when at the door appeared

—Who but his Wife the Bad? Whereof one dose,
One grain, one mite of the medicament,
240   Sufficed him. Up he sprang. One word, too gross

To soil my lips with,—and through ceiling went
Somehow the Husband. "That a storm's dispersed
We know for certain by the sulphury scent!

224| MS:metaphor, the §crossed out and replaced above by§ a < > sheaves §altered to§ sheaf
§punctuation mark, possibly a colon, illegibly crossed out§   225| MS:it— §altered to§ it!
or §altered to§ Or   226| MS:friend!—Go *P1880:*go   227| MS:mother whom
*P1880:*mother, whom   233| MS:decree! And closlier still §two words crossed out and
replaced above by two words§ ever as   234| MS:one—his *P1880:*one, his
237| MS:Pressed on his *P1880:*Pressing his   238| MS:whereof one dose— *P1880:*the Bad?
Whereof one dose,   239| MS:grain one mite §last two words inserted above§ < > medicament
*P1880:*grain, one < > medicament,   241| MS:and §inserted above§ through the §crossed
out§ ceiling *P1880:*cieling *CP1880:*ceiling *1880:*cieling *1889a:*ceiling

"Hail to the Doctor! Who but one so versed
245   In all Dame Nature's secrets had prescribed
The staff thus opportunely? Style him first

"And foremost of physicians!" "I've imbibed
Elixir surely," smiled the prince,—"have gained
New lease of life. Dear Doctor, how you bribed

250   "Death to forego me, boots not: you've obtained
My daughter and her dowry. Death, I've heard,
Was still on earth the strongest power that reigned,

"Except a Bad Wife!" Whereunto demurred
Nowise the Doctor, so refused the fee
255   —No dowry, no bad wife!

                         "You think absurd
This tale?"—the Rabbi added: "True, our Talmud
Boasts sundry such: yet—have our elders erred
In thinking there's some water there, not all mud?"
I tell it, as the Rabbi told it me.

244| MS:the Staff-prescriber §crossed out and replaced above by three words§ Doctor! Who
but   246| MS:thus §over perhaps *so*§   248| MS:surely" smiled the prince "and
§crossed out and replaced above by§ have   *P1880:*surely," smiled the prince,—"have
253| MS:a Bad Wife!—" Whereunto   *P1880:*a Bad Wife!" Whereunto
254| MS:the Doctor, and §crossed out and replaced above by§ so   255| MS:dowry, and
§crossed out§ no bad §inserted above§   256| MS:tale",—the   *P1880:*tale."—
*CP1880:*tale." §altered to§ tale?"—the   257| MS:Has sundry   *P1880:*Boasts sundry

57

PAN AND LUNA

Si credere dignum est.—*Georgic.* iii. 390.

> O worthy of belief I hold it was,
> Virgil, your legend in those strange three lines!
> No question, that adventure came to pass
> One black night in Arcadia: yes, the pines,
> 5   Mountains and valleys mingling made one mass
> Of black with void black heaven: the earth's confines,
> The sky's embrace,—below, above, around,
> All hardened into black without a bound.
>
> Fill up a swart stone chalice to the brim
> 10   With fresh-squeezed yet fast-thickening poppy-juice:
> See how the sluggish jelly, late a-swim,
> Turns marble to the touch of who would loose
> The solid smooth, grown jet from rim to rim,
> By turning round the bowl! So night can fuse
> 15   Earth with her all-comprising sky. No less,
> Light, the least spark, shows air and emptiness.
>
> And thus it proved when—diving into space,
> Stript of all vapour, from each web of mist
> Utterly film-free—entered on her race
> 20   The naked Moon, full-orbed antagonist
> Of night and dark, night's dowry: peak to base,

PAN AND LUNA   *Epigraph*| MS:est—*Georgic*   *P1880:*est.—*Georgic*   [1]| MS:Oh,
worthy   *P1880:* Well worthy   *CP1880:*Well §crossed out and replaced both above and in the
margin by§ O   [3]| MS:question the §crossed out and replaced above by§ that
[4]| MS:That midnight §first word and first three letters of second word crossed out and
replaced above by two words§ One black   [5]| MS:vallies   *1889a:*valleys
[9]| Who §crossed out§ fills §altered to§ Fill <> stone §inserted above§
[10]| MS:poppy-juice,   *P1880:*poppy-juice: [11]| MS:Sees §last letter crossed out§
[13]| MS:smoothness, §last four letters crossed out§ grown §inserted above, crossed out, then
ness marked for reinstatement, then reinstatement marks crossed out§ grown §inserted above§
[19]| MS:film-free, entered   *P1880:*film-free—entered   [20]| MS:moon   *P1880:*naked
Moon   [21]| MS:dark her dowry   *P1880:*dark, night's dowry

Upstarted mountains, and each valley, kissed
To sudden life, lay silver-bright: in air
Flew she, revealed, Maid-Moon with limbs all bare.

25 Still as she fled, each depth—where refuge seemed—
Opening a lone pale chamber, left distinct
Those limbs: mid still-retreating blue, she teemed
Herself with whiteness,—virginal, uncinct
By any halo save what finely gleamed
30 To outline not disguise her: heaven was linked
In one accord with earth to quaff the joy,
Drain beauty to the dregs without alloy.

Whereof she grew aware. What help? When, lo,
A succourable cloud with sleep lay dense:
35 Some pine-tree-top had caught it sailing slow,
And tethered for a prize: in evidence
Captive lay fleece on fleece of piled-up snow
Drowsily patient: flake-heaped how or whence,
The structure of that succourable cloud,
40 What matter? Shamed she plunged into its shroud.

Orbed—so the woman-figure poets call
Because of rounds on rounds—that apple-shaped
Head which its hair binds close into a ball
Each side the curving ears—that pure undraped
45 Pout of the sister paps—that . . . Once for all,
Say—her consummate circle thus escaped
With its innumerous circlets, sank absorbed,
Safe in the cloud—O naked Moon full-orbed!

---

²⁴| MS:maid-moon <> left §crossed out and replaced above by§ all   *P1880:*revealed,
Maid-Moon   ²⁷| MS:limbs—the still-retreating blue: she   *CP1880:*limbs—the §dash and
last word replaced in margin by colon and one word§ limbs: mid <> blue: §altered to§ blue,
she   ³⁰| MS:To cir §perhaps for *circle,* crossed out§   ³¹| MS:to tas §perhaps for
taste, crossed out§   ³⁵| MS:slow   *P1880:*slow, §comma added in margin§
³⁷| MS:Captive, her §comma and last word crossed out and replaced above by§ lay
⁴¹| MS:woman-figured-moon we §altered to§ woman-figure poets   ⁴²| MS:of all her
§two words crossed out and replaced above by two words§ rounds on   ⁴⁸| MS:cloud—
that §crossed out and replaced above by§ O <> moon   *P1880:*naked Moon

But what means this? The downy swathes combine,
50   Conglobe, the smothery coy-caressing stuff
Curdles about her! Vain each twist and twine
Those lithe limbs try, encroached on by a fluff
Fitting as close as fits the dented spine
Its flexile ivory outside-flesh: enough!
55   The plumy drifts contract, condense, constringe,
Till she is swallowed by the feathery springe.

As when a pearl slips lost in the thin foam
Churned on a sea-shore, and, o'er-frothed, conceits
Herself safe-housed in Amphitrite's dome,—
60   If, through the bladdery wave-worked yeast, she meets
What most she loathes and leaps from,—elf from gnome
No gladlier,—finds that safest of retreats
Bubble about a treacherous hand wide ope
To grasp her—(divers who pick pearls so grope)—

65   So lay this Maid-Moon clasped around and caught
By rough red Pan, the god of all that tract:
He it was schemed the snare thus subtly wrought
With simulated earth-breath,—wool-tufts packed
Into a billowy wrappage. Sheep far-sought
70   For spotless shearings yield such: take the fact
As learned Virgil gives it,—how the breed
Whitens itself for ever: yes, indeed!

51| MS:her: vain   *P1880:*her! Vain   52| MS:try—encroached   *P1880:*try, encroached
55| MS:constringe   *P1880:*constringe,   59| MS:Herself received by §two words crossed out and replaced above by two words§ safe-housed in   60| MS:wave's-worked §altered to§ wave-worked   62-63| MS:finds that safest of retreats/ §last four words added above creating a new line§ Bubbles about §last two words added below with a line connecting them to the following word§ a   *1889a:*Bubble   64| MS:her (divers who §inserted above§ picking §last three letters crossed out§ pearl   *P1880:*her—(divers <> pearls
65| MS:So was the maid-moon   *P1880:*So lay this Maid-Moon
66| MS:all §inserted above§ that same §crossed out§ tract,—   *P1880:*tract:
67| MS:snare and subtly   *P1880:*snare thus subtly   68| MS:What §crossed out and replaced above by§ With   69| MS:wrappage,—sheep   *P1880:*wrappage. Sheep
71| MS:it,—thus §crossed out and replaced above by§ how

If one forefather ram, though pure as chalk
From tinge on fleece, should still display a tongue
75 Black 'neath the beast's moist palate, prompt men baulk
The propagating plague: he gets no young:
They rather slay him,—sell his hide to caulk
Ships with, first steeped in pitch,—nor hands are wrung
In sorrow for his fate: protected thus,
80 The purity we love is gained for us.

So did Girl-moon, by just her attribute
Of unmatched modesty betrayed, lie trapped,
Bruised to the breast of Pan, half-god half-brute,
Raked by his bristly boar-sward while he lapped
85 —Never say, kissed her! that were to pollute
Love's language—which moreover proves unapt
To tell how she recoiled—as who finds thorns
Where she sought flowers—when, feeling, she touched—horns!

Then—does the legend say?—first moon-eclipse
90 Happened, first swooning-fit which puzzled sore
The early sages? Is that why she dips
Into the dark, a minute and no more,
Only so long as serves her while she rips
The cloud's womb through and, faultless as before,
95 Pursues her way? No lesson for a maid
Left she, a maid herself thus trapped, betrayed?

Ha, Virgil? Tell the rest, you! "To the deep
Of his domain the wildwood, Pan forthwith

---

⁷³| MS:fore-father *1889a:*forefather ⁷⁵| MS:neath *P1880:*'neath
⁷⁶| MS:young— *P1880:*young: ⁸¹| MS:So lay §crossed out and replaced above by§
the §crossed out and replaced by§ did girl-moon *P1880:*did Girl-Moon *1889a:*did Girl-
moon ⁸²| MS:lay §altered to§ lie ⁸³| MS:half god half brute, *1889a:*half-god
half-brute, ⁸⁴| MS:boar- §last word and hyphen inserted above§ < > while fierce
§crossed out§ ⁸⁸| MS:when feeling she < > horns. *CP1880:*when §comma inserted§
when, feeling §comma inserted§ feeling, she < > horns! ⁸⁹| MS:say?—the §crossed
out§ < > moon- §last word and hyphen inserted above§ -eclipse *P1880:*moon-eclipse
⁹⁰| MS:swooning-fit that §crossed out and replaced above by§ which
⁹⁴| MS:and, lucid §crossed out and replaced above by§ faultless ⁹⁶| MS:a maid §last
two words inserted above§ ⁹⁷| MS:rest, §two letters, possibly *th*, crossed out§

Called her, and so she followed"—in her sleep,
100   Surely?—"by no means spurning him." The myth
Explain who may! Let all else go, I keep
—As of a ruin just a monolith—
Thus much, one verse of five words, each a boon:
Arcadia, night, a cloud, Pan, and the moon.

---

^{101|} MS:go—I *P1880:*go, I   ^{104|} MS:midnight, §first three letters crossed out§ a
§inserted above§

"Touch him ne'er so lightly, into song he broke:
Soil so quick-receptive,—not one feather-seed,
Not one flower-dust fell but straight its fall awoke
Vitalizing virtue: song would song succeed
5   Sudden as spontaneous—prove a poet-soul!"

                        Indeed?
Rock's the song-soil rather, surface hard and bare:
Sun and dew their mildness, storm and frost their rage
Vainly both expend,—few flowers awaken there:
Quiet in its cleft broods—what the after age
10   Knows and names a pine, a nation's heritage.

"TOUCH HIM NE'ER SO LIGHTLY"   3| *1880:*flower dust   *1889a:*flower-dust
9| MS:after-age   *P1880:*after age

JOCOSERIA

Edited by Allan C. Dooley

JOCOSERIA

Wanting is—what?
Summer redundant,
Blueness abundant,
—Where is the blot?
5 Beamy the world, yet a blank all the same,
—Framework which waits for a picture to frame:
What of the leafage, what of the flower?
Roses embowering with nought they embower!
Come then, complete incompletion, O comer,
10 Pant through the blueness, perfect the summer!
Breathe but one breath
Rose-beauty above,
And all that was death
Grows life, grows love,
15 Grows love!

―――――――――――――――――――――――――――――――――――――――

"WANTING IS—WHAT?"   MS:§ll. 1-15 flush left§   1889a:§ll. 1-4, 11-15 indented§
4| MS:the spot?   1889a:the blot?   10| MS:the Summer!   P1883:the summer!

JOCOSERIA

1883

DONALD

"Will you hear my story also,
    —Huge Sport, brave adventure in plenty?"
The boys were a band from Oxford,
    The oldest of whom was twenty.

5 The bothy we held carouse in
    Was bright with fire and candle;
Tale followed tale like a merry-go-round
    Whereof Sport turned the handle.

In our eyes and noses—turf-smoke:
10   In our ears a tune from the trivet,
Whence "Boiling, boiling," the kettle sang,
    "And ready for fresh Glenlivet."

So, feat capped feat, with a vengeance:
    Truths, though,—the lads were loyal:
15 "Grouse, five score brace to the bag!
    Deer, ten hours' stalk of the Royal!"

Of boasting, not one bit, boys!
    Only there seemed to settle
Somehow above your curly heads,
20   —Plain through the singing kettle,

Palpable through the cloud,
    As each new-puffed Havanna
Rewarded the teller's well-told tale,—
    This vaunt "To Sport—Hosanna!

25 "Hunt, fish, shoot,
          Would a man fulfil life's duty!
      Not to the bodily frame alone
          Does Sport give strength and beauty,

      "But character gains in—courage?
30   Ay, Sir, and much beside it!
      You don't sport, more's the pity:
          You soon would find, if you tried it,

      "Good sportsman means good fellow,
          Sound-hearted he, to the centre;
35   Your mealy-mouthed mild milksops
          —There's where the rot can enter!

      "There's where the dirt will breed,
          The shabbiness Sport would banish!
      Oh no, Sir, no! In your honoured case
40   All such objections vanish.

      "'Tis known how hard you studied:
          A Double-First—what, the jigger!
      Give me but half your Latin and Greek,
          I'll never again touch trigger!

45   "Still, tastes are tastes, allow me!
          Allow, too, where there's keenness
      For Sport, there's little likelihood
          Of a man's displaying meanness!"

      So, put on my mettle, I interposed.
50   "Will you hear my story?" quoth I.
      "Never mind how long since it happed,
          I sat, as we sit, in a bothy;

47| MS:For Sport there's *P1883:*For Sport, there's   54| MS:level, *P1883:*level:

"With as merry a band of mates, too,
    Undergrads all on a level:
55 (One's a Bishop, one's gone to the Bench,
    And one's gone—well, to the Devil.)

"When, lo, a scratching and tapping!
    In hobbled a ghastly visitor.
Listen to just what he told us himself
60   —No need of our playing inquisitor!"

———————

Do you happen to know in Ross-shire
    Mount . . . Ben . . . but the name scarce matters:
Of the naked fact I am sure enough,
    Though I clothe it in rags and tatters.

65 You may recognise Ben by description;
    Behind him—a moor's immenseness:
Up goes the middle mount of a range,
    Fringed with its firs in denseness.

Rimming the edge, its fir-fringe, mind!
70   For an edge there is, though narrow;
From end to end of the range, a stripe
    Of path runs straight as an arrow.

And the mountaineer who takes that path
    Saves himself miles of journey
75 He has to plod if he crosses the moor
    Through heather, peat and burnie.

But a mountaineer he needs must be,
    For, look you, right in the middle
Projects bluff Ben—with an end in *ich*—
80   Why planted there, is a riddle:

---

[61] MS:in Ross shire   *P1883:*in Ross-shire   [62] MS:Mount Ben . . but   *P1883:*Mount
Ben . . . but   *1889a:*Mount . . . Ben . . . but   [63] MS:enough   *P1883:*enough,

Since all Ben's brothers little and big
    Keep rank, set shoulder to shoulder,
And only this burliest out must bulge
    Till it seems—to the beholder

85 From down in the gully,—as if Ben's breast
    To a sudden spike diminished,
Would signify to the boldest foot
    "All further passage finished!"

Yet the mountaineer who sidles on
90   And on to the very bending,
Discovers, if heart and brain be proof,
    No necessary ending.

Foot up, foot down, to the turn abrupt
    Having trod, he, there arriving,
95 Finds—what he took for a point was breadth,
    A mercy of Nature's contriving.

So, he rounds what, when 'tis reached, proves straight,
    From one side gains the other:
The wee path widens—resume the march,
100   And he foils you, Ben my brother!

But Donald—(that name, I hope, will do)—
    I wrong him if I call "foiling"
The tramp of the callant, whistling the while
    As blithe as our kettle's boiling.

105 He had dared the danger from boyhood up,
    And now,—when perchance was waiting
A lass at the brig below,—'twixt mount
    And moor would he stand debating?

85| MS:breast,   *1889a:* breast   109| MS:twenty five,   *P1883:* twenty-five,

Moreover this Donald was twenty-five,
110   A glory of bone and muscle:
Did a fiend dispute the right of way,
         Donald would try a tussle.

Lightsomely marched he out of the broad
         On to the narrow and narrow;
115 A step more, rounding the angular rock,
         Reached the front straight as an arrow.

He stepped it, safe on the ledge he stood,
         When—whom found he full-facing?
What fellow in courage and wariness too,
120   Had scouted ignoble pacing,

And left low safety to timid mates,
         And made for the dread dear danger,
And gained the height where—who could guess
         He would meet with a rival ranger?

125 'Twas a gold-red stag that stood and stared,
         Gigantic and magnific,
By the wonder—ay, and the peril—struck
         Intelligent and pacific:

For a red deer is no fallow deer
130   Grown cowardly through park-feeding;
He batters you like a thunderbolt
         If you brave his haunts unheeding.

I doubt he could hardly perform *volte-face*
         Had valour advised discretion:
135 You may walk on a rope, but to turn on a rope
         No Blondin makes profession.

Yet Donald must turn, would pride permit,
         Though pride ill brooks retiring:

116| MS:stood   *P1883:*stood,   137| MS:would his pride   *P1883:*would pride

Each eyed each—mute man, motionless beast—
140   Less fearing than admiring.

These are the moments when quite new sense,
     To meet some need as novel,
Springs up in the brain: it inspired resource:
     —"Nor advance nor retreat but—grovel!"

145 And slowly, surely, never a whit
     Relaxing the steady tension
Of eye-stare which binds man to beast,—
     By an inch and inch declension,

Sank Donald sidewise down and down:
150   Till flat, breast upwards, lying
At his six-foot length, no corpse more still,
     —"If he cross me! The trick's worth trying."

Minutes were an eternity;
     But a new sense was created
155 In the stag's brain too; he resolves! Slow, sure,
     With eye-stare unabated,

Feelingly he extends a foot
     Which tastes the way ere it touches
Earth's solid and just escapes man's soft,
160   Nor hold of the same unclutches

Till its fellow foot, light as a feather whisk,
     Lands itself no less finely:
So a mother removes a fly from the face
     Of her babe asleep supinely.

165 And now 'tis the haunch and hind foot's turn
     —That's hard: can the beast quite raise it?

Yes, traversing half the prostrate length,
　　His hoof-tip does not graze it.

Just one more lift! But Donald, you see,
170　　Was sportsman first, man after:
A fancy lightened his caution through,
　　—He well-nigh broke into laughter.

"It were nothing short of a miracle!
　　Unrivalled, unexampled—
175　All sporting feats with this feat matched
　　Were down and dead and trampled!"

The last of the legs as tenderly
　　Follows the rest: or never
Or now is the time! His knife in reach,
180　　And his right-hand loose—how clever!

For this can stab up the stomach's soft,
　　While the left-hand grasps the pastern.
A rise on the elbow, and—now's the time
　　Or never: this turn's the last turn!

185　I shall dare to place myself by God
　　Who scanned—for He does—each feature
Of the face thrown up in appeal to Him
　　By the agonizing creature.

Nay, I hear plain words: "Thy gift brings this!"
190　　Up he sprang, back he staggered,
Over he fell, and with him our friend
　　—At following game no laggard.

Yet he was not dead when they picked next day
　　From the gully's depth the wreck of him;
195　His fall had been stayed by the stag beneath
　　Who cushioned and saved the neck of him.

172| 　MS:laughter: 　*1883a:*laughter 　*1889a:*laughter. 　　196| 　MS:him. 　*1889a:*him

But the rest of his body—why, doctors said,
 Whatever could break was broken;
Legs, arms, ribs, all of him looked like a toast
200 In a tumbler of port-wine soaken.

"That your life is left you, thank the stag!"
 Said they when—the slow cure ended—
They opened the hospital door, and thence
  —Strapped, spliced, main fractures mended,

205 And minor damage left wisely alone,—
 Like an old shoe clouted and cobbled,
Out—what went in a Goliath well-nigh,—
  Some half of a David hobbled.

"You must ask an alms from house to house:
210 Sell the stag's head for a bracket,
With its grand twelve tines—I'd buy it myself—
  And use the skin for a jacket!"

He was wiser, made both head and hide
 His win-penny: hands and knees on,
215 Would manage to crawl—poor crab—by the roads
  In the misty stalking-season.

And if he discovered a bothy like this,
 Why, harvest was sure: folk listened.
He told his tale to the lovers of Sport:
220 Lips twitched, cheeks glowed, eyes glistened.

And when he had come to the close, and spread
 His spoils for the gazers' wonder,
With "Gentlemen, here's the skull of the stag
  I was over, thank God, not under!"—

---

§emended to§ him. §see Editorial Notes§ 207| MS:a Goliah of Gath, *P1883:*of Gath,—
*CP1883:*a Goliath well nigh,— *1883:*well-nigh,— 215| MS:roads, *P1883:*roads
216| MS:stalking-season; *P1883:*stalking-season. 218| MS:folks *1889a:*folk

225. The company broke out in applause;
    "By Jingo, a lucky cripple!
Have a munch of grouse and a hunk of bread,
    And a tug, besides, at our tipple!"

And "There's my pay for your pluck!" cried This,
230   "And mine for your jolly story!"
Cried That, while 'Tother—but he was drunk—
    Hiccupped "A trump, a Tory!"

I hope I gave twice as much as the rest;
    For, as Homer would say, "within grate
235 Though teeth kept tongue," my whole soul growled
    "Rightly rewarded,—Ingrate!"

224| MS:over—thank God—not under!" *P1883:*over, thank God, not under!"—
225| MS:applause: *P1883:*applause;   227| MS:hunk of bread, *1889a:*hunk of
§emended to§ hunk of bread, §see Editorial Notes§   233| MS:rest: *P1883:*rest;

SOLOMON AND BALKIS

Solomon King of the Jews and the Queen of Sheba Balkis
Talk on the ivory throne, and we well may conjecture their talk is
Solely of things sublime: why else has she sought Mount Zion,
Climbed the six golden steps, and sat betwixt lion and lion?

5   She proves him with hard questions: before she has reached the
         middle
He smiling supplies the end, straight solves them riddle by riddle;
Until, dead-beaten at last, there is left no spirit in her,
And thus would she close the game whereof she was first beginner:

"O wisest thou of the wise, world's marvel and well-nigh monster,
10   One crabbed question more to construe or *vulgo* conster!
Who are those, of all mankind, a monarch of perfect wisdom
Should open to, when they knock at *spheteron do*—that's his dome?"

The King makes tart reply: "Whom else but the wise his equals
Should he welcome with heart and voice?—since, king though he be,
         such weak walls
15   Of circumstance—power and pomp—divide souls each from other
That whoso proves kingly in craft I needs must acknowledge my
         brother.

"Come poet, come painter, come sculptor, come builder—whate'er
         his condition,
Is he prime in his art? We are peers! My insight has pierced the
         partition
And hails—for the poem, the picture, the statue, the building—my
         fellow!
20   Gold's gold though dim in the dust: court-polish soon turns it yellow.

"But tell me in turn, O thou to thy weakling sex superior,
That for knowledge hast travelled so far yet seemest no whit the
         wearier,—

SOLOMON AND BALKIS   ¹| MS:of Sheba, Balkis,   *1889a:*of Sheba Balkis
⁶| MS:end, and solves   *P1883:*end, straight solves   ¹²| MS:that's, his   *1889a:*that's his

Who are those, of all mankind, a queen like thyself, consummate
In wisdom, should call to her side with an affable 'Up hither, come,
    mate!' "

25 "The Good are my mates—how else? Why doubt it?" the Queen
    upbridled:
"Sure even above the Wise,—or in travel my eyes have idled,—
I see the Good stand plain: be they rich, poor, shrewd or simple,
If Good they only are. . . . Permit me to drop my wimple!"

And in that bashful jerk of her body, she—peace, thou scoffer!—
30 Jostled the King's right-hand stretched courteously help to proffer,
And so disclosed a portent: all unaware the Prince eyed
The Ring which bore the Name—turned outside now from inside!

The truth-compelling Name!—and at once "I greet the Wise—Oh,
Certainly welcome such to my court—with this proviso:
35 The building must be my temple, my person stand forth the statue,
The picture my portrait prove, and the poem my praise—you cat,
    you!"

But Solomon nonplussed? Nay! "Be truthful in turn!" so bade he:
"See the Name, obey its hest!" And at once subjoins the lady
—"Provided the Good are the young, men strong and tall and proper,
40 Such servants I straightway enlist,—which means . . ." but the blushes
    stop her.

"Ah, Soul," the Monarch sighed, "that wouldst soar yet ever crawlest,
How comes it thou canst discern the greatest yet choose the smallest,
Unless because heaven is far, where wings find fit expansion,
While creeping on all-fours suits, suffices the earthly mansion?

45 "Aspire to the Best! But which? There are Bests and Bests so many,
With a *habitat* each for each, earth's Best as much Best as any!

24| MS:wisdom should *P1883:*wisdom, should   28| MS:are . . Permit *P1883:*are. . . .
Permit   36| MS:The poem my picture prove   *P1883:*The picture my portrait prove
40| MS:means . ." but *P1883:*means . . ." but   45| MS:the Best—but   *P1883:*the Best—
But   46| MS:for each,—earth's <> any. *P1883:*for each, earth's <> any!

On Lebanon roots the cedar—soil lofty, yet stony and sandy—
While hyssop, of worth in its way, on the wall grows low but handy.

"Above may the Soul spread wing, spurn body and sense beneath her;
Below she must condescend to plodding unbuoyed by æther.
In heaven I yearn for knowledge, account all else inanity;
On earth I confess an itch for the praise of fools—that's Vanity.

"It is nought, it will go, it can never presume above to trouble me;
But here,—why, it toys and tickles and teases, howe'er I redouble me
In a doggedest of endeavours to play the indifferent. Therefore,
Suppose we resume discourse? Thou hast travelled thus far: but
    wherefore?

"Solely for Solomon's sake, to see whom earth styles Sagest?"
Through her blushes laughed the Queen. "For the sake of a Sage? The
    gay jest!
On high, be communion with Mind—there, Body concerns not Balkis:
Down here,—do I make too bold? Sage Solomon,—one fool's small
    kiss!"

54| MS:and it tickles and teazes   *P1883:*and tickles   *1889a:*teases
55| MS:indifferent; therefore,   *P1883:*indifferent. Therefore,

CRISTINA AND MONALDESCHI

Ah, but how each loved each, Marquis!
    Here's the gallery they trod
    Both together, he her god,
    She his idol,—lend your rod,
5 Chamberlain!—ay, there they are—"*Quis*
    Separabit?"—plain those two
    Touching words come into view,
    Apposite for me and you:

Since they witness to incessant
10   Love like ours: King Francis, he—
    Diane the adored one, she—
    Prototypes of you and me.
Everywhere is carved her Crescent
    With his Salamander-sign—
15   Flame-fed creature: flame benign
    To itself or, if malign,

Only to the meddling curious,
    —So, be warned, Sir! Where's my head?
    How it wanders! What I said
20   Merely meant—the creature, fed
Thus on flame, was scarce injurious
    Save to fools who woke its ire,
    Thinking fit to play with fire.
    'Tis the Crescent you admire?

25 Then, be Diane! I'll be Francis.
    Crescents change,—true!—wax and wane,
    Woman-like: male hearts retain
    Heat nor, once warm, cool again.
So, we figure—such our chance is—

CRISTINA AND MONALDESCHI Title| MS:Christina   *CP1883:*Cristina
8| MS:you; *P1883:*you! *1883a:*you *1889a:*you: 22| MS:ire *1883:*ire,
28| MS:again: *P1883:*again.

30   I as man and you as . . . What?
   Take offence? My Love forgot
   He plays woman, I do not?

I—the woman? See my habit,
   Ask my people! Anyhow,
35   Be we what we may, one vow
   Binds us, male or female. Now,—
Stand, Sir! Read! "*Quis separabit?*"
   Half a mile of pictured way
   Past these palace-walls to-day
40   Traversed, this I came to say.

You must needs begin to love me;
   First I hated, then, at best,
   —Have it so!—I acquiesced;
   Pure compassion did the rest.
45   From below thus raised above me,
   Would you, step by step, descend,
   Pity me, become my friend,
   Like me, like less, loathe at end?

That's the ladder's round you rose by!
50   That—my own foot kicked away,
   Having raised you: let it stay,
   Serve you for retreating? Nay.
Close to me you climbed: as close by,
   Keep your station, though the peak
55   Reached proves somewhat bare and bleak!
   Woman's strong if man is weak.

Keep here, loving me forever!
   Love's look, gesture, speech, I claim;
   Act love, lie love, all the same—
60   Play as earnest were our game!

30| MS:as . . What?   *P1883:*as. . . What?   *1889a:*as . . . What?
55| MS:bleak!   *1889a:*bleak §emended to§ bleak! §see Editorial Notes§

Lonely I stood long: 'twas clever
    When you climbed, before men's eyes,
    Spurned the earth and scaled the skies,
    Gained my peak and grasped your prize.

65 Here you stood, then, to men's wonder;
    Here you tire of standing? Kneel!
    Cure what giddiness you feel,
    This way! Do your senses reel?
Not unlikely! What rolls under?
70   Yawning death in yon abyss
    Where the waters whirl and hiss
    Round more frightful peaks than this.

Should my buffet dash you thither . . .
    But be sage! No watery gave
75   Needs await you: seeming brave
    Kneel on safe, dear timid slave!
You surmised, when you climbed hither,
    Just as easy were retreat
    Should you tire, conceive unmeet
80   Longer patience at my feet?

Me as standing, you as stooping,—
    Who arranged for each the pose?
    Lest men think us friends turned foes,
    Keep the attitude you chose!
85 Men are used to this same grouping—
    I and you like statues seen.
    You and I, no third between,
    Kneel and stand! That makes the scene.

Mar it—and one buffet . . . Pardon!
90   Needless warmth—wise words in waste!
    'Twas prostration that replaced

73| MS:thither . .   *P1883:*Shoud <> thither. . . .   *CP1883:*Should   *1889a:*thither . . .
86| MS:seen; *P1883:*seen.   89| MS:buffet . . Pardon! *P1883:*buffet . . . Pardon!
90| MS:waste. *P1883:*waste!

Kneeling, then? A proof of taste.
Crouch, not kneel, while I mount guard on
Prostrate love—become no waif,
95   No estray to waves that chafe
Disappointed—love's so safe!

Waves that chafe? The idlest fancy!
Peaks that scare? I think we know
Walls enclose our sculpture: so
100   Grouped, we pose in Fontainebleau.
Up now! Wherefore hesitancy?
Arm in arm and cheek by cheek,
Laugh with me at waves and peak!
Silent still? Why, pictures speak.

105   See, where Juno strikes Ixion,
Primatice speaks plainly! Pooh—
Rather, Florentine Le Roux!
I've lost head for who is who—
So it swims and wanders! Fie on
110   What still proves me female! Here,
By the staircase!—for we near
That dark "Gallery of the Deer."

Look me in the eyes once! Steady!
Are you faithful now as erst
115   On that eve when we two first
Vowed at Avon, blessed and cursed
Faith and falsehood? Pale already?
Forward! Must my hand compel
Entrance—this way? Exit—well,
120   Somehow, somewhere. Who can tell?

96| MS:Disappointed—you so   *P1883:*Disappointed—love so
*1889a:*Disappointed—love's so   105| MS:strikes Ixion—   *P1883:*strikes Ixion,

What if to the self-same place in
    Rustic Avon, at the door
    Of the village church once more,
    Where a tombstone paves the floor
¹²⁵ By that holy-water basin
    You appealed to—"As, below,
    This stone hides its corpse, e'en so
    I your secrets hide"? What ho!

Friends, my four! You, Priest, confess him!
¹³⁰   I have judged the culprit there:
    Execute my sentence! Care
    For no mail such cowards wear!
Done, Priest? Then, absolve and bless him!
    Now—you three, stab thick and fast,
¹³⁵   Deep and deeper! Dead at last?
    Thanks, friends—Father, thanks! Aghast?

What one word of his confession
    Would you tell me, though I lured
    With that royal crown abjured
¹⁴⁰   Just because its bars immured
Love too much? Love burst compression,
    Fled free, finally confessed
    All its secrets to that breast
    Whence . . . let Avon tell the rest!

---

^{126|} MS:to—"As below   *P1883:* to—"As, below,
^{144|} MS:Whence . . let   *P1883:*Whence . . . let

MARY WOLLSTONECRAFT AND FUSELI

Oh but is it not hard, Dear?
    Mine are the nerves to quake at a mouse:
If a spider drops I shrink with fear:
    I should die outright in a haunted house;
5 While for you—did the danger dared bring help—
From a lion's den I could steal his whelp,
With a serpent round me, stand stock-still,
Go sleep in a churchyard,—so would will
Give me the power to dare and do
10 Valiantly—just for you!

Much amiss in the head, Dear,
    I toil at a language, tax my brain
Attempting to draw—the scratches here!
    I play, play, practise and all in vain:
15 But for you—if my triumph brought you pride,
I would grapple with Greek Plays till I died,
Paint a portrait of you—who can tell?
Work my fingers off for your "Pretty well:"
Language and painting and music too,
20 Easily done—for you!

Strong and fierce in the heart, Dear,
    With—more than a will—what seems a power
To pounce on my prey, love outbroke here
    In flame devouring and to devour.
25 Such love has laboured its best and worst
To win me a lover; yet, last as first,
I have not quickened his pulse one beat,
Fixed a moment's fancy, bitter or sweet:
Yet the strong fierce heart's love's labour's due,
30 Utterly lost, was—you!

MARY WOLLSTONECRAFT AND FUSELI   ¹| MS:O *1889a:*Oh   ¹⁹| MS:too—
*P1883:*too,   ²³| MS:prey, has love broke here *P1883:*prey love out broke here
*CP1883:*outbroke   ²⁸| MS:sweet, *P1883:*sweet:

ADAM, LILITH, AND EVE

One day it thundered and lightened.
Two women, fairly frightened,
Sank to their knees, transformed, transfixed,
At the feet of the man who sat betwixt;
5   And "Mercy!" cried each—"if I tell the truth
Of a passage in my youth!"

Said This: "Do you mind the morning
I met your love with scorning?
As the worst of the venom left my lips,
10   I thought 'If, despite this lie, he strips
The mask from my soul with a kiss—I crawl
His slave,—soul, body and all!' "

Said That: "We stood to be married;
The priest, or someone, tarried;
15   'If Paradise-door prove locked?' smiled you.
I thought, as I nodded, smiling too,
'Did one, that's away, arrive—nor late
Nor soon should unlock Hell's gate!' "

It ceased to lighten and thunder.
20   Up started both in wonder,
Looked round and saw that the sky was clear,
Then laughed "Confess you believed us, Dear!"
"I saw through the joke!" the man replied
They re-seated themselves beside.

ADAM, LILITH, AND EVE   ¹⁸| MS:gate!'   *1889a:*gate!' §emended to§ gate!' "
§see Editorial Notes§

IXION

High in the dome, suspended, of Hell, sad triumph, behold us!
    Here the revenge of a God, there the amends of a Man.
Whirling forever in torment, flesh once mortal, immortal
    Made—for a purpose of hate—able to die and revive,
5 Pays to the uttermost pang, then, newly for payment replenished,
    Doles out—old yet young—agonies ever afresh;
Whence the result above me: torment is bridged by a rainbow,—
    Tears, sweat, blood,—each spasm, ghastly once, glorified now.
Wrung, by the rush of the wheel ordained my place of reposing,
10   Off in a sparklike spray,—flesh become vapour thro' pain,—
Flies the bestowment of Zeus, soul's vaunted bodily vesture,
    Made that his feats observed gain the approval of Man,—
Flesh that he fashioned with sense of the earth and the sky and the ocean,
    Framed should pierce to the star, fitted to pore on the plant,—
15 All, for a purpose of hate, re-framed, re-fashioned, re-fitted
    Till, consummate at length,—lo, the employment of sense!
Pain's mere minister now to the soul, once pledged to her pleasure—
    Soul, if untrammelled by flesh, unapprehensive of pain!
Body, professed soul's slave, which serving beguiled and betrayed her,
20   Made things false seem true, cheated thro' eye and thro' ear,
Lured thus heart and brain to believe in the lying reported,—
    Spurn but the traitorous slave, uttermost atom, away,
What should obstruct soul's rush on the real, the only apparent?
    Say I have erred,—how else? Was I Ixion or Zeus?
25 Foiled by my senses I dreamed; I doubtless awaken in wonder:
    This proves shine, that—shade? Good was the evil that seemed?
Shall I, with sight thus gained, by torture be taught I was blind once?
    Sisuphos, teaches thy stone—Tantalos, teaches thy thirst
Aught which unaided sense, purged pure, less plainly demonstrates?
30   No, for the past was dream: now that the dreamers awake,
Sisuphos scouts low fraud, and to Tantalos treason is folly.
    Ask of myself, whose form melts on the murderous wheel,

IXION   ¹| MS:dome suspended of   *P1883:*dome, suspended, of   ⁷| MS:me:
whose §crossed out§ torment   ¹⁹| MS:beguiles and betrays   *P1883:*beguiled and
betrayed   ²⁰| MS:Makes < > cheats thro' the eye and the ear,   *P1883:*Made < >
cheated thro' eye and thro' ear,   ²¹| MS:Lures   *P1883:*Lured

What is the sin which throe and throe prove sin to the sinner!
    Say the false charge was true,—thus do I expiate, say,
35 Arrogant thought, word, deed,—mere man who conceited me
      godlike,
    Sat beside Zeus, my friend—knelt before Heré, my love!
What were the need but of pitying power to touch and disperse it,
    Film-work—eye's and ear's—all the distraction of sense?
How should the soul not see, not hear,—perceive and as plainly
40   Render, in thought, word, deed, back again truth—not a lie?
"Ay, but the pain is to punish thee!" Zeus, once more for a pastime,
    Play the familiar, the frank! Speak and have speech in return!
I was of Thessaly king, there ruled and a people obeyed me:
    Mine to establish the law, theirs to obey it or die:
45 Wherefore? Because of the good to the people, because of the honour
    Thence accruing to me, king, the king's law was supreme.
What of the weakling, the ignorant criminal? Not who, excuseless,
    Breaking my law braved death, knowing his deed and its due—
Nay, but the feeble and foolish, the poor transgressor, of purpose
50   No whit more than a tree, born to erectness of bole,
Palm or plane or pine, we laud if lofty, columnar—
    Loathe if athwart, askew,—leave to the axe and the flame!
Where is the vision may penetrate earth and beholding acknowledge
    Just one pebble at root ruined the straightness of stem?
55 Whose fine vigilance follows the sapling, accounts for the failure,
    —Here blew wind, so it bent: there the snow lodged, so it broke?
Also the tooth of the beast, bird's bill, mere bite of the insect
    Gnawed, gnarled, warped their worst: passive it lay to offence.
King—I was man, no more: what I recognized faulty I punished,
60   Laying it prone: be sure, more than a man had I proved,
Watch and ward o'er the sapling at birthtime had saved it, nor simply
    Owned the distortion's excuse,—hindered it wholly: nay, more—
Even a man, as I sat in my place to do judgment, and pallid
    Criminals passing to doom shuddered away at my foot,
65 Could I have probed thro' the face to the heart, read plain a
      repentance,
    Crime confessed fools' play, virtue ascribed to the wise,

---

44| MS:theirs to perform it   *P1883:*theirs to obey it
66| MS:fool's-play   *P1883:*fool's play

Had I not stayed the consignment to doom, not dealt the renewed
    ones
    Life to retraverse the past, light to retrieve the misdeed?
Thus had I done, and thus to have done much more it behoves thee,
70   Zeus who madest man—flawless or faulty, thy work!
What if the charge were true, as thou mouthest,—Ixion the cherished
    Minion of Zeus grew vain, vied with the godships and fell,
Forfeit thro' arrogance? Stranger! I clothed, with the grace of our
    human,
    Inhumanity—gods, natures I likened to ours.
75 Man among men I had borne me till gods forsooth must regard me
    —Nay, must approve, applaud, claim as a comrade at last.
Summoned to enter their circle, I sat—their equal, how other?
    Love should be absolute love, faith is in fulness or nought.
"I am thy friend, be mine!" smiled Zeus: "If Heré attract thee,"
80   Blushed the imperial cheek, "then—as thy heart may suggest!"
Faith in me sprang to the faith, my love hailed love as its fellow,
    "Zeus, we are friends—how fast! Heré, my heart for thy heart!"
Then broke smile into fury of frown, and the thunder of "Hence,
    fool!"
    Then thro' the kiss laughed scorn "Limbs or a cloud, was to
    clasp?"
85 Then from Olumpos to Erebos, then from the rapture to torment,
    Then from the fellow of gods—misery's mate, to the man!
—Man henceforth and forever, who lent from the glow of his nature
    Warmth to the cold, with light coloured the black and the blank.
So did a man conceive of your passion, you passion-protesters!
90   So did he trust, so love—being the truth of your lie!
You to aspire to be Man! Man made you who vainly would ape him:
    You are the hollowness, he—filling you, falsifies void.
Even as—witness the emblem, Hell's sad triumph suspended,
    Born of my tears, sweat, blood—bursting to vapour above—
95 Arching my torment, an iris ghostlike startles the darkness,
    Cold white—jewelry quenched —justifies, glorifies pain.

67| MS:doom, and §crossed out and replaced above by§ not   72| MS:with thy godship
*P1883:*with the godships   73| MS:arrogance? Stranger, I   *P1883:*arrogance? Stranger! I
78| MS:Love is §crossed out and replaced above by two words§ should be
86| MS:man   *P1883:*man!

Strive, mankind, though strife endure through endless obstruction,
    Stage after stage, each rise marred by as certain a fall!
Baffled forever—yet never so baffled but, e'en in the baffling,
100   When Man's strength proves weak, checked in the body or soul—
Whatsoever the medium, flesh or essence,—Ixion's
    Made for a purpose of hate,—clothing the entity Thou,
—Medium whence that entity strives for the Not-Thou beyond it,
    Fire elemental, free, frame unencumbered, the All,—
105   Never so baffled but—when, on the verge of an alien existence,
    Heartened to press, by pangs burst to the infinite Pure,
Nothing is reached but the ancient weakness still that arrests strength,
    Circumambient still, still the poor human array,
Pride and revenge and hate and cruelty—all it has burst through,
110   Thought to escape,—fresh formed, found in the fashion it fled,—
Never so baffled but—when Man pays the price of endeavour,
    Thunderstruck, downthrust, Tartaros-doomed to the wheel,—
Then, ay, then, from the tears and sweat and blood of his torment,
    E'en from the triumph of Hell, up let him look and rejoice!
115 What is the influence, high o'er Hell, that turns to a rapture
    Pain—and despair's murk mists blends in a rainbow of hope?
What is beyond the obstruction, stage by stage tho' it baffle?
    Back must I fall, confess "Ever the weakness I fled"?
No, for beyond, far, far is a Purity all-unobstructed!
120   Zeus was Zeus—not Man: wrecked by his weakness, I whirl.
Out of the wreck I rise—past Zeus to the Potency o'er him!
    I—to have hailed him my friend! I—to have clasped her—my
        love!
Pallid birth of my pain,—where light, where light is, aspiring
    Thither I rise, whilst thou—Zeus, keep the godship and sink!

97| MS:Strive, my Kind, though strife endeavour thro'   *P1883:*kind <> strife endure
*1889a:*Strive, mankind <> through   98| MS:fall,   *P1883:*fall!   102| MS:entity
*Thou,   P1883:*entity Thou,   103| MS:it   *P1883:*it,   107| MS:still to arrest
*P1883:*still that arrests   109| MS:burst from,   *P1883:*burst through,
110| MS:fresh-formed   *P1883:*fresh formed   112| MS:downthrust, Tartaros-doomed on
the   *P1883:* downthrust, Tartaros-doomed to the   119| MS:all-unobstructed.
*P1883:*all-unobstructed!   121| MS:him—   *P1883:*him!   124| MS:the weakness and
*P1883:*the §illegible word scraped away§ and   *CP1883:*the godship and

JOCHANAN HAKKADOSH

"This now, this other story makes amends
And justifies our Mishna," quoth the Jew
Aforesaid. "Tell it, learnedest of friends!"

———————————

A certain morn broke beautiful and blue
5   O'er Schiphaz city, bringing joy and mirth,
—So had ye deemed; while the reverse was true,

Since one small house there gave a sorrow birth
In such black sort that, to each faithful eye,
Midnight, not morning settled on the earth.

10   How else, when it grew certain thou wouldst die
Our much-enlightened master, Israel's prop,
Eximious Jochanan Ben Sabbathai?

Old, yea but, undiminished of a drop,
The vital essence pulsed through heart and brain;
15   Time left unsickled yet the plenteous crop

On poll and chin and cheek, whereof a skein
Handmaids might weave—hairs silk-soft, silver-white,
Such as the wool-plant's; none the less in vain

Had Physic striven her best against the spite
20   Of fell disease: the Rabbi must succumb;
And, round the couch whereon in piteous plight

He lay a-dying, scholars,—awe-struck, dumb
Throughout the night-watch,—roused themselves and spoke
One to the other: "Ere death's touch benumb

JOCHANAN HAKKADOSH   *Title*| MS:Hagadosch §altered to§ Hakkadosch Jochanan
P1883: HAKKADOSH JOCHANAN   *CP1883:*§marked for transposition to§ *JOCHANAN
HAKKADOSH*   ²| MS:our Mischna §altered to§ our Mishna   ³| *P1883:*learnedst
*CP1883:*learnedest   ¹⁰| MS:die, *P1883:*die   ¹³| MS:yea, but *P1883:*yea but

25   "His active sense,—while yet 'neath Reason's yoke
      Obedient toils his tongue,—befits we claim
      The fruit of long experience, bid this oak

      "Shed us an acorn which may, all the same,
      Grow to a temple-pillar,—dear that day!—
30   When Israel's scattered seed finds place and name

      "Among the envious nations. Lamp us, pray,
      Thou the Enlightener! Partest hence in peace?
      Hailest without regret—much less, dismay—

      "The hour of thine approximate release
35   From fleshly bondage soul hath found obstruct?
      Calmly envisagest the sure increase

      "Of knowledge? Eden's tree must hold unplucked
      Some apple, sure, has never tried thy tooth,
      Juicy with sapience thou hast sought, not sucked?

40   "Say, does age acquiesce in vanished youth?
      Still towers thy purity above—as erst—
      Our pleasant follies? Be thy last word—truth!"

      The Rabbi groaned; then, grimly, "Last as first
      The truth speak I—in boyhood who began
45   Striving to live an angel, and, amerced

      "For such presumption, die now hardly man.
      What have I proved of life? To live, indeed,
      That much I learned: but here lies Jochanan

      "More luckless than stood David when, to speed
50   His fighting with the Philistine, they brought
      Saul's harness forth: whereat, 'Alack, I need

25| MS:His *CP1883:*"His   28| MS:Shed *CP1883:*"Shed   31| MS:Among
CP1883:"Among   34| MS:The *CP1883:*"The   37| MS:Of *CP1883:*"Of
40| MS:Say <> youth, *CP1883:*"Say <> youth?   46| MS:For *P1883:*"For
51| MS:whereat, "Alack *P1883:* whereat, 'Alack

"'Armour to arm me, but have never fought
With sword and spear, nor tried to manage shield,
Proving arms' use, as well-trained warrior ought.

55 "'Only a sling and pebbles can I wield!'
So he: while I, contrariwise, 'No trick
Of weapon helpful on the battle-field

"'Comes unfamiliar to my theoric:
But, bid me put in practice what I know,
60 Give me a sword—it stings like Moses' stick,

"'A serpent I let drop apace.' E'en so,
I,—able to comport me at each stage
Of human life as never here below

"Man played his part,—since mine the heritage
65 Of wisdom carried to that perfect pitch,
Ye rightly praise,—I, therefore, who, thus sage,

"Could sure act man triumphantly, enrich
Life's annals with example how I played
Lover, Bard, Soldier, Statist,—(all of which

70 "Parts in presentment failing, cries invade
The world's ear—'Ah, the Past, the pearl-gift thrown
To hogs, time's opportunity we made

"'So light of, only recognized when flown!
Had we been wise!')—in fine, I—wise enough,—
75 What profit brings me wisdom never shown

52| MS:Armour *P1883:*"Armour *1889a:*"'Armour 55| MS:Only <> wield!'
P1883:"Only <> wield!' *1889a:*"'Only 56| MS:contrariwise, "No *P1883:*
contrariwise, 'No 58| MS:Comes *P1883:*"Comes *1889a:*"'Comes 61| MS:A
<> apace: E'en *P1883:*"A <> apace.' E'en *1889a:*"'A 64| MS:Man *P1883:*"Man
66| MS:Ye all avow,—I *P1883:*Ye rightly praise,—I 67| MS:Needs must act
P1883:"Could sure act 69| MS:Lover, Bard, Soldier, Statist,—all *P1883:* Lover, Bard,
Soldier, Statist,—(all 70| MS:Parts *P1883:*"Parts 73| MS:So *P1883:*"So
1889a:"'So 74| MS:wise!'—in *P1883:* wise!')—in 75| MS:profits brings
§inserted above§ me a §crossed out§ wisdom *P1883:*profits brings me wisdom *1883a:*profit

"Just when its showing would from each rebuff
Shelter weak virtue, threaten back to bounds
Encroaching vice, tread smooth each track too rough

"For youth's unsteady footstep, climb the rounds
80 Of life's long ladder, one by slippery one,
Yet make no stumble? Me hard fate confounds

"With that same crowd of wailers I outrun
By promising to teach another cry
Of more hilarious mood than theirs, the sun

85 "I look my last at is insulted by.
What cry,—ye ask? Give ear on every side!
Witness yon Lover! 'How entrapped am I!

"'Methought, because a virgin's rose-lip vied
With ripe Khubbezleh's, needs must beauty mate
90 With meekness and discretion in a bride:

"'Bride she became to me who wail—too late—
Unwise I loved!' That's one cry. 'Mind's my gift:
I might have loaded me with lore, full weight

"'Pressed down and running over at each rift
95 O' the brain-bag where the famished clung and fed.
I filled it with what rubbish!—would not sift

76| MS:Just <> would §crossed out and replaced above by§ had §crossed out; *would* marked
for retention§ *P1883:*"Just   77| MS:Sheltered §altered to§ Shelter <> threatened
§altered to§ threaten   78| MS:tread §altered to§ trod §*tread* marked for retention§
79| MS:For <> climb §altered to§ clomb §*climb* marked for retention§ *P1883:*"For
81| MS:make §altered to§ made §*make* marked for retention§ no stumble,—me
*P1883:*stumble? Me   82| MS:With   *P1883:*"With <> I begun §crossed out and replaced
above by§ outrun   85| MS:I   *P1883:*"I   86| MS:Howso §crossed out and replaced
above by two words§ What cry   88| MS:'Methought   *P1883:*"Methought
1889a:"'Methought   91| MS:Bride   *P1883:*"Bride   *1889a:*"'Bride
93| MS:loaded §word illegibly crossed out and replaced by§ me   94| MS:And §crossed
out and replaced above by§ Pressed   *P1883:*"Pressed   *1889a:*"'Pressed
96| MS:filled mine §crossed out and replaced above by§ it

"'The wheat from chaff, sound grain from musty—shed
Poison abroad as oft as nutriment—
And sighing say but as my fellows said,

100   "'*Unwise I learned!*' That's two. 'In dwarf's-play spent
Was giant's prowess: warrior all unversed
In war's right waging, I struck brand, was lent

"'For steel's fit service, on mere stone—and cursed
Alike the shocked limb and the shivered steel,
105   Seeing too late the blade's true use which erst

"'How was I blind to! My cry swells the peal—
Unwise I fought!' That's three. But wherefore waste
Breath on the wailings longer? Why reveal

"A root of bitterness whereof the taste
110   Is noisome to Humanity at large?
First we get Power, but Power absurdly placed

"In Folly's keeping, who resigns her charge
To Wisdom when all Power grows nothing worth:
Bones marrowless are mocked with helm and targe

115   "When, like your Master's, soon below the earth
With worms shall warfare only be. Farewell,
Children! I die a failure since my birth!"

"Not so!" arose a protest as, pell-mell,
They pattered from his chamber to the street,
120   Bent on a last resource. Our Targums tell

97| MS:The <> from blemished—shed   *P1883:* "The <> from musty—shed   *1889a:* "'The
99| MS:fellow   *P1883:*fellows   100| MS:*Unwise* <> dwarf's-play   *P1883:* "Unwise
1889a: "'*Unwise* <> dwarfs-play §emended to§ dwarf's-play §see Editorial Notes§
101| MS:A §crossed out§ Was §added in margin§ giant's   103| MS:For woodland service
P1883: "For steel's fit service   *1889a:* "'For   104| MS:shocked hand §crossed out and
replaced above by§ limb   106| MS:How   *P1883:* "How   *1889a:* "'How
109| MS:That root   *P1883:* "A root   112| MS:In   *P1883:* "In   115| MS:When
P1883: "When   118| MS:arose the §crossed out and replaced above by§ a

That such resource there is. Put case, there meet
The Nine Points of Perfection—rarest chance—
Within some saintly teacher whom the fleet

Years, in their blind implacable advance,
125   O'ertake before fit teaching born of these
Have magnified his scholars' countenance,—

If haply folk compassionating please
To render up—according to his store,
Each one—a portion of the life he sees

130   Hardly worth saving when 'tis set before
Earth's benefit should the Saint, Hakkadosh,
Favoured thereby, attain to full fourscore—

If such contribute (Scoffer, spare thy "Bosh!")
A year, a month, a day, an hour—to eke
135   Life out, —in him away the gift shall wash

That much of ill-spent time recorded, streak
The twilight of the so-assisted sage
With a new sunrise: truth, though strange to speak!

Quick to the doorway, then, where youth and age,
140   All Israel, thronging, waited for the last
News of the loved one. "'Tis the final stage:

"Art's utmost done, the Rabbi's feet tread fast
The way of all flesh!" So announced that apt
Olive-branch Tsaddik: "Yet, O Brethren, cast

126| MS:Have gratified §altered to§ magnified his   131| MS:the sick Hagadosch, §altered
to§ Hakkadosch,   *P1883:*the Saint, Hakkadosh,   134| MS:An hour, a day, a week,
§crossed out§ month, A §inserted above§ year—to §marked for transposition to§ A year, a
month, a day, An hour—to *P1883:*an   142| MS:Art's *P1883:*"Art's

145 "No eye to earthward! Look where heaven has clapped
Morning's extinguisher—yon ray-shot robe
Of sun-threads—on the constellation mapped

"And mentioned by our Elders,—yea, from Job
Down to Satam,—as figuring forth—what?
150 Perpend a mystery! Ye call it *Dob*—

"'The Bear': I trow, a wiser name than that
Were *Aish*—'The Bier': a corpse those four stars hold,
Which—are not those Three Daughters weeping at,

"*Banoth*? I judge so: list while I unfold
155 The reason. As in twice twelve hours this Bier
Goes and returns, about the East-cone rolled,

"So may a setting luminary here
Be rescued from extinction, rolled anew
Upon its track of labour, strong and clear,

160 "About the Pole—that Salem, every Jew
Helps to build up when thus he saves some Saint
Ordained its architect. Ye grasp the clue

"To all ye seek? The Rabbi's lamp-flame faint
Sinks: would ye raise it? Lend then life from yours,
165 Spare each his oil-drop! Do I need acquaint

"The Chosen how self-sacrifice ensures
Ten-fold requital?—urge ye emulate
The fame of those Old Just Ones death procures

145| MS:No *P1883:* "No   148| MS:And *P1883:* "And   149| MS:to myself §crossed
out and replaced above by§ Satam   151| MS:'The *P1883:* "'The   152| MS:Is
§crossed out and replaced above by§ Were §crossed out; *Is* marked for retention§ *Aish*
P1883: Were *Aish*   154| MS:*Banoth* *P1883:* "*Banoth*   156| MS:the earth-cone rolled,
P1883: the east-cone rolled,   *1889a:* the East-cone   157| MS:So *P1883:* "So
159| MS:labour, fresh and *P1883:* labour, strong and   160| MS:About *1883:* "About
161| MS:saint *P1883:* some Saint   163| MS:To < > lampt-light §second half of
compount crossed out and replaced above by§ flame *P1883:* "To
166| MS:The faithful how *P1883:* "The Chosen how

"Such praise for, that 'tis now men's sole debate
170 Which of the Ten, who volunteered at Rome
To die for glory to our Race, was great

"Beyond his fellows? Was it thou—the comb
Of iron carded, flesh from bone, away,
While thy lips sputtered thro' their bloody foam

175 "Without a stoppage (O brave Akiba!)
'Hear, Israel, our Lord God is One'? Or thou,
Jischab?—who smiledst, burning, since there lay,

"Burning along with thee, our Law! I trow,
Such martyrdom might tax flesh to afford:
180 While that for which I make petition now,

"To what amounts it? Youngster, wilt thou hoard
Each minute of long years thou look'st to spend
In dalliance with thy spouse? Hast thou so soared,

"Singer of songs, all out of sight of friend
185 And teacher, warbling like a woodland bird,
There's left no Selah, 'twixt two psalms, to lend

"Our late-so-tuneful quirist? Thou, averred
The fighter born to plant our lion-flag
Once more on Zion's mount,—doth, all-unheard,

190 "My pleading fail to move thee? Toss some rag
Shall staunch our wound, some minute never missed
From swordsman's lustihood like thine! Wilt lag

169| MS:Such fame for   *P1883:* "Such praise for   172| MS:Beyond   *P1883:* "Beyond
175| MS:Without one §crossed out and replaced above by§ a stopping §altered to§ stoppage
P1883: "Without   178| MS:Burning   *P1883:* "Burning   181| MS:To   *P1883:* "To
184| MS:Singer   *P1883:* "Singer   185| MS:And master, warbling   *P1883:* And teacher,
warbling   187| MS:Our   *P1883:* "Our   190| MS:My   *P1883:* "My

"In liberal bestowment, show close fist
When open palm we look for,—thou, wide-known
195 For statecraft? whom, 'tis said, an if thou list,

"The Shah himself would seat beside his throne,
So valued were advice from thee" . . . But here
He stopped short: such a hubbub! Not alone

From those addressed, but, far as well as near,
200 The crowd broke into clamour: "Mine, mine, mine—
Lop from my life the excrescence, never fear!

"At me thou lookedst, markedst me! Assign
To me that privilege of granting life—
Mine, mine!" Then he: "Be patient! I combine

205 "The needful portions only, wage no strife
With Nature's law nor seek to lengthen out
The Rabbi's day unduly. 'Tis the knife

"I stop,—would cut its thread too short. About
As much as helps life last the proper term,
210 The appointed Fourscore,—that I crave and scout

"A too-prolonged existence. Let the worm
Change at fit season to the butterfly!
And here a story strikes me, to confirm

193| MS:In   *P1883:*"In   195| MS:state-craft   *1889a:*statecraft
196| MS:The   *P1883:*"The   197| MS:but §altered to§ But   198| MS:hubbub! for
§crossed out§ Not alone   199| MS:but far <> near   *1889a:*but, far <> near,
202| MS:At   *P1883:*"At   204| MS:he: Be patient: I   *P1883:*he: "Be patient! I
205| MS:The   *P1883:*"The   208| MS:I <> about   *P1883:*"I <> About
209| MS:helps it last   *P1883:*helps life last   210| MS:appointed Fourscore,—so much
§last two words crossed out and replaced above by two words§ that I crave,— §dash
overwritten by§ and   *1889a:*crave and   211| MS:A   *P1883:*"A
212| MS:at its §crossed out and replaced above by§ fit   212| MS:me to confirm
*P1883:*confirm,   *CP1883:*me, to confirm

"This judgment. Of our worthies, none ranks high
215 As Perida who kept the famous school:
None rivalled him in patience: none! For why?

"In lecturing it was his constant rule,
Whatever he expounded, to repeat
—Ay, and keep on repeating, lest some fool

220 "Should fail to understand him fully—(feat
Unparalleled, Uzzean!)—do ye mark?—
Five hundred times! So might he entrance beat

"For knowledge into howsoever dark
And dense the brain-pan. Yet it happed, at close
225 Of one especial lecture, not one spark

"Of light was found to have illumed the rows
Of pupils round their pedagogue. 'What, still
Impenetrable to me? Then—here goes!'

"And for a second time he sets the rill
230 Of knowledge running, and five hundred times
More re-repeats the matter—and gains *nil.*

"Out broke a voice from heaven: 'Thy patience climbs
Even thus high. Choose! Wilt thou, rather, quick
Ascend to bliss—or, since thy zeal sublimes

214| MS:This *P1883:* *P1883:*"This   215| MS:As Perida that §crossed out and replaced
above by§ who   216| MS:Who §crossed out and replaced above by§ None <> patience?
§question mark crossed out§ : None   *P1883:*patience: none   217| MS:In *P1883:*"In
220| MS:Should <> fully—feat *P1883:*"Should <> fully—(feat   221| MS:Unparalleled,
Uzzean!—do *P1883:* Unparalleled, Uzzean!)—do   223| MS:For *P1883:*"For
224| MS:dense the §crossed out and replaced above by§ were §crossed out; *the* marked for
retention§ brain-pan §altered to§ brain-pans §last letter crossed out§
226| MS:Of *P1883:*"Of   227| MS:pedagogue. "What *P1883:* pedagogue. 'What
228| MS:goes!" *P1883:*goes!'   229| MS:And <> sets §last letter crossed out and
restored§ *P1883:*"And   231| MS:More he §crossed out and replaced above by§ did
§crossed out; *he* marked for retention§ repeats §last letter crossed out and restored§ <>
gained §altered to§ gains *P1883:*More re-repeats   232| MS:This drew §last two words
crossed out and replaced above by one word§ Outbroke <> heaven: "Thy *P1883:*"Out
broke <> heaven: 'Thy   234| MS:to heaven §crossed out and replaced above by§ bliss

235 "'Such drudgery, will thy back still bear its crick,
Bent o'er thy class,—thy voice drone spite of drouth,—
Five hundred years more at thy desk wilt stick?'

"'To heaven with me!' was in the good man's mouth,
When all his scholars,—cruel-kind were they!—
240 Stopped utterance, from East, West, North and South,

"Rending the welkin with their shout of 'Nay—
No heaven as yet for our instructor! Grant
Five hundred years on earth for Perida!'

"And so long did he keep instructing! Want
245 Our Master no such misery! I but take
Three months of life marital. Ministrant

"Be thou of so much, Poet! Bold I make,
Swordsman, with thy frank offer!—and conclude,
Statist, with thine! One year,—ye will not shake

250 "My purpose to accept no more. So rude?
The very boys and girls, forsooth, must press
And proffer their addition? Thanks! The mood

"Is laudable, but I reject, no less,
One month, week, day of life more. Leave my gown,
255 Ye overbold ones! Your life's gift, you guess,

235| MS:Such drudging §altered to§ drudgery *CP1883:*"Such *1889a:*"'Such
237| MS:stick?" *P1883:*stick?' 238| MS:"To <> me!" was *P1883:*"'To <> me!' was
239| MS:scholars, stopped it—cruel §last three words crossed out and replaced above by three words§ —cruel-kind were 241| MS:Rending *P1883:*"Rending 244| MS:And *P1883:*"And 246| MS:A year §last two words crossed out and replaced above by two words§ Three months <> marital; ministrant *P1883:*marital. Ministrant 247| MS:Be thou §added in margin§ Shalt thou §last two words crossed out and replaced above by three words§ Of so much §crossed out§ likewise, §crossed out and replaced above by§ thou, §crossed out§ *P1883:*"Be <> of 249| MS:thine—four §crossed out and replaced above by§ one years §altered to§ year *P1883:*thine! One 250| MS:My <> to accept no more. §last three words crossed out and replaced above by three words§ extend the life. §last three words crossed out; original reading restored§ So rude— *P1883:*"My <> rude?
253| MS:Is <> I refuse, no *P1883:*"Is <> I reject, no 254| MS:One parti §crossed out§ week or day *P1883:*One month, week, day 255| MS:overbold ones §crossed out and

104

"Were good as any? Rudesby, get thee down!
Set my feet free, or fear my staff! Farewell,
Seniors and saviours, sharers of renown

"With Jochanan henceforward!" Straightway fell
260　Sleep on the sufferer; who awoke in health,
Hale everyway, so potent was the spell.

———————

O the rare Spring-time! Who is he by stealth
Approaches Jochanan?—embowered that sits
Under his vine and figtree mid the wealth

265　Of garden-sights and sounds, since intermits
Never the turtle's coo, nor stays nor stints
The rose her smell. In homage that befits

The musing Master, Tsaddik, see, imprints
A kiss on the extended foot, low bends
270　Forehead to earth, then, all-obsequious, hints

"What if it should be time? A period ends—
That of the Lover's gift—his quarter-year
Of lustihood: 'tis just thou make amends,

"Return that loan with usury: so, here
275　Come I, of thy Disciples delegate,
Claiming our lesson from thee. Make appear

"Thy profit from experience! Plainly state
How men should Love!" Thus he: and to him thus
The Rabbi: "Love, ye call it?—rather, Hate!

---

replaced above by word illegibly crossed out; *ones* restored§　256| 　MS:Were <> down—
P1883: "Were <> down!　258| 　MS:saviours! Sharers　*P1883:* saviours, sharers
259| 　MS:With　*P1883:* "With　261| 　MS:everyway—so　*P1883:* everyway, so
262| 　MS:rare Spring time　*P1883:* rare Spring-time　267| 　MS:The §added in margin§
Rose §altered to§ rose her display §crossed out and replaced above by§ smell
274| 　MS:Return　*P1883:* "Return　276| 　MS:Claiming MS:their lesson
P1883: Claiming our lesson　277| 　MS:Thy　*P1883:* "Thy　278| 　MS:love　*CP1883:*
should Love　279| 　MS:The Rabbi. "Love　*P1883:* The Rabbi: "Love

280   "What wouldst thou? Is it needful I discuss
      Wherefore new sweet wine, poured in bottles caked
      With old strong wine's deposit, offers us

      "Spoilt liquor we recoil from, thirst-unslaked?
      Like earth-smoke from a crevice, out there wound
285   Languors and yearnings: not a sense but ached

      "Weighed on by fancied form and feature, sound
      Of silver word and sight of sunny smile:
      No beckoning of a flower-branch, no profound

      "Purple of noon-oppression, no light wile
290   O' the West wind, but transformed itself till—brief—
      Before me stood the phantasy ye style

      "Youth's love, the joy that shall not come to grief,
      Born to endure, eternal, unimpaired
      By custom the accloyer, time the thief.

295   "Had Age's hard cold knowledge only spared
      That ignorance of Youth! But now the dream,
      Fresh as from Paradise, alighting fared

      "As fares the pigeon, finding what may seem
      Her nest's safe hollow holds a snake inside
300   Coiled to enclasp her. See, Eve stands supreme

      "In youth and beauty! Take her for thy bride!
      What Youth deemed crystal, Age finds out was dew
      Morn set a-sparkle, but which noon quick dried

280| MS:What   *P1883:* "What   283| MS:Spoilt   *P1883:* "Spoilt   284| MS:crevice, influence wound—   *1889a:* crevice, out there wound   286| MS:Weighed *P1883:* "Weighed   289| MS:Purple   *P1883:* "Purple   292| MS:Youth's *P1883:* "Youth's   295| MS:Had   *P1883:* "Had   296| MS:dream *P1883:* dream, 297| MS:from Paradise alighting   *P1883:* from Paradise, alighting   298| MS:As   *P1883:* "As 300| MS:her. See, she §crossed out and replaced above by§ Eve   301| MS:In < > beauty. Take   *P1883:* "In < > beauty! Take   303| MS:sets §altered to§ set a-sparkle, and §crossed out and replaced above by§ but < > noon has dried   *1889a:* noon quick dried

"While Youth bent gazing at its red and blue
305 Supposed perennial,—never dreamed the sun
Which kindled the display would quench it too.

"Graces of shape and colour—everyone
With its appointed period of decay
When ripe to purpose!'still, these dead and done,

310 "'Survives the woman-nature—the soft sway
Of undefinable omnipotence
O'er our strong male-stuff, we of Adam's clay.'

"Ay, if my physics taught not why and whence
The attraction! Am I like the simple steer
315 Who, from his pasture lured inside the fence

"Where yoke and goad await him, holds that mere
Kindliness prompts extension of the hand
Hollowed for barley, which drew near and near

"His nose—in proof that, of the horned band,
320 The farmer best affected him? Beside,
Steer, since his calfhood, got to understand

"Farmers a many in the world so wide
Were ready with a handful just as choice
Or choicer—maize and cummin, treats untried.

304| MS:While   *P1883:* "While   306| MS:kindled glory soon §last two words crossed out
and replaced above by two words§ the display   307| MS:Graces   *P1883:* "Graces
309| MS:purpose! Still   *P1883:* purpose! 'Still   310| MS:Survives   *P1883:* "Survives
1889a: " 'Survives   312| MS:clay.   *P1883:* clay.'   313| MS:Ay   *P1883:* "Ay
314| MS:like a §altered to§ the   315| MS:from the §crossed out and replaced above by§
his   316| MS:Where   *P1883:* "Where   318| MS:barley which drew
§crossed out and replaced above by§ draws   *P1883:* drew   *CP1883:* barley, which
319| MS:His   *P1883:* "His   320| MS:affected §altered to§ affects him? Note §inserted
above§ beside,   *P1883:* affected him? Beside   321| MS:This steer, since calfhood, gets
P1883: Steer, long since < > got   *1889a:* Steer, since his calfhood
322| MS:Farmers   *P1883:* "Farmers   323| MS:Are ready   *P1883:* Were ready

325   "Shall I wed wife, and all my days rejoice
   I gained the peacock? 'Las me, round I look,
   And lo—'With me thou wouldst have blamed no voice

   "'Like hers that daily deafens like a rook:
   I am the phœnix!'—'I, the lark, the dove,
330   —The owl,' for aught knows he who blindly took

   "Peacock for partner, while the vale, the grove,
   The plain held bird-mates in abundance. There!
   Youth, try fresh capture! Age has found out Love

   "Long ago. War seems better worth man's care.
335   But leave me! Disappointment finds a balm
   Haply in slumber." "This first step o' the stair

   "To knowledge fails me, but the victor's palm
   Lies on the next to tempt him overleap
   A stumbling-block. Experienced, gather calm,

340   "Thou excellence of Judah, cured by sleep
   Which ushers in the Warrior, to replace
   The Lover! At due season I shall reap

   "Fruit of my planting!" So, with lengthened face,
   Departed Tsaddik: and three moons more waxed
345   And waned, and not until the Summer-space

325| MS:Shall   *P1883:* "Shall   328| MS:Like < > like the §crossed out and replaced
above by§ a   *P1883:* "Like   *1889a:* " 'Like   330| MS:aught I §crossed out§ know §altered
to§ knows he §inserted§ who   331| MS:Peacock   *P1883:* "Peacock
334| MS:Long < > care—   *P1883:* "Long < > care.   337| MS:To < > fails us, but
P1883: "To < > fails me, but   337-39| MS:§incorrectly spaced; bracketed as new stanza§
339| MS:This §altered to§ The stumbling-block experience. Gather calm,
P1883: A stumbling-block   *1889a:* stumbling block. Experienced, gather
340| MS:Thou   *P1883:* "Thou   341| MS:the Warrior, to thy wish §last three words
crossed out§ to replace   342| MS:Returning §crossed out and replaced above by two
words§ The Lover. at §altered to§ At   343| MS:Fruit of my sowing!" §first syllable crossed
out and replaced above by *plant*§ Slow §crossed out and replaced above by§ So   *P1883:* "Fruit
345| MS:the summer-space   *1889a:* the Summer-space

Waned likewise, any second visit taxed
The Rabbi's patience. But at three months' end,
Behold, supine beneath a rock, relaxed

The sage lay musing till the noon should spend
350   Its ardour. Up comes Tsaddik, who but he,
With "Master, may I warn thee, nor offend,

"That time comes round again? We look to see
Sprout from the old branch—not the youngling twig—
But fruit of sycamine: deliver me,

355   "To share among my fellows, some plump fig,
Juicy as seedy! That same man of war,
Who, with a scantling of his store, made big

"Thy starveling nature, caused thee, safe from scar,
To share his gains by long acquaintanceship
360   With bump and bruise and all the knocks that are

"Of battle dowry,—he bids loose thy lip,
Explain the good of battle! Since thou know'st
Let us know likewise! Fast the moments slip,

"More need that we improve them!"—"Ay, we boast,
365   We warriors in our youth, that with the sword
Man goes the swiftliest to the uttermost—

346| MS:Was ended §last two words crossed out and replaced above by two words§
Waned likewise   350| MS:ardour. In §altered to§ Up comes   352| MS:That
P1883: "That   354| MS:But §added in margin§ Fruit of the §crossed out§ sycamine < >
me *CP1883:* me,   355| MS:To < > fellows some *P1883:* "To *CP1883:* fellows, some
356| MS:Juicy and §crossed out and replaced above by§ as seedy. That < > war
P1883: seedy! That *CP1883:* war,   357| MS:Who with < > store made
P1883: Who, with < > store, made   358| MS:Thy *P1883:* "Thy   361| MS:Of < >
dowry. Therefore, loose *P1883:* dowry: therefore *1889a:* dowry,—he bids loose
362| MS:knowst, *CP1883:* know'st, *1889a:* know'st   363| MS:likewise. Fast the moments
fly, §overwritten with§ slip, *CP1883:* likewise! Fast   364| MS:More *P1883:* "More < >
boast *CP1883:* boast,   365| MS:youth that *P1883:* youth, that

"Takes the straight way thro' lands yet unexplored
To absolute Right and Good,—may so obtain
God's glory and man's weal too long ignored,

370 "Too late attained by preachments all in vain—
The passive process. Knots get tangled worse
By toying with: does cut cord close again?

"Moreover there is blessing in the curse
Peace-praisers call war. What so sure evolves
375 All the capacities of soul, proves nurse

"Of that self-sacrifice in men which solves
The riddle—*Wherein differs Man from beast?*
Foxes boast cleverness and courage wolves:

"Nowhere but in mankind is found the least
380 Touch of an impulse 'To our fellows—good
I' the highest !—not diminished but increased

"'By the condition plainly understood
—Such good shall be attained at price of hurt
I' the highest to ourselves!' Fine sparks, that brood

385 "Confusedly in Man, 'tis war bids spurt
Forth into flame: as fares the meteor-mass,
Whereof no particle but holds inert

367| MS:Takes *P1883:*'Takes *CP1883:*"Takes *1889a:*Takes §emended to§ "Takes §see Editorial Notes§ 369| MS:and world's §crossed out and replaced above by§ man's 370| MS:Too <> vain, *P1883:*vain,— *CP1883:*"Too *1889a:*vain— 373| MS:Moreover *P1883:*"Moreover 376| MS:Of <> Man *P1883:*"Of <> men 379| MS:Nowhere *P1883:*"Nowhere 380| MS:of the impulse—'To *P1883:*of an impulse 'To 381| MS:highest—not *P1883:*highest!—not 382| MS:By *P1883:*"By *1889a:*"'By 384| MS:ourselves': those sparks that *P1883:*ourselves!' Fine sparks that *CP1883:*sparks, that 385| MS:Confusedly *P1883:*"Confusedly 386| MS:as in some §last two words crossed out and replaced above by two words§ fires the *P1883:*fares §see Editorial Notes§ 387| MS:Wherein *P1883:*Whereof

"Some seed of light and heat, however crass
The enclosure, yet avails not to discharge
390   Its radiant birth before there come to pass

"Some push external,—strong to set at large
Those dormant fire-seeds, whirl them in a trice
Through heaven and light up earth from marge to marge:

"Since force by motion makes—what erst was ice—
395   Crash into fervency and so expire,
Because some Djinn has hit on a device

"For proving the full prettiness of fire!
Ay, thus we prattle—young: but old—why, first,
Where's that same Right and Good—(the wise inquire)—

400   "So absolute, it warrants the outburst
Of blood, tears, all war's woeful consequence,
That comes of the fine flaring? Which plague cursed

"The more your benefited Man—offence,
Or what suppressed the offender? Say it did—
405   Show us the evil cured by violence,

"Submission cures not also! Lift the lid
From the maturing crucible, we find
Its slow sure coaxing-out of virtue, hid

388| MS:Some   *P1883:* "Some   390| MS:Its §overwritten by§ The radiant <> comes
*P1883:*Its radiant <> come   391| MS:Some <> external, setting them §last two words
crossed out and replaced above by three words§ —strong to set   *P1883:* "Some
392| MS:whirls §altered to§ whirl   393| MS:lights §altered to§ light <> to marge,—
*P1883:*marge: 394| MS:Since   *P1883:* "Since   396| MS:on the device   *P1883:*on a
device   397| MS:For   *P1883:* "For   398| MS:So do we fable—young   *P1883:*Ay,
thus we prattle—young   400| MS:So <> warrants such §crossed out and replaced above
by§ the   *P1883:* "So   401| MS:all thr §crossed out and replaced above by§ war's
402| MS:That §crossed out and replaced above by§ As §crossed out; *That* marked for retention§
<> Which amerced   *P1883:*Which plague cursed   403| MS:The <> benefitted
P1883: "The   *1889a:*benefited   404| MS:the offender?—Say §last three words crossed
out and replaced above by three words§ offence? Which, if   *P1883:*the offender? Say
406| MS:Submission   *P1883:* "Submission   408| MS:virtue, hid   *P1883:*virtue hid
*CP1883:*virtue, hid   *1889a:*virtue hid §emended to§ virtue, hid §see Editorial Notes§

111

"In that same meteor-mass, hath uncombined
410 Those particles and, yielding for result
Gold, not mere flame, by so much leaves behind

"The heroic product. E'en the simple cult
Of Edom's children wisely bids them turn
Cheek to the smiter with'*sic Jesus vult.*'

415 "Say there's a tyrant by whose death we earn
Freedom, and justify a war to wage:
Good!—were we only able to discern

"Exactly how to reach and catch and cage
Him only and no innocent beside!
420 Whereas the folk whereon war wreaks its rage

"—How shared they his ill-doing? Far and wide
The victims of our warfare strew the plain,
Ten thousand dead, whereof not one but died

"In faith that vassals owed their suzerain
425 Life: therefore each paid tribute,—honest soul,—
To that same Right and Good ourselves are fain

"To call exclusively our end. From bole
(Since ye accept in me a sycamine)
Pluck, eat, digest a fable—yea, the sole

409| MS:In *P1883:* "In 410| MS:particles, and yielded *P1883:* particles and, yielding
411| MS:flame, and §crossed out§ so leaving §inserted above§ far left §crossed out§ *P1883:*
flame, by so much leaves 412| MS:The *P1883:* "The 415| MS:Say*P1883:* "Say
416| MS:Freedon, which justifies a *P1883:* Freedom, and justify a 418| MS:Exactly
P1883: "Exactly 419| MS:beside: *P1883:* beside! 420| MS:whereon we wreak our
rage *P1883:* whereon war wreaks its rage 421| MS:—How shared §altered to§ share
P1883: shared *CP1883:* "—How 424| MS:In < > vassal §altered to§ vassals owed his
§altered to§ their *P1883:* "In 425| MS:Life—therefore each §inserted above§ paid its
§crossed out§ tribute *P1883:* Life: therefore 427| MS:To claim exclusively
P1883: "To 1889a:* "To call exclusively 428| MS:—Since in me ye accept §marked for
transposition to§ —Since ye accept in me a sycamine— *P1883:* (Since < > sycamine)
429| MS:a simile— §crossed out and replaced above by two words§ a fable—yea, the

430 "Fig I afford you! 'Dost thou dwarf my vine?'
(So did a certain husbandman address
The tree which faced his field), 'Receive condign

"'Punishment, prompt removal by the stress
Of axe I forthwith lay unto thy root!'
435 Long did he hack and hew, the root no less

"As long defied him, for its tough strings shoot
As deep down as the boughs above aspire:
All that he did was—shake to the tree's foot

"Leafage and fruitage, things we most require
440 For shadow and refreshment: which good deed
Thoroughly done, behold the axe-haft tires

"His hand, and he desisting leaves unfreed
The vine he hacked and hewed for. Comes a frost,
One natural night's work, and there's little need

445 "Of hacking, hewing: lo, the tree's a ghost!
Perished it starves, black death from topmost bough
To farthest-reaching fibre! Shall I boast

"My rough work,—warfare,—helped more? Loving, now—
That, by comparison, seems wiser, since
450 The loving fool was able to avow

"He could effect his purpose, just evince
Love's willingness,—once 'ware of what she lacked,
His loved one,—to go work for that, nor wince

430| MS:Fig <> you. 'Dost   *P1883:*"Fig <> you! 'Dost   433| MS:Punishment and
removal   *P1883:*"Punishment, prompt removal   *1889a:*"'Punishment   436| MS:As long
§added in margin§ Defied <> for the §crossed out and replaced above by§ its   *P1883:*"As
<> defied   439| MS:Leafage   *P1883:*"Leafage   442| MS:His   *P1883:*"His
445| MS:Of   *P1883:*"Of   446| MS:stares   *P1883:*starves   448| MS:My   *P1883:*"My
451| MS:He   *P1883:*"He   452| MS:once certain what   *P1883:*once ware of what
*1889a:*once 'ware   453| MS:The loved <> that nor   *P1883:*His loved <> that, nor

"At self-expenditure: he neither hacked
455   Nor hewed, but when the lady of his field
Required defence because the sun attacked,

"He, failing to obtain a fitter shield,
Would interpose his body, and so blaze,
Blest in the burning. Ah, were mine to wield

460   "The intellectual weapon—poet-lays,—
How preferably had I sung one song
Which . . . but my sadness sinks me: go your ways!

"I sleep out disappointment." "Come along,
Never lose heart! There's still as much again
465   Of our bestowment left to right the wrong

"Done by its earlier moiety—explain
Wherefore, who may! The Poet's mood comes next.
Was he not wishful the poetic vein

"Should pulse within him? Jochanan, thou reck'st
470   Little of what a generous flood shall soon
Float thy clogged spirit free and unperplexed

"Above dry dubitation! Song's the boon
Shall make amends for my untoward mistake
That Joshua-like thou couldst bid sun and moon—

475   "Fighter and Lover,—which for most men make
All they descry in heaven,—stand both stock-still
And lend assistance. Poet shalt thou wake!"

454| MS:At any self-expenditure—nor hacked   *P1883:* "At self-expenditure: he
neither hacked   *1883:* 'At   *1889a:* "At   455| MS:of the field   *P1883:* of his field
457| MS:He   *P1883:* "He   460| MS:The   *P1883:* "The   463| MS:I   *P1883:* "I
466| MS:Done   *P1883:* "Done   469| MS:Should   *P1883:* "Should
472| MS:Above   *P1883:* "Above   475| MS:Fighter   *CP1883:* "Fighter

Autumn brings Tsaddik. "Ay, there speeds the rill
Loaded with leaves: a scowling sky, beside:
480 The wind makes olive-trees up yonder hill

"Whiten and shudder—symptoms far and wide
Of gleaning-time's approach; and glean good store
May I presume to trust we shall, thou tried

"And ripe experimenter! Three months more
485 Have ministered to growth of Song: that graft
Into thy sterile stock has found at core

"Moisture, I warrant, hitherto unquaffed
By boughs, however florid, wanting sap
Of prose-experience which provides the draught

490 "Which song-sprouts, wanting, wither: vain we tap
A youngling stem all green and immature:
Experience must secrete the stuff, our hap

"Will be to quench Man's thirst with, glad and sure
That fancy wells up through corrective fact:
495 Missing which test of truth, though flowers allure

"The goodman's eye with promise, soon the pact
Is broken, and 'tis flowers,—mere words,—he finds
When things,—that's fruit,—he looked for. Well, once cracked

481| MS:Whiten   *P1883:* "Whiten   484| MS:And   *P1883:* "And   485| *P1883:* of
Song—that   *CP1883:* of Song: that   487| MS:Moisture   *P1883:* "Moisture
488| MS:boughs however blossomed—wanting   *P1883:* however florid, wanting
CP1883: boughs, however   490| MS:Mere song-shoots wanting—wither   *P1883:* "Mere
song-sprouts, wanting, wither   *1889a:* "Which song-sprouts   491| *1883:* immature
1889a: immature: 492| MS:secrete   *1889a:* secret   §emended to§ secrete §see Editorial
Notes§   493| MS:MS:Will be to bathe us §last two words crossed out and replaced above
by two words§ quench our thirsting, §last syllable and comma crossed out and replaced above
by§ with, glad   *P1883:* "Will < > quench Man's thirst   495| MS:Wanting which < >
truth—though   *P1883:* truth, though   *1889a:* Missing which   496| MS:The
P1883: "The   498| MS:for. Well, 'tis cracked   *P1883:* for. Well, once cracked

"The nut, how glad my tooth the kernel grinds!
500   Song may henceforth boast substance! Therefore, hail
Proser and poet, perfect in both kinds!

"Thou from whose eye hath dropped the envious scale
Which hides the truth of things and substitutes
Deceptive show, unaided optics fail

505   "To transpierce,—hast entrusted to the lute's
Soft but sure guardianship some unrevealed
Secret shall lift mankind above the brutes

"As only knowledge can?" "A fount unsealed"
(Sighed Jochanan) "should seek the heaven in leaps
510   To die in dew-gems—not find death, congealed

"By contact with the cavern's nether deeps,
Earth's secretest foundation where, enswathed
In dark and fear, primæval mystery sleeps—

"Petrific fount wherein my fancies bathed
515   And straight turned ice. My dreams of good and fair
In soaring upwards had dissolved, unscathed

"By any influence of the kindly air,
Singing, as each took flight, 'The Future—that's
Our destination, mists turn rainbows there,

499| MS:The nut, and §crossed out and replaced above by three words§ glad my tooth the
kernel is mankind's: §last two words crossed out and replaced above by one word§ grinds:
P1883: "The nut, how glad <> grinds!   500| MS:substance! too. So, §last two words
crossed out and replaced above by one word§ Therefore,   501| MS:Rabbi, prose-poet,
perfect   *P1883:* Proser and poet, perfect   502| MS:Thou   *P1883:* "Thou
505| MS:To pierce thro',—hast   *P1883:* To transpierce,—hast   *CP1883:* "To
508| MS:As   *P1883:* "As   509| MS:(Replied the sage) "should   *P1883:* (Sighed
Jochanan) "should   511| MS:By   *P1883:* "By   513| MS:fear primæval
P1883: fear, primæval   514| MS:Petrific   *P1883:* "Petrific   516| MS:By §crossed out
and replaced above by§ In   517| MS:By   *P1883:* "By   518| MS:flight, 'The
1889a: flight, The §emended to§ flight, 'The §see Editorial Notes§

520   "Which sink to fog, confounded in the flats
      O' the Present.' Day's the song-time for the lark,
      Night for her music boasts but owls and bats.

      "And what's the Past but night—the deep and dark
      Ice-spring I speak of, corpse-thicked with its drowned
525   Dead fancies which no sooner touched the mark

      "They aimed at—fact—than all at once they found
      Their film-wings freeze, henceforth unfit to reach
      And roll in æther, revel—robed and crowned

      "As truths, confirmed by falsehood all and each—
530   Sovereign and absolute and ultimate!
      Up with them, skyward, Youth, ere Age impeach

      "Thy least of promises to re-instate
      Adam in Eden! Sing on, ever sing,
      Chirp till thou burst!—the fool cicada's fate,

535   "Who holds that after Summer next comes Spring,
      Than Summer's self sun-warmed, spice-scented more.
      Fighting was better! There, no fancy-fling

      "Pitches you past the point was reached of yore
      By Sampsons, Abners, Joabs, Judases,
540   The mighty men of valour who, before

521| MS:the Present. Day's the singing-time §altered to§ song-time for the §inserted above§
larks §altered to§ lark,   *P1883:*the Present! Day's §emended to§ Present.' Day's §see Editorial
Notes§   523| MS:And   *P1883:*"And   525| MS:Fallen fancies   *P1883:*Dead fancies
526| MS:They   *P1883:*"They   527| MS:freeze—henceforth   *P1883:*freeze, henceforth
528| MS:æther,—revel, robed   *P1883:* æther,revel—robed   529| MS:As truths
confirmed   *P1883:*"As   *1889a:*truths, confirmed   532| MS:Thy   *P1883:*"Thy
533| MS:in Eden: sing on   *P1883:*in Eden! Sing on   534| MS:burst—the <> fate—
*P1883:*burst!—the <> fate,   535| MS:Who   *CP1883:*"Who   536| MS:Sun-warmed,
spice-scented more than §altered to§ Than Summer's self. §marked for transposition to§ Than
Summer's self sun-warmed, spice-scented more.   538| MS:Pitches   *P1883:*"Pitches

"Our little day, did wonders none profess
To doubt were fable and not fact, so trust
By fancy-flights to emulate much less.

"Were I a Statesman, now! Why, that were just
545 To pinnacle my soul, mankind above,
A-top the universe: no vulgar lust

"To gratify—fame, greed, at this remove
Looked down upon so far—or overlooked
So largely, rather—that mine eye should rove

550 "World-wide and rummage earth, the many-nooked,
Yet find no unit of the human flock
Caught straying but straight comes back hooked and crooked

"By the strong shepherd who, from out his stock
Of aids proceeds to treat each ailing fleece,
555 Here stimulate to growth, curtail and dock

"There, baldness or excrescence,—that, with grease,
This, with up-grubbing of the bristly patch
Born of the tick-bite. How supreme a peace

"Steals o'er the Statist,—while, in wit, a match
560 For shrewd Ahithophel, in wisdom . . . well,
His name escapes me—somebody, at watch

"And ward, the fellow of Ahithophel
In guidance of the Chosen!"—at which word
Eyes closed and fast asleep the Rabbi fell.

541| MS:Our *P1883:* "Our   545| MS:pinnacle one's soul *P1883:* pinnacle my soul
547| MS:To *P1883:* "To   549| MS:rather, that one's eye *P1883:* rather—that mine eye
550| MS:World-wide *P1883:* "World-wide   552| MS:But, caught astray, should §crossed
out and replaced above by§ straight come §altered to§ comes *P1883:* Caught straying but
straight   553| MS:By *P1883:* "By   554| MS:aids should wisely treat *P1883:* aids
proceeds to treat   556| MS:There *P1883:* "There   559| MS:Steals *P1883:* "Steals
560| MS:shrewd Ahitophel, in wisdom . . well, *P1883:* shrewd Ahithophel, in wisdom . . . well,
561| MS:somebody at *P1883:* somebody, at   562| MS:And ward the < > Ahitophel
P1883: "And ward, the < > Ahithophel   563| MS:the Chosen"—at *P1883:* the Chosen!"—at

565 "Cold weather!" shivered Tsaddik. "Yet the hoard
Of the sagacious ant shows garnered grain,
Ever abundant most when fields afford

"Least pasture, and alike disgrace the plain
Tall tree and lowly shrub. 'Tis so with us
570 Mortals: our age stores wealth ye seek in vain

"While busy youth culls just what we discuss
At leisure in the last days: and the last
Truly are these for Jochanan, whom thus

"I make one more appeal to! Thine amassed
575 Experience, now or never, let escape
Some portion of! For I perceive aghast

"The end approaches, while they jeer and jape,
These sons of Shimei: 'Justify your boast!
What have ye gained from Death by twelve months' rape?'

580 "Statesman, what cure hast thou for—least and most—
Popular grievances? What nostrum, say,
Will make the Rich and Poor, expertly dosed,

"Forget disparity, bid each go gay
That, with his bauble,—with his burden, this?
585 Propose an alkahest shall melt away

567| MS:And §crossed out and replaced above by§ Ever most abundant §marked for
transposition to§ abundant most when the §crossed out§ fields   568| MS:No §crossed
out and replaced above by§ Least   *P1883:*"Least   569| MS:lowly plant. 'Tis
*P1883:*lowly shrub. 'Tis   570| MS:Mortals, our age has wealth   *P1883:*Mortals: our age
stores wealth   571| MS:While youth is busy—culls what   *P1883:*"While busy youth culls
just what   573| MS:for Jochanan whom   *P1883:*for Jochanan, whom
574| MS:I <> to. Thine   *P1883:*"I <> to! Thine   576| MS:of! since I   *P1883:*of! For I
577| MS:The end approaches, and they <> jape   *P1883:*"The end approaches, while
they <> jape,   578| MS:of Shimei: "Justify <> boast—   *P1883:*of Shimei: 'Justify <>
boast!   579| MS:rape?"   *P1883:*rape?'   580| MS:Statesman   *P1883:*"Statesman
583| MS:Forget   *P1883:*"Forget   584| MS:this?—   *P1883:*this?
585| MS:Propose a remedy to rub away   *P1883:*Propose an alkahest shall melt away

119

"Men's lacquer, show by prompt analysis
Which is the metal, which the make-believe,
So that no longer brass shall find, gold miss

"Coinage and currency? Make haste, retrieve
590   The precious moments, Master!" Whereunto
There snarls an "Ever laughing in thy sleeve,

"Pert Tsaddik? Youth indeed sees plain a clue
To guide man where life's wood is intricate:
How shall he fail to thrid its thickest through

595   "When every oak-trunk takes the eye? Elate
He goes from bole to brushwood, plunging finds—
Smothered in briars—that the small's the great!

"All men are men: I would all minds were minds!
Whereas 'tis just the many's mindless mass
600   That most needs helping: labourers and hinds

"We legislate for—not the cultured class
Which law-makes for itself nor needs the whip
And bridle,—proper help for mule and ass,

"Did the brutes know! In vain our statesmanship
605   Strives at contenting the rough multitude:
Still the ox cries ' 'Tis me thou shouldst equip

586| MS:All varnish §crossed out and replaced above by§ lacquer   *P1883*:Men's lacquer
587| MS:metal which   *CP1883*:metal, which   588| MS:no more shall brass find than
gold   *P1883*:no longer brass shall find, gold   589| MS:Coinage   *P1883*:"Coinage
591| MS:He tartly §crossed out and replaced above by two words§ snarls an   *P1883*:There
snarls   592| MS:Pert   *P1883*:"Pert   593| MS:guide him where the §crossed out and
replaced above by§ life's wood's §altered to§ wood most §crossed out and replaced above by§
is   *P1883*:guide man where   595| MS:When   *P1883*:"When
598| MS:All <> men—I   *P1883*:"All <> men: I   599| MS:Unluckily 'tis <> the
mindless   *P1883*:Whereas 'tis <> the many's mindless   601| MS:We
P1883:"We   603| MS:help §inserted above§   604| MS:Did <> know. In
P1883:"Did <> know! In   606| MS:me you §crossed out and replaced above by§ thou

"'With equine trappings!' or, in humbler mood,
'Cribful of corn for me! and, as for work—
Adequate rumination o'er my food!'

610 "Better remain a Poet! Needs it irk
Such an one if light, kindled in his sphere,
Fail to transfuse the Mizraim cold and murk

"Round about Goshen? Though light disappear,
Shut inside,—temporary ignorance
615 Got outside of, lo, light emerging clear

"Shows each astonished starer the expanse
Of heaven made bright with knowledge! That's the way,
The only way—I see it at a glance—

"To legislate for earth! As poet. . . . Stay!
620 What is . . . I would that . . . were it . . . I had been . . .
O sudden change, as if my arid clay

"Burst into bloom! . . ." "A change indeed, I ween,
And change the last!" sighed Tsaddik as he kissed
The closing eyelids. "Just as those serene

625 "Princes of Night apprised me! Our acquist
Of life is spent, since corners only four
Hath Aisch, and each in turn was made desist

607| MS:With   *P1883:*"With   *1889a:*"'With   608| MS:me—and   *P1883:*me! and
610| MS:Better   *P1883:*"Better   611| MS:one that light kindled <> sphere   *P1883:*one
if light, kindled <> sphere,   612| MS:Fails <> Mizraim §illegible word, possibly *mass*,
crossed out and replaced above by§ cold   *P1883:*Fail   613| MS:Round <> disappear
P1883:"Round <> disappear,   614| MS:Inside,—contemporaneous ignorance
*P1883:*Shut inside,—temporary ignorance   615| MS:emerges   *P1883:*emerging
616| MS:And shows the astonished   *P1883:*"Shows each astonished   617| MS:way
*P1883:*way,   619| MS:To <> earth: as poet . . Stay!   *P1883:*"To <> earth! As poet. . . .
Stay!   620| MS:is . . I <> that . . were it . . I had been . .   *P1883:* is . . . I <> that . . .
were it . . . I had been . . .   621| MS:This sudden   *P1883:*O sudden
622| MS:Burst <> bloom! . ." "A <> indeed! I   *P1883:*"Burst <> bloom! . . ." "A <> indeed,
I   623| MS:'Tis change   *P1883:*And change   625| MS:Princes   *P1883:*"Princes
626| MS:spent. Of corners   *P1883:*spent since corners   *CP1883:*spent, since

"In passage round the Pole (O Mishna's lore—
Little it profits here!) by strenuous tug
630　Of friends who eked out thus to full fourscore

"The Rabbi's years. I see each shoulder shrug!
What have we gained? Away the Bier may roll!
To-morrow, when the Master's grave is dug,

"In with his body I may pitch the scroll
635　I hoped to glorify with, text and gloss,
My Science of Man's Life: one blank's the whole!

"Love, war, song, statesmanship—no gain, all loss,
The stars' bestowment! We on our return
To-morrow merely find—not gold but dross,

640　"The body not the soul. Come, friends, we learn
At least thus much by our experiment—
That—that . . . well, find what, whom it may concern!"

But next day through the city rumours went
Of a new persecution; so, they fled
645　All Israel, each man,—this time,—from his tent,

Tsaddik among the foremost. When, the dread
Subsiding, Israel ventured back again
Some three months after, to the cave they sped

Where lay the Sage,—a reverential train!
650　Tsaddik first enters. "What is this I view?
The Rabbi still alive? No stars remain

628| MS:In < > Mischna's §altered to§ Mishna's　*P1883:*"In　629| MS:profits!) by a
strenuous　*P1883:*profits here!) by strenuous　631| MS:The < > years: I　*P1883:*years. I
CP1883:"The　634| MS:In　*P1883:*"In　635| MS:to blacken with both text
*P1883:*to glorify with, text　636| MS:of Man's Life—one　*P1883:*of Man's Life: one
637| MS:Love　*P1883:*"Love　638| MS:bestowment! Tsaddik §crossed out and replaced
above by two words§ We on on §altered to§ our　639| MS:finds §altered to§ find
640| MS:The　*P1883:*"The　642| MS:that . . well　*P1883:*that . . . well
644| MS:so they　*P1883:*so, they　646| MS:foremost. When, their §altered to§ the

122

"Of Aisch to stop within their courses. True,
I mind me, certain gamesome boys must urge
Their offerings on me: can it be—one threw

655 "Life at him and it stuck? There needs the scourge
To teach that urchin manners! Prithee, grant
Forgiveness if we pretermit thy dirge

"Just to explain no friend was ministrant,
This time, of life to thee! Some jackanapes,
660 I gather, has presumed to foist his scant

"Scurvy unripe existence—wilding grapes
Grass-green and sorrel-sour—on that grand wine,
Mighty as mellow, which, so fancy shapes

"May fitly image forth this life of thine
665 Fed on the last low fattening lees—condensed
Elixir, no milk-mildness of the vine!

"Rightly with Tsaddik wert thou now incensed
Had he been witting of the mischief wrought
When, for elixir, verjuice he dispensed!"

670 And slowly woke,—like Shushan's flower besought
By over-curious handling to unloose
The curtained secrecy wherein she thought

652| MS:Of   *P1883:* "Of   655| MS:Life at me <> stuck? Beseech thee, g §last two words
and letter crossed out and replaced above by three words§ There needs the   *P1883:* "Life at
him and   656| MS:that rude boy §last two words crossed out and replaced above by one
word§ urchin   658| MS:Just <> ministrant   *P1883:* "Just <> ministrant,
659| MS:time of   *P1883:* time, of   661| MS:Scurvy   *P1883:* "Scurvy
663| MS:which my fancy   *1889a:* which, so fancy   664| MS:Into an image of that §last
two words crossed out and replaced above by two words§ fit for life   *P1883:* "May fitly image
forth this life   665| MS:Fed low upon the fattening   *P1883:* Fed on the last low fattening
666| MS:no mere mildness <> vine.   *P1883:* no milk-mildness <> vine!   667| MS:Justly
with   *P1883:* "Righly with   *CP1883:* "Rightly   670| MS:wakened,— §altered to§
wakening,—like a bell-flower brought   *P1883:* woke,—like Shushan's flower besought

Her captive bee, mid store of sweets to choose,
Would loll, in gold pavilioned lie unteased,
675   Sucking on, sated never,—whose, O whose

Might seem that countenance, uplift, all eased
Of old distraction and bewilderment,
Absurdly happy? "How ye have appeased

"The strife within me, bred this whole content,
680   This utter acquiescence in my past,
Present and future life,—by whom was lent

"The power to work this miracle at last,—
Exceeds my guess. Though—*ignorance confirmed
By knowledge* sounds like paradox, I cast

685   "Vainly about to tell you—fitlier termed—
Of calm struck by encountering opposites,
Each nullifying either! Henceforth wormed

"From out my heart is every snake that bites
The dove that else would brood there: doubt, which kills
690   With hiss of 'What if sorrows end delights?'

"Fear which stings ease with 'Work the Master wills!'
Experience which coils round and strangles quick
Each hope with 'Ask the Past if hoping skills

673| *P1883:*choose   *CP1883:*choose,   674| MS:loll in gold, pavilioned lie unteazed,
*1889a:*loll, in gold pavilioned lie unteased,   675| MS:on, dreamin §crossed out and
replaced above by§ sated   679| MS:The *P1883:*"The   680| MS:past *1889a:*past,
682| MS:The *P1883:*"The   683| MS:I nowise §last two words crossed out and replaced
above by two words§ Exceeds my guess nor yet— §last two words and dash crossed out and
replaced above by one word and dash§ Though—ignorance confirmed *P1883:ignorance
confirmed*   684| MS:By knowledge *P1883:By knowledge*   685| MS:Vainly
P1883:"Vainly   686| MS:Of calm from these encountering *P1883:*This calm struck by
encountering *1889a:*Of calm   687| MS:either, whereby—wormed *P1883:*either!
Henceforth wormed   688| MS:From *P1883:*'From *CP1883:*"From
689| MS:that stoops to brood there—doubt *P1883:*that else would brood there: doubt
691| MS:Fear that §crossed out and replaced above by§ which *P1883:*"Fear
692| MS:Experience that §crossed out and replaced above by§ which

"'To work accomplishment, or proves a trick
695   Wiling thee to endeavour! Strive, fool, stop
Nowise, so live, so die—that's law! why kick

"'Against the pricks?' All out-wormed! Slumber, drop
Thy films once more and veil the bliss within!
Experience strangle hope? Hope waves a-top

700   "Her wings triumphant! Come what will, I win,
Whoever loses! Every dream's assured
Of soberest fulfilment. Where's a sin

"Except in doubting that the light, which lured
The unwary into darkness, meant no wrong
705   Had I but marched on bold, nor paused immured

"By mists I should have pressed thro', passed along
My way henceforth rejoicing? Not the boy's
Passionate impulse he conceits so strong,

"Which, at first touch, truth, bubble-like, destroys,—
710   Not the man's slow conviction 'Vanity
Of vanities—alike my griefs and joys!'

"Ice!—thawed (look up) each bird, each insect by—
(Look round) by all the plants that break in bloom,
(Look down) by every dead friend's memory

694| MS:To <> accomplishment—or   *P1883:* "To <> accomplishment, or
695| MS:endeavour! Strive thou, stop   *P1883:* endeavour! Strive, fool, stop
696| MS:law: why   *P1883:* law! why   697| MS:Against the pricks?' While now—Oh,
slumber   *P1883:* "Against the pricks?' All out-warmed! Slumber   *CP1883:* out-wormed
700| MS:Her   *P1883:* "Her <> win   *CP1883:* win,   701| MS:loses, every dream
P1883: loses! Every dream's   702| MS:fulfilment. There's no sin   *1889a:* fulfilment.
Where's a sin   703| MS:Except <> light which   *P1883:* "Except   *CP1883:* light, which
704| MS:into dark had done no   *P1883:* into darkness did no   *CP1883:* darkness, did
705| MS:Had I §altered to§ he but followed still, not paused   *P1883:* Had I but marched on
bold, nor paused   706| MS:By mists I §altered to§ he should   *P1883:* "By mists I should
707| MS:My §altered to§ His way <> rejoicing! Not   *P1883:* My way   *1889a:* rejoicing? Not
709| MS:But truth, at first touch, bubble-like   *P1883:* "Which at first touch, truth, bubble-like
CP1883: "Which, at   710| MS:man's cold conviction   *P1883:* man's slow conviction
712| MS:Ice—thawed   *P1883:* "Ice!—thawed   713| MS:by every §crossed out and
replaced above by two words§ all the plant §altered to§ plants <> breaks §altered to§ break

715 "That smiles 'Am I the dust within my tomb?'
Not either, but both these—amalgam rare—
Mix in a product, not from Nature's womb,

"But stuff which He the Operant—who shall dare
Describe His operation?—strikes alive
720 And thaumaturgic. I nor know nor care

"How from this tohu-bohu—hopes which dive,
And fears which soar—faith, ruined through and through
By doubt, and doubt, faith treads to dust—revive

"In some surprising sort,—as see, they do!—
725 Not merely foes no longer but fast friends.
What does it mean unless—O strange and new

"Discovery!—this life proves a wine-press—blends
Evil and good, both fruits of Paradise,
Into a novel drink which—who intends

730 "To quaff, must bear a brain for ecstasies
Attempered, not this all-inadequate
Organ which, quivering within me, dies

"—Nay, lives!—what, how,—too soon, or else too late—
I was—I am . . ." ("He babbleth!" Tsaddik mused)
735 "O Thou Almighty who canst re-instate

715| MS:That smiles 'Is man the < > within his tomb?' *P1883:* "That smiles 'am I the < >
within my tomb?' *CP1883:* smiles 'Am 716| MS:but these both—amalgam
P1883: but both these—amalgam 718| MS:But pestled by §last two words crossed out
and replaced above by one word§ stuff the Operant, pestling—who *P1883:* "But stuff which
He the Operant who *CP1883:* the Operant—who 721| MS:How *P1883:* "How
722| MS:And doubts §crossed out and replaced above by§ fears < > faith ruined
P1883: faith, ruined 723| MS:and doubt faith *P1883:* and doubt, faith
724| MS:In < > do,— *P1883:* "In < > do!— 725| MS:friends— *1889a:* friends.
727| MS:Discovery *P1883:* "Discovery 730| MS:To *P1883:* "To
733| MS:—Nay < > late? *P1883:* "—Nay < > late—

"Truths in their primal clarity, confused
By man's perception, which is man's and made
To suit his service,—how, once disabused

"Of reason which sees light half shine half shade,
740 Because of flesh, the medium that adjusts
Purity to his visuals, both an aid

"And hindrance,—how to eyes earth's air encrusts,
When purged and perfect to receive truth's beam
Pouring itself on the new sense it trusts

745 "With all its plenitude of power,—how seem
The intricacies now, of shade and shine,
Oppugnant natures—Right and Wrong, we deem

"Irreconcilable? O eyes of mine,
Freed now of imperfection, ye avail
750 To see the whole sight, nor may uncombine

"Henceforth what, erst divided, caused you quail—
So huge the chasm between the false and true,
The dream and the reality! All hail,

"Day of my soul's deliverance—day the new,
755 The never-ending! What though every shape
Whereon I wreaked my yearning to pursue

736| MS:Truths <> primal clearness §crossed out and replaced above by§ clarity, unconfused §first two letters crossed out§ *P1883:*"Truths   739| MS:Of *P1883:*"Of
742| MS:And hindrance,—eyes which earth's dense air   *P1883:*"And hindrance,—how to eyes earth's air   743| MS:Once purged <> receive the beam   *P1883:*When purged <> receive truth's beam   745| MS:With <> seem   *P1883:*"With   *1889a:*seen §emended to§ seem §see Editorial Notes§   746| MS:Then, the intricacies of   *1889a:*The intricacies now, of   747| MS:right and wrong   *P1883:*natures—Right and Wrong
748| MS:Irreconcilable   *P1883:*" Irreconcilable   750| MS:To grasp §crossed out and replaced above by§ see the whole truth§crossed out and replaced above by§ sight
751| MS:Henceforth   *P1883:*"Henceforth   754| MS:Day <> Day   *P1883:*"Day <> day

"Even to success each semblance of escape
From my own bounded self to some all-fair
All-wise external fancy, proved a rape

760 "Like that old giant's, feigned of fools—on air,
Not solid flesh? How otherwise? To love
That lesson was to learn not here—but there—

"On earth, not here! 'Tis there we learn,—there prove
Our parts upon the stuff we needs must spoil,
765 Striving at mastery, there bend above

"The spoiled clay potsherds, many a year of toil
Attests the potter tried his hand upon,
Till sudden he arose, wiped free from soil

"His hand cried 'So much for attempt—anon
770 Performance! Taught to mould the living vase,
What matter the cracked pitchers dead and gone?'

"Could I impart and could thy mind embrace
The secret, Tsaddik!" "Secret none to me!"
Quoth Tsaddik, as the glory on the face

775 Of Jochanan was quenched. "The truth I see
Of what that excellence of Judah wrote,
Doughty Halaphta. This a case must be

757| MS:Even to success what tempted like §last three words crossed out and replaced above by three words§ each semblance of   *P1883:*"Even   760| MS:Like < > air   *P1883:*"Like   *CP1883:*air,   763| MS:On   *P1883:*"On   765| MS:mastery,—there   *P1883:*mastery, there   766| MS:The   *P1883:*"The   767| MS:tries   *P1883:*tried   768| MS:arises, free   *P1883:*arose, wiped free   769| MS:Wipes hand, cries < > for endeavour—now §last two words crossed out and replaced above by two words§ attempt—anon   *P1883:*"His hand, cried   772| MS:Could   *P1883:*"Could   775| *P1883:*"Of   *CP1883:*Of   777| MS:case may be   *P1883:*case must be

"Wherein, though the last breath have passed the throat,
So that 'The man is dead' we may pronounce,
780   Yet is the Ruach—(thus do we denote

"The imparted Spirit)—in no haste to bounce
From its entrusted Body,—some three days
Lingers ere it relinquish to the pounce

"Of hawk-clawed Death his victim. Further says
785   Halaphta, 'Instances have been, and yet
Again may be, when saints, whose earthly ways

"'Tend to perfection, very nearly get
To heaven while still on earth: and, as a fine
Interval shows where waters pure have met

790   "'Waves brackish, in a mixture, sweet with brine,
That's neither sea nor river but a taste
Of both—so meet the earthly and divine

"'And each is either.' Thus I hold him graced—
Dying on earth, half inside and half out,
795   Wholly in heaven, who knows? My mind embraced

"Thy secret, Jochanan, how dare I doubt?
Follow thy Ruach, let earth, all it can,
Keep of the leavings!" Thus was brought about

778| MS:Wherein <> throat   *P1883:*"Wherein <> throat,   780| MS:the Ruach §altered
to§ Ruah   *P1883:*the Ruach   781| MS:The   *P1883:*"The   783| MS:Lingers till
§crossed out and replaced above by§ ere   784| MS:Of hawk-faced §inserted above;
second half of compound crossed out and replaced above by§ clawed <> victim: further
P1883:"Of <> victim. Further   786| MS:saints who   *P1883:*saints, whose
787| MS:Tend   *P1883:*"Tend   *1889a:*"'Tend   788| MS:and as   *P1883:*and, as
790| MS:Waves <> mixture,—sweet   *P1883:*"Waves <> mixture, sweet   *1889a:*"'Waves
793| MS:And <> either. Thus I hold was §crossed out and replaced above by§ him graced
P1883:"And <> graced—   *1889a:*"'And <> either.' Thus   794| MS:Our Rabbi, §crossed
out§ who was §crossed out and replaced above by§ died §last two words crossed out and
replaced above by§ dying §crossed out§ Dying on earth, §last three words inserted above§ half
inside and §inserted above§   796| MS:Thy <> Jochanan, why §crossed out and replaced
above by§ how   *P1883:*"Thy   797| MS:thy Ruach §altered to§ Ruah, let §inserted above§
*P1883:*thy Ruach   798| MS:of its §crossed out and replaced above by§ the

The sepulture of Rabbi Jochanan:
800 Thou hast him,—sinner-saint, live-dead, boy-man,—
Schiphaz, on Bendimir, in Farzistan!

NOTE,—This story can have no better authority than that of the treatise,
existing dispersedly in fragments of Rabbinical writing, משך של רכים בדים,
from which I might have helped myself more liberally. Thus, instead of the
simple reference to "Moses' stick," —but what if I make amends by attempting
5   three illustrations, when some thirty might be composed on the same subject,
equally justifying that pithy proverb ממשה עד משה לא קם משה.

I.

Moses the Meek was thirty cubits high,
    The staff he strode with—thirty cubits long:
    And when he leapt, so muscular and strong
Was Moses that his leaping neared the sky
5   By thirty cubits more: we learn thereby
    He reached full ninety cubits—am I wrong?—
    When, in a fight slurred o'er by sacred song,
With staff outstretched he took a leap to try
The just dimensions of the giant Og.
10   And yet he barely touched—this marvel lacked
Posterity to crown earth's catalogue
    Of marvels—barely touched—to be exact—
The giant's ankle-bone, remained a frog
    That fain would match an ox in stature: fact!

800| MS:There §altered to§ Thou sleeps the Hagadosch, both §last four words crossed out and replaced above by five words§ hast him, sinner-saint, live dead, boy and §crossed out§ man,— *P1883:*him,—sinner-saint, live-dead, boy-man,—   801| MS:§added below last line of poem§ L. D. I. E. Dec. 22 '82. §crossed out; see Editorial Notes§

Note   2| MS:§no punctuation after Hebrew§ *P1883:*§comma inserted§
6| MS:equally to §crossed out§ justifying   MS:§in B's hand following Hebrew at end of note§ (Let the three sonnets follow)

SONNET I   §in B's hand above poem§ Print these sonnets in a smaller type, after the Note.   7| MS:flight not found in §last three words crossed out and replaced above by three words§ slurred o'er by   8| MS:out-stretched   *1889a:*outstretched
13| MS:ancle-bone   *1889a:*ankle-bone

II.

And this same fact has met with unbelief!
    How saith a certain traveller? "Young, I chanced
    To come upon an object—if thou canst,
Guess me its name and nature! 'Twas, in brief,
5 White, hard, round, hollow, of such length, in chief,
    —And this is what especially enhanced
    My wonder—that it seemed, as I advanced,
Never to end. Bind up within thy sheaf
Of marvels, this—Posterity! I walked
10   From end to end,—four hours walked I, who go
A goodly pace,—and found—I have not baulked
    Thine expectation, Stranger? Ay or No?
'Twas but Og's thigh-bone, all the while, I stalked
    Alongside of: respect to Moses, though!"

III.

Og's thigh-bone—if ye deem its measure strange,
    Myself can witness to much length of shank
    Even in birds. Upon a water's bank
Once halting, I was minded to exchange
5 Noon heat for cool. Quoth I "On many a grange
    I have seen storks perch—legs both long and lank:
    Yon stork's must touch the bottom of this tank,
Since on its top doth wet no plume derange
Of the smooth breast. I'll bathe there!" "Do not so!"
10   Warned me a voice from heaven. "A man let drop
    His axe into that shallow rivulet—
As thou accountest—seventy years ago:
It fell and fell and still without a stop
    Keeps falling, nor has reached the bottom yet."

SONNET II   ¹| MS:Yet §crossed out and replaced above by§ And   ⁵| MS:round,
broad, and §last two words crossed out and replaced above by one word§ hollow, of that
§crossed out and replaced above by§ such   ⁶| MS:—Which circumstance §last two
words crossed out and replaced above by four words§And this is what   ¹¹| MS:balked
*1889a:*baulked   ¹²| MS:or No?—   *P1883:*expectations   *CP1883:*expectation
*1889a:*or No?   ¹³| MS:'Twas   *1889a:*Twas §emended to§ 'Twas §see Editorial Notes§
¹⁴| MS:though!   *1889a:*though!"

SONNET III   ³| MS:a river's §crossed out and replaced above by§ water's
⁵| MS:Noon's §altered to§ Noon   ⁸| MS:top wet doth §marked for transposition to§
top doth wet   ¹⁴| MS:yet."   *1889a:*yet.' §emended to§ yet." §see Editorial Notes§

NEVER THE TIME AND THE PLACE

Never the time and the place
  And the loved one all together!
This path—how soft to pace!
  This May—what magic weather!
5 Where is the loved one's face?
In a dream that loved one's face meets mine,
  But the house is narrow, the place is bleak
Where, outside, rain and wind combine
  With a furtive ear, if I strive to speak,
10 With a hostile eye at my flushing cheek,
With a malice that marks each word, each sign!
O enemy sly and serpentine,
  Uncoil thee from the waking man!
   Do I hold the Past
15   Thus firm and fast
  Yet doubt if the Future hold I can?
This path so soft to pace shall lead
Thro' the magic of May to herself indeed!
Or narrow if needs the house must be,
20 Outside are the storms and strangers: we—
Oh, close, safe, warm sleep I and she,
 —I and she!

NEVER THE TIME AND THE PLACE   *Title* MS:§no title§ *P1883:*§title added in B's hand, with note *?Heading*§ *1883:*§title present§

PAMBO

Suppose that we part (work done, comes play)
    With a grave tale told in crambo
—As our hearty sires were wont to say—
    Whereof the hero is Pambo?

5   Do you happen to know who Pambo was?
    Nor I—but this much have heard of him:
He entered one day a college-class,
    And asked—was it so absurd of him?—

"May Pambo learn wisdom ere practise it?
10   In wisdom I fain would ground me:
Since wisdom is centred in Holy Writ,
    Some psalm to the purpose expound me!"

"That psalm," the Professor smiled, "shall be
    Untroubled by doubt which dirtieth
15   Pellucid streams when an ass like thee
    Would drink there—the Nine-and-thirtieth.

"Verse first: *I said I will look to my ways*
    That I with my tongue offend not.
How now? Why stare? Art struck in amaze?
20   Stop, stay! The smooth line hath an end knot!

"He's gone!—disgusted my text should prove
    Too easy to need explaining?
Had he waited, the blockhead might find I move
    To matter that pays remaining!"

25   Long years went by, when—"Ha, who's this?
    Do I come on the restive scholar

PAMBO   9| MS:practice *CP1883:*practise   10| MS:me. *P1883:*me:
17| MS:"Verse First *1889a:*first   22| MS:explaining; *P1883:*explaining?
24| MS:remaining." *P1883:*remaining!"

I had driven to Wisdom's goal, I wis,
    But that he slipped the collar?

"What? Arms crossed, brow bent, thought-immersed?
30   A student indeed! Why scruple
To own that the lesson proposed him first
    Scarce suited so apt a pupil?

"Come back! From the beggarly elements
    To a more recondite issue
35 We pass till we reach, at all events,
    Some point that may puzzle . . . Why I 'pish' you?"

From the ground looked piteous up the head:
    "Daily and nightly, Master,
Your pupil plods thro' that text you read,
40   Yet gets on never the faster.

"At the self-same stand,—now old, then young!
    I will look to my ways—were doing
As easy as saying!—*that I with my tongue*
    Offend not—and 'scape pooh-poohing

45 From sage and simple, doctor and dunce?
    Ah, nowise! Still doubts so muddy
The stream I would drink at once,—but once!
    That—thus I resume my study!"

Brother, brother, I share the blame,
50   *Arcades sumus ambo!*
Darkling, I keep my sunrise-aim,
    Lack not the critic's flambeau,
And *look to my ways*, yet, much the same,
    Offend with my tongue—like Pambo!

---

²⁹| MS:"What < > thought-immersed— *P1883:*thought-immersed?   *1889a:*'What §emended to§ "What §see Editorial Notes§   ³⁶| MS:puzzle . . why *P1883:*puzzle . . . why   ⁴⁷| MS:stream I am fain to drink at once, *P1883:*stream I would drink at once,—but once!   ⁵⁰| MS:*ambo.* *P1883: ambo!*
⁵¹| MS:sunrise aim, *P1883:*sunrise-aim,   ⁵³| MS:yet, all the *CP1883:*yet, much the
⁵⁴| MS:Offend with my tongue *P1883: Offend with my tongue*

FERISHTAH'S FANCIES

Edited by Allan C. Dooley

FERISHTAH'S FANCIES

FERISHTAH'S FANCIES   §MS in Balliol College Library, Oxford. Ed. P1884, CP1884,
1884, 1885, 1885a, 1889a.   See Editorial Notes and Table of Editions§

"His genius was jocular, but, when disposed, he could be very serious."—
Article "Shakespear," JEREMY COLLIER'S *Historical & c. Dictionary,* 2nd edition, 1701.

"You, Sir, I entertain you for one of my Hundred; only, I do not like the
fashion of your garments: you will say they are Persian: but let them be
changed."—*King Lear,* act iii. sc. 6.

Epigraph 1 ¹| MS:His *P1884:*'His *1889a:*"His ²| MS:serious. *Article,*
"Shakespear." Jeremy < > *Historical etc.* §inserted above§ *P1884:*serious'—Article 'Shakespear,'
< > *&c.* *1889a:*serious."—Article "Shakespear," ²⁻³| MS:*Dictionary, 1688.*
*P1884:*1688 *CP1884:Dictionary,* 2d. Edition, §inserted above§ 1701. §replacing date§
*1884:*2ⁿᵈ < > 1701 *1889a:*1701.

Epigraph 2 ¹| MS:You *P1884:*'You *1889a:*"You ²| MS:say, they are Persian;
but 1885a:say they are Persian: but ³| MS:changed. *King Lear. Act P1884:*changed'
< > *Lear,* Act *1889a:*changed."—*King Lear,* act

FERISHTAH'S FANCIES

1884

PROLOGUE

Pray, Reader, have you eaten ortolans
    Ever in Italy?
Recall how cooks there cook them: for my plan's
    To—Lyre with Spit ally.
5 They pluck the birds,—some dozen luscious lumps,
    Or more or fewer,—
Then roast them, heads by heads and rumps by rumps,
    Stuck on a skewer.
But first,—and here's the point I fain would press,—
10   Don't think I'm tattling!—
They interpose, to curb its lusciousness,
    —What, 'twixt each fatling?

First comes plain bread, crisp, brown, a toasted square:
    Then, a strong sage-leaf:
15 (So we find books with flowers dried here and there
    Lest leaf engage leaf.)
First, food—then, piquancy—and last of all
    Follows the thirdling:
Through wholesome hard, sharp soft, your tooth must bite
20   Ere reach the birdling.
Now, were there only crust to crunch, you'd wince:
    Unpalatable!
Sage-leaf is bitter-pungent—so's a quince:
    Eat each who's able!
25 But through all three bite boldly—lo, the gust!
    Flavour—no fixture—
Flies, permeating flesh and leaf and crust
    In fine admixture.

PROLOGUE   [27]| MS:Flies permeating   *1889a:*Flies, permeating
[28]| MS:In your §crossed out and replaced above by§ fine admixture.

So with your meal, my poem: masticate
30   Sense, sight and song there!
Digest these, and I praise your peptics' state,
    Nothing found wrong there.
Whence springs my illustration who can tell?
    —The more surprising
35 That here eggs, milk, cheese, fruit suffice so well
    For gormandizing.

A fancy-freak by contrast born of thee,
    Delightful Gressoney!
Who laughest "Take what is, trust what may be!"
40   That's Life's true lesson,—eh?

Maison Delapierre,
Gressoney St. Jean, Val d'Aosta
September 12, '83

39| MS:Who smilest "Take < > be"!   *P1884:*Who laughest "Take < > be!"

THE EAGLE

Dervish—(though yet un-dervished, call him so
No less beforehand: while he drudged our way,
Other his worldly name was: when he wrote
Those versicles we Persians praise him for,
5   —True fairy-work—Ferishtah grew his style)—
Dervish Ferishtah walked the woods one eve,
And noted on a bough a raven's nest
Whereof each youngling gaped with callow beak
Widened by want; for why? beneath the tree
10   Dead lay the mother-bird. "A piteous chance!
"How shall they 'scape destruction?" sighed the sage
—Or sage about to be, though simple still.
Responsive to which doubt, sudden there swooped
An eagle downward, and behold he bore
15   (Great-hearted) in his talons flesh wherewith
He stayed their craving, then resought the sky.
"Ah, foolish, faithless me!" the observer smiled,
"Who toil and moil to eke out life, when lo

Providence cares for every hungry mouth!"
20   To profit by which lesson, home went he,
And certain days sat musing,—neither meat
Nor drink would purchase by his handiwork.
Then,—for his head swam and his limbs grew faint,—
Sleep overtook the unwise one, whom in dream
25   God thus admonished: "Hast thou marked my deed?
Which part assigned by providence dost judge
Was meant for man's example? Should he play
The helpless weakling, or the helpful strength
That captures prey and saves the perishing?
30   Sluggard, arise: work, eat, then feed who lack!"

THE EAGLE   *Titl*| MS:1. *The Eagle*   *P1884: 1. THE EAGLE*   *1889a: THE*
¹⁶| MS:cravings   *P1884:*craving   ²⁵| MS:admonished. "Hast
*P1884:*admonished: "Hast   ²⁹| MS:Which captures   *P1884:*That captures

Waking, "I have arisen, work I will,
Eat, and so following. Which lacks food the more,
Body or soul in me? I starve in soul:
So may mankind: and since men congregate
35   In towns, not woods,—to Ispahan forthwith!"

Round us the wild creatures, overhead the trees,
Underfoot the moss-tracks,—life and love with these!
I to wear a fawn-skin, thou to dress in flowers:
All the long lone Summer-day, that greenwood life of ours!
40   Rich-pavilioned, rather,—still the world without,—
Inside—gold-roofed silk-walled silence round about!
Queen it thou on purple,—I, at watch and ward
Couched beneath the columns, gaze, thy slave, love's guard!

So, for us no world? Let throngs press thee to me!
45   Up and down amid men, heart by heart fare we!
Welcome squalid vesture, harsh voice, hateful face!
God is soul, souls I and thou: with souls should souls have place.

42| MS:Queen it §inserted above§ Thou §altered to§ thou on queenly §crossed out§
purple,—I at   *P1884:*purple,—I, at   43| MS:gaze, love's slave, thy guard!
*P1884:*gaze, thy slave, love's guard!

THE MELON-SELLER

Going his rounds one day in Ispahan,—
Half-way on Dervishhood, not wholly there,—
Ferishtah, as he crossed a certain bridge,
Came startled on a well-remembered face.
5   "Can it be? What, turned melon-seller—thou?
Clad in such sordid garb, thy seat yon step
Where dogs brush by thee and express contempt?
Methinks, thy head-gear is some scooped-out gourd!
Nay, sunk to slicing up, for readier sale,
10   One fruit whereof the whole scarce feeds a swine?
Wast thou the Shah's Prime Minister, men saw
Ride on his right-hand while a trumpet blew
And Persia hailed the Favourite? Yea, twelve years
Are past, I judge, since that transcendency,
15   And thou didst peculate and art abased;
No less, twelve years since, thou didst hold in hand
Persia, couldst halve and quarter, mince its pulp
As pleased thee, and distribute—melon-like—
Portions to whoso played the parasite,
20   Or suck—thyself—each juicy morsel. How

Enormous thy abjection,—hell from heaven,
Made tenfold hell by contrast! Whisper me!
Dost thou curse God for granting twelve years' bliss
Only to prove this day's the direr lot?"

25   Whereon the beggar raised a brow, once more
Luminous and imperial, from the rags.
"Fool, does thy folly think my foolishness
Dwells rather on the fact that God appoints
A day of woe to the unworthy one,

THE MELON-SELLER   *Title*| MS:2. *The Melon-Seller*   P1884: 2. THE MELON-SELLER
1889a: THE   9| sunk for §crossed out and replaced above by§ to slicing
13| MS:the Favorite   *1889a:*the Favourite   15| MS:abased: *P1884:*abased;
20| MS:each luscious morsel *P1884:*each juicy morsel   21| MS:heaven *P1884:*heaven,

30 Than that the unworthy one, by God's award,
Tasted joy twelve years long? Or buy a slice,
Or go to school!"

To school Ferishtah went;
And, schooling ended, passed from Ispahan
To Nishapur, that Elburz looks above
35 —Where they dig turquoise: there kept school himself,
The melon-seller's speech, his stock in trade.
Some say a certain Jew adduced the word
Out of their book, it sounds so much the same,
אֶת־הַטּוֹב נְקַבֵּל מֵאֵה הָאֱלֹהִים
40 אֶת־הָרָע לֹא נְקַבֵּל: In Persian phrase,
"Shall we receive good at the hand of God
And evil not receive?" But great wits jump.

Wish no word unspoken, want no look away!
What if words were but mistake, and looks—too sudden, say!
45 Be unjust for once, Love! Bear it—well I may!

Do me justice always? Bid my heart—their shrine—
Render back its store of gifts, old looks and words of thine
—Oh, so all unjust—the less deserved, the more divine?

39-40| §Hebrew emended to restore diacritical marks; see Editorial Notes§
40-42| MS:§Hebrew§ So, great wits jump! / §rule§   *P1884:* §Hebrew§ But great wits jump. /
§rule§   *1885:* §Hebrew§ In Persian phrase, / "Shall we receive good at the hand of God /
And evil not receive?" But <> jump. / §rule§   47| MS:gifts, those looks
*P1884:*gifts, old looks   48| MS:—Oh so <> divine! *P1884:*—Oh, so <> divine?

SHAH ABBAS

Anyhow, once full Dervish, youngsters came
To gather up his own words, 'neath a rock
Or else a palm, by pleasant Nishapur.

Said someone, as Ferishtah paused abrupt,
5   Reading a certain passage from the roll
Wherein is treated of Lord Ali's life:
"Master, explain this incongruity!
When I dared question 'It is beautiful,
But is it true?'—thy answer was 'In truth
10 Lives beauty.' I persisting—'Beauty—yes,
In thy mind and in my mind, every mind
That apprehends: but outside—so to speak—
Did beauty live in deed as well as word,
Was this life lived, was this death died—not dreamed?'
15 'Many attested it for fact' saidst thou.
'Many!' but mark, Sir! Half as long ago
As such things were,—supposing that they were,—

Reigned great Shah Abbas: he too lived and died
—How say they? Why, so strong of arm, of foot
20 So swift, he stayed a lion in his leap
On a stag's haunch,—with one hand grasped the stag,
With one struck down the lion: yet, no less,
Himself, that same day, feasting after sport,
Perceived a spider drop into his wine,
25 Let fall the flagon, died of simple fear.
So all say,—so dost thou say?"

                    "Wherefore not?"
Ferishtah smiled: "though strange, the story stands
Clear-chronicled: none tells it otherwise:
The fact's eye-witness bore the cup, beside."

───

SHAH ABBAS   *Title*| MS:3. *Belief* *P1884:*3. *SHAH ABBAS*   *1889a: SHAH*
⁴| MS:paused awhile   *P1884:*paused abrupt,   ⁶| of §word illegibly crossed out§
Lord §inserted above§ Ali's   ¹⁵| 'Many §word illegibly crossed out§
attested it for §last two words inserted above§ fact

30   "And dost thou credit one cup-bearer's tale,
    False, very like, and futile certainly,
    Yet hesitate to trust what many tongues
    Combine to testify was beautiful
    In deed as well as word? No fool's report
35   Of lion, stag and spider, but immense
    With meaning for mankind,—thy race,—thyself?"

    Whereto the Dervish: "First amend, my son,
    Thy faulty nomenclature, call belief
    Belief indeed, nor grace with such a name
40   The easy acquiescence of mankind
    In matters nowise worth dispute, since life
    Lasts merely the allotted moment. Lo—
    That lion-stag-and-spider tale leaves fixed
    The fact for us that somewhen Abbas reigned,
45   Died, somehow slain,—a useful registry,—
    Which therefore we—'believe'? Stand forward, thou,
    My Yakub, son of Yusuf, son of Zal!
    I advertise thee that our liege, the Shah
    Happily regnant, hath become assured,
50   By opportune discovery, that thy sires,
    Son by the father upwards, track their line
    To—whom but that same bearer of the cup
    Whose inadvertency was chargeable
    With what therefrom ensued, disgust and death
55   To Abbas Shah, the over-nice of soul?
    Whence he appoints thee,—such his clemency,—
    Not death, thy due, but just a double tax
    To pay, on thy particular bed of reeds
    Which flower into the brush that makes a broom

36| MS:race, thyself?"   *1889a:*race,—thyself?"   37| MS:the Dervish "First   *P1884:*the
Dervish: "First   39| MS:Belief §word illegibly crossed out and replaced above by§ indeed   45| Was §crossed out and replaced above by illegible word, crossed out in turn§ Died, §added
in margin§ somehow slain,—an useful §crossed out and then marked for retention§
*P1884:*slain,—a useful   48| MS:liege the   *1885:*liege, the   49| MS:become
apprised,   *P1884:*become assured,   50| MS:discovery how §crossed out and replaced
above by§ that thy   54| MS:With that offence wherefrom came death-disgust
*P1884:*With what therefrom ensued, disgust and death   55| MS:soul: *P1884:*soul?
59| MS:into a brush which §crossed out and replaced above by§ that   *P1884:*into the brush

60   Fit to sweep ceilings clear of vermin. Sure,
     Thou dost believe the story nor dispute
     That punishment should signalize its truth?
     Down therefore with some twelve dinars! Why start,
     —The stag's way with the lion hard on haunch?
65   'Believe the story?'—how thy words throng fast!—
     'Who saw this, heard this, said this, wrote down this,
     That and the other circumstance to prove
     So great a prodigy surprised the world?
     Needs must thou prove me fable can be fact
70   Or ere thou coax one piece from out my pouch!' "

     "There we agree, Sir: neither of us knows,
     Neither accepts that tale on evidence
     Worthy to warrant the large word—belief.
     Now I get near thee! Why didst pause abrupt,
75   Disabled by emotion at a tale
     Might match—be frank!—for credibility
     The figment of the spider and the cup?
     —To wit, thy roll's concerning Ali's life,
     Unevidenced—thine own word! Little boots
80   Our sympathy with fiction! When I read
     The annals and consider of Tahmasp
     And that sweet sun-surpassing star his love,
     I weep like a cut vine-twig, though aware
     Zurah's sad fate is fiction, since the snake
85   He saw devour her,—how could such exist,
     Having nine heads? No snake boasts more than three!
     I weep, then laugh—both actions right alike.
     But thou, Ferishtah, sapiency confessed,

---

[60] MS:ceilings <> vermin: sure *P1884:*ceilings <> vermin. Sure,   [63] MS:with twelve
<> Why that start, *P1884:*with some twelve <> Why start,   [64] MS:stag's own with
*P1884:*stag's way with   [66] MS:down this *1889a:*down this,
[67] MS:circumstance in proof *P1884:*circumstance to prove   [69] must you prove
*P1884:*must thou prove   [70] MS:ere you coax <> from out my §last two words inserted
above§ pouch of mine!' " §last two words crossed out§   [73] MS:the big word
*P1884:*the large word   [80] MS:Thy sympathy *P1884:*Our sympathy
[81] MS:of Thamasp *1885a:*of Tahmasp   [83] MS:vine-twig though *P1884:*vine-twig,
though   [87] MS:actions good alike. *P1884:*actions right alike.

When at the Day of Judgment God shall ask
90   'Didst thou believe?'—what wilt thou plead? Thy tears?
(Nay, they fell fast and stain the parchment still)
What if thy tears meant love? Love lacking ground
—Belief,—avails thee as it would avail
My own pretence to favour since, forsooth,
95   I loved the lady—I, who needs must laugh
To hear a snake boasts nine heads: they have three!"

"Thanks for the well-timed help that's born, behold,
Out of thy words, my son,—belief and love!
Hast heard of Ishak son of Absal? Ay,
100   The very same we heard of, ten years since,
Slain in the wars: he comes back safe and sound,—
Though twenty soldiers saw him die at Yezdt,—
Just as a single mule-and-baggage boy
Declared 'twas like he some day would,—for why?
105   The twenty soldiers lied, he saw him stout,
Cured of all wounds at once by smear of salve,
A Mubid's manufacture: such the tale.
Now, when his pair of sons were thus apprised
Effect was twofold on them. 'Hail!' crowed This:
110   'Dearer the news than dayspring after night!
The cure-reporting youngster warrants me
Our father shall make glad our eyes once more,
For whom, had outpoured life of mine sufficed
To bring him back, free broached were every vein!'
115   'Avaunt, delusive tale-concocter, news
Cruel as meteor simulating dawn!'
Whimpered the other: 'Who believes this boy

89| MS:of Judgement §altered to§ of Judgment   92| MS:if they §altered to§ thy tears
§inserted above§ meant thy §crossed out§ love? Thy §inserted above§ Love lacked §word
illegibly crossed out§ ground   *P1884*:love? Love lacking ground   93| MS:would myself
§crossed out and replaced above by§ avail   95| MS:lady—I who   *P1884*:lady—I, who
106| MS:Free of   *P1884*:Cured of   108| MS:apprised,   *1885:*apprised
109| MS:crowed this   *P1884*:crowed This: 111| MS:This §altered to§ The
112| MS:eyes again, §crossed out and replaced above by two words§ once more,
113| MS:He whom   *P1884*:For whom   114| MS:bring back safely, broached   *P1884*:bring
him back, free broached   117| MS:other. 'Who <> boy,   *P1884*:other. 'Who   *1889a:*boy

Must disbelieve his twenty seniors: no,
Return our father shall not! Might my death
120 Purchase his life, how promptly would the dole
Be paid as due!' Well, ten years pass,—aha,
Ishak is marching homeward,—doubts, not he,
Are dead and done with! So, our townsfolk straight
Must take on them to counsel. 'Go thou gay,
125 Welcome thy father, thou of ready faith!
Hide thee, contrariwise, thou faithless one,
Expect paternal frowning, blame and blows!'
So do our townsfolk counsel: dost demur?"

"Ferishtah like those simpletons—at loss
130 In what is plain as pikestaff? Pish! Suppose
The trustful son had sighed 'So much the worse!
Returning means—retaking heritage
Enjoyed these ten years, who should say me nay?'
How would such trust reward him? Trustlessness
135 —O' the other hand—were what procured most praise
To him who judged return impossible,
Yet hated heritage procured thereby.
A fool were Ishak if he failed to prize
Mere head's work less than heart's work: no fool he!"

140 "Is God less wise? Resume the roll!" They did.

119| MS:Return my §crossed out and replaced above by§ our   123| MS:with: so the §crossed out and replaced above by§ our townsfolk needs   *P1884:*with! So our townsfolk straight   *CP1884:*So, our   128| MS:do the §crossed out and replaced above by§ our < > counsel: I demur."   *P1884:*counsel: dost demur?   132| MS:means retaking *1885:*means—retaking   134| MS:How should §crossed out and replaced above by§ will §crossed out§ that §crossed out and replaced above by two words§ would such   135| MS:hand, were what procured §altered to§ procures   *P1884:*hand—were < > procured   136| MS:To who should judge < > impossible   *P1884:*To him who judged < > impossible,   137| And §crossed out and replaced above by§ Yet hate   *P1884:*hated   139| MS:Mere mind's work more §crossed out and replaced above by§ less < > he!" *1889a:*he!' §emended to§ he!" §see Editorial Notes§

You groped your way across my room i' the dear dark dead of night;
At each fresh step a stumble was: but, once your lamp alight,
Easy and plain you walked again: so soon all wrong grew right!

What lay on floor to trip your foot? Each object, late awry,
Looked fitly placed, nor proved offence to footing free—for why?
The lamp showed all, discordant late, grown simple symmetry.

Be love your light and trust your guide, with these explore my heart!
No obstacle to trip you then, strike hands and souls apart!
Since rooms and hearts are furnished so,—light shows you,—needs love start?

---

¹⁴¹| MS:room in §crossed out and replaced above by§ i'   ¹⁴²| MS:At §added in margin§
Each fresh §inserted above§ step §two words, possibly *you took* crossed out§ —a §crossed out
and replaced above by§ you §crossed out, *a* marked for retention§ stumble §word illegibly
crossed out and replaced above by§ was: ¹⁴³| MS:plain your §crossed out and replaced
above by§ you walking §altered to§ walked again: and §crossed out and replaced above by§ so
< > wrong seemed §crossed out and replaced above by§ grew   ¹⁴⁴| What was §crossed
out and replaced above by§ lay < > to §crossed out and replaced above by§ could §crossed
out; *to* marked for retention§ trip you §altered to§ your foot §inserted above§
¹⁴⁶| MS:discordant here §crossed out and replaced above by§ there, now simple
P1884: discordant late, grown simple   ¹⁴⁷| MS:these walk bold my   *P1884:* these explore
my   ¹⁴⁸| MS:trip your §altered to§ you foot §crossed out and replaced above by§ then,
no shock strikes hands apart!   *P1884:* then, strike souls and hands
CP1884: §last three words marked for transposition§   *1884:* strike hands and souls apart!
¹⁴⁹| MS:So rooms < > furnished, §word, possibly *when*, crossed out and replaced above by§ —
since, light < > you,— §word illegibly crossed out and replaced above by§ needs
P1884: Since rooms < > furnished so, light

THE FAMILY

A certain neighbour lying sick to death,
Ferishtah grieved beneath a palm-tree, whence
He rose at peace: whereat objected one
"Gudarz our friend gasps in extremity.
5 Sure, thou art ignorant how close at hand
Death presses, or the cloud, which fouled so late
Thy face, had deepened down not lightened off."

"I judge there will be respite, for I prayed."

"Sir, let me understand, of charity!
10 Yestereve, what was thine admonishment?
'All-wise, all-good, all-mighty—God is such!'
How then should man, the all-unworthy, dare
Propose to set aside a thing ordained?
To pray means—substitute man's will for God's:
15 Two best wills cannot be: by consequence,
What is man bound to but—assent, say I?
Rather to rapture of thanksgiving; since
That which seems worst to man to God is best,
So, because God ordains it, best to man.
20 Yet man—the foolish, weak and wicked—prays!
Urges 'My best were better, didst Thou know'!"

"List to a tale. A worthy householder
Of Shiraz had three sons, beside a spouse
Whom, cutting gourds, a serpent bit, whereon
25 The offended limb swelled black from foot to fork.
The husband called in aid a leech renowned
World-wide, confessed the lord of surgery,

THE FAMILY　　　*Title*| MS:4. *The Father's Family*　P1884:4. THE FAMILY　1889a: THE
2| MS:Ferishtah sat beneath　P1884:Ferishtah grieved beneath　　³| MS:rose and
smiled: whereat　P1884:rose at peace: whereat　　8| P1884:prayed.'　CP1884:prayed."
8-9| P1884:§no ¶§　CP1884:§¶ called for in margin¶　　18| MS:man is best to God, §last
four words marked for transposition to§ to God is best,　23| MS:sons beside
P1884:sons, beside　　27| MS:World-wide, the lord confessed §last three
words marked for transposition to§ confessed the lord

And bade him dictate—who forthwith declared
'Sole remedy is amputation.' Straight
30 The husband sighed 'Thou knowest: be it so!'
His three sons heard their mother sentenced: 'Pause!'
Outbroke the elder: 'Be precipitate
Nowise, I pray thee! Take some gentler way,
Thou sage of much resource! I will not doubt
35 But science still may save foot, leg and thigh!'
The next in age snapped petulant: 'Too rash!
No reason for this maiming! What, Sir Leech,
Our parent limps henceforward while we leap?
Shame on thee! Save the limb thou must and shalt!'
40 'Shame on yourselves, ye bold ones!' followed up
The brisk third brother, youngest, pertest too:
'The leech knows all things, we are ignorant;
What he proposes, gratefully accept!
For me, had I some unguent bound to heal
45 Hurts in a twinkling, hardly would I dare
Essay its virtue and so cross the sage
By cure his skill pronounces folly. Quick!
No waiting longer! There the patient lies:
Out then with implements and operate!' "

50 "Ah, the young devil!"

                  "Why, his reason chimed
Right with the Hakim's,"

                      "Hakim's, ay—but chit's?
How? what the skilled eye saw and judged of weight
To overbear a heavy consequence,
That—shall a sciolist affect to see?
55 All he saw—that is, all such oaf should see,
Was just the mother's suffering."

                     "In my tale,

29| MS:amputation." Straight, *1885:* amputation." Straight   35| MS:Thy science
*P1884:*But science   42| MS:"The   *P1884:*'The   44| MS:had I an §crossed out and
replaced above by§ some   54| MS:That—should a   *P1884:*That—shall a

Be God the Hakim: in the husband's case,
Call ready acquiescence—aptitude
Angelic, understanding swift and sure:
60 Call the first son—a wise humanity,
Slow to conceive but duteous to adopt:
See in the second son—humanity,
Wrong-headed yet right-hearted, rash but kind.
Last comes the cackler of the brood, our chit
65 Who, aping wisdom all beyond his years,
Thinks to discard humanity itself:
Fares like the beast which should affect to fly
Because a bird with wings may spurn the ground,
So, missing heaven and losing earth—drops how
70 But hell-ward? No, be man and nothing more—
Man who, as man conceiving, hopes and fears,
And craves and deprecates, and loves, and loathes,
And bids God help him, till death touch his eyes
And show God granted most, denying all."

---

75 Man I am and man would be, Love—merest man and nothing more.
Bid me seem no other! Eagles boast of pinions—let them soar!
I may put forth angel's plumage, once unmanned, but not before.

60| MS:The first son—dutiful humanity,   *P1884:*Call the < > son—a wise humanity,
61| MS:but ready to try: §crossed out and replaced above by§adopt: *P1884:*but duteous to
62| MS:second—rude humanity,   *P1884:*second son—humanity,
63| MS:Wrong-headed yet §inserted above§ righteous §altered to§ right-hearted, reason's
type: *P1884:*right-hearted, rash but kind: *1885:*kind   *1889a:*kind.
64| MS:our fool   *P1884:*our chit   65| MS:Who aping < > years   *P1884:*Who, aping
< > years,   66| MS:Discards man's best—humanity   *P1884:*Thinks to discard humanity
67| MS:should affect §inserted above§   68| MS:bird with wings §last two words inserted
above§ may §word, possibly *flying*, crossed out§ spurn   69| MS:drops where
*P1884:*drops how   70| MS:hell-wards   *1885:*hell-ward   73| MS:him till
*P1884:*him, till   75| MS:be, Love, §crossed out and replaced above by§ weak merest
*P1884:*be, Love, merest   *CP1884:*be, Love—merest   76| MS:of wings, and
§last two words crossed out and replaced above by§ pinions—

Now on earth, to stand suffices,—nay, if kneeling serves, to kneel:
Here you front me, here I find the all of heaven that earth can feel:
80   Sense looks straight,—not over, under,—perfect sees beyond appeal.

Good you are and wise, full circle: what to me were more outside?
Wiser wisdom, better goodness? Ah, such want the angel's wide
Sense to take and hold and keep them! Mine at least has never tried.

79| MS:heaven §word, possibly *on*, crossed out and replaced above by§ that earth: §colon crossed out§ can

THE SUN

"And what might that bold man's announcement be"—
Ferishtah questioned—"which so moved thine ire
That thou didst curse, nay, cuff and kick—in short,
Confute the announcer? Wipe those drops away
5   Which start afresh upon thy face at mere
Mention of such enormity: now, speak!"

"He scrupled not to say—(thou warrantest,
O patient Sir, that I unblamed repeat
Abominable words which blister tongue?)
10   God once assumed on earth a human shape:
(Lo, I have spitten!) Dared I ask the grace,
Fain would I hear, of thy subtility,
From out what hole in man's corrupted heart
Creeps such a maggot: fancies verminous
15   Breed in the clots there, but a monster born
Of pride and folly like this pest—thyself
Only canst trace to egg-shell it hath chipped."

The sun rode high. "During our ignorance"—
Began Ferishtah—"folk esteemed as God
20   Yon orb: for argument, suppose him so,—
Be it the symbol, not the symbolized,
I and thou safelier take upon our lips.
Accordingly, yon orb that we adore
—What is he? Author of all light and life:
25   Such one must needs be somewhere: this is he.
Like what? If I may trust my human eyes,
A ball composed of spirit-fire, whence springs
—What, from this ball, my arms could circle round?
All I enjoy on earth. By consequence,
30   Inspiring me with—what? Why, love and praise.

THE SUN   *Title*| MS:5. *Incarnation*   *P1884:*5. THE SUN   *1889a: THE*
4| MS:Refute §altered to§ Confute   8| MS:O saintly Sir   *1884:*O patient Sir
9| *1884:*tongue?)—   *1885:*tongue?)   17-18| MS:§¶§   *1889a:*§¶ lost in paging;
emended to restore ¶; see Editorial Notes§

I eat a palatable fig—there's love
In little: who first planted what I pluck,
Obtains my little praise, too: more of both
Keeps due proportion with more cause for each:

35 So, more and ever more, till most of all
Completes experience, and the orb, descried
Ultimate giver of all good, perforce
Gathers unto himself all love, all praise,
Is worshipped—which means loved and praised at height.

40 Back to the first good: 'twas the gardener gave
Occasion to my palate's pleasure: grace,
Plain on his part, demanded thanks on mine.
Go up above this giver,—step by step,
Gain a conception of what—(how and why,

45 Matters not now)—occasioned him to give,
Appointed him the gardener of the ground,—
I mount by just progression slow and sure
To some prime giver—here assumed yon orb—
Who takes my worship. Whom have I in mind,

50 Thus worshipping, unless a man, my like
Howe'er above me? Man, I say—how else,
I being man who worship? Here's my hand
Lifts first a mustard-seed, then weight on weight
Greater and ever greater, till at last

55 It lifts a melon, I suppose, then stops—
Hand-strength expended wholly: so, my love
First lauds the gardener for the fig his gift,
Then, looking higher, loves and lauds still more,
Who hires the ground, who owns the ground, Sheikh, Shah,

60 On and away, away and ever on,
Till, at the last, it loves and lauds the orb
Ultimate cause of all to laud and love.
Where is the break, the change of quality
In hand's power, soul's impulsion? Gift was grace,

65 The greatest as the smallest. Had I stopped

34| MS:each, *1884:*each: 39| *P1884:*height *CP1884:*height.
45| MS:now) occasioned <> give,— *1884:*now)—occasioned <> give,
59| MS:§line added between present ll. 58 and 60§

Anywhere in the scale, stayed love and praise
As so far only fit to follow gift,
Saying 'I thanked the gardener for his fig,
But now that, lo, the Shah has filled my purse
70   With tomans which avail to purchase me
A fig-tree forest, shall I pay the same
With love and praise, the gardener's proper fee?'
Justly would whoso bears a brain object
'Giving is giving, gift claims gift's return,
75   Do thou thine own part, therefore: let the Shah
Ask more from who has more to pay.' Perchance
He gave me from his treasure less by much
Than the soil's servant: let that be! My part
Is plain—to meet and match the gift and gift
80   With love and love, with praise and praise, till both
Cry 'All of us is thine, we can no more!'
So shall I do man's utmost—man to man:
For as our liege the Shah's sublime estate
Merely enhaloes, leaves him man the same,
85   So must I count that orb I call a fire
(Keep to the language of our ignorance)
Something that's fire and more beside. Mere fire
—Is it a force which, giving, knows it gives,
And wherefore, so may look for love and praise
90   From me, fire's like so far, however less
In all beside? Prime cause this fire shall be,
Uncaused, all-causing: hence begin the gifts,
Thither must go my love and praise—to what?
Fire? Symbol fitly serves the symbolized
95   Herein,—that this same object of my thanks,
While to my mind nowise conceivable
Except as mind no less than fire, refutes

72| MS:garder's §altered to§ gardener's   74| MS:gift gets gift's *P1884:*gift claims gift's
76| MS:pay. Perchance *1889a:*pay.' Perchance   77| MS:gave thee from
*1889a:*gave me from   78| MS:be! Thy part *1889a:*be! My part
82| MS:So shalt thou do *1889a:*So shall I do   86| MS:of the Ignorance)
*P1884:*of our ignorance)   87| MS:beside: mere *1889a:*beside. Mere
89| MS:wherefore, and may *P1884:*wherefore, so may   90| MS:me, one like
*P1884:*me, fire's like   97| MS:mind as well as fire *P1884:*mind no less than fire

Next moment mind's conception: fire is fire—
While what I needs must thank, must needs include
100 Purpose with power,—humanity like mine,
Imagined, for the dear necessity,
One moment in an object which the next
Confesses unimaginable. Power!
—What need of will, then? nought opposes power:
105 Why, purpose? any change must be for worse:
And what occasion for beneficence
When all that is, so is and so must be?
Best being best now, change were for the worse.
Accordingly discard these qualities
110 Proper to imperfection, take for type
Mere fire, eject the man, retain the orb,—
The perfect and, so, inconceivable,—
And what remains to love and praise? A stone
Fair-coloured proves a solace to my eye,
115 Rolled by my tongue brings moisture curing drouth,
And struck by steel emits a useful spark:
Shall I return it thanks, the insentient thing?
No,—man once, man for ever—man in soul
As man in body: just as this can use
120 Its proper senses only, see and hear,
Taste, like or loathe according to its law
And not another creature's—even so
Man's soul is moved by what, if it in turn
Must move, is kindred soul: receiving good
125 —Man's way—must make man's due acknowledgment,
No other, even while he reasons out
Plainly enough that, were the man unmanned,

100| MS:power: humanity *P1884:*power,—humanity   101| MS:Imagined for < >
necessity *P1884:*Imagined, for < > necessity,   103| MS:unimaginable. Power—
P1884: unimaginable. Power!   104| MS:then? what opposes power? *1885:*then? nought
opposes power: 105| MS:worse. *P1884:*worse.   107| MS:so is perforce—for why?
*P1884:*so is and so must be; *1885:*be? *1885a:*Whea *1889a:*When   108| MS:change is
§crossed out and replaced above by§ were   112| MS:and so inconceivable,—
P1884: and, so, inconceivable,—   114| MS:a pleasure to *P1884:*a solace to
125| MS:way, must < > acknowledgement, *P1884:*way—must *CP1884:*§second *e* in
acknowledgement queried in margin§ *1884:* acknowledgement, *1889a:* acknowledgment,

Made angel of, angelic every way,
The love and praise that rightly seek and find
130   Their man-like object now,—instructed more,
Would go forth idly, air to emptiness.
Our human flower, sun-ripened, proffers scent
Though reason prove the sun lacks nose to feed
On what himself made grateful: flower and man,
135   Let each assume that scent and love alike
Being once born, must needs have use! Man's part
Is plain—to send love forth,—astray, perhaps:
No matter, he has done his part."

                  "Wherefrom
What is to follow—if I take thy sense—
140   But that the sun—the inconceivable
Confessed by man—comprises, all the same,
Man's every-day conception of himself—
No less remaining unconceived!"

                 "Agreed"!

"Yet thou, insisting on the right of man
145   To feel as man, not otherwise,—man, bound
By man's conditions neither less nor more,
Obliged to estimate as fair or foul,
Right, wrong, good, evil, what man's faculty
Adjudges such,—how canst thou,—plainly bound
150   To take man's truth for truth and only truth,—

131| MS:idly—air   *P1884:*idly, air   132| MS:sun-ripened, offers scent
*P1884:*sun-ripened, proffers scent   133| MS:prove there §crossed out and replaced
above by two words§ the sun lacks a §crossed out§ nose   134| MS:With §over illigible
word; crossed out and replaced above by§ On what §words crossed out and replaced above by
three words§ himself made grateful   135| MS:Let §added in margin§ Each §word,
possibly *would*, crossed out§ assume   *P1884:*each   136| MS:use: §word, possibly *our*,
crossed out and replaced above by word illegibly crossed out; replaced in turn by§ man's
*P1884:*use! Man's   137| MS:send §word, possibly *scent*, crossed out and replaced above
by§ love   138| MS:matter, we §altered to§ he have §altered to§ has done our §altered to§
his   144| MS:§¶ called for in margin§   *P1884:*§¶§   147| MS:as foul or fair,
*P1884:*as fair or foul,   148| MS:Wrong, right, good   *P1884:*Right, wrong, good
149| MS:cans't thou,—thiswise bound   *P1884:*canst   *1889a:*thou,—plainly bound

Dare to accept, in just one case, as truth
Falsehood confessed? Flesh simulating fire—
Our fellow-man whom we his fellows know
For dust—instinct with fire unknowable!
155 Where's thy man-needed truth—its proof, nay print
Of faintest passage on the tablets traced
By man, termed knowledge? 'Tis conceded thee,
We lack such fancied union—fire with flesh:
But even so, to lack is not to gain
160 Our lack's suppliance: where's the trace of such
Recorded?"

       "What if such a tracing were?
If some strange story stood,—whate'er its worth,—
That the immensely yearned-for, once befell,
—The sun was flesh once?—(keep the figure!)"

                                  "How?
165 An union inconceivable was fact?"

" Son, if the stranger have convinced himself
Fancy is fact—the sun, besides a fire,
Holds earthly substance somehow fire pervades
And yet consumes not,—earth, he understands,
170 With essence he remains a stranger to,—
Fitlier thou saidst 'I stand appalled before
Conception unattainable by me
Who need it most'—than this—'What? boast he holds
Conviction where I see conviction's need,
175 Alas,—and nothing else? then what remains

151| MS:in this §crossed out and replaced above by§ just   154| MS:dust—becomes the fire *P1884:*dust—instinct with fire   155| MS:man's-needed *P1884:*man-needed
164| MS:§¶§ "What— *P1884:*§¶§ "How?   168| MS:substance fire somehow §marked for transposition to§ substance somehow fire
170| MS:Such §crossed out and replaced above by§ With   173| MS:than §words, possibly '*Dares he*, crossed out and replaced above by two words§ this—'What? Boast
175| MS:Alas,— §added in margin§ And < > else, §altered to§ else? and therefore §last two words crossed out and replaced above by one word§ then what

But that I straightway curse, cuff, kick the fool!' "

———————

Fire is in the flint: true, once a spark escapes,
Fire forgets the kinship, soars till fancy shapes
Some befitting cradle where the babe had birth—
180 Wholly heaven's the product, unallied to earth.
Splendours recognized as perfect in the star!—
In our flint their home was, housed as now they are.

176| MS:But fall to anger, §last three words crossed out and replaced above by three words§
that I straightway curse   181| MS:Recognized §altered to§ recognized §word, possibly *its,*
crossed out§ splendours §altered to§ Splendours §marked for transposition to§ Splendours
recognized as §inserted above§   182| MS:home is, §altered to§ was, §word illegibly
crossed out above§ housed now as §marked for transposition to§ as now

MIHRAB SHAH

Quoth an inquirer, "Praise the Merciful!
My thumb which yesterday a scorpion nipped—
(It swelled and blackened)—lo, is sound again!
By application of a virtuous root
5   The burning has abated: that is well:
But now methinks I have a mind to ask,—
Since this discomfort came of culling herbs
Nor meaning harm,—why needs a scorpion be?
Yea, there began, from when my thumb last throbbed,
10 Advance in question- framing, till I asked
Wherefore should any evil hap to man—
From ache of flesh to agony of soul—
Since God's All-mercy mates All-potency?
Nay, why permits He evil to Himself—
15 Man's sin, accounted such? Suppose a world
Purged of all pain, with fit inhabitant—
Man pure of evil in thought, word and deed—
Were it not well? Then, wherefore otherwise?
Too good result? But He is wholly good!
20 Hard to effect? Ay, were He impotent!
Teach me, Ferishtah!"

Said the Dervish: "Friend,

MIHRAB SHAH   *Title*| MS:6. *Pain*   *P1884:*6. *MIHRAB SHAH*   *1889a:MIHRAB*
¹| MS:enquirer   *1889a:*inquirer   ⁵| MS:burning hath   *P1884:*burning has
⁶| MS:But much it comes into my §last five words crossed out and replaced above by five
words§ now methinks I have a mind   ⁷| MS:this discomfited §altered to§ discomfort me
§crossed out and replaced above by two words§ came of   ⁹| MS:And so §last two crossed
out and replaced above by two words§ Yea, there began, the while §last two words crossed out
and replaced above by two words§ from when my thumb thus §crossed out and replaced above
by *fir,* crossed out and replaced by§ last   ¹⁰| MS:Advance upon that §last two words
crossed out and replaced above by one word§ in question-framing, §-*framing,* inserted above§
till   ¹³| MS:Since the §crossed out and replaced above by§ God's All-mercy is §crossed
out and replaced above by§ mates   ¹⁴| MS:permits he §altered to§ He <> himself—
§altered to§ Himself—   ¹⁶| MS:inhabitant   *P1884:*inhabitant—
¹⁸| MS:well? §words illegibly crossed out and replaced above by two words§ Then, wherefore
¹⁹| MS:result? §words, possibly *Is not,* crossed out and replaced above by one word§
But he §altered to§ He is §inserted above§ <> good? §altered to§ good!
²¹| MS:the Dervish: "Sure   *P1884:*the Dervish: "Friend,

My chance, escaped to-day, was worse than thine:
I, as I woke this morning, raised my head,
Which never tumbled but stuck fast on neck.
25 Was not I glad and thankful!"

"How could head
Tumble from neck, unchopped—inform me first!
Unless we take Firdausi's tale for truth,
Who ever heard the like?"

"The like might hap
By natural law: I let my staff fall thus—
30 It goes to ground, I know not why. Suppose,
Whene'er my hold was loosed, it skyward sprang
As certainly, and all experience proved
That, just as staves when unsupported sink,
So, unconfined, they soar?"

"Let such be law—
35 Why, a new chapter of sad accidents
Were added to humanity's mischance,
No doubt at all, and as a man's false step
Now lays him prone on earth, contrariwise,
Removal from his shoulder of a weight
40 Might start him upwards to perdition. Ay!
But, since such law exists in just thy brain,

---

²⁴| MS:but §word illegibly crossed out and replaced above by second word, illegibly crossed out and replaced by two words§ stuck fast on neck—   *P1884:*neck.   ²⁶| MS:Drop off §last two words crossed out and replaced above by one word§ Tumble < > unchopped—instruct §crossed out and replaced above by§ inform me   ²⁷| MS:§line added between present ll. 26 and 28§ we both §crossed out and replaced above by§ take Firdusi §altered to§ Firdusi's and his tale §last three words crossed out§ tale for   *1885a:*take Firdausi's
²⁸| MS:like?" §¶§ "Yet such §last two words crossed out and replaced above by two words§ The like   ³⁴| MS:they rise?" §crossed out and replaced above by§ soar?" §¶§ "Were §crossed out and replaced above by§ Let such the §crossed out and replaced above by§ be
³⁶| MS:humanity's §inserted above§   ³⁸| MS:earth, so—how say I? §last four words crossed out and replaced above by one word§ contrariwise?   ⁴⁰| MS:Might §crossed out and replaced above by§ May §crossed out; *Might* marked for retention§ < > perdition,—Ay! *P1884:*perdition. Ay!   ⁴¹| MS:But since < > brain   *1885:*But, since < > brain,

163

I shall not hesitate to doff my cap
For fear my head take flight."

          "Nor feel relief
Finding it firm on shoulder. Tell me, now!
45   What were the bond 'twixt man and man, dost judge,
Pain once abolished? Come, be true! Our Shah—
How stands he in thy favour? Why that shrug?
Is not he lord and ruler?"

          "Easily!
His mother bore him, first of those four wives
50   Provided by his father, such his luck:
Since when his business simply was to breathe
And take each day's new bounty. There he stands—
Where else had I stood, were his birth-star mine?
No, to respect men's power, I needs must see
55   Men's bare hands seek, find, grasp and wield the sword
Nobody else can brandish! Bless his heart,
'Tis said, he scarcely counts his fingers right!"

    "Well, then—his princely doles! from every feast
Off go the feasted with the dish they ate
60   And cup they drank from,—nay, a change besides
Of garments" . . .

        "Sir, put case, for service done,—

43| *CP1884:*relief, *1884:*relief   44| MS:now— *P1884:*now!   45| MS:dost think, *P1884:*dost judge,   46| MS:true! The §crossed out and replaced above by§ Our Khan— *P1884:*true! Our Shah—   47| MS:favour? Why, that *P1884:*favour? Why that 48| MS:§¶§ "Easily: *P1884:*§¶§ "Easily!   49| MS:of fifty §crossed out and replaced above by two words§ those four wives   50| MS:Accepted §crossed out and replaced above by§ Provided by   52| MS:take, §comma crossed out§ each day, §altered to§ day's, its §crossed out and replaced above by§ new   53| MS:Wherelse <> stood if his birth §last three words crossed out§ were his birth-star §last three words inserted above§ mine? *1885:*Where else   54| MS:No,—to respect §word illegibly crossed out and replaced above by§ men's power *P1884:*No, to   55| MS:A §crossed out and replaced above by§ Men's <> hand §altered to§ hands get and §last two words crossed out and replaced above by two words§ seek, find, grasp   58| MS:doles— §altered to§ doles! from   60| MS:The §crossed out and replaced above by§ And <> from, with §crossed out and replaced above by§ —nay, <> besides §struck through and restored§   61| MS:done, *P1884:*done,—

Or best, for love's sake,—such and such a slave
Sold his allowance of sour lentil soup
To therewith purchase me a pipe-stick,—nay,
If he, by but one hour, cut short his sleep
To clout my shoe,—that were a sacrifice!"

"All praise his gracious bearing."

                              "All praise mine—
Or would praise did they never make approach
Except on all-fours, crawling till I bade
'Now that with eyelids thou hast touched the earth,
Come close and have no fear, poor nothingness!'
What wonder that the lady-rose I woo
And palisade about from every wind,
Holds herself handsomely? The wilding, now,
Ruffled outside at pleasure of the blast,
That still lifts up with something of a smile
Its poor attempt at bloom" . . .

                         "A blameless life,
Where wrong might revel with impunity—
Remember that!"

                         "The falcon on his fist—
Reclaimed and trained and belled and beautified
Till she believes herself the Simorgh's match—
She only deigns destroy the antelope,

65
70
75
80

62| MS:sake, such and   *P1884:*sake,—such and   64| MS:a melon §crossed out and
replaced above by§ pipe-stick   67| MS:his pleasant §crossed out and replaced above by§
gracious bearing . ." §¶§   *P1884:*bearing." §¶§   70| MS:§line added between present ll.
69 and 71§ with §word, possibly *faces*, crossed out and replaced above by§ eyelids
72| MS:lady-rose I guard §crossed out and replaced above by§ woo
73| MS:And garden-wall §crossed out and replaced above by§ palisade about
80| MS:trained and dressed §crossed out and replaced above by§ belled and
81| MS:Till it §replaced above by§ she believes itself §altered to§ herself the Simorgh's
mate— §crossed out and replaced above by§ self §crossed out; *mate* marked for retention§
1884O:§*mate*— altered to *match*—§   *1885:*match—   82| MS:§line added between
present ll. 81 and 83§ Strives §crossed out and replaced in margin by§ Deigns §crossed out§
She §inserted above§ only deigns §inserted above§ to §crossed out§ destroy §crossed out and
replaced above by word illegibly crossed out; *destroy* marked for retention§ the

Stoops at no carrion-crow: thou marvellest?"

"So be it, then! He wakes no love in thee
85 For any one of divers attributes
Commonly deemed loveworthy. All the same,
I would he were not wasting, slow but sure,
With that internal ulcer" . . .

       "Say'st thou so?
How should I guess? Alack, poor soul! But stay—
90 Sure in the reach of art some remedy
Must lie to hand: or if it lurk,—that leech
Of fame in Tebriz, why not seek his aid?
Couldst not thou, Dervish, counsel in the case ?

"My counsel might be—what imports a pang
95 The more or less, which puts an end to one
Odious in spite of every attribute
Commonly deemed loveworthy?"

       "Attributes?
Faugh!—nay, Ferishtah,—'tis an ulcer, think!
Attributes, quotha? Here's poor flesh and blood,
100 Like thine and mine and every man's, a prey
To hell-fire! Hast thou lost thy wits for once?"

83| MS:carrion-crow—thou *P1884:*carrion-crow: thou   85| MS:of all those §last two
words crossed out and replaced above by one word§ divers attributes
86| MS:Commonly thought §crossed out and replaced above by§ judged love-worthy
*P1884:*Commonly deemed love-worthy *1889a:*loveworthy   87| MS:not §inserted
above§   88| MS:ulcer . . ." §¶§ *P1884:*ulcer" . . . §¶§   89| MS:guess? Alas §altered
to§ Alack   91| MS:hand—or *P1884:*hand: or   92| MS:in Syria,— §crossed out
and marked for retention§ why *P1884:*in Tebriz, why   93| MS:Thou, Dervish, could'st
§altered to§ Could'st not §last four words marked for transposition to§ Could'st not Thou,
Dervish *P1884:*Couldst not thou   94| MS:"My §crossed out and replaced above by§
"His §crossed out; "*My* marked for retention§ <> might §word above illegibly crossed out§
95| MS:less which *P1884:*less, which   96| MS:§words illegibly crossed out and replaced
above by one word§ Odious despite §altered to two words§ in spite §word illegibly crossed out
and replaced above by two words§ of every attributes §altered to§ attribute
97| MS:love-worthy." §¶§ *P1884:*love-worthy?" §¶§   98| MS:Faugh,—nay
*P1884:*Faugh!—nay   101| MS:To torture . . hast *P1884:*To hell-fire! Hast

"Friend, here they are to find and profit by!
Put pain from out the world, what room were left
For thanks to God, for love to Man? Why thanks,—
¹⁰⁵ Except for some escape, whate'er the style,
From pain that might be, name it as thou mayst?
Why love,—when all thy kind, save me, suppose,
Thy father, and thy son, and . . . well, thy dog,
To eke the decent number out—we few
¹¹⁰ Who happen—like a handful of chance stars
From the unnumbered host—to shine o'erhead
And lend thee light,—our twinkle all thy store,—
We only take thy love! Mankind, forsooth?
Who sympathizes with their general joy
¹¹⁵ Foolish as undeserved? But pain—see God's
Wisdom at work!—man's heart is made to judge
Pain deserved nowhere by the common flesh
Our birthright,—bad and good deserve alike
No pain, to human apprehension! Lust,
¹²⁰ Greed, cruelty, injustice, crave (we hold)
Due punishment from somebody, no doubt:
But ulcer in the midriff! that brings flesh
Triumphant from the bar whereto arraigned
Soul quakes with reason. In the eye of God
¹²⁵ Pain may have purpose and be justified:

102| MS:"Son, here *P1884:*"Friend, here   104| MS:to Man? Why, thanks *P1884:* to
Man? Why thanks *1885:*thanks,—   108| MS:father—and thy son—and . . well, thy dog
*CP1884:*dog, *1885:*father, and thy son, and *1889a:*and . . . well
113| MS:love? Mankind *P1884:*love! Mankind   116| MS:to see *P1884:*to judge
118| *P1884:*alike. *CP1884:*alike   119-24| MS:§ll. 119-121 added between present ll. 118
and 122 and in margin; l. 123 and revised beginning of l. 124 added between present ll. 122
and 124. See Editorial Notes§   119| MS:apprehension! Scorn, §crossed out and
replaced above by§ Lust,   120| MS:Hate, any human proves any fact you please! §entire
line crossed out and replaced above by new line§ Greed, cruelty, injustice crave alike §last
word crossed out and replaced above by two words§ —we hold— *P1884:*crave (we hold)
121| MS:A feared §last two words crossed out and replaced below by one word§ Due
punishment   122| MS:midriff! That brings the §crossed out§ flesh *P1884:*that
124| MS:Straight to a level: §last three words crossed out and replaced in margin by four
words§ Man's §crossed out§ soul §altered to§ Soul quakes with reason. In the eyes of
*1889a:*eye   125| MS:may §inserted above§ has §altered to§ have a
§crossed out§ purpose and is §crossed out and replaced above by§ be

Man's sense avails to only see, in pain,
A hateful chance no man but would avert
Or, failing, needs must pity. Thanks to God
And love to man,—from man take these away,
130 And what is man worth? Therefore, Mihrab Shah,
Tax me my bread and salt twice over, claim
Laila my daughter for thy sport,—go on!
Slay my son's self, maintain thy poetry
Beats mine,—thou meritest a dozen deaths!
135 But—ulcer in the stomach,—ah, poor soul,
Try a fig-plaster: may it ease thy pangs!"

So, the head aches and the limbs are faint!
      Flesh is a burthen—even to you!
Can I force a smile with a fancy quaint?
140   Why are my ailments none or few?

In the soul of me sits sluggishness:
      Body so strong and will so weak!
The slave stands fit for the labour—yes,
      But the master's mandate is still to seek.

126| MS:Our eyes are §last three words crossed out and replaced above by four words§ Man's sense avails to only made to §last two words crossed out§ see   127| MS:A hatefulness §altered to§ hateful thing §crossed out and replaced above by§ chance <> would remove §crossed out and replaced above by§ avert   128| MS:failing to remove §last two words crossed out and replaced above by§ —that, needs §crossed out§ must   *P1884:*failing, needs must   129| MS:To God §last two words crossed out§ and §altered to§ And <> man, §comma crossed out§ —from man §inserted above§ take   130| MS:And §added in margin§ What <> worth? Let pain continue thus! §last four words crossed out and replaced above by four words§ Mihrab Khan,—say wherefore §last four words crossed out and replaced above by three words in margin§ Therefore, Mihrab Khan,   *P1884:*what <> Mihrab Shah,
131| MS:over, §words illegibly crossed out and replaced above by§ Laila §crossed out and replaced by§ claim   132| MS:thy slave,—go on;   *P1884:* thy sport,—go on!
133| MS:thy Rhuibayat §crossed out and replaced above by§ poetry
136| MS:pangs!   *P1884:*pangs!"   141| MS:sits §illegible word altered to§ sluggishness:

145   You, now—what if the outside clay
       Helped, not hindered the inside flame?
   My dim to-morrow—your plain to-day,
       Yours the achievement, mine the aim?

   So were it rightly, so shall it be!
150   Only, while earth we pace together
   For the purpose apportioned you and me,
       Closer we tread for a common tether.

   You shall sigh "Wait for his sluggish soul!
       Shame he should lag, not lamed as I!"
155   May not I smile "Ungained her goal:
       Body may reach her—by-and-by?"

150| MS:while thus §crossed out and replaced above by§ earth <> to-gether   *P1884:*together
151| MS:§two words, the first possibly *Earth*, crossed out and replaced above by three words§
For the purpose   152| MS:for the §crossed out and replaced above by§ a
153| MS:shall say §altered to§ sigh <> soul—   *P1884:*soul?   *CP1884:*soul!
154| MS:Why §crossed out and replaced above by two words§ Shame he
should he §crossed out§ lag <> I?" §punctuation altered to§ I!"
155| MS:I shall say §last three words crossed out and replaced above by four words§
May not I smile <> goal!   *P1884:*goal: 156| MS:Body, so §crossed out and replaced
above by§ may <> bye and bye?"   *P1884:*Body may   *1889a:*by-and-by?"

A CAMEL-DRIVER

"How of his fate, the Pilgrims' soldier-guide
Condemned" (Ferishtah questioned), "for he slew
The merchant whom he convoyed with his bales
—A special treachery?"

        "Sir, the proofs were plain:
5 Justice was satisfied: between two boards
The rogue was sawn asunder, rightly served."

"With all wise men's approval—mine at least."

"Himself, indeed, confessed as much. 'I die
Justly' (groaned he) 'through over-greediness
10 Which tempted me to rob: but grieve the most
That he who quickened sin at slumber,—ay,
Prompted and pestered me till thought grew deed,—
The same is fled to Syria and is safe,
Laughing at me thus left to pay for both.
15 My comfort is that God reserves for him
Hell's hottest' . . ."

      "Idle words."

        "Enlighten me!
Wherefore so idle? Punishment by man
Has thy assent,—the word is on thy lips.
By parity of reason, punishment
20 By God should likelier win thy thanks and praise."

"Man acts as man must: God, as God beseems.
A camel-driver, when his beast will bite,

A CAMEL-DRIVER   *Title*] MS:7. *A camel-driver* *P1884:*7. *A CAMEL-DRIVER* *1889a:A*
9| MS:he) 'for over-greediness *P1884:*he) 'through over-greediness
12| MS:deed, *P1884:*deed,—   13| MS:to Syria §not cancelled, but replaced
above by§ Tebriz §crossed out§   18| MS:Hath *P1884:*Has

Thumps her athwart the muzzle: why?"

                    "How else
Instruct the creature—mouths should munch, not bite?

²⁵ "True, he is man, knows but man's trick to teach.
Suppose some plain word, told her first of all,
Had hindered any biting?"

                "Find him such,
And fit the beast with understanding first!
No understanding animals like Rakhsh
³⁰ Nowadays, Master! Till they breed on earth,
For teaching—blows must serve."

                 "Who deals the blow—
What if by some rare method,—magic, say,—
He saw into the biter's very soul,
And knew the fault was so repented of
³⁵ It could not happen twice?"

                   "That's something: still,
I hear, methinks, the driver say 'No less
Take thy fault's due! Those long-necked sisters, see,
Lean all a-stretch to know if biting meets
Punishment or enjoys impunity.
⁴⁰ For their sakes—thwack!'"

                "The journey home at end,
The solitary beast safe-stabled now,
In comes the driver to avenge a wrong
Suffered from six months since,—apparently
With patience, nay, approval: when the jaws
⁴⁵ Met i' the small of the arm, 'Ha, Ladykin,

---

²⁴| MS:creature mouths <> munch not   *P1884:*creature, mouths   *1885:*creature—mouths
*1889a:*munch, not   ²⁹| MS:animals as §altered to§ like Ruksh
*1885a:*like Rakhsh   ⁴⁰| MS:thwack!" §¶§   *1889a:*thwack!'" §¶§
⁴²| MS:avenge his wrong   *P1884:*avenge a wrong

Still at thy frolics, girl of gold?' laughed he:
'Eat flesh? Rye-grass content thee rather with,
Whereof accept a bundle!' Now,—what change!
Laughter by no means! Now 'tis 'Fiend, thy frisk
50   Was fit to find thee provender, didst judge?
Behold this red-hot twy-prong, thus I stick
To hiss i' the soft of thee!' "

                    "Behold? behold
A crazy noddle, rather! Sure the brute
Might wellnigh have plain speech coaxed out of tongue,
55   And grow as voluble as Rakhsh himself
At such mad outrage. 'Could I take thy mind,
Guess thy desire? If biting was offence
Wherefore the rye-grass bundle, why each day's
Patting and petting, but to intimate
60   My playsomeness had pleased thee? Thou endowed,
With reason, truly!' "

              "Reason aims to raise
Some makeshift scaffold-vantage midway, whence
Man dares, for life's brief moment, peer below:
But ape omniscience? Nay! The ladder lent
65   To climb by, step and step, until we reach
The little foothold-rise allowed mankind
To mount on and thence guess the sun's survey—
Shall this avail to show us world-wide truth
Stretched for the sun's descrying ? Reason bids
70   'Teach, Man, thy beast his duty first of all
Or last of all, with blows if blows must be,—

47| MS:flesh? Content <> with, §comma added§ rye-grass §marked for transposition to§
flesh? rye-grass Content   *P1884:*flesh? Rye-grass content   51| MS:red-hot implement I
*P1884:*red-hot twy-prong thus I   54| MS:well nigh   *1889a:*wellnigh   55| MS:as
Ruksh   *1885a:*as Rakhsh   62| MS:makeshift midway scaffold-vantage, whence
*1889a:*makeshift scaffold-vantage midway, whence   63| MS:It may, for <> below
*P1884:*below: *1889a:*Man dares, for   64| MS:—Aping omniscience? What—the   *P1884:*But
apes omniscience? Nay! The   *1889a:*ape   67| MS:and there guess   *1889a:*and thence
guess   68| MS:show the world-wide   *P1884:*show them world-wide   *1889a:*show us world-wide

How else accomplish teaching?' Reason adds
'Before man's First, and after man's poor Last,
God operated and will operate.'
75 —Process of which man merely knows this much,—
That nowise it resembles man's at all,
Teaching or punishing."

"It follows, then,
That any malefactor I would smite
With God's allowance, God himself will spare
80 Presumably. No scapegrace? Then, rejoice
Thou snatch-grace safe in Syria!"

"Friend, such view
Is but man's wonderful and wide mistake.
Man lumps his kind i' the mass: God singles thence
Unit by unit. Thou and God exist—
85 So think!—for certain: think the mass—mankind—
Disparts, disperses, leaves thyself alone!
Ask thy lone soul what laws are plain to thee,—
Thee and no other,—stand or fall by them!
That is the part for thee: regard all else
90 For what it may be—Time's illusion. This
Be sure of—ignorance that sins, is safe.
No punishment like knowledge! Instance, now!
My father's choicest treasure was a book

Wherein he, day by day and year by year,
95 Recorded gains of wisdom for my sake

74| MS:operate: *P1884:*operate.'   75| MS:Process §added in margin§ Of which dread
process §last two words crossed out§ <> much— *P1884:*—Process of <> much,—
78| MS:That those the malefactors thou §crossed out and replaced above by§ I wouldst
§altered to§ would slay *P1884:*That any malefactor I would smite   80| MS:Presumably:
no §inserted above§ scape-grace? Nay, rejoice *P1884:*Presumably. No scape-grace? Then,
rejoice *1889a:*scapegrace   81| MS:§¶§ "Friend, your view *P1884:*§¶§ "Friend, such
view   86| MS:leaves you both alone: *P1884:*leaves thyself alone!   88| MS:by
these! *P1884:*by them!   90| MS:be—an §altered to§ Time's   91| MS:Only §crossed
out§ be §altered to§ Be<> that sins, §last two words inserted above§ is safe: *P1884:*safe.
92| MS:§line added between present ll. 91 and 93§ knowledge! Look ye now! *P1884:*knowledge!
Instance, now!   94| MS:he day <> by year *P1884:*he, day <> by year,

When I should grow to manhood. While a child,
Coming upon the casket where it lay
Unguarded,—what did I but toss the thing
Into a fire to make more flame therewith,
100 Meaning no harm? So acts man three-years old!
I grieve now at my loss by witlessness,
But guilt was none to punish. Man mature—
Each word of his I lightly held, each look
I turned from—wish that wished in vain—nay, will
105 That willed and yet went all to waste—'tis these
Rankle like fire. Forgiveness? rather grant
Forgetfulness! The past is past and lost.
However near I stand in his regard,
So much the nearer had I stood by steps
110 Offered the feet which rashly spurned their help.
That I call Hell; why further punishment?"

When I vexed you and you chid me,
    And I owned my fault and turned
My cheek the way you bid me,
115   And confessed the blow well earned,—

My comfort all the while was
    —Fault was faulty—near, not quite!
Do you wonder why the smile was?
    O'erpunished wrong grew right.

96| MS:manhood: while   *P1884:*manhood. While   101| MS:at that loss   *P1884:*at my loss   105| MS:all to §inserted above§   106| MS:fire: forgiveness? Could it §last two words crossed out and replaced above by two words§ That must be   *P1884:*fire. Forgiveness? rather grant   107| MS:Forgetfulness! Past is past, and lost is lost.   *P1884:*Forgetfulness! The past is past and lost.   110| MS:which saw §word illegibly crossed out and replaced above by§ yet spurned   *P1884:*which rashly spurned   111| MS:call Hell; what §word illegibly crossed out and replaced above by§ further punishment?   *P1884:*call Hell; why further   *1889a:*punishment?"   111-12| MS:L. D. I. E. Sept. 23. '83. §added in margin and crossed out; see Editorial Notes§   114| MS:My Cheek §last two words inserted above§ The   *P1884:*the   118| MS:Did you   *P1884:*Do you   119| MS:wrong grown §crossed out and replaced above by§ grew

120   But faults you ne'er suspected,
           Nay, praised, no faults at all,—
       Those would you had detected—
           Crushed eggs whence snakes could crawl!

120| MS:But the §crossed out§ faults §altered to§ fault §restored to§ faults
121| MS:§two words, possibly *Marked for,* crossed out and replaced above by one word§ Nay,
praise §altered to§ praised, no faults §altered to§ fault §restored to§ faults
122| MS:Such §crossed out and replaced above by§ Those   123| MS:eggs §word
illegibly crossed out and replaced above by§ whence snakes could §crossed out and replaced
above by§ can §crossed out; *could* marked for retention§

TWO CAMELS

Quoth one: "Sir, solve a scruple! No true sage
I hear of, but instructs his scholar thus:
'Wouldst thou be wise? Then mortify thyself!
Baulk of its craving every bestial sense!
5   Say "If I relish melons—so do swine!
Horse, ass and mule consume their provender
Nor leave a pea-pod: fasting feeds the soul.'"
Thus they admonish: while thyself, I note,
Eatest thy ration with an appetite,
10   Nor fallest foul of whoso licks his lips
And sighs—'Well-saffroned was that barley soup!'
Can wisdom co-exist with—gorge-and-swill,
I say not,—simply sensual preference
For this or that fantastic meat and drink?
15   Moreover, wind blows sharper than its wont
This morning, and thou hast already donned
Thy sheepskin over-garment: sure the sage
Is busied with conceits that soar above
A petty change of season and its chance
20   Of causing ordinary flesh to sneeze?

TWO CAMELS   *Title|* MS:8. *Two Camels* *P1884:*8. TWO CAMELS *1889a:*TWO
¹| MS:Quoth §added in margin§ One said §crossed out§ "I have §last two words crossed out
and replaced above by two words§ Sir, solve <> No one §crossed out and replaced above by§
true *P1884:*one: "Sir   ³| MS:'Would'st <> thyself: *P1884:*thyself!   *1889a:*'Wouldst
⁴| MS:sense: *P1884:*sense!   ⁵| MS:Say, do §crossed out and replaced above by§ 'If
*1885:*Say 'If   *1889a:*Say "If   ⁶| MS:The §crossed out and replaced above by§ Horse, <>
mule §two words illegibly crossed out and replaced above by one word§ consume
⁷| MS:soul.'   *1889a:*soul.'"   ⁸| MS:So §crossed out and replaced above by§ Thus <>
admonish: but §crossed out and replaced above by§ while   ¹⁰| MS:foul on §altered to§ of
¹¹| MS:sighs—'Well-flavoured §second word of compound crossed out and replaced above by§
saffroned <> lentil §crossed out and replaced above by§ barley
¹²| MS:with visceral §crossed out§ —gorge-and-swill *1885:*-swill,
¹³| MS:§word, possibly *Sensuality,* crossed out§ I <> sensual §inserted above§
¹⁴| MS: meat or §altered to§ and   ¹⁵| MS:wind is §crossed out and replaced above by§
blows   ¹⁶| MS:and I have §last two words crossed out and replaced above by one word,
illegibly crossed out and replaced by two words§ thou hast   ¹⁸| MS:with such thoughts as
§last three words crossed out and replaced above by two words§ conceits that

I always thought, Sir" . . .

             "Son," Ferishtah said,
"Truth ought to seem as never thought before.
How if I give it birth in parable?
A neighbour owns two camels, beasts of price

25   And promise, destined each to go, next week,
Swiftly and surely with his merchandise
From Nishapur to Sebzevar, no truce
To tramp, but travel, spite of sands and drouth,
In days so many, lest they miss the Fair.

30   Each falls to meditation o'er his crib
Piled high with provender before the start.
Quoth this: 'My soul is set on winning praise
From goodman lord and master,—hump to hoof,
I dedicate me to his service. How?

35   Grass, purslane, lupines and I know not what,
Crammed in my manger? Ha, I see—I see!
No, master, spare thy money! I shall trudge
The distance and yet cost thee not a doit
Beyond my supper on this mouldy bran.'

40   'Be magnified, O master, for the meal
So opportunely liberal!' quoth that.
'What use of strength in me but to surmount

21| MS:thought, Sir" . . . §¶§ "My §crossed out§ Son   *1889a:*thought, "Sir" . . §¶§ §emended to§ thought, "Sir . . . §¶§ §see Editorial Notes§   22| MS:ought to §inserted above§ seems §altered to§ seem to me §last two words crossed out§ as   24| MS:Thy §crossed out and replaced above by§ A   25| MS:promise, both he §last two words crossed out§ destines §altered to§ destined   26| MS:merchandize *1889a:*merchandise   26-27| MS:§two lines added at bottom of leaf, heavily revised and illegibly crossed out§   27| MS:§line added above present l. 28§ to Sebzevah, no *1885a:*Sebzevar, no   28| MS:From §word illegibly crossed out§ to Khelib §last four words crossed out and replaced above by four words§ To tramp, but travel,   29| MS:lest he miss *P1884:*lest they miss   30| MS:Both §crossed out and replaced above by§ Each fall §altered to§ falls < > o'er their §crossed out and replaced above by§ his   31| MS:before they §altered to§ the   32| MS:Quoth one §altered to§ this   33| MS:goodman §inserted above§ < > master that is,— §last two words crossed out§ hump to hoof, §crossed out and replaced above by§ pad, *P1884:*to hoof,   37| MS:master, §inserted above§ save thy shekels §crossed out and replaced above by§ dinars §word illegibly crossed out§ ! I can trudge *P1884:*master, spare thy money! I shall trudge   39| MS:bran." *P1884:*bran.'   40| MS:"Be *P1884:*'Be   41| MS:liberal," < > that: *P1884:*liberal!' < > that.   42| MS:"The §crossed out and replaced above by§ "What < > me is §crossed out and replaced above by§ but to

Sands and simooms, and bend beneath thy bales
No knee until I reach the glad bazaar?
45   Thus I do justice to thy fare: no sprig
Of toothsome chervil must I leave unchewed!
Too bitterly should I reproach myself
Did I sink down in sight of Sebzevar,
Remembering how the merest mouthful more
50   Had heartened me to manage yet a mile!'
And so it proved: the too-abstemious brute
Midway broke down, his pack rejoiced the thieves,
His carcass fed the vultures: not so he
The wisely thankful, who, good market-drudge,
55   Let down his lading in the market-place,
No damage to a single pack. Which beast,
Think ye, had praise and patting and a brand
Of good-and-faithful-servant fixed on flank?
So, with thy squeamish scruple. What imports
60   Fasting or feasting? Do thy day's work, dare
Refuse no help thereto, since help refused
Is hindrance sought and found. Win but the race—
Who shall object 'He tossed three wine cups off,

43| MS:bend no iota §last two words crossed out§ beneath   95| MS:Thy bales §last two words crossed out and replaced above by two words§ No knee until   45| MS:Lo, I *P1884:*Thus I   46| MS:Of juicy §inserted above§ chervil will §crossed out and replaced above by§ must I leave unmunched! §crossed out and replaced above by§ unchewed, *P1884:*Of toothsome chervil <> unchewed!   47| MS:bitterly I should §marked for transposition to§ bitterly should I   48| MS:of Khelib walls *P1884:*of Sebzevah, *1885a:*of Sebzebar,   49| MS:how a §crossed out and replaced above by§ the mere §altered to§ merest   50| MS:mile!" *P1884:*mile!'   54| MS:market-§second word of compound illegibly crossed out and replaced above by§ drudge,   55| MS:lading at the master's feet, *P1884:*lading in the market-place,   57| MS:you *P1884:*ye   58| MS:fixed §inserted above§ on his §crossed out§ flank?   59| MS:Thou, with <> scruple,—what of thee, *P1884:*So, with <> what imports *1885:*scruple. What   60| MS:feasting,—do thy service §crossed out and replaced above by two words§ day's work,— dare *P1884:*feasting? Do <> work, dare   61| MS:thereto,—since *1885:*thereto, since   62| MS:found. Win thou §crossed out and replaced above by§ but the §replaced above by§ thy §crossed out; *the* marked for retention§   63| MS:Who §crossed out and then marked for retention§ <> object §word above illegibly crossed out§ "He drank §crossed out and replaced above by two words§ tossed off three wine §inserted above§ cups, of wine, §last two words crossed out§ *P1884:*object 'He tossed three wine cups off,

And, just at starting, Lilith kissed his lips'?

65 "More soberly,—consider this, my Son!
Put case I never have myself enjoyed,
Known by experience what enjoyment means,
How shall I—share enjoyment?—no, indeed!—
Supply it to my fellows,—ignorant,
70 As so I should be of the thing they crave,
How it affects them, works for good or ill.
Style my enjoyment self-indulgence—sin—
Why should I labour to infect my kind
With sin's occasion, bid them too enjoy,
75 Who else might neither catch nor give again
Joy's plague, but live in righteous misery?
Just as I cannot, till myself convinced,
Impart conviction, so, to deal forth joy
Adroitly, needs must I know joy myself.
80 Renounce joy for my fellows' sake? That's joy
Beyond joy; but renounced for mine, not theirs?
Why, the physician called to help the sick,
Cries 'Let me, first of all, discard my health!'
No, Son: the richness hearted in such joy
85 Is in the knowing what are gifts we give,
Not in a vain endeavour not to know!
Therefore, desire joy and thank God for it!
The Adversary said,—a Jew reports,—
הֲנָם יְדָא אִיּוֹב אֱלֹהִים:

64| MS:And, Lillith §crossed out§ just §inserted above§ at starting, Lilith §inserted above§ kissed him §altered to§ his lips? §word illegibly crossed out§ "   *P1884:*lips?'
64-65| MS:§no ¶§ *P1884:*§¶§   65| MS:More <> Son!   *1889a:*"More <> Son §emended to§ Son! §see Editorial Notes§   65-66| MS: Sept. '83—Jan. 15. '84. L. D. I. E. §added in margin and crossed out; see Editorial Notes§   68| MS:enjoyment,—no, indeed,— *P1884:*enjoyment?—no, indeed!—   75| MS:else would deeply never catch *P1884:*else might neither catch   76| MS:The plague   *P1884:*Joy's plague
81| MS:but for mine renounced, not theirs—   *P1884:*but renounced for mine, not theirs?
83| MS:Cries, "first of all, let me §marked for transposition to§ Cries, "let me, first of all <> health!"   *P1884:*Cries 'Let <> health!   *CP1884:*health!'   84| MS:son—the <> in the joy   *P1884:*No, Son: the <>in such joy   85| MS:what it is we   *P1884:*what are gifts we
86| MS:know!   *1889a:*know §emended to§ know! §see Editorial Notes§
89| §Hebrew emended to restore diacritical marks; see Editorial Notes§

90 In Persian phrase, 'Does job fear God for nought?'
Job's creatureship is not abjured, thou fool!
He nowise isolates himself and plays
The independent equal, owns no more
Than himself gave himself, so why thank God?
95 A proper speech were this מאלהים
'Equals we are, Job, labour for thyself,
Nor bid me help thee: bear, as best flesh may,
Pains I inflict not nor avail to cure:
Beg of me nothing thou thyself mayst win
100 By work, or waive with magnanimity,
Since we are peers acknowledged,—scarcely peers,
Had I implanted any want of thine
Only my power could meet and gratify.'
No: rather hear, at man's indifference—
105 'Wherefore did I contrive for thee that ear
Hungry for music, and direct thine eye
To where I hold a seven-stringed instrument,
Unless I meant thee to beseech me play?' "

Once I saw a chemist take a pinch of powder
110 —Simple dust it seemed—and half-unstop a phial:
—Outdropped harmless dew. "Mixed nothings make"—quoth he—

90| MS:In Persian Phrase, §last three words inserted above§ "Does <> nought?"
P1884:'Does <> nought?'   91| MS:Mark you, §crossed out§ Job's creatureship forsooth
§inserted above; marked for transposition to end of line§ is not abjured,   *P1884:*creatureship
is not abjured, thou fool!   93| MS:equal: throws away   *P1884:*equal, owns no more
94| MS:What himself <> so his to give!   *P1884:*Than himself <> so why thank God?
95| MS:proper rule for you and me, that same!   *P1884:*proper speech were this §Hebrew§
96| MS:Equals we are,—so labour   *P1884:*'Equals we are, Job, labour   97| MS:thee,
bear as   *P1884:*thee: bear, as   98| MS:cure,   *P1884:*cure: 99| MS:thou may'st
win thyself   *1885:*thou thyself may'st win   *1889a:*mayst   101| MS:So we <> scarcely
peers   *P1884:*Since we   *1885:*scarcely peers,   102| MS:implanted every want
*P1884:*implanted any want   103| MS:gratify.   *P1884:*gratify.'   104| MS:I should
exclaim at thine ingratitude—   *P1884:*No: rather hear, at man's indifference—
105| MS:Wherefore did I §two words illegibly crossed out and replaced above by two words§
contrive for   108| MS:play?   *P1884:*play?' "   110| MS:and then §crossed out and
replaced above by first part of compound§ half-unstop a phial   *P1884:*phial: *1889a:*phial.
§emended to§ phial: §see Editorial Notes§   111| MS:—Out-dropped <> make" quoth
he   *P1884:*—Out dropped <> make"—quoth   *1885:*he—   *1889a:*—Outdropped

"Something!" So they did: a thunderclap, but louder—
Lightning-flash, but fiercer—put spectators' nerves to trial:
Sure enough, we learned what was, imagined what might be.

115　　Had I no experience how a lip's mere tremble,
Look's half hesitation, cheek's just change of colour,
These effect a heartquake,—how should I conceive
What a heaven there may be? Let it but resemble
Earth myself have known! No bliss that's finer, fuller,
120　　Only—bliss that lasts, they say, and fain would I believe.

---

¹¹²|　MS:A §crossed out and replaced above by word illegibly crossed out§ lightning-flash,
§altered to§ Lightning-flash, §second part of compound crossed out and restored§ but more
§inserted above and crossed out§ fiercer §altered to§ fierce §*fiercer* restored§
¹¹⁶|　MS:cheek §altered to§ cheek's that §crossed out§ just changed §altered to§ change of
§inserted above§ colour,　　¹¹⁷|　MS:effect a §last two words crossed out and replaced
above by words illegibly crossed out; *effect a* marked for retention§　　¹¹⁹|　MS:Earth that I
have　*P1884:*Earth myself have　　¹²⁰|　MS:say,—§words illegibly crossed out
and replaced above by four words§ and fain would I

CHERRIES

"What, I disturb thee at thy morning-meal:
Cherries so ripe already? Eat apace!
I recollect thy lesson yesterday.
Yet—thanks, Sir, for thy leave to interrupt" . . .

5   "Friend, I have finished my repast, thank God!"

"There now, thy thanks for breaking fast on fruit!—
Thanks being praise, or tantamount thereto.
Prithee consider, have not things degree,
Lofty and low? Are things not great and small,
10   Thence claiming praise and wonder more or less ?
Shall we confuse them, with thy warrant too,
Whose doctrine otherwise begins and ends
With just this precept 'Never faith enough
In man as weakness, God as potency'?
15   When I would pay soul's tribute to that same,
Why not look up in wonder, bid the stars
Attest my praise of the All-mighty One?
What are man's puny members and as mean
Requirements weighed with Star-King Mushtari?

CHERRIES   *Title*| MS:9. *Gratitude   P1884:*9. *CHERRIES   1889a: CHERRIES*
¹| MS:Ah §crossed out and replaced above by§ What   *P1884:* "What   ²⁻⁷| MS:§written
in two locations in margin and marked for insertion between present ll. 1 and 8§
²| MS:so §two words illegibly crossed out and replaced above by two words§ ripe already? Eat
§crossed out and replaced above by§ Champ apace—   *P1884:*already? Eat apace!
⁴| MS:thanks Sir for <> interrupt.   *P1884:*thanks, Sir, for <> interrupt." . .
*1885:*interrupt" . . .   ⁵| MS:Friend <> God.   *P1884:* "Friend <> God!"
⁶| MS:There <> fruit!   *P1884:* "There <> fruit!—   ⁸| MS:Still, Sir §last two words
crossed out and replaced above by one word§ Prithee consider, things have not degree,
§marked for transposition to§ consider, have not things degree,
⁹| MS:small   *P1884:*small,   ¹⁰| MS:§added between present ll. 9 and 11§
¹³| MS:With §crossed out§ In just <> "Never   *P1884:*With <> 'Never
¹⁴| MS:weakness—God as potency?"   *P1884:*weakness, God as potency'?
¹⁶| MS:in rapture §crossed out and replaced above by§ wonder   ¹⁷| MS:my homage to
§last two words crossed out and replaced above by two words§ praise of the Allmighty
*P1884:*the All-mighty   ¹⁹| MS:Requirements by the side of Mazzaroth? §crossed out and
replaced above by§ Mushtari—The §crossed out§ Star-King? §marked for transposition to§
Star-King Mushtari?   *P1884:*Requirements weighed with Star-King

20   There is the marvel!"

                        "Not to man—that's me.
        List to what happened late, in fact or dream.
        A certain stranger, bound from far away,
        Still the Shah's subject, found himself before
        Ispahan palace-gate. As duty bade,
25   He enters in the courts, will, if he may,
        See so much glory as befits a slave
        Who only comes, of mind to testify
        How great and good is shown our lord the Shah.
        In he walks, round he casts his eye about,
30   Looks up and down, admires to heart's content,
        Ascends the gallery, tries door and door,
        None says his reverence nay: peeps in at each,
        Wonders at all the unimagined use,
        Gold here and jewels there,—so vast, that hall—
35   So perfect yon pavilion!—lamps above
        Bidding look up from luxuries below,—
        Evermore wonder topping wonder,—last—
        Sudden he comes upon a cosy nook,
        A nest-like little chamber, with his name,
40   His own, yea, his and no mistake at all,

---

²⁰| MS:me, *P1884:*me.   ²⁰⁻²¹| MS:§line inserted§ Who I §replaced above by§ now have
finished my repast—thank God!— §line crossed out§   ²¹| MS:late in *P1884:*late, in
²²| MS:stranger, far away but still *P1884:*stranger, bound from far away,   ²³| MS:Our
§crossed out and replaced above by§ Shah master's subject *P1884:*Still the Shah's subject
²⁴| MS:Ishpahan §added in margin§ The §crossed out§ palace-gate. "By §quotation marks
crossed out§ duty bound" §quotation marks crossed out§ quoth he, §last two words crossed
out§ *P1884:*palace-gate. As duty bade,   ²⁵| MS:"He <> courts and, will §inserted
above§ if §crossed out and marked for retention§ I §crossed out and replaced above by§ he
may, *P1884:*He <> courts, will, if   ²⁷| MS:only §inserted above§ comes that he, §last
two words crossed out§ in haste, §last two words crossed out and replaced above by two words§
of mind   ²⁸| MS:is shown §last two words inserted above§ the Shah our lord."
*P1884:*shown our lord the Shah.   ³⁰| MS:content: *P1884:*content,
³¹| MS:galleries §altered to§ gallery   ³²| MS:Peeps in at each,—none says his reverence
nay: §marked for transposition to§ None says his reverence nay: peeps in at each—,
*P1884:*each,   ³⁵| MS:pavilion,—lamps *P1884:* pavilion!—lamps
³⁷| MS: wonder upon §crossed out and replaced above by§ topping
³⁸| MS:What §crossed out§ comes he suddenly §altered to§ Sudden upon §marked for
transposition to§ Sudden he comes upon—a cosy §inserted above§ *P1884:*upon a
⁴⁰| MS:own, name, §crossed out and replaced above by§ yea,

Plain o'er the entry: what, and he descries
Just those arrangements inside,—oh, the care!—
Suited to soul and body both,—so snug
The cushion—nay, the pipe-stand furnished so!
45 Whereat he cries aloud,—what think'st thou, Friend?
'That these my slippers should be just my choice,
Even to the colour that I most affect,
Is nothing: ah, that lamp, the central sun,
What must it light within its minaret
50 I scarce dare guess the good of! Who lives there?
That let me wonder at,—no slipper-toys
Meant for the foot, forsooth, which kicks them—thus!'

"Never enough faith in omnipotence,—
Never too much, by parity, of faith
55 In impuissance, man's—which turns to strength
When once acknowledged weakness every way.
How? Hear the teaching of another tale.

"Two men once owed the Shah a mighty sum,
Beggars they both were: this one crossed his arms
60 And bowed his head,—'whereof,'—sighed he,—'each hair
Proved it a jewel, how the host's amount
Were idly strewn for payment at thy feet!'
'Lord, here they lie, my havings poor and scant!

---

^{41|} MS:entry,—what   *1889a:*entry: what   ^{43|} MS:Suitable §altered to§ Suited
^{44|} MS:cushioning §altered to§ cushion—nay   ^{45|} MS:cried <> think you, Son?
*P1884:*cries <> think'st thou, Friend?   ^{46|} MS:That   *P1884:*'That   ^{48|} MS:oh
*P1884:*ah   ^{50|} MS:of: who   *P1884:*of! Who   ^{51|} MS:slipper toys   *1889a:*slipper-
toys   ^{52|} MS:foot—forsooth—which <> thus!"   *P1884:*foot, forsooth, which <> thus!'
^{52-53|} MS:§no ¶§   *1889a:*§¶ added§   ^{53|} MS: Never<> Omnipotence,—
*P1884:*omnipotence,—   *1889a:* "Never   ^{54|} MS:Never enough §crossed out and
replaced above by two words§ too much <> of trust   *P1884:*of faith   ^{55|} MS:In man's
mere impuissance, turning strength   *P1884:*In impuissance, man's—which turns to strength
^{57|} MS:§added in margin§   ^{57-58|} MS:§no ¶§   *P1884:*§¶ added§
^{58|} MS:Two <> owed the Shah §two words crossed out and replaced above by two words§ our
Khan a <> sum,   *P1884:*owed the Shah a   *1889a:* "Two <> sum §emended to§ sum, §see
Editorial Notes§   ^{59|} MS:were: that one   *P1884:*were: this one   ^{60|} MS:head,—
"whereof,"—sighed he,—"each   *P1884:* head,—'whereof,'—sighed he,—'each
^{61|} MS:jewel, all the   *P1884:*jewel, how the   ^{62|} MS:idly poured for <> feet."
*P1884:*idly strewn for <> feet!'   ^{63|} MS:"Well, here they are, my havings, Royal Sir,
P1884:'Lord, here they lie, my havings poor and scant!

184

All of the berries on my currant-bush,
65 What roots of garlic have escaped the mice,
And some five pippins from the seedling tree,—
Would they were half-a-dozen! anyhow,
Accept my all, poor beggar that I am!'
'Received in full of all demands!' smiled back
70 The apportioner of every lot of ground
From inch to acre. Littleness of love
Befits the littleness of loving thing.
What if he boasted 'Seeing I am great,
Great must my corresponding tribute be'?
75 Mushtari,—well, suppose him seven times seven
The sun's superior, proved so by some sage:
Am I that sage? To me his twinkle blue
Is all I know of him and thank him for,
And therefore I have put the same in verse—
80 'Like yon blue twinkle, twinks thine eye, my Love!'

"Neither shalt thou be troubled overmuch
Because thy offering,—littleness itself,—
Is lessened by admixture sad and strange
Of mere man's-motives,—praise with fear, and love
85 With looking after that same love's reward.
Alas, Friend, what was free from this alloy,—
Some smatch thereof,—in best and purest love
Proffered thy earthly father? Dust thou art,

65| MS:garlick   *1889a:*garlic   66| MS:And all three §replaced above by§ five apples on
the <> tree,   *P1884:*And some five pippins from the <> tree,—   67| MS:anyhow
*P1884:*anyhow,   68| MS:Here is my <> am!"   *P1884:*Accept my <> am!'   ·
69| MS:"Received <> demands" smiled   *P1884:*'Received <> demands!' smiled
72| MS:thing—   *P1884:*thing.   73| MS:boasted "Seeing   *P1884:*boasted 'Seeing
74| MS:be?"   *P1884:*be?' §emended to§ be'? §see Editorial Notes§   75| MS: Mazzaroth
§crossed out and replaced above by§ Mushtari   79| MS:verse.   *P1884:*verse—
80| MS:"Like <> Love!"   *P1884:*'Like <> Love!'   81-82| MS:§no ¶§   *P1884:*§¶ added§
81| MS:Neither shalt thou §last two words inserted above§   *1889a:*"Neither
82| MS:the   *P1884:*thy   84| MS:Of poor §crossed out and replaced above by§ mere
85| MS:With Looking §altered to§ looking for the very §last three words crossed out and
replaced above by three words§ after that same <> reward: *P1884:*reward.
86| MS:Alas, friend, §crossed out and replaced above by§ Son, what   *P1884:*Alas, Friend, what
88| MS:thy father? Dust thou wast and art   *P1884:*thy earthly father? Dust thou art,

Dust shalt be to the end. Thy father took
90   The dust, and kindly called the handful—gold,
Nor cared to count what sparkled here and there,
Sagely unanalytic. Thank, praise, love
(Sum up thus) for the lowest favours first,
The commonest of comforts! aught beside
95   Very omnipotence had overlooked
Such needs, arranging for thy little life.
Nor waste thy power of love in wonderment
At what thou wiselier lettest shine unsoiled
By breath of word. That this last cherry soothes
100   A roughness of my palate, that I know:
His Maker knows why Mushtari was made."

———————

Verse-making was least of my virtues: I viewed with despair
Wealth that never yet was but might be—all that verse-making were
If the life would but lengthen to wish, let the mind be laid bare.
105   So I said "To do little is bad, to do nothing is worse"—And made verse.

Love-making,—how simple a matter! No depths to explore,
No heights in a life to ascend! No disheartening Before,
No affrighting Hereafter,—love now will be love evermore.
So I felt "To keep silence were folly:"—all language above, I made love.

———————

89| MS:And shalt *P1884:*Dust shalt   90| MS:and wisely §crossed out and replaced above by§ kindly   91| MS:count the sparkles *P1884:*count what sparkled
94| MS:commonest of §inserted above§ comforts, aught *P1884:*comforts! aught
95| MS: Very Omnipotence *P1884:*omnipotence   96| MS:Arranging for thy daily littleness: §altered to two words§ little life: *P1884:*Such needs, arranging for thy little life.
99| MS:this banana §crossed out and replaced above by two words§ last cherry
100| MS:A dryness §crossed out and replaced above by§ roughness in §altered to§ of
101| MS:His maker knows §last three words inserted above§ Why Mazzaroth §crossed out and replaced above by§ Mushtari was made. *P1884:*His Maker < > why *1889a:*made."
101-2| MS:Jan. 15. L. D. I. E. §added in margin and crossed out§   103| MS:be— §two words illegibly crossed out and replaced above by two words§ all that   109| MS:felt "Only silence < > folly",—all *P1884:*felt "To keep silence < > folly:"—all

PLOT-CULTURE

"Ay, but, Ferishtah,"—a disciple smirked,—
"That verse of thine 'How twinks thine eye, my Love,
Blue as yon star-beam!' much arrides myself
Who haply may obtain a kiss therewith
5 This eve from Laila where the palms abound—
My youth, my warrant—so the palms be close!
Suppose when thou art earnest in discourse
Concerning high and holy things,—abrupt
I out with—'Laila's lip, how honey-sweet!'—
10 What say'st thou, were it scandalous or no?
I feel thy shoe sent flying at my mouth
For daring—prodigy of impudence—
Publish what, secret, were permissible.
Well,—one slide further in the imagined slough,—
15 Knee-deep therein, (respect thy reverence!)—
Suppose me well aware thy very self
Stooped prying through the palm-screen, while I dared
Solace me with caressings all the same?
Unutterable, nay—unthinkable,
20 Undreamable a deed of shame! Alack,
How will it fare shouldst thou impress on me
That certainly an Eye is over all
And each, to mark the minute's deed, word, thought,
As worthy of reward or punishment?
25 Shall I permit my sense an Eye-viewed shame,

PLOT-CULTURE   *Title*⌐ MS:10. §word illegibly crossed out and replaced by§ *Plot-culture*
*P1884:*10. PLOT-CULTURE *1889a:PLOT-CULTURE*   4⌐ MS:may §inserted above§
5⌐ MS:from Leila §crossed out and replaced above by§ Laila < > palms §words illegibly crossed
out and replaced above by one word§ abound—   9⌐ MS:with—'Leila's §altered to§ Laila's
10⌐ MS:How §altered to§ What   11⌐ MS:my teeth §crossed out and replaced by§ mouth
14⌐ MS:one step §crossed out and replaced above by§ slide   15⌐ MS:§line added
between present ll. 14 and 16§   17⌐ MS:palm-screen, and §crossed out and replaced
above by§ while   20⌐ MS:shame! Alas! §crossed out and replaced above by§ Alack!
*P1884:*shame! Alack,   22⌐ MS:Thy §altered to§ That §two words illegibly crossed out and
replaced above by one word§ certainly an eye §altered to§ Eye   23⌐ MS:each to see
§altered to§ mark the minute's act §crossed out and replaced above by§ deed   *P1884:*each, to
25⌐ MS:§two words, possible *And sir,* crossed out§ —Shall < > sense a §crossed out and
replaced above by two words§ an Eye-viewed thing—   *P1884:*an Eye-viewed shame,

187

Broad daylight perpetration,—so to speak,—
I had not dared to breathe within the Ear,
With black night's help about me? Yet I stand
A man, no monster, made of flesh not cloud:
30 Why made so, if my making prove offence
To Maker's eye and ear?"

      "Thou wouldst not stand
Distinctly Man,"—Ferishtah made reply,
"Not the mere creature,—did no limit-line
Round thee about, apportion thee thy place
35 Clean-cut from out and off the illimitable,—
Minuteness severed from immensity.
All of thee for the Maker,—for thyself,
Workings inside the circle that evolve
Thine all,——the product of thy cultured plot.
40 So much of grain the ground's lord bids thee yield
Bring sacks to granary in Autumn! spare
Daily intelligence of this manure,
That compost, how they tend to feed the soil:
There thou art master sole and absolute
45 —Only, remember doomsday! Twitt'st thou me
Because I turn away my outraged nose
Shouldst thou obtrude thereon a shovelful
Of fertilizing kisses? Since thy sire
Wills and obtains thy marriage with the maid,
50 Enough! Be reticent, I counsel thee,
Nor venture to acquaint him, point by point,
What he procures thee. Is he so obtuse?

---

²⁷| MS:the Ear *P1884:*the Ear,   ²⁹| MS:cloud, *P1884:*cloud: ³⁰| MS:if the
§crossed out and replaced above by§ my   ³¹| MS:To Maker's §inserted above§ eye and
ear? of Maker? §last two words and punctuation crossed out§ *P1884:*ear?" < > would'st
*1889a:*wouldst   ³²| MS:reply *1889a:*reply,   ³⁵| MS:illimitable,
P1884: illimitable,—   ³⁹| MS:plot: *P1884:*plot.   ⁴⁰| MS:yield— *P1884:*yield:
⁴¹| MS:in Autumn: spare *P1884:*in Autumn! spare   ⁴³| MS:they hope to < > soil,—
*P1884:*they tend < > soil: ⁴⁵| MS:doomsday! Twitst *P1884:* doomsday! Twit'st
1889a: doomsday! Twitt'st   ⁴⁸| MS:kisses? §word, possibly *Why,* §crossed out and
replaced above by§ Since   ⁴⁹| MS:the slut, *P1884:*the maid,
⁵⁰| MS:counsel this, *P1884:*counsel thee,   ⁵²| MS:What pleasures §crossed out§ he
< > he ignorant? *P1884:*thee. Is he so obtuse

Keep thy instruction to thyself! My ass—
Only from him expect acknowledgment
55 The while he champs my gift, a thistle-bunch,
How much he loves the largess: of his love
I only tolerate so much as tells
By wrinkling nose and inarticulate grunt,
The meal, that heartens him to do my work,
60 Tickles his palate as I meant it should."

———————————

Not with my Soul, Love!—bid no Soul like mine
　　　Lap thee around nor leave the poor Sense room!
Soul,—travel-worn, toil-weary,—would confine
　　　Along with Soul, Soul's gains from glow and gloom,

65 Captures from soarings high and divings deep.
Spoil-laden Soul, how should such memories sleep?
Take Sense, too—let me love entire and whole—
　　　Not with my Soul!

Eyes shall meet eyes and find no eyes between,
70 　　　Lips feed on lips, no other lips to fear!
No past, no future—so thine arms but screen
　　　The present from surprise! not there, 'tis here—
Not then, 'tis now:—back, memories that intrude!
Make, Love, the universe our solitude,
75 And, over all the rest, oblivion roll—
　　　Sense quenching Soul!

55| MS:champs his provender §last two words crossed out and replaced above by four words§
my gift, a thistle-bunch,　　56| MS:largess,—and §crossed out§ of his §inserted above§
*P1884:*largess: of　　58| MS:The §crossed out and replaced above by§ By < > nose, the
§crossed out§ inarticulate grunt. §marked for transposition to§ grunt inarticulate
§transposition cancelled, *and* inserted above after *nose,* period altered to comma§
*P1884:*nose and　　59| MS:meal that strengthens §crossed out and replaced above by§
heartens　*P1884:*meal, that　　59-60| MS:L. D. I. E. Jan. 17 '84. §added in margin; crossed
out§　　60| MS:palate likewise: so I meant.　*P1884:*palate as I meant it should." §MS ends;
added below last line of poem is the instruction§ (*Leave room for a small poem's insertion here*)

189

A PILLAR AT SEBZEVAR

"Knowledge deposed, then!"—groaned whom that most grieved
As foolishest of all the company.
"What, knowledge, man's distinctive attribute,
He doffs that crown to emulate an ass
5   Because the unknowing long-ears loves at least
Husked lupines, and belike the feeder's self
—Whose purpose in the dole what ass divines?

"Friend," quoth Ferishtah, "all I seem to know
Is—I know nothing save that love I can
10   Boundlessly, endlessly. My curls were crowned
In youth with knowledge,—off, alas, crown slipped
Next moment, pushed by better knowledge still
Which nowise proved more constant: gain, to-day,
Was toppling loss to-morrow, lay at last
15   —Knowledge, the golden?—lacquered ignorance!
As gain—mistrust it! Not as means to gain:
Lacquer we learn by: cast in fining-pot,
We learn,—when what seemed ore assayed proves dross,—
Surelier true gold's worth, guess how purity
20   I' the lode were precious could one light on ore
Clarified up to test of crucible.
The prize is in the process: knowledge means
Ever-renewed assurance by defeat
That victory is somehow still to reach,
25   But love is victory, the prize itself:
Love—trust to! Be rewarded for the trust
In trust's mere act. In love success is sure,
Attainment—no delusion, whatsoe'er
The prize be: apprehended as a prize,

A PILLAR AT SEBZEVAR   *Title*| MS:11. *A Pillar at Khorasan* *P1884:*11. *A PILLAR AT SEBZEVAH 1885a:SEBZEVAR 1889a:A*   ²| MS:company— *P1884:*company.
⁸| MS:"Son," quoth *P1884:*"Friend," quoth ¹¹| MS:knowledge,—down §crossed out and replaced above by§ off, alas, it §crossed out and replaced above by§ crown ¹⁴| MS:Proved toppling *P1884:*Was toppling ¹⁵| MS:golden? Lacquered *P1884:*golden?—lacquered ¹⁶| MS:not *P1884:*it! Not ²⁴| MS:to gain: *P1884:*to reach:

30   A prize it is. Thy child as surely grasps
    · An orange as he fails to grasp the sun
    Assumed his capture. What if soon he finds
    The foolish fruit unworthy grasping? Joy
    In shape and colour,—that was joy as true—
35   Worthy in its degree of love—as grasp
    Of sun were, which had singed his hand beside.
    What if he said the orange held no juice
    Since it was not that sun he hoped to suck?
    This constitutes the curse that spoils our life
40   And sets man maundering of his misery,
    That there's no meanest atom he obtains
    Of what he counts for knowledge but he cries
    'Hold here,—I have the whole thing,—know, this time,
    Nor need search farther!' Whereas, strew his path
45   With pleasures, and he scorns them while he stoops:
    'This fitly call'st thou pleasure, pick up this
    And praise it, truly? I reserve my thanks
    For something more substantial.' Fool not thus
    In practising with life and its delights!
50   Enjoy the present gift, nor wait to know
    The unknowable. Enough to say 'I feel
    Love's sure effect, and, being loved, must love
    The love its cause behind,—I can and do!'
    Nor turn to try thy brain-power on the fact,
55   (Apart from as it strikes thee, here and now—
    Its how and why, i'the future and elsewhere)
    Except to—yet once more, and ever again,
    Confirm thee in thy utter ignorance:
    Assured that, whatsoe'er the quality

36| MS:were—which *P1884:*were, which   40| MS:of the §crossed out and replaced
above by§ his   46| MS:fitly call you pleasure *P1884:*fitly call'st thou pleasure
48| MS:substantial." Fool *P1884:*substantial.' Fool   51| MS:—The *P1884:*The
52| MS:The §crossed out and replaced above by§ sure effect, of §crossed out§ love §altered
to§ Love's §marked for transposition to§ Love's sure effect, and   53| MS:do, *P1884:*
do!'   54| MS:try my brain-power <> fact *P1884:*thr thy brain-power <> fact,
55| MS:—Apart from how it strikes me, here *P1884:*(Apart from as it strikes thee, here
56| MS:elsewhere— *P1884:*elsewhere)   57| MS:to—this once *P1884:*to—yet once
58| MS:Confirm me in my utter ignorance— *P1884:*Confirm thee in thy utter ignorance:

60 Of love's cause, save that love was caused thereby,
This—nigh upon revealment as it seemed
A minute since—defies thy longing looks,
Withdrawn into the unknowable once more.
Wholly distrust thy knowledge, then, and trust
65 As wholly love allied to ignorance!
There lies thy truth and safety. Love is praise,
And praise is love! Refine the same, contrive
An intellectual tribute—ignorance
Appreciating ere approbative
70 Of knowledge that is infinite? With us
The small, who use the knowledge of our kind
Greater than we, more wisely ignorance
Restricts its apprehension, sees and knows
No more than brain accepts in faith of sight,
75 Takes first what comes first, only sure so far.
By Sebzevar a certain pillar stands
So aptly that its gnomon tells the hour;
What if the townsmen said 'Before we thank
Who placed it, for his serviceable craft,
80 And go to dinner since its shade tells noon,
Needs must we have the craftsman's purpose clear
On half a hundred more recondite points
Than a mere summons to a vulgar meal!'
Better they say 'How opportune the help!
85 Be loved and praised, thou kindly-hearted sage

61| MS:That *P1884:*This   65| MS:ignorance: *P1884:*ignorance!
66| MS:safety. Love be §crossed out and replaced above by§ is   67| MS:praise be
§crossed out and replaced above by§ is   69| MS:approving §altered to§ approbative of
§crossed out§   70| MS:Of §added in margin§ Knowledge <> us, the small, §last two
words crossed out§ *P1884:*knowledge *1889a:*us   71| MS:The small, §last two words
and punctuation added in margin§ Who §three words illegibly crossed out and replaced
above by one word§ thank the *P1884:*who *1889a:*who use the   72| MS:we, the wiser
*1889a:*we, more wisely   76| MS:A certain pillar stands by §two words illegibly crossed out
and replaced above by two words illegibly crossed out§ Khorasan *P1884:*by Sebzevah
*1885a:*by Sebzevar *1889a:*By Sebzevar a certain pillar stands   78| MS:Think you §last
two words crossed out and replaced above by two words§ What if <> say §altered to§ said
79| MS:it, by §crossed out and replaced above by§ for   80| MS:dinner now §crossed out
and replaced above by§ since its shade points §crossed out and replaced above by§ tells
83| MS:meal?' *P1884:*meal!'   84| MS:said—'How *P1884:*said 'How
*1889a:*say   85| MS:kindly-hearted one *P1884:* kindly-hearted sage

Whom Hudhud taught,—the gracious spirit-bird,—
How to construct the pillar, teach the time!'
So let us say—not 'Since we know, we love,'
But rather 'Since we love, we know enough.'
90   Perhaps the pillar by a spell controlled
Mushtari in his courses? Added grace
Surely I count it that the sage devised,
Beside celestial service, ministry
To all the land, by one sharp shade at noon
95   Falling as folk foresee. Once more then, Friend—
(What ever in those careless ears of thine
Withal I needs must round thee)—knowledge doubt
Even wherein it seems demonstrable!
Love,—in the claim for love, that's gratitude
100 For apprehended pleasure, nowise doubt!
Pay its due tribute,—sure that pleasure is,
While knowledge may be, at the most. See, now!
Eating my breakfast, I thanked God.—'For love
Shown in the cherries' flavour? Consecrate
105 So petty an example?' There's the fault!
We circumscribe omnipotence. Search sand
To unearth water: if first handful scooped
Yields thee a draught, what need of digging down
Full fifty fathoms deep to find a spring
110 Whereof the pulse might deluge half the land?
Drain the sufficient drop, and praise what checks
The drouth that glues thy tongue,—what more would help
A brimful cistern? Ask the cistern's boon

90| MS:What if §last two words crossed out and replaced above one word by§ Perhaps
94| MS:To Thee §crossed out and replaced above by§ all the town §crossed out and replaced
above by§ land   95| MS:as I foresee.' Once more, my Son §altered to§ friend—
*P1884:*foresee. Once more, then, Friend—   *1885:*as folk foresee   *1889a:*more then
96| MS:What   *P1884:*(What   97| MS:thee—knowledge   *P1884:* thee)—knowledge
99| MS:the right §crossed out and replaced above by§ claim to §altered to§ for <> gratitude,
*P1884:*gratitude   101| MS:*is,*   *P1884:*is,   102| MS:now—   *P1884:*now!
104| MS:flavour?—Consecrate   *P1884:* flavour? Consecrate   107| MS:water! if
*P1884:*water: if   109| MS:§word illegibly crossed out and replaced above by two words§
Full fifty   110| MS:pulse would deluge §words illegibly crossed out§ ?   *P1884:*deluge half the
land?   *1885:*pulse might deluge   113| MS:cistern? §twow words illegibly crossed out and
replaced above by three words§ ask the cistern's boon §two words illegibly crossed out§

When thou wouldst solace camels: in thy case,
Relish the drop and love the loveable!"

"And what may be unloveable?"

"Why, hate!
If out of sand comes sand and nought but sand
Affect not to be quaffing at mirage,
Nor nickname pain as pleasure. That, belike,
Constitutes just the trial of thy wit
And worthiness to gain promotion,—hence,
Proves the true purpose of thine actual life.
Thy soul's environment of things perceived,
Things visible and things invisible,
Fact, fancy—all was purposed to evolve
This and this only—was thy wit of worth
To recognize the drop's use, love the same,
And loyally declare against mirage
Though all the world asseverated dust
Was good to drink? Say, 'what made moist my lip,
That I acknowledged moisture:' thou art saved!

"For why? The creature and creator stand
Rightly related so. Consider well!
Were knowledge all thy faculty, then God
Must be ignored: love gains him by first leap.
Frankly accept the creatureship: ask good
To love for: press bold to the tether's end
Allotted to this life's intelligence!
'So we offend?' Will it offend thyself
If,—impuissance praying potency,—

114| MS:wouldst sate §crossed out and replaced above by§ solace   115| MS:loveable!
*P1884:*loveable!"   116| MS:'And <> unloveable?'—Why *P1884:*"And <> unloveable?"
§¶§ Why   121| MS:hence *P1884:*hence,   122| MS:Proved §altered to§ Proves
130| MS:to quaff §crossed out and replaced above by§ drink. Say, what <> lip *P1884:*drink?
Say, 'what <> lip,   131| MS:moisture: thou *P1884:*moisture:' thou
132| MS:For *1889a:*"For   133| MS:well: *P1884:*well!   139| MS:So you offend?
Will it offend yourself *P1884:*'So we offend?' Will it offend thyself
140| MS:That,—impuissance *P1884:* If,—impuissance

Thy child beseech that thou command the sun
Rise bright to-morrow—thou, he thinks supreme
In power and goodness, why shouldst thou refuse?
Afterward, when the child matures, perchance
The fault were greater if, with wit full-grown,
The stripling dared to ask for a dinar,
Than that the boy cried 'Pluck Sitara down
And give her me to play with!' 'Tis for him
To have no bounds to his belief in thee:
For thee it also is to let her shine
Lustrous and lonely, so best serving him!"

Ask not one least word of praise!
    Words declare your eyes are bright?
What then meant that summer day's
Silence spent in one long gaze?
    Was my silence wrong or right?

Words of praise were all to seek!
    Face of you and form of you,
Did they find the praise so weak
When my lips just touched your cheek—
    Touch which let my soul come through?

145, 150, 155, 160 are line numbers.

141| MS: Your child beseeches that you bid the *P1884:*Thy child beseech that thou command the 142| MS:to-morrow—you, he *P1884:*to-morrow—thou, he 143| MS:should you refuse? *P1884:*should'st thou refuse? *1889a:*shouldst 145| MS:greater that, with *P1884:* greater if, with 149| MS:in you— *P1884:*in thee— *1885:*thee: 150| MS:For whom it *1885:*For thee it 151| MS:him! *P1884:*him!" 156| MS:Silence *P1884:*Was my silence 157| MS:Word <> is all *P1884:*Words <> were all 158| form of you *P1884:*form of you, 160| MS:cheek, *P1884:*cheek—

A BEAN-STRIPE: ALSO, APPLE-EATING

"Look, I strew beans" . . .

                    (Ferishtah, we premise,
Strove this way with a scholar's cavilment
Who put the peevish question: " Sir, be frank!
A good thing or a bad thing—Life is which?
5   Shine and shade, happiness and misery
Battle it out there: which force beats, I ask?
If I pick beans from out a bushelful—
This one, this other,—then demand of thee
What colour names each justly in the main,—
10   'Black' I expect, and 'White' ensues reply:
No hesitation for what speck, spot, splash
Of either colour's opposite, intrudes
To modify thy judgment. Well, for beans
Substitute days,—show, ranged in order, Life—
15   Then, tell me its true colour! Time is short,
Life's days compose a span,—as brief be speech!
Black I pronounce for, like the Indian Sage,—
Black—present, past and future, interspersed
With blanks, no doubt, which simple folk style Good
20   Because not Evil: no, indeed? Forsooth
Black's shade on White is White too! What's the worst
Of Evil but that, past, it overshades
The else-exempted present?—memory,
We call the plague! 'Nay, but our memory fades
25   And leaves the past unsullied!' Does it so?
Why, straight the purpose of such breathing-space,

A BEAN-STRIPE: ALSO, APPLE-EATING   *Title*| MS:12. *A Bean-Stripe* *P1884:*12. *A BEAN-STRIPE: ALSO, APPLE-EATING* *1889a:A*   ¹| MS: beans . ." §¶§ *P1884:*beans" . . . §¶§   ⁴| MS:thing—which is Life? §marked for transposition to§ thing—Life is which?   ¹⁰| MS:reply,— §punctuation crossed out and replaced by colon§ ¹⁵| MS:Instruct §crossed out and replaced above by two words§ Then, tell me of §crossed out§ its true §inserted above§   ²⁰| MS:indeed? Forsooth, *1889a:*indeed? Forsooth ²⁴| MS:plague! Oh, but the §crossed out and replaced above by§ our *P1884:*plague! 'Nay, but   ²⁵| MS:unsullied! Does *P1884:*unsullied!' Does

Such respite from past ill, grows plain enough!
What follows on remembrance of the past?
Fear of the future! Life, from birth to death,
30 Means—either looking back on harm escaped,
Or looking forward to that harm's return
With tenfold power of harming. Black, not White,
Never the whole consummate quietude
Life should be, troubled by no fear!—nor hope—
35 I'll say, since lamplight dies in noontide, hope
Loses itself in certainty. Such lot
Man's might have been: I leave the consequence
To bolder critics of the Primal Cause;
Such am not I: but, man—as man I speak:
40 Black is the bean-throw: evil is the Life!")

" Look, I strew beans"—resumed Ferishtah—"beans
Blackish and whitish; what they figure forth
Shall be man's sum of moments, bad and good,
That make up Life,—each moment when he feels
45 Pleasure or pain, his poorest fact of sense,
Consciousness anyhow: there's stand the first;
Whence next advance shall be from points to line,
Singulars to a series, parts to whole,
And moments to the Life. How look they now,
50 Viewed in the large, those little joys and griefs
Ranged duly all a-row at last, like beans
—These which I strew? This bean was white, this—black,
Set by itself,—but see if, good and bad
Each following either in companionship,
55 Black have not grown less black and white less white,
Till blackish seems but dun, and whitish—grey,

---

³¹| MS:to that §crossed out and replaced above by§ such harm's *P1884:*to that harm's
³²| MS:power to plague§last two words crossed out and replaced above by two words§ of
harming. Black, never §crossed out and replaced above by§ not   ³⁴| MS:fear—nay,
§crossed out and replaced above by§ nor   ³⁷| MS:Might Man's §marked for
transposition to§ Man's might   ⁴⁰| *P1884:*the Life!" *1885:*the Life!")
⁴⁴| MS:Which §crossed out and replaced above by§ That   ⁴⁵| MS:poorest
primal fact, *P1884:*poorest fact of sense,   ⁴⁹| MS:looks §altered to§ look it §altered
to§ they §crossed out and replaced above by§ they

And the whole line turns—well, or black to thee
Or white belike to me—no matter which:
The main result is—both are modified
60 According to our eye's scope, power of range
Before and after. Black dost call this bean?
What, with a whiteness in its wake, which—see—
Suffuses half its neighbour?—and, in turn,
Lowers its pearliness late absolute,
65 Frowned upon by the jet which follows hard—
Else wholly white my bean were. Choose a joy!
Bettered it was by sorrow gone before,
And sobered somewhat by the shadowy sense
Of sorrow which came after or might come.
70 Joy, sorrow,—by precedence, subsequence—
Either on each, make fusion, mix in Life
That's both and neither wholly: grey or dun?
Dun thou decidest? grey prevails, say I:
Wherefore? Because my view is wide enough,
75 Reaches from first to last nor winks at all:
Motion achieves it: stop short—fast we stick,—
Probably at the bean that's blackest.

                                    "Since—
Son, trust me,—this I know and only this—
I am in motion, and all things beside
80 That circle round my passage through their midst,—
Motionless, these are, as regarding me:
—Which means, myself I solely recognize.
They too may recognize themselves, not me,
For aught I know or care: but plain they serve
85 This, if no other purpose—stuff to try
And test my power upon of raying light

61| MS:after. Black you call   *P1884:*after. Black dost call   64| MS:its late absolute of
§crossed out§ pearliness, §marked for transposition to§ its pearliness late absolute,
72| MS:wholly—grey   *P1884:*wholly: grey   73| MS:Dun you decide for? grey
*P1884:*Dun thou decidest? grey   76| MS:fast you stick,—   *P1884:*fast we stick,—
77| *P1884:*§¶§ Since—   *1889a:*§¶§ "Since—   84| MS:care—so §crossed out and
replaced above by§ but   *P1884:*care: but   85| MS:This purpose, if no other—stuff
§marked for transposition to§ This, if no other purpose—stuff I §altered to§ to

198

And lending hue to all things as I go
Moonlike through vapour. Mark the flying orb!
Think'st thou the halo, painted still afresh
90   At each new cloud-fleece pierced and passaged through,
This was and is and will be evermore
Coloured in permanence? The glory swims
Girdling the glory-giver, swallowed straight
By night's abysmal gloom, unglorified
95   Behind as erst before the advancer: gloom?
Faced by the onward-faring, see, succeeds
From the abandoned heaven a next surprise,
And where's the gloom now?—silver-smitten straight,
One glow and variegation! So with me,
100   Who move and make,—myself,—the black, the white,
The good, the bad, of life's environment.
Stand still! black stays black: start again! there's white
Asserts supremacy: the motion's all
That colours me my moment: seen as joy?
105   I have escaped from sorrow, or that was
Or might have been: as sorrow?—thence shall be
Escape as certain: white preceded black,
Black shall give way to white as duly,—so,
Deepest in black means white most imminent.
110   Stand still,—have no before, no after!—life
Proves death, existence grows impossible
To man like me. 'What else is blessed sleep
But death, then?' Why, a rapture of release
From toil,—that's sleep's approach: as certainly,
115   The end of sleep means, toil is triumphed o'er:
These round the blank inconsciousness between
Brightness and brightness, either pushed to blaze
Just through that blank's interposition. Hence

89| MS:Think you *P1884:*Think'st thou   96| MS:onward-faring, let §crossed out and
replaced above by§ straight §crossed out and replaced by§ see,   97| MS:heaven the next
*P1884:*heaven a next   100| MS:I §altered to§ Who   104| MS:joy?—   *1889a:*joy?
110| MS:after,—life *P1884:*after!—life   111| MS:existence were §crossed out and
replaced above by§ grows   113| MS:then?' Why,—a *P1884:*then?' Why, a
114| MS:approach,—as certainly *P1884:*approach: as certainly,   117| MS:A §crossed out§
Brightness and a §crossed out§ brightness: either §inserted above§ *P1884:*and brightness, either

The use of things external: man—that's I—
120   Practise thereon my power of casting light,
And calling substance,—when the light I cast,
Breaks into colour,—by its proper name
—A truth and yet a falsity: black, white,
Names each bean taken from what lay so close
125   And threw such tint: pain might mean pain indeed
Seen in the passage past it,—pleasure prove
No mere delusion while I paused to look,—
Though what an idle fancy was that fear
Which overhung and hindered pleasure's hue!
130   While how, again, pain's shade enhanced the shine
Of pleasure, else no pleasure! Such effects
Came of such causes. Passage at an end,—
Past, present, future pains and pleasures fused
So that one glance may gather blacks and whites
135   Into a life-time,—like my bean-streak there,
Why, white they whirl into, not black—for me!"

"Ay, but for me? The indubitable blacks,
Immeasurable miseries, here, there
And everywhere i' the world—world outside thine
140   Paled off so opportunely,—body's plague,
Torment of soul,—where's found thy fellowship
With wide humanity all round about
Reeling beneath its burden? What's despair?
Behold that man, that woman, child—nay, brute!

120] MS:§word, possibly *Shine*, corssed out and replaced above by Practice thereupon §altered to§ thereon   125] MS:such shadow §crossed out and replaced above by§ tint,—pain must §crossed out and replaced above by§ might §word inserted above and crossed out§ *P1884:*tint: pain might   129] MS:hindered truth of §last two words crossed out and replaced above by one word§ pleasure's hue, *P1884:*hue!   130] MS:again, its §crossed out and replaced above by§ pain's   136] MS:Why, §added in margin§ White < > into, §word, possibly *never*, crossed out and replaced above by§ not < > me! *P1884:*white < > me!"   136-37] MS:§no ¶§ *P1884:*§¶§   137] MS: "Ay §quotation marks crossed out§ < > for you? The *P1884:* "Ay < > for me? The   139] MS:outside mine §crossed out and replaced above by§ yours *P1884:*outside thine   141] MS:found my §crossed out and replaced above by§ your fellowship *P1884:*found thy fellowship   144] MS:Look at §last two words crossed out and replaced above by one word§ Behold < > woman, nay, that child! §last three words crossed out and replaced above by three words§ child—nay, brute!

145 Will any speck of white unblacken life
Splashed, splotched, dyed hell-deep now from end to end
For him or her or it—who knows? Not I!"

"Nor I, Son! 'It' shall stand for bird, beast, fish,
Reptile, and insect even: take the last!
150 There's the palm-aphis, minute miracle
As wondrous every whit as thou or I:
Well, and his world's the palm-frond, there he's born,
Lives, breeds and dies in that circumference,
An inch of green for cradle, pasture-ground,
155 Purlieu and grave: the palm's use, ask of him!
'To furnish these,' replies his wit: ask thine—
Who see the heaven above, the earth below,
Creation everywhere,—these, each and all
Claim certain recognition from the tree
160 For special service rendered branch and bole,
Top-tuft and tap-root:—for thyself, thus seen,
Palms furnish dates to eat, and leaves to shade,
—Maybe, thatch huts with,—have another use
Than strikes the aphis. So with me, my Son!
165 I know my own appointed patch i' the world,
What pleasures me or pains there: all outside—
How he, she, it, and even thou, Son, live,
Are pleased or pained, is past conjecture, once
I pry beneath the semblance,—all that's fit,
170 To practise with,—reach where the fact may lie
Fathom-deep lower. There's the first and last

147| MS:knows? Not I!" §crossed out and replaced above by§ you §quotation marks crossed
out§ *P1884:*knows? Not I!" 147-48| MS:§no ¶§ *P1884:*§¶§ 148| MS:Nor
P1884:"Nor 151| MS:whit as you or *P1884:*whit as thou or 155| MS:use, do you
ask? *P1884:*use, ask of him! 156| MS:ask yours— *P1884:*ask thine—
160| MS:bole *P1884:*bole, 161| MS:for yourself, say you, *P1884:*for thyself, thus seen,
162| MS:Palms are for §last two words crossed out and replaced above by one word§ furnish
163| MS:with, quite §crossed out and replaced above by§ —have 166| MS:pleasures
there or pains me §marked for transposition to§ pleasures me or pains there
167| MS:even you *P1884:*even thou 169| MS:You §crossed out and replaced above by§
I <> fit *P1884:*fit, 170| MS:We §crossed out and replaced above by§
To <> with, to §crossed out and replaced above by§ —reach

Of my philosophy. Blacks blur thy white?
Not mine! The aphis feeds, nor finds his leaf
Untenable because a lance-thrust, nay,
175   Lightning strikes sere a moss-patch close beside,
Where certain other aphids live and love.
Restriction to his single inch of white,
That's law for him, the aphis: but for me,
The man, the larger-souled, beside my stretch
180   Of blacks and whites, I see a world of woe
All round about me: one such burst of black
Intolerable o'er the life I count
White in the main, and, yea—white's faintest trace
Were clean abolished once and evermore.
185   Thus fare my fellows, swallowed up in gloom
So far as I discern: how far is that?
God's care be God's! 'Tis mine—to boast no joy
Unsobered by such sorrows of my kind
As sully with their shade my life that shines."

190   "Reflected possibilities of pain,
Forsooth, just chasten pleasure! Pain itself,—
Fact and not fancy, does not this affect
The general colour?"

           "Here and there a touch
Taught me, betimes, the artifice of things—

172| MS:philosophy. Blacks blot §altered to§ blur your   *P1884:*blur thy
174| MS:Untenable, because   *1889a:* Untenable because   175| MS:struck stiff §crossed out and replaced above by§ sere a moss-tuft §second word of compound crossed out and replaced above by§ patch close beside   *P1884:*strikes <> beside,   176| MS:lived and loved.   *P1884:*live and love.   179| MS:For man   *P1884:*The man   183| MS:and lo, §inserted above§ white §altered to§ white's §word illegibly crossed out§ faintest   *P1884:*and, yea—white's   184| MS:evermore— §dash crossed outr and replaced by period§
185| MS:So §altered to§ Thus <> fellows—swallowed   *P1884:*fellows, swallowed
186| MS:as I see—but §last two words crossed out and replaced above by§ discern:
189| MS:As §added in margin§ Sullying §altered to§ Sully with their §inserted above§ <> my sun of §last two words crossed out§ life <> shines.   *P1884:*sully <> shines."
189-90| MS:§no ¶§   *P1884:*§¶§   190| MS:'Reflected   *P1884:*"Reflected
191| MS:pleasure? Pain   *P1884:* pleasure! Pain   192| MS:fancy, how §crossed out§ does not §inserted above§   193| MS:colour?' Here   *P1884:*colour?" §¶§ "Here

195   That all about, external to myself,
       Was meant to be suspected,—not revealed
       Demonstrably a cheat,—but half seen through,
       Lest white should rule unchecked along the line:
       Therefore white may not triumph. All the same,
200   Of absolute and irretrievable
       And all-subduing black,—black's soul of black
       Beyond white's power to disintensify,—
       Of that I saw no sample: such may wreck
       My life and ruin my philosophy
205   To-morrow, doubtless: hence the constant shade
       Cast on life's shine,—the tremor that intrudes
       When firmest seems my faith in white. Dost ask
       'Who is Ferishtah, hitherto exempt
       From black experience? Why, if God be just,
210   Were sundry fellow-mortals singled out
       To undergo experience for his sake,
       Just that the gift of pain, bestowed on them,
       In him might temper to the due degree
       Joy's else-excessive largess?' Why, indeed!
215   Back are we brought thus to the starting-point—
       Man's impotency, God's omnipotence,
       These stop my answer. Aphis that I am,
       How leave my inch-allotment, pass at will
       Into my fellow's liberty of range,
220   Enter into his sense of black and white,
       As either, seen by me from outside, seems
       Predominatingly the colour? Life,
       Lived by my fellow, shall I pass into

---

[197] MS:Demonstrably the cheat, best §crossed out and replaced above by§ but half seen-
through   *P1884:*Demonstrably a cheat,—but half seen through   *1889a:*through,
[198] MS:should prove §crossed out and replaced above by§ rule   [199] MS:Therefore I
may   *P1884:*Therefore white may   [203] MS:see *P1884:*saw   [205] MS:doubtless,—
hence   *P1884:*doubtless: hence   [207] MS:seems philosophy: §crossed out and replaced
above by four words§ my faith in white. You ask   *P1884:*white. Dost ask
[209] MS:From all man's §last two words crossed out§ black endurance,— §crossed out and
replaced above by§ experience? Why,   [210] MS:singled from §crossed out§ out
[211] MS:To §two words illegibly crossed out and replaced above by one word§ undergo < >
for your §crossed out and replaced above by§ his   [213] MS:In you §crossed out and
replaced above by§ him   [220] MS:white *P1884:*white,

And myself live there? No—no more than pass
225 From Persia, where in sun since birth I bask
Daily, to some ungracious land afar,
Told of by travellers, where the might of snow
Smothers up day, and fluids lose themselves
Frozen to marble. How I bear the sun,
230 Beat though he may unduly, that I know:
How blood once curdled ever creeps again,
Baffles conjecture: yet since people live
Somehow, resist a clime would conquer me,
Somehow provided for their sake must dawn
235 Compensative resource, 'No sun, no grapes,—
Then, no subsistence!'—were it wisely said?
Or this well-reasoned—'Do I dare feel warmth
And please my palate here with Persia's vine,
Though, over-mounts,—to trust the traveller,—
240 Snow, feather thick, is falling while I feast?
What if the cruel winter force his way
Here also?' Son, the wise reply were this:
When cold from over-mounts spikes through and through
Blood, bone and marrow of Ferishtah,—then,
245 Time to look out for shelter—time, at least,
To wring the hands and cry 'No shelter serves!'
Shelter, of some sort, no experienced chill
Warrants that I despair to find."

"No less,
Doctors have differed here; thou say'st thy say;

225| MS:where since birth I bask in sun   *P1884:*where in sun since birth I bask
227| MS:the frosty §crossed out and replaced above by§ might of   228| MS:up sunshine
§crossed out and replaced above by two words§ day, and   233| MS:resist that §crossed
out and replaced above by§ a   234| MS:Somehow must be provided <> sake §marked
for transposition to§ Somehow provided <> sake must be   *P1884:*must seem   *1885:*must
dawn   238| MS:here by §crossed out and replaced above by§ with Persia's palms §crossed
out§ vine,   239| MS:While §crossed out and replaced above by§ Though
241| MS:winter find §crossed out and replaced above by§ force   246| MS:'no   *1889a:*cry
'No   248| MS:despair with §crossed out and replaced above by two words§ to find. 'No
*P1884:*find." §¶§ "No   249| MS:§line added in margin§ here; yesteryear §crossed out
and replaced above by four words§ you say your say;   *P1884:*here; thou say'st thy say;

250 Another man's experience masters thine,
Flat controverted by the sourly-Sage,
The Indian witness who, with faculty
Fine as Ferishtah's, found no white at all
Chequer the world's predominating black,
255 No good oust evil from supremacy,
So that Life's best was that it led to death.
How of his testimony?"

                "Son, suppose
My camel told me: 'Threescore days and ten
I traversed hill and dale, yet never found
260 Food to stop hunger, drink to stay my drouth;
Yet, here I stand alive, which take in proof
That to survive was found impossible!'
'Nay, rather take thou, non-surviving beast'
(Reply were prompt), 'on flank this thwack of staff
265 Nowise affecting flesh that's dead and dry!
Thou wincest? Take correction twice, amend
Next time thy nomenclature! Call white—white!'
The sourly-Sage, for whom life's best was death,
Lived out his seventy years, looked hale, laughed loud,
270 Liked—above all—his dinner,—lied, in short."

    "Lied is a rough phrase: say he fell from truth

250| MS:masters mine §crossed out§ you, *P1884:*masters thine, 251| MS:the sourly-§inserted above§ sagely §altered to§ Sage, sour, §crossed out§ 252| MS:That §altered to§ The 257| MS:testimony?' Son *P1884:*testimony?" §¶§ "Son 259| MS:never ate §crossed out§ found 260| MS:to appease me §last two words crossed out and replaced above by two words§ stop hunger 261| MS:And §crossed out and replaced above by§ Lo, here *P1884:*Yet, here 262| MS:Survival §crossed out and replaced above by three words§ That living thusly §last four words crossed out§ That to survive §last three words inserted above§ was found §inserted below§ impossibility!' §altered to§ impossible!' 263| MS:beast, *P1884:*beast,' *1889a:*beast' 264| MS:prompt) 'this thwack of staff on flank §marked for transposition to§ prompt) 'on flank this thwack of staff *1889a:*prompt), 'on 267| MS:white—white!" *P1884:*white—white!' 268| MS:sourly-Sage for < > best is §crossed out and replaced above by§ was death *1885:*sourly-Sage, for < > death, 269| MS:out the seventy *P1884:*out his seventy 270| MS:—Above all—liked §altered to§ Liked §marked for transposition to§ —Liked—above all—his < > short. *P1884:*short." 271| MS:is thy §crossed out and replaced above by§ a < > phrase,—say *P1884:*phrase: say

In climbing towards it!—sure less faulty so
Than had he sat him down and stayed content
With thy safe orthodoxy, 'White, all white,
275   White everywhere for certain I should see
Did I but understand how white is black,
As clearer sense than mine would.' Clearer sense,—
Whose may that be? Mere human eyes I boast,
And such distinguish colours in the main,
280   However any tongue, that's human too,
Please to report the matter. Dost thou blame
A soul that strives but to see plain, speak true,
Truth at all hazards? Oh, this false for real,
This emptiness which feigns solidity,—
285   Ever some grey that's white, and dun that's black,—
When shall we rest upon the thing itself
Not on its semblance?—Soul—too weak, forsooth,
To cope with fact—wants fiction everywhere!
Mine tires of falsehood: truth at any cost!"

290   "Take one and try conclusions—this, suppose!
God is all-good, all-wise, all-powerful: truth?
Take it and rest there. What is man? Not God:
None of these absolutes therefore,—yet himself,
A creature with a creature's qualities.
295   Make them agree, these two conceptions! Each
Abolishes the other. Is man weak,
Foolish and bad? He must be Ahriman,

272| MS:it,—sure   *P1884:* it!—sure   274| MS:orthodoxy 'White, all   *1889a:* orthodoxy, 'White, all   275| MS:everywhere be certain   *1885:*everywhere for certain
276| MS:understand that §crossed out and replaced above by three words§ how white is black, §two words illegibly crossed out and replaced above by§ white §crossed out§
277| MS:would.' §¶ called for in margin, then cancelled§ Clearer
279| MS:colours well as you, §last three words crossed out and replaced above by three words§ in the main,   280| MS:However §word, possibly *straining,* crossed out and replaced above by§ any   282| MS:speak truth,   *P1884:*speak true,
284| MS:emptiness that §crossed out and replaced above by§ which
285| MS:Ever this §crossed out and replaced above by§ some grey from §crossed out and replaced above by§ that's < > dun from §crossed out and replaced above by§ that's
288| MS:fact sees §crossed out and replaced above by§ wants   297| MS:and evil §crossed out and replaced above by§ bad? He is §crossed out and replaced above by two words§ must be

206

Co-equal with an Ormuzd, Bad with Good,
Or else a thing made at the Prime Sole Will,
300 Doing a maker's pleasure—with results
Which—call, the wide world over, 'what must be'—
But, from man's point of view, and only point
Possible to his powers, call—evidence
Of goodness, wisdom, strength—we mock ourselves
305 In all that's best of us,—man's blind but sure
Craving for these in very deed not word,
Reality and not illusion. Well,—
Since these nowhere exist—nor there where cause
Must have effect, nor here where craving means
310 Craving unfollowed by fit consequence
And full supply, aye sought for, never found—
These—what are they but man's own rule of right?
A scheme of goodness recognized by man,
Although by man unrealizable,—
315 Not God's with whom to will were to perform:
Nowise performed here, therefore never willed.
What follows but that God, who could the best,
Has willed the worst,—while man, with power to match
Will with performance, were deservedly
320 Hailed the supreme—provided . . . here's the touch

298| MS:§line added in margin§ with the Maker, Bad <> Good   *P1884:*with an Ormuzd, Bad
<> Good,   299| MS:else the §crossed out and replaced above by§ a <> the maker's will,
*P1884:*the Prime Sole Will,   300| MS:Doing the master's pleasure   *P1884:*Doing a
maker's   301| MS:Which we §crossed out and replaced above by dash§
302| MS:view, the only   *P1884:*view, and only   304| MS:strength—you mock yourself
*P1884:*strength—we mock ourselves   *1889a:*strength? we §emended to§ strength—we §see
Editorial Notes§   308| MS:Since they §crossed out and replaced above by§ these no-
where   *P1884:*nowhere   311| MS:supply, still §crossed out and replaced above by§ aye
312| MS:This §altered to§ These—what is it §last two words crossed out and replaced above by
two words§ are they but man's §word illegibly crossed out and replaced above by§ own <>
Right?   *P1884:*right?   313| MS:§line added between present ll. 312 and 314§ A scheme
§added in margin§ §two words, possibly *An image,* crossed out§ of   314| MS:By man the
weak §last two words crossed out and replaced below by one word§ Although §marked for
transposition to§ Although by man unrealizable,   *P1884:*unrealizable,—
315| MS:will is §crossed out and replaced above by§ were   317| MS:follows then §crossed
out§ but <> Best,   *P1884:*best,   318| MS:Has willed §last two words crossed out and
replaced above by one word§ Wants §crossed out; *Has willed* marked for retention§
320| MS:God the <> provided . . here's   *P1884:*Hailed the <> provided . . . here's

That breaks the bubble . . . this concept of man's
Were man's own work, his birth of heart and brain,
His native grace, no alien gift at all.
The bubble breaks here. Will of man create?
325   No more than this my hand which strewed the beans
Produced them also from its finger-tips.
Back goes creation to its source, source prime
And ultimate, the single and the sole."

"How reconcile discordancy,—unite
330   Notion and notion—God that only can
Yet does not,—man that would indeed
But just as surely cannot,—both in one?
What help occurs to thy intelligence?"

"Ah, the beans,—or,—example better yet,—
335   A carpet-web I saw once leave the loom
And lie at gorgeous length in Ispahan!
The weaver plied his work with lengths of silk
Dyed each to match some jewel as it might,
And wove them, this by that. 'How comes it, friend,'—
340   (Quoth I)—'that while, apart, this fiery hue,
That watery dimness, either shocks the eye,
So blinding bright, or else offends again
By dulness,—yet the two, set each by each,
Somehow produce a colour born of both,

321| MS:bubble . . this *P1884:*bubble . . . this   322| MS:Was §altered to§ Were < > own §word illegibly crossed out and replaced above by§ work, his §inserted above§ birth of his §crossed out§ heart   323| MS:all: *P1884:*all.   325| MS:§word illegibly crossed out§ no §altered to§ No   326| MS:also §inserted above§ §word above illegibly crossed out§   327| MS:source, the §crossed out and replaced above by§ source
328| MS:The §crossed out and replaced above by§ And < > the only §crossed out and replaced above by§ single < > sole: *P1884:*sole. *1885:*sole."
328-29| MS:§no ¶ *1885:*§¶§   329| MS:How *1885:*"How   332| MS:surely does §crossed out and replaced above by§ can   333| MS:to our intelligence? *1885:*to thy intelligence?"   333-34| MS:§no ¶§ *P1884:*§¶§   334| MS:Ah, the beans,—only §crossed out and replaced above by two words§ or,—example better yet,— §inserted above§ §words illegibly crossed out§ *1885:*"Ah   336| MS:in Ispahan: *1885:*in Ispahan!
342| MS:As §altered to§ So   343| MS:Pathetically §crossed out and replaced above by§ By blank §altered to§ blankness,—yet §inserted above§ *P1884:*By dulness,—yet

345   A medium profitable to the sight?'
      'Such medium is the end whereat I aim,'—
      Answered my craftsman: 'there's no single tinct
      Would satisfy the eye's desire to taste
      The secret of the diamond: join extremes,
350   Results a serviceable medium-ghost,
      The diamond's simulation. Even so
      I needs must blend the quality of man
      With quality of God, and so assist
      Mere human sight to understand my Life,
355   What is, what should be,—understand thereby
      Wherefore I hate the first and love the last,—
      Understand why things so present themselves
      To me, placed here to prove I understand.
      Thus, from beginning runs the chain to end,
360   And binds me plain enough. By consequence,
      I bade thee tolerate,—not kick and cuff
      The man who held that natures did in fact
      Blend so, since so thyself must have them blend
      In fancy, if it take a flight so far."

365   "A power, confessed past knowledge, nay, past thought,
      —Thus thought thus known!"

                "To know of, think about—
      Is all man's sum of faculty effects
      When exercised on earth's least atom, Son!
      What was, what is, what may such atom be?
370   No answer! Still, what seems it to man's sense?
      An atom with some certain properties
      Known about, thought of as occasion needs,
      —Man's—but occasions of the universe?

346] MS:'That medium   *P1884:*'Such medium   347] MS:Answered the §crossed out and replaced above by§ my craftsman: 'There's   *P1884:*there's   354] MS:My human <> understand the world,   *P1884:*Mere human <> understand my Life,   359] MS:So §altered to§ Thus   363] MS:must let §crossed out and replaced above by§ have 364] MS:far.   *P1884:*far."   365-478] MS:§entire section inserted into MS; see Editorial Notes§   366] MS:thought and known!"   *1885:*thought thus known!" 369] MS:is; what   *P1884:*is, what   370] MS:How answer? Still   *P1884:*No answer! Still

Unthinkable, unknowable to man.
375 Yet, since to think and know fire through and through
Exceeds man, is the warmth of fire unknown,
Its uses—are they so unthinkable?
Pass from such obvious power to powers unseen,
Undreamed of save in their sure consequence:
380 Take that, we spoke of late, which draws to ground
The staff my hand lets fall: it draws, at least—
Thus much man thinks and knows, if nothing more."

"Ay, but man puts no mind into such power!
He neither thanks it, when an apple drops,
385 Nor prays it spare his pate while underneath.
Does he thank Summer though it plumped the rind?
Why thank the other force—whate'er its name—
Which gave him teeth to bite and tongue to taste
And throat to let the pulp pass? Force and force,
390 No end of forces! Have they mind like man?"

"Suppose thou visit our lord Shalim-Shah,
Bringing thy tribute as appointed. 'Here
Come I to pay my due!' Whereat one slave
Obsequious spreads a carpet for thy foot,
395 His fellow offers sweetmeats, while a third
Prepares a pipe: what thanks or praise have they?
Such as befit prompt service. Gratitude
Goes past them to the Shah whose gracious nod
Set all the sweet civility at work;
400 But for his ordinance, I much suspect,
My scholar had been left to cool his heels
Uncarpeted, or warm them—likelier still—
With bastinado for intrusion. Slaves
Needs must obey their master: 'force and force,
405 No end of forces,' act as bids some force
Supreme o'er all and each: where find that one?

376| MS:Exceeds him, is *P1884:*Exceeds man, is   379| MS:their plain consequence:
*P1884:*their sure consequence: 383| MS:power: *P1884:*power!
402| MS:liker *P1884:*liklier

How recognize him? Simply as thou didst
The Shah—by reasoning 'Since I feel a debt,
Behoves me pay the same to one aware
410 I have my duty, he his privilege.'
Didst thou expect the slave who charged thy pipe
Would serve as well to take thy tribute-bag
And save thee further trouble?"

       "Be it so!
The sense within me that I owe a debt
415 Assures me—somewhere must be somebody
Ready to take his due. All comes to this—
Where due is, there acceptance follows: find
Him who accepts the due! and why look far?
Behold thy kindred compass thee about!
420 Ere thou wast born and after thou shalt die,
Heroic man stands forth as Shahan-Shah.
Rustem and Gew, Gudarz and all the rest,
How come they short of lordship that's to seek?
Dead worthies! but men live undoubtedly
425 Gifted as Sindokht, sage Sulayman's match,
Valiant like Kawah: ay, and while earth lasts
Such heroes shall abound there—all for thee
Who profitest by all the present, past,
And future operation of thy race.
430 Why, then, o'erburdened with a debt of thanks,
Look wistful for some hand from out the clouds
To take it, when, all round, a multitude
Would ease thee in a trice?"

      "Such tendered thanks

413| MS:farther *1889a:*further   421| MS:as Shalim-Shah. *1885a:*as Shahan-Shah.
422| MS:rest *P1884:*rest,   423| MS:Where come <> seek? *P1884:*How come
*1889a:*seek §emended to§ seek? §see Editorial Notes§   424| MS:worthies! But
*P1884:*but   425| MS:sage Sulayman's peer, *P1884:* sage Sulayman's match,
427| MS:shall perform there *P1884:*shall abound there   430| MS:Why then
*P1884:*Why, then   432| MS:To help thee, when *P1884:*To take it, when
433| MS:§¶§ "Such load of thanks *P1884:*§¶§ "Such tendered thanks

Would tumble back to who craved riddance, Son!
435 —Who but my sorry self? See! stars are out—
Stars which, unconscious of thy gaze beneath,
Go glorifying, and glorify thee too
—Those Seven Thrones, Zurah's beauty, weird Parwin!
Whether shall love and praise to stars be paid
440 Or—say—some Mubid who, for good to thee
Blind at thy birth, by magic all his own
Opened thine eyes, and gave the sightless sight,
Let the stars' glory enter? Say his charm
Worked while thyself lay sleeping: as he went
445 Thou wakedst: 'What a novel sense have I!
Whom shall I love and praise?' 'The stars, each orb
Thou standest rapt beneath,' proposes one:
'Do not they live their life, and please themselves,
And so please thee? What more is requisite?'
450 Make thou this answer: 'If indeed no mage
Opened my eyes and worked a miracle,
Then let the stars thank me who apprehend
That such an one is white, such other blue!
But for my apprehension both were blank.
455 Cannot I close my eyes and bid my brain
Make whites and blues, conceive without stars' help,
New qualities of colour? were my sight
Lost or misleading, would yon red—I judge
A ruby's benefaction—stand for aught
460 But green from vulgar glass? Myself appraise
Lustre and lustre; should I overlook
Fomalhaut and declare some fen-fire king,
Who shall correct me, lend me eyes he trusts
No more than I trust mine? My mage for me!

436| MS:Stars, all §crossed out and replaced above by§ which unconscious   *P1884*:Stars
which, unconscious   437| MS:Go glorying, and   *1889a*:Go glorifying, and
438| MS:—The §altered to§ —Those   440| MS:who, discovering §crossed out and
replaced above by three words§ for good to   442| MS:the §words illegibly crossed out
and replaced above by two words§ sightless sight,   443| MS:enter? Say, his
P1884:enter? Say his   444| MS:while thou layedst   *1889a*:while thyself lay
453| MS:blue: *P1884*:blue!   456| MS:conceive, without   *P1884*:conceive without
459| MS:benefaction—pass §crossed out and replaced above by§ stand
461| MS:and lustre: should   *P1884*: and lustre; should

465 I never saw him: if he never was,
     I am the arbitrator!' No, my Son!
     Let us sink down to thy similitude:
     I eat my apple, relish what is ripe—
     The sunny side, admire its rarity
470 Since half the tribe is wrinkled, and the rest
     Hide commonly a maggot in the core,—
     And down Zerdusht goes with due smack of lips:
     But—thank an apple? He who made my mouth
     To masticate, my palate to approve,
475 My maw to further the concoction—Him
     I thank,—but for whose work, the orchard's wealth
     Might prove so many gall-nuts—stocks or stones
     For aught that I should think, or know, or care."

     Why from the world," Ferishtah smiled, "should thanks
480   Go to this work of mine? If worthy praise,
     Praised let it be and welcome: as verse ranks,
           So rate my verse: if good therein outweighs
           Aught faulty judged, judge justly! Justice says:
     Be just to fact, or blaming or approving:
485 But—generous? No, nor loving!

     "Loving! what claim to love has work of mine?
           Concede my life were emptied of its gains
     To furnish forth and fill work's strict confine,
           Who works so for the world's sake—he complains
490   With cause when hate, not love, rewards his pains.
     I looked beyond the world for truth and beauty:
     Sought, found and did my duty."

469| MS:sunny half §crossed out and replaced above by§ side   475| MS:concoction—him §altered to§ Him   478| MS:think or know or   *P1884:*think, or know, or
478-79| MS: §rule§   *P1884:* §no rule; emended to restore rule; see Editorial Notes§
479| MS:world" Ferishtah smiled "should   *1889a:* world," Ferishtah smiled, "should
481| MS:ranks   *P1884:*ranks,   483| MS:MS:faulty found §crossed out and replaced above by§ judged   484| MS:approving,   *P1884:*approving: 486| MS:Loving < > has verse §crossed out and replaced above by§ work   *P1884:*"Loving   487| MS:were stript §crossed out and replaced above by§ emptied of all its   *P1884:*of its
490| MS:hate—not love—rewards   *P1884:*hate, not love, rewards   491| MS:for Truth and Beauty,   *P1884:*truth and beauty: 492| MS:duty.   *P1884:*duty."

EPILOGUE

Oh, Love—no, Love! All the noise below, Love,
    Groanings all and moanings—none of Life I lose!
All of Life's a cry just of weariness and woe, Love—
    "Hear at least, thou happy one!" How can I, Love, but choose?

5   Only, when I do hear, sudden circle round me
        —Much as when the moon's might frees a space from cloud—
Iridescent splendours: gloom—would else confound me—
        Barriered off and banished far—bright-edged the blackest shroud!

Thronging through the cloud-rift, whose are they, the faces
10   Faint revealed yet sure divined, the famous ones of old?
"What"—they smile—"our names, our deeds so soon erases
        Time upon his tablet where Life's glory lies enrolled?

"Was it for mere fool's-play, make-believe and mumming,
        So we battled it like men, not boylike sulked or whined?
15   Each of us heard clang God's 'Come!' and each was coming:
        Soldiers all, to forward-face, not sneaks to lag behind!

"How of the field's fortune? That concerned our Leader!
        Led, we struck our stroke nor cared for doings left and right:
Each as on his sole head, failer or succeeder,
20   Lay the blame or lit the praise: no care for cowards: fight!"

Then the cloud-rift broadens, spanning earth that's under
        Wide our world displays its worth, man's strife and strife's success:
All the good and beauty, wonder crowning wonder,
        Till my heart and soul applaud perfection, nothing less.

25   Only, at heart's utmost joy and triumph, terror
        Sudden turns the blood to ice: a chill wind disencharms

---

EPILOGUE   13| MS:it then §crossed out§ for mere §inserted above§
17| MS:our Leader;   *P1884:*our Leader!

All the late enchantment! What if all be error—
    If the halo irised round my head were, Love, thine arms?

Palazzo Giustinian-Recanati, Venice:
December 1, 1883.

27| MS:All §word, possibly *warm,* crossed out and replaced above by the   28| MS:§ends
with date§ Venice, Dec. 1 '83.   *P1884:*Palazzo Giustinian-Recanati, Venice: / December 1, 1883.

DRAMATIC IDYLS, SECOND SERIES

Emendations to the Text

The following emendations have been made to the 1889a copy-text:

Clive, l. 127: In the proofs and the 1880 edition, this line begins with a single quotation mark. The quotation mark is missing in the copy-text, though space was left for it. The P1880-1880 punctuation has been restored.

Clive, l. 161: Only in the copy-text is the exclamation mark at the end of the line omitted. The exclamation mark has been restored.

Clive, l. 162: In the copy-text, the hyphen between the words *Rogue's* and *March* is missing; the MS-1880 reading is restored.

Clive, l. 195: The apostrophe in *Lordship's* is missing in 1889a, though space for it remains. The correct MS-1880 reading is restored.

Pietro of Abano, l. 14: Only in the copy-text is there a comma, instead of a semicolon, after the word *question*. The semicolon in MS-1880 has been restored.

Pietro of Abano, l. 264: MS-1880 correctly read *wields*; 1889a reads *wield* with an extra space where the *s* should be. The MS-1880 reading is restored.

Pietro of Abano, l. 363: In the copy-text, the necessary single quotation mark at the beginning of the line is missing, though space for it remains. The MS-1880 quotation mark has been restored. Interestingly, this correction was made in later impressions of 1889, though at whose direction is unknown.

Pietro of Abano, l. 407: MS-1880 end this line with an exclamation mark; there is no punctuation in the copy-text. The exclamation mark is restored.

Composition

B's volume of six narrative poems, *Dramatic Idyls*, published in 1879, was such a popular and critical success that B was encouraged to write six more idyls. *Dramatic Idyls, Second Series*, published in 1880, was reasonably successful, but it was not so popular as his first effort, now retitled *Dramatic Idyls, First Series*, and no second edition was published.

All of the idyls in the second series were written in 1880, and in his manuscript B gives the date of composition for all six poems. In order of completion the dates are as follows: "Pietro of Abano," 20 January; "Echetlos," 2 February; "Muléykeh," 22 February; "Clive," 27 February; "Doctor —," 10 March; and "Pan and Luna," 9 April. These dates indicate that B wrote with remarkable speed. As with the manuscript of his first six dramatic idyls, his manuscript for the second series is clean and lightly corrected. Most of the changes are minor alterations of wording and punctuation, and have the appearence of subsequent revisions, not substitutions during composition. The typical alteration involves crossing out the original passage and substituting the preferred reading above the line. Because of the speed with which the poems were composed and the relative scarcity of revisions, one may conclude that B wrote these idyls with almost unerring facility. The changes that he made on the proofs are also infrequent and, by and large, insignificant. He made final and equally inconsequential revisions for the collected works of 1889.

B gives his definition of the word *idyl* in a letter to Wilfred Meynell, published in an article in A*thenaeum*, in which he refers to poems in his first series: "An idyl, as you know, is a succinct little story complete in itself; not necessarily concerning pastoral matters, by any means, though from the prevalency of such topics in the Idyls of Theocritus, such is the general notion. These of mine are called 'Dramatic' because the story is told by some actor in it, not by the poet himself" (Wilfred Meynell, "The 'Detachment' of Browning," *Athenaeum* [4 January 1890], 18). In his study of B's later poetry, Clyde de L. Ryals remarks that "the poet did not accurately describe what he had accomplished" (*Browning's Later Poetry, 1871-1889* [Ithaca, NY, 1975], 168) since most of the idyls in the first series are told by narrators who are not actors in the poems. The objection is equally relevant to the six idyls in the second series. Only one of these poems, "Clive," is told, throughout, by a character in the narrative.

"Clive" is a poem of which B was especially proud. In a letter to Edmund Gosse of 15 March 1885, he selected it as one of his poems he would "not object to be judged by" (Hood, 235-36). In this letter, he writes that "Clive" is idyllic "in the Greek sense." Because the poem is obviously not Greek in the sense that it is pastoral, the sense in which he believed it to be Greek is unclear. One must conclude that he defined the word *idyl* very loosely; it appears that, in his mind, to qualify as an idyl, Greek or otherwise, a narrative poem must have only the characteristics of succinctness and completeness. (For further discussion of B's title, see *Dramatic Idyls, First Series, Composition.*)

Text and Publication

The manuscript of *Dramatic Idyls, Second Series* (*Reconstruction,* E94) is in the library of Balliol College, Oxford. It is bound in brown morocco together with the manuscripts of *Dramatic Idyls* and *Jocoseria*: on the front cover, stamped in gold, is Browning's family coat of arms.

The eight poems of *Dramatic Idyls, Second Series* were written on lined 8" by 20" paper, which B folded into folios. He numbered the folios of each poem separately, and the compositors renumbered the leaves (excepting the title page and the contents page) 1 through 52. The half-titles in the printed editions are not in the MS; titles appear at the top of the page, above the first line of each narrative poem. At the end of each, B indicates a date of composition, and supplies his characteristic abbreviation "L.D.I.E."—*Laus Deo in excelsis* ("Praise God in the highest").

On the title page in the poet's hand are the words "Dramatic Idyls. / (second series) / by Robert Browning. / (print in all respects like the first series published last year)." Centered on the second leaf of the manuscript is "Contents," followed by the titles of the six narrative poems in the second series. Following the list of titles is his direction to the printers: "In somewhat smaller type than the poems which follow—", and beneath this is the text of the introductory lyric "You are sick." The same instruction to the printer occurs at the top of the leaf bearing the epilogue, "Touch him ne'er so lightly." The names of compositors and other printers' marks appear throughout the MS, which B sent in for typesetting on 20 April 1880 (Hood, 190).

A set of author's proofs (*Reconstruction,* E95; identified as P1880 in our variant lists) of the first edition of *Dramatic Idyls, Second Series* survived and is owned by Texas Christian University in Fort Worth, Texas. On these sheets the poet made a few alterations and additions (CP1880 in the variants). The first edition of *Dramatic Idyls, Second Series* was published by Smith, Elder, and Co. on 15 June 1880 in a volume of 147 numbered pages, bound in brown cloth boards. It sold for five shillings. (For a full bibliographical description of the edition see Broughton, A111.) The poet made further corrections for the collected edition of 1888-89, where *Dramatic Idyls, Second Series* appears in the fifteenth volume, pages 81-164.

Reception

B's sequel to *Dramatic Idyls, First Series* was not, by and large, enthusiastically greeted; even some of his staunchest supporters make unkind remarks about it. Mrs. Sutherland Orr, who speaks highly of the first idyls, believes that "the new inspiration slowly subsided through the second series of *Idyls*, 1880, and *Jocoseria*, 1883" (Orr, *Life*, 324). De-Vane agrees that it is probably just "to say with Mrs. Orr that the second group of *Dramatic Idyls* shows the slow subsidence of the inspiration which make the first series a new and striking volume" (*Hbk.*, 445).

Contemporary reviews voiced familiar complaints which over the course of B's career became standard. An anonymous reviewer for the *Times* (23 August 1880) remarked: "His lines are commonly, as formerly, broken-backed. No better test of an instinct for rhythm could be proposed to a lad aspiring after the vocation of a poet than to set him the task of reading aloud, for instance, 'Pietro of Abano', so as to keep the flow of a tune" (Litzinger and Smalley, 465). An unsigned review for *The British Quarterly* (1 July 1880) reads as follows: "Mr. Browning, as everyone knows, is not seldom abstruse; more concerned to make manifest the hidden and recondite and unexpected relations of his subject than to deal with the more general and apparent aspects of it" (Broughton, C567). *The Pall Mall Gazette* paid an ambiguous compliment in finding his second series superior to the first inasmuch as "none of the poems in the present volume is founded upon the psychology of crime and bloodshed, a morbid fondness for which has, not without reason, been brought as a reproach against their author" (Broughton, C586.1).

In *An Introduction to the Study of Browning*, an early attempt at assessing B's achievement, Arthur Symonds repeats the criticism that B's second attempt is inferior to the first: "The volume differs considerably from its precursor, and it contains nothing quite equal to the best of the earlier poems. There is more variety, perhaps, but the human interest is less intense, the stories less moving and absorbing" ([London, 1886], 188). Even into the twentieth century a notion of "subsidence" and inferiority persisted. J. M. Cohen, for example, found little to admire in the two series of idylls and in *Jocoseria*: "The contents of these three books are on a lower level of inspiration than any other group of Browning's poems. Each one of these dozen and a half stories in verse is marred by the Browning mannerisms, and not one of them is brought to life by any urgency in its telling" (*Robert Browning* [London, 1952], 156).

And yet from the beginning some readers expressed admiration for *Dramatic Idyls, Second Series.* The anonymous reviewer for *Scribner's Monthly* (November 1880) held that "Mr. Browning appeals much more strongly in his second volume of Dramatic Idyls than in his first to the sympathy of lovers of poetry" (Broughton, C590), and G. K. Chesterton offered the most extravagant praise that either book of idylls has received:

> Another collection followed in 1879, the first series of *Dramatic Idyls*, which contain such masterpieces as "Pheidippides" and "Iván Ivánovitch." Upon its heels, in 1880, came the second series of *Dramatic Idyls*, including "Muléykeh" and "Clive," possibly the two best stories in poetry, told in the best manner of storytelling. Then only did the marvelous fountain begin to slacken in quantity, but never in quality.
>
> (*Robert Browning* [New York, 1903], 127)

More recently, Clyde de L. Ryals, in his reading of B's later works, quotes DeVane's criticism and disagrees with it: "Although commentators have found the second series of idyls inferior to the first, I personally see no evidence of 'the slow subsidence of the inspiration which made the first series a new and striking volume'" (Ryals, op. cit., 174).

"YOU ARE SICK"

Text]   In the MS, this short poem appears under the "Contents" for *Dramatic Idyls, Second Series* where it is undated. DeVane remarks that it "serves as a prologue" in reminding the reader that idylls which follow will concern "what Browning believes to be the proper province of poetry—man's soul" (*Hbk.*, 446).

ECHETLOS

Sources]   For *Dramatic Idyls, First Series* B wrote "Pheidippides," a poem about a famous Greek hero who played a crucial role in the battle of

Marathon. One of his sources for this poem was Pausanius' *Description of Greece*, and probably it was while he was working on "Pheidippides" that B discovered in Pausanius the following passage concerning another, more obscure hero, Echetlos:

> The Marathonians worship both those who died in the fighting, calling them heroes, and secondly Marathon, from whom the parish derives its name, and then, Heracles, saying that they were the first among the Greeks to acknowledge him as a god. They say too that there chanced to be present in the battle a man of rustic appearance and dress. Having slaughtered many of the foreigners with a plough he was seen no more after the engagement. When the Athenians made enquiries at the oracle the god merely ordered them to honour Echetlaeus (*He of the Plough-tail*) as a hero. A trophy too of white marble has been erected.
>
> (*Description of Greece*, tr. W. H. S. Jones [London, 1931], 1.32.4).

Earlier in his book Pausanius describes a portico in Athens with several wall-paintings, one of which depicts the battle of Marathon along with pictures of Callimachus and Miltiadés and "a hero called Echetlus, of whom I shall make mention later" (1.15.4). From these two scant references in Pausanius, B has fleshed out his portrait of the "unknown soldier" of Marathon.

At the battle of Marathon (490 B.C.) the Greeks defeated the numerically superior Persian invaders on a plain northeast of Athens. Not only the poet but his wife, in her childhood, had written about this famous battle. At the age of fourteen Elizabeth had penned a precocious four-book epic *The Battle of Marathon*. B relied upon Herodotus for general information about the conflict's vicissitudes, as in this extract:

> The two armies fought together on the plain of Marathon for a length of time; and in the mid battle, where the Persians themselves and the Sacæ had their place, the barbarians were victorious, and broke and pursued the Greeks into the inner country; but on the two wings the Athenians and the Platæans defeated the enemy. Having done so, they suffered the routed barbarians to fly at their ease, and joining the two wings in one, fell upon those who had broken their own centre, and fought and conquered them.
>
> (*History of Herodotus*, 3rd ed., tr. George Rawlinson [London, 1875], 6.113).

Though citing several warriors from both sides, Herodotus says nothing of the anonymous, shadowy hero who assists the Greeks and disappears afterwards. For a description of the conflict and other details in the idyl, B obviously drew on Herodotus; yet that writer hardly helped him with Themistocles (see l. 29) and certainly not with the latter's experience after the battle of Salamis; hence the poet turned to what was for him the more familiar source of Plutarch's *The Lives of Noble Grecians and Romans*, at least for data about Themistocles. Even so, he gave remarkably free rein to his imagination.

2]   *Barbarians*   The Greeks considered anyone not a Greek to be a barbarian.

10]   *helmed*   Protected by head armor.

11]   *clown's*   Pertaining to a peasant.

13]   *weak mid-line*   See Herodotus's description of the battle in *Sources* above.

    tunnies   Tuna.

15]   *Kallimachos Polemarch*   A polemarch was a Greek civil officer who was also given military authority. Herodotus relates that five of the ten generals were in favor of fighting the Persians, and five wished to avoid conflict. Callimachus, the polemarch, cast the eleventh, deciding vote in favor of battle (6.109). The information that Callimachus was put in charge of the Greek's right wing and that he died in the skirmish is given by Herodotus (6.111 and 114).

18]   *Sakian*   The Sacæ were a Scythian tribe who fought with the Persians.

    Mede   In the sixth century B.C. the Medes were conquered by the Persians under Cyrus the Great. Media, the land of the Medes, became a province of the Persian empire.

21]   *blood-plashed*   Blood-splashed.

22]   *thonged*   Equipped with a strip of hide.

23]   *share*   Plowshare.

25]   *Oracle*   At Delphi in Greece an oracle, a priestess of Apollo, answered questions put to her by those in search of truth. Her answers, though often ambiguous, were presumably infallible.

27]   *Holder of the Plowshare*   B's translation of the Greek word *Echetlos*.

28-9]   *Míltiadés . . . Paros*   Herodotus relates that Miltiadés, a Greek general who fought at Marathon, later led an unsuccessful expedition against the island of Paros, where he sustained a serious injury to his thigh. Upon returning home, he was brought to trial on the charge of "having dealt deceitfully with the Athenians." He avoided a sentence of death, but was fined fifty talents. "Soon afterwards his thigh completely gangrened and mortified: and so Míltiadés died; and the fifty talents were paid by his son Cimon" (6.132-36).

29-30]   *Themistokles*   The Athenian military leader who was responsible for the decisive naval victory of the Greeks over the Persians at the battle of Salamis (480 B.C.). Later, having been banished from Athens, he ingratiated himself with his erstwhile enemy, Xerxes, the Persian monarch, and lived in Persia.

30]   *Satrap*   Persian provincial governor.

   Sardis   The capital city of Lydia, part of the Persian empire in the fifth century B.C.

CLIVE

Sources]   An account of the card game that led to the duel recounted in "Clive" appears in two printed sources which B consulted. The first is Sir John Malcom's *The Life of Robert, Lord Clive* ([London, 1836], 1.46-7):

> Soon after his arrival at this place [Fort St. David], he was engaged in a duel with an officer, to whom he had lost some money at cards, but who, with his companion, was clearly proved to have played unfairly. Clive was not the only loser; but the others were terrified into payment by the threats of those who had won their money. This example had no effect on him; he persisted in refusing to pay, and was called out by one of them who deemed himself insulted by his conduct. They met without seconds: Clive fired, and missed his antagonist, who immediately came close up to him, and held the pistol to his head, desiring him to ask his life, with which he complied. The next demand was, to recant his assertions respecting unfair play. On compliance with this being refused, his opponent threatened to shoot him. 'Fire, and be d—d,' said the dauntless young man; 'I said you cheated; I say so still, and I will never pay you.' The astonished officer threw away his pistol, saying, Clive was mad. The latter received from young companions many compliments for the spirit he had shown; but he not only declined coming forward against the officer with whom he had fought, but never afterwards spoke of his behaviour at the card-table. 'He has given me life,' he said, 'though I am resolved on never paying money which was unfairly won, or again associating with him, I shall never do him an injury.'

In his review of Malcom's book for the *Edinburgh Review*, Thomas Macaulay mentions the incident in a cursory fashion: "His personal courage, of which he had, while still a writer, given signal proof by a desperate duel with a military bully who was the terror of Fort St. David, speedily made him conspicuous even among hundreds of brave men" ("Lord Clive," *Macaulay's Prose and Poetry* [Cambridge, Mass., 1967], 312).

B knew Malcom's and Macaulay's remarks, but relied on a much fuller account he had heard in Paris years before the poem was composed. He explains his first encounter with the story in a letter to Tennyson of 7 August 1880 (see Thomas J. Collins, "The Sources of Browning's 'Clive': New Evidence," *Browning Newsletter* 3 [1969], 6-7):

> If you look at one of my poems in the present book, I want to make a remark on it—"Clive" is the poem; and some of the reviewers say that my account of the incident which is its subject differs from the same in the version of Sir J. Malcom. So it does—and this is why. More than thirty years ago, as I was traveling in company with Mrs. Jameson in France, she told me the story exactly as I repeat it—having heard Macaulay so tell it a few weeks before at Ld. Lansdowne's. I supposed it would be so told in the Clive essay, which I only read last year—   when I found there was just a reference to "a desperate duel in which Clive proved his courage." On referring to Malcom's Life, I came upon it,—clumsily told, with the inconsistent ending that, while the Officer "threw down his pistol declaring Clive must be mad,"—Clive threatened those present at the encounter in case they mentioned the matter to the Officer's disadvantage—which it would have puzzled them to do. The same author slurs over Clive's suicide in such a fashion that you might count it a natural death. I conjecture, therefore, that Macaulay had authority for saying that the cheat was confessed. All this I set down because when I comment on a fact—a fact I find it and leave it, or what would the comment be worth?

Several errors occur in this letter: the quotations from Macaulay and Malcolm are inaccurate, and, more importantly, Malcom says nothing about Clive's having threatened bystanders, a detail which B added. Still, the letter shows that he believed the oral story, which he heard at second hand, to be more complete and reliable than either of the printed sources, and also that he trusted in its authenticity.

Still another version of his hearing the story from Mrs. Jameson is given in the *Diary: 1872-1885* of B's friend Alfred Domett ([London, 1953], 237-38). Domett's version is on several points at variance with B's own account.

The characters in B's framing narration, Clive's old friend and his son, are fictional.

2] *Clive . . . India* As a young man Robert Clive (1725-74) went to India as a clerk in the British East India Company. His colleagues soon discovered his talents for military strategy and leadership. In various encounters—between British and French forces, as well as British and Indian forces—he met with such astonishing success that the boast he "gave England India" seems hardly an exaggeration. Near the end of his life Clive was investigated by Parliament on various charges of corruption in office, but he was never officially convicted; indeed, Parliament commended him for service to his country. Throughout his life he was a prey to melancholia; a year after his exoneration by Parliament, at the age of forty-nine, he took his own life.

8] *Plassy* At the battle of Plassey (B's spelling is idiosyncratic) in 1757, Clive defeated Surajah Dowlah, a Muslim leader supported by the French, and established British supremacy in India.

10] *thrids* Threads.

12] *forthright* A straight path.

    meander A winding path.

13] *rood* A unit of measurement varying from 6 to 8 yards.

16] *rummer-glass* A large drinking glass.

23] *writing on the wall* From Dan. 5:1-28. After King Belshazzar has drunk from golden vessels plundered from the temple of Jerusalem, a hand appears and writes mysterious words upon a wall. Daniel interprets these words as a portent of the king's doom.

27] *smock-frocked* A smock-frock is a coarse linen garment worn by farm laborers.

31] *Poor as Job and meek as Moses* Proverbial phrases. One of the afflictions with which God tests the faith of Job is loss of his possessions. Presumably Moses' reputation for meekness was earned when, having been ordered by God to be His spokesman, he objects that he is an ineffective speaker. See Exod. 4:10-16.

34] *magnific* "Imposing by vastness or dignity." The *OED* cites this line of B's.

39] *quill-driving* A *quill-driver* is a contemptuous term for a clerk.

40] *Arcot* Clive's successful defense of the town of Arcot against French and Indian attackers (1751) was one of the early exploits that made him internationally famous.

47]   *bee's-wing*   A filmy crust formed on aged port.

50]   *cuirasses*   Covers with a breastplate, a piece of armor which protects the body from neck to waist.

70]   *Alexanders, Cæsars, Marlboroughs*   The Macedonian king Alexander the Great (356-323 B.C.); the Roman emperor Julius Cæsar (100-44 B.C.); and the British general John Churchill, Duke of Marlborough (1650-1722) are all world-renowned military leaders.

70-1]   *Pitt?— / Frederick the Fierce*   The statesman William Pitt (1708-78) was an eloquent defender of Clive. After Clive returned from his second stay in India, Pitt extolled his remarkable exploits in Parliament. Macaulay writes: "Pitt, whose influence in the House of Commons and in the country was unbounded, was eager to mark his regard for one whose exploits had contributed so much to the lustre of that memorable period. The great orator had already in Parliament described Clive as a heaven-born general, as a man who, bred to the labour of the desk, had displayed a military genius which might excite the admiration of the King of Prussia" (Macaulay, op. cit., 348). Frederick the Fierce is Frederick the Great (1712-86), the Prussian king to whom Macaulay refers.

72]   *bore the bell away*   Took first place.

77]   *sleep-stuff*   Opium. Clive took opium. Macaulay writes of him: "During his long residence in tropical climates, he had contracted several painful distempers. In order to obtain ease he called in the help of opium; and he was gradually enslaved by this treacherous ally" (Macaulay, op. cit., 371).

86]   *Ticket*   To characterize, label.

91]   *factor-days*   A *factor* is a clerk.

92]   *St. David's*   A British fort, near the city of Madras.

101]   *Cock o' the Walk*   A person with an inflated sense of his importance.

        Mars   The Roman god of war.

103]   *baize*   A coarse cotton fabric often used as a cover for card tables.

111]   *force a card*   A dealer who forces a card contrives to make his opponent select a card of the dealer's choice, though the opponent thinks that he is picking at random.

112]   *Thyrsis . . . Chloe*   Conventional names for lovers in pastorals.

121]   *Sirrah*   A terms of contempt which implies that the person addressed is of inferior rank.

142]   *clerkling*   A petty clerk.

158]   *sharper*   Cheater.

162]   *Rogue's-March*   A tune played when a soldier is disgraced by being drummed out of the regiment.

184] *Twenty-five* The conversation between Clive and the idyl's narrator takes place a week before Clive's suicide in 1774 (see l. 238). Clive first arrived in India in 1744, and, according to Malcolm, the duel took place shortly after Clive's arrival. Consequently, more than twenty-five years have elapsed between the event and Clive's telling of it.

207] *nick* To take advantage of the opportune moment.

222] *Rent . . . Frenchman's will."* The British, French, and Dutch all had trading companies which paid money to Indian royalty for the right to conduct business. Before Clive completely altered the situation, the French were the most powerful foreign power in India.

229] *Lord Plassy* Clive was given an aristocratic title. For *Plassy*, see line 8.

MULÉYKEH

Source] The story which B tells in this idyl appeared in print in 1847, thirty-three years earlier than the publication of *Dramatic Idyls, Second Series*, in a book by Rollo Springfield entitled *The Horse and His Rider: Sketches and Anecdotes of the Noble Quadruped, and of Equestrian Nations* ([London, 1847], 199-201).

A Bedouin, named Jabal, possessed a mare of great celebrity. Hassad Pacha, then governor of Damascus, wished to buy the animal, and repeatedly made the owner the most liberal offers, which Jabal steadily refused. The pacha then had recourse to threats, but with no better success. At length one Jafar, a Bedouin of another tribe, presented himself to the pacha, and asked what would he give the man who should make him master of Jabal's mare. "I will fill his horse's nosebag with gold," replied Hassad, whose pride and covetousness had been irritated to the highest degree by the obstinacy of the mare's owner. The result of this interview having gone abroad, Jabal became more watchful than ever; and always secured his mare at night with an iron chain, one end of which was fastened round her hind fetlock, whilst the other, after passing through the tent cloth, was attached to a picket driven into the ground under the felt that served himself and his wife for a bed. But one midnight Jafar crept into the tent, and, insinuating his body between Jabal and his wife, he pressed gently now against the one, now against the other, so that the sleepers made room for him right and left, neither of them doubting that the pressure came from the other. This being done, Jafar slit the felt with a sharp knife, drew out the picket, loosed the mare, and sprang on her back. Just before starting off with his prize, he caught up Jabal's lance, and poking him with the butt end, cried out, "I am Jafar! I have stolen your noble mare, and I give you notice in time." This warning, be it observed, was in accordance with the usual practice of the Desert on such occasions: to rob a hostile tribe is considered an honourable exploit, and the man who accomplishes it is desirous of all the glory that may flow from the deed. Poor Jabal, when he heard the words, rushed out of the tent and gave the alarm; then mounting his brother's mare, and accompanied by some of his tribe, he pursued the robber for four hours. The brother's mare was of the same stock as Jabal's, but was not equal to her; nevertheless, she outstripped those of all the other pursuers, and was even on the point of overtaking the robber, when Jabal shouted to him, "Pinch her right ear, and give her a touch with the heel." Jafar did so, and away went the mare like lightning, speedily rendering all further pursuit hopeless. The *pinch in the ear* and the *touch with the heel*, were the secret sign by which Jabal had been used to urge the mare to her utmost speed. Every Bedouin trains the animal he rides, to obey some sign of this kind, to which he has recourse only on urgent occasions, and which he makes a close secret, not to be divulged even to his son. Jabal's comrades were amazed and indignant at his strange conduct; "O thou father of a jackass!" they cried, "thou hast helped the thief to rob thee of thy jewel!" But he silenced their upbraidings, by saying, "I would rather lose her than sully her reputation. Would you have me suffer it to be said among the tribes, that another mare had proved fleeter than mine? I have at least this comfort left me, that I can say she never met with her match."

It is not known that B read Springfield's book, but the two stories are so nearly identical it seems clear that he had access to Springfield's story in some form.

B could neither read nor speak Arabic, and he employed Arabic names largely to lend to his poem an aura of exoticism and authenticity. Like many of his contemporaries, he had a taste for orientalism (see, e.g., *Ferishtah Fancies*), but it is to be wondered if he was always aware of the precise meanings of the terms he employed. The names of places in Arabia which are mentioned in the poem do not exist today under the same name, and the proper names he employs are nowadays, with the exception of Hóseyn, rarely used.

1] *Hóseyn* Arabic: beautiful, handsome, decent. A name sacred to the Shia sect of Islam, it refers to the grandson of the Prophet Muhammad.
2] *salt* "Taken as a type of necessary adjunct to food, and hence as a symbol of hospitality" (*OED*). The implication is that Hóseyn is too poor to entertain guests.
7] *Sinán* Arabic: spearhead. Among the most powerful names for Arab males.
11] *Muléykeh* Arabic: little queen, precious.
12] *Pearl* DeVane's observation that "the name 'Muléykeh' Browning took to be Arabian for 'pearl'" (*Hbk.*, 452) is questionable; *pearl* may just as probably be intended, not as a translation, but as a metaphor for a possession of unusual value.
21] *Duhl the son of Sheybán* Duhl (Arabic: to overwhelm or overpower) Ben Sheyban is the name of a warrior who led his tribe against the Persians.
32] *Múzennem* Arabic: marked, spotted. A term used to describe fine camels and horses, B uses it as a generic noun for well-bred horses.
61] *Holy House* The holy temple on Temple Mount in Jerusalem. When Muhammad resided in Medina, a city with a substantial Jewish population, he adopted the custom of facing the Temple Mount during prayer. Later, c. 624 A.D, he directed his followers to pray toward Mecca.
68] *headstall* Part of a bridle.
71] *Buhéyseh* Arabic: date, the fruit of palm trees. Mainly used as a female name.
87] *Ed-Dárraj* Arabic: bird similar to a bobwhite. This area was so called for its large population of such birds.
88] *El-Sabán* Arabic: soap maker. This area was known for its soap industry.
104] *Bénu-Asád* Arabic: sons of lion. This tribe was among the most powerful supporters of Hóseyn.
105] *Er-Rass* Arabic: summit. Used by B as a place name.

PIETRO OF ABANO

Sources and Influences] "Pietro of Abano" fuses fact and fiction. Pietro was a real man (c.1250-c.1316), an Italian physician who was born in Padua. The narrative of which B makes him the central character is a fiction written by a Spanish nobleman who also lived in the thirteenth and fourteenth century. This nobleman, Don Juan Manuel, told his story about one Don Illan, a medieval magician. B changed the protag-

onist of the tale from an imaginary to a real man, and altered some of
the details to create his idyl.

He was aware of Pietro at least as early as 1846. In a letter to EBB
of 8 February of that year, he discusses the Italian quatrain which,
years later, he quotes in a footnote to line 40 of his poem.

> Poor dear wonderful persecuted Pietro d'Abano wrote this qua-
> train on the people's plaguing him about his mathematical stud-
> ies and wanting to burn him—he helped to build Padua Cathe-
> dral, wrote a Treatise on Magic still extant, and passes for a
> conjuror in his country to this day—when there is a storm the
> mothers tell the children that he is in the air: his pact with the
> evil one obliged him to drink no *milk*: no natural human food!
> You know Tieck's novel about him? Well, this quatrain is said, I
> believe truly, to have been discovered in a well near Padua some
> fifty years ago.
>
> (*Correspondence*, 12.49).

The novel by Ludwig Tieck (1773-1853) to which the poet refers is
Pietro von Abano oder Petrus Apone (1825), an English translation of
which appeared in *Blackwoods Edinburgh Magazine* in August of 1839.

In an entry in one of his favorite sources, the French encyclopae-
dia *Biographie Universelle*, B found a discussion of the frequently am-
biguous and controversial reports of Pietro's habits and life:

> ABANO (Pietro of), physician and astrologer, born in 1250 in the
> village of Abano, near Padua. The Latin name of this village is
> Aponus, which is why Pietro is often called Petrus de Apono or
> Aponensis in Latin. He is also sometimes referred to as Petrus de
> Padua. In his youth he went off to learn the Greek language,
> some say to Constantinople, others say just to some of the islands
> subject to the republic of Venice. Wanting to devote himself to
> the study of medicine and mathematics, he returned to Padua
> and stayed there for several years. He also spent several years in
> Paris, where he was received as a Doctor of Philosophy and of
> Medicine. Padua called him home to teach medicine and it was in
> his name that a chair was founded there. At that time he acquired
> a great reputation as a physician of which, some claim, he some-
> times took advantage to exact considerable sums of money from
> his patients. But the tales told of his acts of avarice seem exagger-
> ated. Generally, many fables have been ascribed to him. Among
> other personal habits, he is attributed with having such a horror

of milk that he couldn't see it being consumed without his stomach turning. One sees in his work that he had read all of the medical books known in his time. One also sees that he would mix real knowledge with forensic astrology. He had more than four hundred astrological figures painted on the vault of the public hall in Padua. A fire destroyed them in 1420 and they were repainted by the famous Giotto. His infatuation for this false science and his real knowledge of natural philosophy and mathematics (sciences which were not very cultivated in his time) made him pass for a magician; he was also accused of heresy. These accusations, against which he had already had to defend himself in Paris, were renewed twice in Padua by physicians and other enemies who were jealous of his reputation. Some reproached him for, among other crimes, not believing in demons, whereas other accusers attributed his extraordinary knowledge to seven familiar spirits which, they said, he kept shut up in a bottle. After having escaped the inquisitors once, because of his friends' influence, he escaped them a second time only by dying in 1316; he was sixty-six years old. His trial began and was ardently followed. Despite the precautions he took as he was dying to make, in front of witnesses, and even in his will, a profession of orthodox faith, the inquisition proceeded with its trial, judged him guilty of heresy, sentenced him to be burned, and ordered the magistrates of Padua, under penalty of excommunication, to exhume his cadaver so that he could be burned publicly. Having heard this sentence, Pietro's servant (who was, it was said, more than just his servant) had the body unearthed during the night and secretly taken and buried in another church. The Inquisition wanted to take proceedings against those who conceived of and abetted in this violation, but the podesta and the community of Padua were able to convince the inquisitors to settle for reading the sentence in public and burning the dead body in effigy. In 1420, his fellow citizens rendered him a tardy homage by placing his bust on the door of their public palace . . . .

(editor's translation from the French)

The entry concludes with a list and brief description of Pietro's many books.

It is fairly certain that the numerous fables ascribed to Pietro encouraged the poet to feature him in a fresh one. The evidence suggests that B was probably well aware of *Count Lucanor or the Fifty Pleasant Stories of Patronio* by the Spanish Nobleman Don Juan Manuel (1282-1347) as

232

translated by James York ([New York and London, 1868], 77-84). The short tales in this collection are exempla which dramatize an improving moral, duly appended to each one. The twelfth one in the series—"Of that which happened to a Dean of Santiago, with Don Illan, the Magician, who lived at Toledo"—depicts a man punished for his ingratitude, and it is most probably this tale that B takes as a chief model for his idyl. Its moral is "Who pays thy kindness with ungratefulness, / The more he has to give, he'll give the less." The story is told by Patronio to his friend Count Lucanor.

"My lord," said Patronio, "there was a Dean of Santiago who had a great desire to be initiated in the art of necromancy; and, hearing that Don Illan of Toledo knew more of this art than any other person in that country, came to Toledo with a view of studying under him. On the day of his arrival he proceeded to the house of Don Illan, whom he found reading in a retired chamber, and who received him very graciously, desiring him not to inform him of the motive of his visit until he had first partaken of his repast, which was found excellent, and consisted of every delicacy that could be desired.

"Now, when the repast was concluded, the dean took the magician aside and told him the motive of his visit, urging him very earnestly to instruct him in the art in which he was so great an adept, and which he, the dean, desired so anxiously to be made acquainted with.

"When Don Illan told him that he was a dean and, consequently, a man of great influence, and that he would attain a high position, saying, at the same time, that men, generally speaking, when they reach an elevated position and attain the objects of their ambition, forget easily what others have previously done for them, as also all past obligations and those from whom they received them—failing generally in the performance of their former promises, the dean assured him that such should not be the case with him; saying, no matter to what eminence he might attain, he would not fail to do everything in his power to help his former friends, and the magician in particular.

"In this way they conversed until supper-time approached; and now, the covenant between them being completed, Don Illan said to the dean, that, in teaching him the art he desired to learn, it would be necessary for them to retire to some distant apartment, and, taking him by the hand, led him to a chamber. As they were quitting the dining-room, he called his housekeeper, desiring her to procure some partridges for their supper that night, but not to cook them until she had his special commands. Having said this, he sought the dean and conducted him to a beautifully carved stone staircase by which they descended a considerable distance, appearing as if they had passed under the river Tagus, and arriving at the bottom of the steps, they found a suite of rooms and a very elegant chamber, where were arranged the books and instruments of study; and having here seated themselves, they were debating which should be the first books to read, when two men entered by the door and gave the dean a letter which had been sent to him by his uncle the archbishop, informing him that he was dangerously ill, and that if he wished to see him alive it would be requisite for him to come immediately. The dean was much moved by this news—partly on account of the illness of his uncle, but more through the fear of being obliged to abandon his favourite [*sic.*] study, just commenced—so he wrote a respectful letter to his uncle the archbishop, which he sent by the same messengers. At the end of four days, other men arrived on foot bringing fresh letters to the dean, informing him that the archbishop was dead, and that all those interested in the welfare of the Church were desirous that he should succeed to his late uncle's dignity, telling him, at the same time, it was quite unnecessary for him to inconvenience himself by returning immediately, as his nomination would be better secured were he not present in the church. At the end of seven or eight days, two squires arrived, very richly dressed and accoutred, who, after kissing his hand, delivered to him the letters informing him that he had been appointed archbishop.

At this point, Don Illan requests that the now-vacant deanery be given to his son, but the archbishop appoints his brother instead. And so begins a history of ingratitude and treachery. In due course, the archbishop is named by the Pope to be Bishop of Tolosa. When Don Illan asks that his son be made archbishop, Tolosa chooses one of his own uncles to fill that office. Two years later, Tolosa becomes a cardinal, and again Don Illan's plea that his son be given a vacated position is refused by the cardinal, who appoints another uncle. Finally, the cardinal is made Pope. Patronio continues:

> "Then Don Illan came to him saying, 'You have now no excuse to offer for not fulfilling the promises you have hitherto made me.'

"But the new pope told him not to importune him so much, as there was still time to think of him and his son.

"Don Illan now began to complain in earnest. 'You have,' said he, 'made me very many promises, not one of which you have performed.' He then recalled to his mind how earnestly he had pledged his word at their first interview to do all he could to help him, and never as yet had he done anything. 'I have no longer any faith in your words,' said Don Illan, 'nor do I now expect anything from you.'

"These expressions very much angered the pope, and he replied, tartly, 'If I am again annoyed in this manner I will have you thrown into prison as a heretic and a sorcerer, for I know well that in Toledo, where you lived, you had no other means of support but by practising the art of necromancy.'

"When Don Illan saw how ill the pope had requited him for what he had done, he prepared to depart, the pope refusing to grant him wherewith to support himself on the road. 'Then,' said he to the pope, 'since I have nothing to eat, I must needs fall back upon the partridges I ordered for to-night's supper.' He then called out to his housekeeper, and ordered her to cook the birds for his supper.

"No sooner had he spoken, than the dean found himself again in Toledo, still dean of Santiago, as on his arrival, but so overwhelmed with shame that he knew not what to say.

"'How fortunate is it,' said Don Illan to him, 'that I have thus proved the intrinsic value of your promises in prosperity; for, as it is, I should have considered it a great misfortune had I allowed you to partake of the partridges."

Still other variants and analogues of the story exist. Charlotte Porter, in her "Variants of Browning's 'Pietro of Abano,'" (*Poet-lore* 3 [1891], 577-88), offers four versions other than the one in Don Manuel's book, two of which are barely more than loose analogues vaguely related to B's plot. Of the other two, one of them was perhaps influential. This is a version considerably shorter than Don Manuel's and is given in *Letters to a Friend* by Connop Thirwall (Bishop of St. David's from 1841 to 1875). Here the scene is changed from Toledo to Seville, and the names of characters are altered, so that the Dean of Santiago becomes Diego Perez, and Don Illan becomes, interestingly, Don Manuel. The plot and moral are basically unchanged. Thirwell's letters were printed in 1881, a year after *Dramatic Idyls, Second Series* appeared, but he was acquainted with B, who could have had access to that version. A fourth version quoted by Charlotte Porter is Adelbert von Chamisso "Vetter Anselmo," published in Berlin in 1879; but it hardly qualifies. In fact we lack documentary evidence that B read the tale in *Count Lucanor* or indeed knew any of its variants; but his plot is so closely similar to the one in Don Manuel's book, it is highly probable that he took the latter's original story as his main source for the poem.

1]   *Petrus Aponensis*   Latin: "Peter of Abano."

7]   *Babel*   The name of the city and the tower "whose top may reach unto heaven" which mankind tried unsuccessfully to build in Gen. 11:4.

14]   *Petrus ipse*   Latin: "Peter himself."

21]   *Dog-Star—Sirius*   A bright star in the constellation Canis Major or Great Dog.

22]   *Aroint*   Drive away with an execration. *OED* lists two other poems besides the present one for this usage, EBB's "To Flush" and B's own *The Two Poets of Croisic.*

    pleasance   Pleasure

23]   *vine and fig-tree*   These emblems of peace and comfort appear in Mic. 4:4 and Zech. 3:10.

24]   *Mars*   The planet named after the Roman god of war. In astrology the influence of Mars is responsible for strife and dissension.

25]   *whilom*   Former.

    grisard   "A grey-haired man" (*OED*). B's use of this word as a noun is unique.

26]   *eld*   Old man

38]   *Padua's*   See *Sources and Influences.*

39-40]   *"Calculating . . . are bent."* Besides this two-line translation of Pietro's quatrain, the Brownings are responsible for other English versions. In a letter to Elizabeth dated 8 February 1846, B translates the lines as follows: "Studying my ciphers, with the compass / I reckon— who soon shall be below ground, / Because of my lore they make great "rumpus," / And against me war makes each dull rogue round" (*Correspondence*, 12.50). Added to this letter in EBB's hand is this version: "With my compass I take up my ciphers, poor scholar . . . / Who myself shall be taken down soon under the ground / Since the world, at my learning, roars out in its choler, / And the blockheads have fought me all round—." In *The Reliques of Father Prout* (1866) still another version appears. The Preface to the *Reliques* reports: "From Florence the poet Browning has sent for this edition some lines lately found in the Euganeian hills, traced on a marble slab that covered the bones of Pietro di Abano, held in his old age to be an astrologer." The Preface then quotes the Italian stanza and continues: "Of which epitaph the poet has supplied this vernacular, rendering *verbatim* 'Studying my cyphers with the compass, / I find I shall be soon under the daisy; / Because of my lore folks make such a rumpus, / That every dull dog is thereat *unaisy*' ([London, 1889], iv). It is apparently this version of the quatrain, preferred by "Father Prout" (pen name of Francis Mahony, a friend of the Brownings), to which B refers in his footnote. In a letter to Furnivall dated 21 October 1881, the poet writes still another slightly different version: "All about the vernacular of the epitaph on *Pietro of Albano* [*sic.*] is pure fun of Father Prout's. I told him of the thing at Florence, and did it *impromptu* into this doggerel:— Studying my cyphers with the compass / I gather I soon shall be below ground, / Because of my lore men make great rumpus, / And war on myself makes each dull rogue round" (Peterson, 36-7). Because this version is substantially the one that B sent Elizabeth in 1846, it seems unlikely that, years later, he created it "impromptu" for Father Prout. Furthermore, because the version in the letter to Furnivall is not the same as the one which actually appears in *Reliques*, either Father Prout made changes in the translation, or the poet incorrectly remembered the version he sent to his friend.

48] *bastinadoed* Beat with a stick

52] *sullen* Unyielding.

57] *Mage* Magus, or magician.

63] *tick* Moment, instant.

64] *milk* See *Sources and Influences*.

70] *moly* In Homer's *Odyssey* (10.290-305) the enchantress Circe turns some of Odysseus' men into swine. To protect Odysseus from the same fate, the god Hermes gives him the magic herb moly.

73] *iris mystic-lettered* According to Furnivall, B explained "that there was an old superstition that, if you look into the iris of a man's eye, you see the letters of his name or the word telling his fate'" (*Browning Society Papers*, Pt. 3 [1882-83], "Monthly Abstract," 9*).

78] *provend* Provender, food.

79] *Apollo* Greek god of prophecy and music.

86] *co-adjutor* Assistant.

87] *noddle* Head.

95] *hests* Behests, commands.

97] *fabric* Edifice.

101] *fascinate* Bewitch.

109] *Petri en pulmones!* Latin: "Behold, the lungs of Peter!"

118] *Ipse dixi* Latin: "I have said."

121] *bray . . . mortar* Prov. 27:22: "Though thou shouldst bray a fool in a mortar among wheat with a pestle, yet will not his foolishness depart from him."

124]   *Michael of Constantinople*   Michael VIII, Palaeologus, Emperor of the Byzantine Empire from 1259 to 1282, was distinguished for his learning.

Hans of Halberstadt   A medieval German magician. According to Nathanael Wanley's *Wonders of the Little World*, one of B's favorite books, "Johannes Teutonicus a Canon of Halberstadt in Germany, after he had performed a number of prestigious Feats almost incredible, was transported by the Devil in the likeness of a black Horse, and was both seen and heard upon one and the same Christmas-day to say Mass in Halberstadt, in Mentz and in Collen" ([London, 1678], 518). See B's "Transcendentalism: A Poem in Twelve Books," l. 37.

139]   *to a tittle—*   To the most minute particular.

150]   *de corde natus haud de mente*   Latin: "Born of heart, not of mind."

154]   *punctual*   Dutiful. .

161]   *tristful*   Sad, sorrowful.

166]   *clapperclawing*   Abuse.

168]   *shuffle cards*   Manipulate matters.

171-72]   *Shall I . . . play the dog*   A dog in the manger is a "churlish person who will neither use something himself nor let another use it; in allusion to the fable of the dog that stationed himself in a manger and would not let the ox or horse eat the hay" (*OED*).

173]   *Bene . . .*   The first syllables of the Latin word *benedicite* (see l. 408), or "bless this food," a mock grace for the hay in the manger above (l. 171).

181-82]   *Plato's tractate . . . 'the Fair and Good,'*   The Greek may refer specifically to *The Republic*, but in several of the Platonic dialogues, Socrates argues that beauty and goodness are one.

182]   *Dog of Egypt*   Anubis, an Egyptian god of the underworld, with the head of a dog or jackal.

190]   *kickshaws*   Delicacies.

pother   To worry about, fuss over.

192]   *cark*   Distress, anxiety.

203]   *Sulla*   Roman statesman and general (138-78 B.C.). Appointed dictator in 82 B.C. for an unlimited term, he voluntarily retired from public life three years later.

204]   *The grapes are sour*   One of the famous fables of Aesop (c. 600 B.C.) concerns a fox who cannot reach grapes which he desires to eat; therefore he claims that he doesn't want the grapes anyway because they are sour.

211]   *Hunks*   A miser.

213]   *Jezebel*   The wicked wife of King Ahab (I Kings:16,17) whose name has become an eponym for all wicked women.

214]   *Jam satis!*   Latin: "Enough now!"

233]   *copper*   A penny or halfpenny.

235]   *bedesman*   An archaic spelling. A *beadsman* prays for the souls of the departed.

244]   *fabric, Padua's boast*   See *Sources and Influences.*

249]   *familiar*   A member of the household.

259]   *Tantalus's treasure*   In Greek myth, Tantalus is punished in Hades by being placed in a pool of water with fruit-bearing boughs over his head. When he stoops to quench his thirst, the water recedes, and when he reaches for the fruit to satisfy his hunger, the wind blows them out of his reach.

264]   *wields the ball*   Exerts royal power. The *ball* is a golden orb which, together with a scepter, symbolizes sovereignty.

266]   *put within my lump their leaven*   "Know ye not that a little leaven leaveneth the whole lump?" (I Cor. 5:6)

280]   *half-mooned boot*   Crescent shaped boots were worn by aristocratic and wealthy citizens.

287]   *Elysian*   Heavenly. In Greek mythology, Elysium is the abode of the blessed dead.

291]   *Per Bacco*   Italian: "By Bacchus," the Roman name for Dionysus, the god of wine and revelry.

292]   *lets*   Hindrances.

299]   *Salomo si nôsset!*   Latin: "Had Solomon but known this!" Solomon is a Biblical king famed for his wisdom.

304]   *Teneor vix!*   Latin: "I can hardly restrain myself!"

309]   *boggled*   Raised scruples, demurred.

310]   *hactēnus*   Latin: "Hitherto."

312]   *Nec Ultra Plus*   Latin: "Nothing further."

315]   *spelter*   Zinc.

322]   *Lost the world, and gained . . .*   "For what shall if profit a man, if he shall gain the whole world, and lose his own soul?" (Mark 8:36).

326]   *Pluck . . . burning*   "ye were as a firebrand plucked out of the burning: yet have ye not returned unto me, saith the Lord." (Amos 4:11)

335]   *crozier*   A bishop's staff.
         crow-bill   Forceps.

340]   *earwigged*   "Having a 'maggot' or craze in one's brain. *nonce-use*" (*OED*). B alone used the word in this sense.

342]   *manna*   "And when the dew that lay was gone up, behold, upon the face of the wilderness there lay a small round thing, as small as the hoar frost on the ground. And when the children of Israel saw it, they said one to another, It is manna: for they wist not what it was. And Moses said unto them, this is the bread which the Lord hath given you to eat." (Exod. 16:14,15)

kecks   Retches.

peason   An obsolete or dialectal form of *pease*, or peas.

346]   *Would we . . . fulcrum*   Archimedes, the Greek inventor and mathematician of the third century B.C., boasted that he could move the earth with a lever if he had a place to stand on.

pou sto   Greek: "On which to stand."

362]   *temporal-supreme*   He will prostrate his worldly sovereignty before the Pope's spiritual power.

366]   *doit*   A Dutch coin or, figuratively, a small amount.

370]   *Lateran*   The papal palace in Rome. Saint John Lateran , the cathedral church of the pope, stands next to the palace.

374]   *Purple*   The rank of cardinal. A cardinal's official dress is purple.

Conclave   The name given to the Sacred College of Cardinals, the body which elects a new pope.

Two-thirds   To be elected pope, a candidate must receive a two thirds majority, plus one, of the votes of the cardinals.

coop   "A narrow place of confinement; a cage"; a relevant slang usage, "the place where electors were 'cooped,'" is recorded in 1889 (*OED*).

381]   *Tithon*   Shortened form of Tithonus. The Greek goddess of dawn, Aurora, fell in love with the mortal Tithonus and granted him immortal life; however, because he was not granted eternal youth, he became extremely old. See Tennyson's poem "Tithonus."

383]   *flesh is grass*   "All flesh *is* grass, and all the goodliness thereof *is* as the flower of the field: The grass withereth, the flower fadeth: but the word of our God shall stand for ever." (Isa. 40:6,7)

388]   *sting in death*   1 Cor. 15:56: "The sting of death is sin."

394]   *farrago*   Hodgepodge.

395]   *Conciliator Differentiarum*   Latin title meaning "Concilliator of Differences." The *Biographie Universelle* says of this work that it is one "often reprinted and one which gave Abano the surname of Conciliator. In it, he undertook the difficult task of conciliating the diverse opinions of physicians and philosophers." (See *Sources and Influences*).

397-98]   *De Speciebus / Ceremonialis Ma-gi-æ*   Latin: *Concerning the Kinds of Magic Ceremonials.*

400]   *Fisher's ring*   The pontifical ring is referred to as the fisherman's ring. The first pope, St. Peter, was a fisherman.

foot that boasts the Cross   The pope's red shoes are embroidered on the front with a cross.

407-8]   *Apage, Sathanas / Dicam verbum Salomonis*   Latin: "Away, Satan, I command in the name of Solomon." Jesus rejects the devil with the words "Get thee behind me, Satan." (Luke 4:8)

Dicite! The concluding syllables of the word *benedicite* (see l. 173).

415] *"Idmen, idmen!"* Greek: We know, we know!

416] *cheese at last I'll know from chalk* Cheese and chalk are proverbial opposites.

420] *Scientiæ Com-pen-di-um* Latin: "*Compendium of Science.*"

421] *Admirationem incutit* Latin: "It inspires admiration."

426] *axe and fasces* An axe bound in a bundle of rods (the fasces) was a symbol of the authority of Roman magistrates.

427] *antipope's part* An antipope is one who claims to be the pope as opposed to one canonically chosen.

433] *Tiberius* Roman emperor from 14 to 37 A.D.

434] *Geryon* In Greek myth, a fearsome giant with three heads, three torsos, and six arms. Geryon appears in *Æneid* 6.289.

439] *crystal* Clear water.

440] *Suetonius* Roman historian (*c.* 69-140 A.D.), author of *The Lives of the Twelve Caesars*. The account of Tiberius throwing dice into a fountain is as follows: "When later, on his way to Illyricum, he visited the oracle of Geryon near Patavium, and drew a lot which advised him to seek an answer to his inquiries by throwing golden dice into the fount of Aponus, it came to pass that the dice when he threw showed the highest possible number and even to-day those very dice may be seen under the water" ("Life of Tiberius," 14.3 [New York, 1959], 130-31).

441] *Venus* The most favorable cast of the dice. See "At the Mermaid," l. 114.

444] *lilt* Rhythmical cadence. The following eight measures of music provide the "equivalent" of the last four lines of the poem's concluding stanza.

DOCTOR ——

Sources and Influences] No source for this idyl has been discovered. If the first words of the poem are to be believed, B heard the story from an unidentified rabbi who remarks that there are similar tales in the *Talmud*; however, this particular tale is not to be found there. Examples of sayings similar to the proverb spoken by Satan, "Stronger than Death is a Bad Wife," are found in the *Talmud*; e.g. "Give me all evils, but not an evil wife," and "Who is the poor man whose days are filled with misery? He who must live with an evil-natured wife." (*The Talmudic Anthology*, Louis Newman and Samuel Spitz, eds. [New York, 1947], 539) A similar saying is also found in Eccles. 8:26: "And I find more bitter than death the woman, whose heart is snares and nets, and her hands as bands: whoso pleaseth God shall escape from her; but the sinner shall be taken by her."

A Greek folk tale which is an fairly close analogue to B's story concerns a peasant who is looking for a godfather for his first born child ("Folk Songs and Tales from Modern Greece," *Poet-lore* 9 [1897], 353-66). Because his one requirement is that the chosen man must be supremely just, the peasant disqualifies God (because the blessings that He bestows on mortals are "ill distributed") and St. Peter (because he denies entry to heaven to the poor) but accepts Death who is supremely just and treats everyone alike. To reward the peasant for the honor given him, Death makes him a successful physician.

> "I—a poor peasant?"
>
> "Yes. From this moment you are eminent,—a physician the foremost in the world."
>
> "But I have never studied! Hardly can I read or write!"
>
> "That matters not. Listen. The rich banker, Abraham, is ill. Go boldly to him, prescribe what you will, and assure him of recovery. He will not die, will dream that you have saved his life and reward you generously, and your fame will spread."
>
> "But other patients?"
>
> "Whenever you are called to any one, you have but to look toward the head and foot of your patient. If I stand at his foot, he will recover; if at his head, know that his days and numbered. All your drugs will not avail him."
>
> So the peasant went to the Jew, Abraham, and cured him after all the other doctors had given him up. His fame spread; and soon everyone was talking of the wondrous physician who could tell at a glance if a sick man would live or die.
>
> Soon the peasant-physician became one of the richest men in the country. Rich men, merchants, bishops, kadis, pachas, the Sultan himself sent for him and would have kept him always in attendance.

At this point, the Greek tale takes a different direction from B's. When the peasant's time to die comes, he begs Death to give him more time. Death shows him that the candle of his life is nearly burnt out. The peasant asks that Death put his son's candle in his place. But the peasant's candle burns out and the peasant dies, thus showing that Death is supremely just and favors no one.

This tale obviously has certain similarities to B's idyl, but there is no evidence that B read it. DeVane asserts that the story is "probably founded on Jewish oral legend" (*Hbk.*, 408), and, in the absence of evidence to the contrary, it seems best to accept B's assurance that he tells the tale "as the Rabbi told it me."

1] *the day allowed* "Now there was a day when the sons of God came to present themselves before the Lord, and Satan came also among them." (Job 1:6) Also: "Again there was a day when the sons of God came to present themselves before the Lord, and Satan came also among them to present himself before the Lord." (Job 2:1)

9] *Stronger . . . Wife* See *Sources and Influences.*

12] *style* Title.

41] *Medicus* Latin: "Physician."

42] *spit* Jesus cures a blind man by applying spit to his eyes. See Mark 8:23.

47-8] *walk the world* "And the Lord said unto Satan, whence comest thou? Then Satan answered the Lord, and said, From going to and fro in the earth, and from walking up and down in it" (Job 1:7).

51] *cheese for chalk* Cheese and chalk are proverbial opposites. See "Pietro of Abano," l. 416.

57] *corrupt* Used here with a suggestion of "to convince."

86] *pennyroyal* A variety of mint from which a potent oil is extracted; a strong dose can be lethal.

87] *sherris* Archaic for "sherry"; see "At The Mermaid" (in *Pacchiarotto*, this edition, 13.166, l. 9) for a parallel usage.

Sumat! Latin: "Let him take it."

89] *Galen* A famous Greek physician and author of the second century A.D.

93] *wis* Know.

95] *sciolists* People whose knowledge is superficial.

115] *coucher* "One who couches or crouches." This line is the only example of this usage cited by the *OED.*

131] *vaticination* Prediction.

140] *Machaon* The physician who attended the Greeks during the Trojan War. He was the son of Aesculapius, a famous Greek healer.

redivivus Latin: "Resurrected."

168] *meal of dust* Man. After Adam and Eve are tempted by the serpent to eat the fruit of the tree of the knowledge of good and evil, God says to Adam "for dust thou art, and unto dust shalt thou return." (Gen. 3:19) Also: "And the Lord God said unto the serpent, Because thou hast done this, thou art cursed above all cattle, and above every beast of the field; upon thy belly shalt thou go, and dust shalt thou eat all the days of thy life." (Gen. 3:14)

190] *meteor shot* In astrology, a meteor is a bad omen.

192] *Jove's salutary influence* Jove, or the planet Jupiter, is thought by astrologers to exert a powerfully beneficent influence.

199] *Antic* An actor who performs a grotesque role.

216] *knobstick* A stick with a rounded knob.

218] *Jacob's-Staff* A pilgrim's staff, named for St. James (Latin *Jacobus*) whose church and relics in Santiago (Spanish for St. James) are a famous site of pilgrimage and miraculous cures in Spain.

243] *sulphury scent* Sulphur, or brimstone, is associated with the devil.

248] *Elixir* A life-prolonging potion.

250] *boots* Matters.

256] *Talmud* The body of traditional Jewish law.

PAN AND LUNA

Sources] In the idyl's epigraph, and first and last stanzas, B indicates Virgil's *Georgics* as his source. In the four books of that poem Virgil (70-19 B.C.) writes of farming and rural life. The third book, on the breeding of livestock, appears to have suggested the subject of this idyl.

> Munere sic niveo lanae, si credere dignum est,
> Pan deus Arcadiae captam te, Luna, fefellit,
> In nemora alta vocans; nec tu aspernata vocantem.
>
> (ll. 391-3)

Though he no doubt read the poem in Latin, B owned *The Works of Virgil* as translated into English prose by C. Davidson, who renders the passage: "Thus Pan, the god of Arcadia (if the story be worthy of credit), deceived thee, O moon, captivated with a snowy offering of wool, inviting thee into the deep groves: nor didst thou scorn his invitation." ([New York, 1864], 80) The poet's own translation of part of this passage appears in the idyl's last stanza (ll. 97-100).

Luna is the goddess of the moon, and the idyl's penultimate stanza asks if her legend is, perhaps, a mythic account of the first eclipse of the moon. DeVane reports that "to Virgil the legend was an attempt by men of olden times to explain the first eclipse of the moon" (*Hbk.*, 410). In fact, in the passage which inspired B Virgil says nothing about eclipses. No aetiological explanation, no moral "lesson for a maid," (l. 95) is added. The answer to B's question—"does the legend say?" (l. 89)—is no; indeed, it is precisely the absence of any causal ethical elaboration that seems to have surprised and fascinated the poet.

Some readers find an intensely personal dimension in the poem. DeVane, for example, remarks:

> As we may see in *One Word More*, the *Epilogue* to *Ferishtah's Fancies*, the *Parleying With Daniel Bartoli* and elsewhere, the moon to Browning was always, after 1855, a symbol for his wife, Elizabeth Barrett Browning. It is possible that in *Pan and Luna* Browning meant to hint biography—to recall for himself in this exquisite legend the brief happiness he had enjoyed with his wife.
>
> (DeVane, *Hbk.*, 457)

Or again, Donald S. Hair holds in his "Browning's 'Pan and Luna': An Experiment in Idyl,":

> 'Pan and Luna" is also, in all probability, a very personal poem, for the moon was one of Browning's recurring symbols for his dead wife, and Mrs. Browning had a considerable interest in the figure of Pan. In this story of seizing and carrying off a pale maiden who becomes a willing captive Browning may have seen the story of his own marriage.
>
> (*Browning Society Notes* 4, 2 [1974], 8).

That the poet symbolized his lost wife as the moon is incontestable, but he draws no exact autobiographical parallels and, of course, does not necessarily cast himself in the role of a deceitful, lecherous Pan.

2] *Virgil . . . lines!* See *Sources.*

4] *Arcadia* The Greek birthplace of Pan and traditional setting of much pastoral poetry.

27-8] *teemed / Herself with whiteness* Pursuing his evocation of spreading moonlight, the poet extends a meaning of *teem,* "to pour forth." The *Maid-Moon* poured out white light from herself.

28] *uncinct* Unencircled.

34] *succourable* Helpful as cover for nakedness.

45] *paps* Nipples.

47] *innumerous* Innumerable. "Now only *poetical* or *rhetorical*" (*OED*).

50] *Conglobe* "To gather or form into a ball or globe" (*OED*).

54] *flexile* Flexible, pliant.

55] *constringe* "To become close or dense" B's use of the word in this sense is the only example cited by the *OED*.

56] *springe* Trap, snare.

58] *conceits* Imagines.

59]   *Amphitrite's dome*   The sea. Amphitrite was the wife of the sea god Poseidon. On B's use of *dome* to mean "dwelling," see "Solomon and Balkis," l. 12n., below.

60]   *bladdery*   Bubbly.

66]   *Pan*   The son of Hermes, Pan had goat's horns and hooves. The god of goatherds and shepherds, he was famous for his ugliness and lechery.

69-70]   *take the fact / As learned Virgil gives it*   Lines in the third book of Virgil's Georgics, preceding the three lines on Pan and Luna, give directions for breeding sheep for maximum whiteness. "If the woolen manufacture be thy care; first let prickly woods, and burs, and caltrops, be far away: shun rich pastures: and from the beginning choose flocks that are white with soft wool. And that ram, though he himself be of the purest white, under whose moist palate there lurks but a black tongue, reject, lest he should sully the fleeces of the new-born lambs" (*The Works of Virgil Literally Translated into English Prose*, tr. C. Davidson [New York, 1864], 80).

84]   *boar-sward*   Boar skin.

lapped   Hemmed in, or pressed hard by a rival or hostile force.

"TOUCH HIM NE'ER SO LIGHTLY"

In this epilogue to his idyls, B contrasts two poets: under favorable circumstances, one poet produces flowers; under unfavorable circumstances, another, and apparently superior, poet produces a pine tree. Who are these poets? Possibly B had no particular poets in mind; he seems to be concerned with two kinds of poets, not two individuals. However, that he believed that his poem was misunderstood is demonstrated by the following sequel. On 16 October 1880, B met in Venice a young lady, Edith Bronson, the daughter of his hostess, who asked him to write some lines in her album. (Peterson notes that DeVane incorrectly identifies this lady as Edith Longfellow, the daughter of the American poet [Peterson, 62]). B complied and wrote the following version of "Touch him ne'er so lightly," employing the same meter and rhyme scheme:

> Thus I wrote in London, musing on my betters
> Poets dead and gone: and lo, the critics cried
> "Out on such a boast!"—as if I dreamed that fetters
> Binding Dante, bound up—me! As if true pride
> Were not also humble!
>
> So I smiled and sighed

As I oped your book in Venice this bright morning,
Sweet new friend of mine! And felt the clay or sand
Whatsoe'er my soil be,—break—for praise or scorning—
Out in grateful fancies—weeds, but weeds expand
Almost into flowers—held by such a kindly hand!

This poetic commentary on his original poem indicates that in B's mind Dante is an example of a "pine" poet.

A holograph copy of these lines found their way into print ("Pages from an Album," *Century Magazine* 25 [1882], 159-60). They were also printed in some American editions of B's works, for example, the Houghton Mifflin "Cambridge" edition of 1895 and the Thomas Crowell edition of 1898. When B learned that Furnivall, a founder of the Browning Society, was thinking of publishing the poem, he wrote as follows in a letter dated 9 December 1882:

> I find you propose to publish that little friendly scribble I added to a young lady's Album two years ago—never dreaming that any use would be made of it in the way which took me by surprise at the Club, when I came on what I thought was an advertisement and found was my very own handwriting—though cramped to suit the tiny book. The poem, as a thing for the purpose it was written for, is *spoiled* by this excrescence,—though suitable enough for the young lady's purpose. I should be very glad if you would omit it, and all references to it in your "Scraps" or elsewhere . . . .
>
> (Peterson, 61)

Four days later, upon learning that the poem had already been published, B wrote this letter:

> The scrap may have gone forth past recall—but I rely on you to prevent it being stereotyped: you know I never interfere, if I can possibly help, in the doings of the Society: but this was an exceptional case. A trifle written for a very young person from whose mother I had received a great deal of benevolence, and attention of every sort: I still think the printing, without any application to me, must have been the effect of some editorial manœuvure: at any rate,—my feeling toward the family remaining quite unchanged by what I shall treat as an accident or the result of a misconception,—*I want nothing more to be said on the subject,*—giving useless pain and obtaining no good . . . .
>
> (Peterson, 62)

JOCOSERIA

§Paul D. L. Turner had begun drafting the Editorial Notes to *Jocoseria* at the time of his death; he had progressed as far as "Ixion." The remaining notes, all revisions, and the textual apparatus are by Allan C. Dooley, who accepts all responsibility for errors.§

Emendations

The following emendations have been made to the 1888-89a copy-text:

Donald, l. 196: MS-1883a have the necessary period at the end of this line; 1889a has no punctuation. The MS-1883a reading is restored.

Donald, l. 227: In an apparent compositor's error, the copy text omits the last word and comma of this line. The MS-1883a reading *bread,* is restored. Interestingly, this correction was made in later impressions of 1889, though at whose direction is unknown.

Cristina and Monaldeschi, l. 55: Syntax requires some punctuation at the end of this line; the copy-text has none. The exclamation mark in MS-1883a is restored.

Adam, Lilith, and Eve, l. 18: The speech by the woman called "That" ends with this line, and a narrator speaks the rest of the poem. As in the parallel case at l. 12, closing double quotes are required as the end of the line. No text contains the correct punctuation, which is supplied.

Jochanan Hakkadosh, l. 100: The copy-text lacks an apostrophe in *dwarf's-play,* though space for it remains. The MS-1883a punctuation is restored.

Jochanan Hakkadosh, l. 367: In the copy-text, the initial quotation marks are missing, though space is made for them. The CP1883-1883a reading is restored.

Jochanan Hakkadosh, l. 408: B corrected his proofs back to his MS reading by inserting a comma between *virtue* and *hid*; this clearly shows his intention, and the phrase beginning with *hid* requires the comma. 1888-89a lacks punctuation here; the MS and CP1883-1883a reading is restored.

Jochanan Hakkadosh, l. 492: The copy-text reading *secret* appears to be a compositor's error, since a verb is required by the syntax; the MS-1883a reading *secrete* is restored.

Jochanan Hakkadosh, ll. 518, 521: These two emendations, based on inference as much as evidence, are intended to designate an embedded quotation. Jochanan's *dreams* (l. 515) are *Singing* (l. 518), and B's MS clearly indicates the beginning of their song with a single quotation mark before *The Future* (l. 518). This punctuation is printed in three consecutive texts—P1883, 1883, and 1883a. In no text, however, is there a closing quotation mark to end the speech, and it is presumably for this reason that the 1889a text deletes the opening quotation mark. The logical place for the dreams to cease singing is in l. 521 after *the Present*, at which point the contrast of future and present is completed. The MS has a period after *Present*; the proofs and printed editions have an exclamation mark. It is our belief that at an earlier stage of proof correction, B inserted a single, closing quotation mark here, but his correction was misread as a call for an exclamation mark. Whatever the cause of the problem, the copy-text's removal of the opening quotation mark is no remedy; it makes the passage more superficially consistent, but no clearer. In this edition, the opening quotation mark is restored, and the closing one supplied; the MS period is also restored.

Jochanan Hakkadosh, l. 745: Either through a compositor's error or broken type, the last word of this line is *seen* in all copies of the 1889a text collated. The reading *seem* (found in all earlier texts) is grammatically and semantically more correct, and properly rhymes with ll. 743 and 747 in B's *terza rima* scheme. The MS-1883a reading is restored.

Jochanan Hakkadosh, Sonnet II, l. 13: The copy-text fails to print the apostrophe in *'Twas*; the MS-1883a reading is restored.

Jochanan Hakkadosh, Sonnet III, l. 14: The copy-text prints a single closing quotation mark at the end of this line, where a double quotation mark is required. The correct MS-1883a punctuation is restored.

Pambo, l. 29: Damaged type in the copy-text produces a single misplaced quotation mark at the beginning of this line; the correct double quotation mark of MS-1883a is restored.

Composition

Direct evidence about the dates and circumstances of the writing of the poems in *Jocoseria* is sparse. The earliest reference is in November of 1881, more than a year after the publication of *Dramatic Idyls, Second Series*, when B told a reviewer for the *Athenæum*, "I have written a poem or two, certainly, which may or may not go into a new volume of Idyls" (Hood, 204). Rumors that he had a new volume in preparation led him to tell George Barnett Smith a few weeks later, "I may print such few things as I have, along with others yet unwritten, in a new volume . . . but there is nothing designed, much less accomplished" (Hood, 206). B may have been less than frank, since it appears that "Donald" was finished around 1 December 1881 (see below). Some of the other poems may have been composed in August and September of 1882, when B and his sister stayed at the Hôtel Virard at St. Pierre de Chartreuse in the French Alps (DeVane, *Hbk.*, 460; McAleer, *LL*, 148), and he may have conceived "Cristina and Monaldeschi" while stopping in Paris on his way. Another period of composition ensued after he returned to London in early October; clearly "Jochanan Hakkadosh" required access to his personal library, and in the Balliol MS this poem is dated 22 December 1882. B assembled his printers' copy shortly after this, and informed Furnivall on 9 Jan. 1883:

> I have given (this afternoon) Smith my new book to print. It is a collection of things gravish and gayish—hence the title "Jocoseria"—which is *Batavian* Latin, I think. There are some eleven of these pieces, little and big,—the main of them being the Deerstalking Poem you remember, "Donald," Solomon & Balkis, Christina [*sic*] & Monaldeschi, Ixion, Mary Wollstoncraft & Fuseli, and a long "Hakkadosch [*sic*] Jochanan"—a Rabbinical story: Eleven pieces in all.
>
> (Peterson, 63)

The printers'-copy MS, then, contained one more poem than the published volume; this was "Gerousios Oinos," which was set in type for *Jocoseria* (see *Reconstruction*, E144) but withdrawn before the Pforzheimer proofs were pulled. Evidence in the MS shows that the poem was to precede "Pambo." DeVane's speculation that B removed the poem because it might have offended his fellow poets is plausible, if unsubtantiated (DeVane, *Hbk.*, 565-66). "Gerousios Oinos" was not published in the poet's lifetime, and first appeared in the *Cornhill Magazine* N. S. 36 (1914):575-76. It is included in the final volume of this edition.

Text and Publication

There are five stages in the textual development of *Jocoseria*: the manuscript at Balliol College, Oxford; a set of page proofs in the Pforzheimer Library in New York; the first edition published by Smith, Elder in 1883, which exists in two impressions; and Volume 15 of *The*

Poetical Works of 1888-1889. The collation of these texts is recorded in our variant lists.

The Balliol Manuscript (MS)   The MS at Balliol consists of 78 leaves: B's handwritten title-page and 42 of his typical folios, inconsistently numbered and sometimes containing only one leaf. The compositors have renumbered the leaves (ignoring the title-page) 1 through 79, and the presence of compositors' names throughout proves that this was the printers'-copy MS. The absence of folio 41 (leaves 75 and 76 in the compositors' numbering) indicates where the excised "Gerousios Oinos" had been when typesetting began—between "Never the Time and the Place" and "Pambo."

The first seven and the last two poems in the MS are fair-copied, with very few revisions; the consistency of the penmanship suggests that B worked with a single pen-point in a short time. "Jochanan Hakkadosh," in contrast, is heavily revised. He numbered the folios containing this poem 1 through 22, and later renumbered them 18 through 39 when assembling the printers' copy. That this is the compositional MS of the poem is further indicated by B's having dated it "Dec. 22 '82." and inscribed it with "L. D. I. E." (for the Latin *Laus Deo in excelsis*, "Praise God in the highest"), his customary expression of thanks for finishing his work. As noted above, the completed MS was sent to Spottiswoode & Co. (Smith, Elder's printers) on 9 January 1883.

The Pforzheimer Proofs (*P1883*)   The page proofs of *Jocoseria* at the Carl H. Pforzheimer Library at the New York Public Library represent an intermediate stage of the proofing process; they form a complete set, and appear to be second author's proofs rather than final or press proofs. The printed readings in the proofs, which were produced (according to a slip attached to page 82) around 1 February 1883, differ from the MS at nearly 500 points. The Pforzheimer proofs also contain 51 further alterations in the poet's hand (noted as *CP1883* in our variant lists). A corrector at the printers has marked numerous mechanical faults in the typesetting, such as high spaces, broken letters, and erroneous signatures. Presumably, this set of proofs was returned to B with his next revises; by 4 February he informed Furnivall, "My business with 'proofs' is all but done" (Peterson, 65). When George Barnett Smith asked for an advance copy of *Jocoseria* to review, the poet sent him the Pforzheimer proofs, with the following letter (now tipped into the bound set):

19. Warwick Crescent, W.
Feb. 17. '83

Dear Mr Barnett Smith,

Your letter arrived as I was on the point of going out in a hurry, and my sister undertook to provisionally answer it. I write now to say for myself that, in all I thought I was bound to observe concerning the publication of any criticisms on my new book, I had mainly your interests in view and not by any means my own—supposing, as I did, that there might be some reason for the objections I mentioned. The whole matter is one about which I am in great ignorance—of the proper etiquette one is bound by on these occasions: and I very cheerfully accept your assurance that there is nothing at all unusual in what you propose to do—and consequently are quite at liberty to do. You must remember that I am not likely to forget your many instances of great kindness to my works—and the works still more interesting to me,—and that this—and this only—was the cause of my desire to caution you on a point where it was possible that I might myself be hindered from affording you the very trifling advantage, as you please to account it, which you have a right to expect. As it is,—I leave the whole business to your discretion, and, for the future—if a future there is to be for my performances in this nature—I will furnish you with "proofs" as soon as they come to hand. What you now have, is certainly in the possession of nobody else whatever—though you may be led to think so by a paragraph which appeared in the "Academy" this morning—inspired by a reading to an audience of two to which I was tempted a few days ago—when my own sister became acquainted with the poems for the very first time. I hear nothing about the Publisher's intention, and have little doubt there is plenty of time before you.

You made some enquiries which I will answer as well as I can. The title is taken from the work of Melander (Schwartzman) reviewed by a curious coincidence in the "Blackwood" of this month: I referred to it in a note to "Paracelsus." The two Hebrew quotations (put in to give a grave look to what is mere fun & invention) being translated amount to—1st—"A collection of many lies"—and the 2nd is an old saying "From Moses to Moses arose none like Moses." I don't think any other matter wants clearing up.

Though B assures Smith there was "plenty of time" in which to write his review, *Jocoseria* was published only three weeks later, on 9 March 1883.

The First Edition (1883)   To the poet's great satisfaction, *Jocoseria* was an immediate success in the marketplace. Less than six weeks after its appearance, the first impression was sold out. On 17 April, B wrote: "This little 'Jocoseria' (joking even in the title) has had the usual luck of the little-deserving,—got itself sold . . . at the rate of 2000 very early, and is now reprinting" (Hood, 218). He signed many presentation volumes on the day of publication, including copies for Tennyson, Furnivall, and Sir Frederick Leighton (*Reconstruction*, C358-73).

The First Edition, Second Impression (1883a)   Smith, Elder & Co. proudly added the words "Second Edition" to the title-page of *Jocoseria*, but collation shows that this second press-run was produced from the initial typesetting, which was left standing. A remark of B's to Furnivall in 1884 suggests that the second impression consisted of just 500 copies: "on the very last of our transactions he [i. e., Smith] good-naturedly remarked 'Had you let me read "Jocoseria" I would have printed 500 additional copies at once'" (Peterson, 93). The new copies were in hand by 2 July 1883, when B dedicated one to Hellen Zimmern (*Reconstruction*, C374). The text differs from the first impression in only a handful of cases, all of which are consistent with dropped types rather than intentional alteration; in all but one case the missing letters and punctuation were corrected in the *Poetical Works* of 1888-89.

Bibliographers have asserted the existence of a third "edition" of *Jocoseria*, but we have found no trace or copy of it. Broughton, Northup, and Pearsall claim that a "3rd ed." was dated 1885 (Broughton, A114). When DeVane (*Hbk.*, 461) says that "*Jocoseria* passed through two separate reprintings" in an unspecified period, he implies a total of three impressions of the first edition. Earlier, Wise had asserted that "three editions of *Jocoseria* have been published, but the text throughout has remained unchanged" (*Complete Bibliography of the Writings of . . . Robert Browning* [London, 1897], 31); he gives no dates, and neither half of this statement appears to be true. The earliest reference to this shadowy "third edition" appears in a bibliography included in W. Sharp's *Life of Robert Browning* (London, 1890), which says of *Jocoseria* "now in third edition." The bibliography was prepared by J. P. Anderson, who also worked with Wise, and perhaps he saw such a book. Yet five years after the second impression, when the fourth volume of the *Poetical*

Works appeared in July 1888, *Jocoseria* was listed as being in its "Second Edition." And a year after Anderson's listing, an advertisement in the second edition of Mrs. Orr's biography of B states: "The following Volumes can still be had: . . . Jocoseria. Second Edition" (Orr, *Life*, [454]). No major research library with extensive Browning holdings, including the Armstrong Browning Library, lists a copy of *Jocoseria* in a third edition; book dealers offer copies of the first and occasionally the second edition, but not a third. Until a clearly marked copy turns up, we must declare the third edition of *Jocoseria* a bibliographical ghost.

Collected Edition (1889a)   In the *Poetical Works* of 1888-1889, *Jocoseria* occupies pages 165-260 of the fifteenth volume. The pattern of B's corrections indicates that the collected edition was set up from a copy of the second impression; there are 83 changes in this final text, many of which are restorations of earlier readings or corrections of typographical errors.

Title

As he explained to Furnivall, B derived his title from the Dutch humanist Otto Melander's *Jocorum atque Seriorum.* This collection of anecdotes, first appearing in 1597, went through numerous editions in the early 17th century. It is not known exactly which B owned (see *Reconstruction*, A1580), but he read the book in his youth and alluded to it contemptuously in *Parcelsus* (1835; this edition, 1.271). Both times, he gives Melander's title as *Jocoseria*, though the title-pages of the early editions read "Iocorum atque Seriorum . . . [etc.]." B's letter to Furnivall in 1883 illuminates further: "The title is Dutch Latin, and barbarous—one would preferably say 'Jocososeria'—indeed the first of my volumes is headed 'Jocosum atque Seriorum Tomus Secundas'— but all the pages have 'Jocoseria', as if the same thing" (Peterson, 65).

The poet apparently took the "Jocoseria" of the running heads as a useful conflation of the two Latin stems (*Joc-* and *Ser-*) used in the original title, and he described his new book to Furnivall as "a collection of things gravish and gayish—hence the title 'Jocoseria' (Peterson, 63; Peterson suggests that both B and Melander allude to Cicero's *ioca seria* [*De Finibus Bonorum et Malorum*, 2.85].). B's "gravish and gayish" may look back to Pope, "An Essay on Man," 4.379-80: "happily to steer / From grave to gay, from lively to severe." A similar phrase appears in E. FitzGerald's introduction to his translation of the *Rubáiyát of Omar Khayyám*: "the Rubáiyát follow one another according to

Alphabetic Rhyme—a strange Farrago of Grave and Gay" (on B and the *Rubáiyát*, see also *Ferishtah's Fancies, Sources and Background* below).

Inaccurate and "barbarous" though it may be, the word pleased B enough to make it his own, and Melander's title echoed once again a year later, when he was finishing *Ferishtah's Fancies*: he considered calling the new collection *Seriora*.

"WANTING IS—WHAT?"

Title]   This lyric serves as prologue to the *Jocoseria* volume, both announcing its general theme (there is always something missing) and pointing forward to the first of its two epilogues, "Never the time and the place." It also serves to preface the collection of dramatic poems with an expression of the poet's personal feeling, as he had done with "Amphibian" in *Fifine at the Fair* (1872; this edition, Vol. 11). What was "wanting," from every aspect of his life, was EBB.

1]   *Wanting*   Missing.

2]   *redundant*   Used in the original sense of Latin *redundans* (= overflowing, pouring forth freely).

4]   *blot*   Blemish, fault, as in *A Blot in the 'Scutcheon* (this edition, 4.9-60).

5]   *Beamy*   Full of sunbeams, sunny, radiant.

7]   *What of*   I. e., what's the good of?

9]   *comer*   Sometimes interpreted as translating the Greek ὁ ἐϱχόμενος (= he that comes), a NT name for the Messiah, as in Matt. 11:3 (E. Berdoe, *The Browning Cyclopaedia* [2nd ed., 1892], 560). But the rhyme-word *love* apostrophizing the *Rose-beauty above* more likely referred to EBB. Cf. B's "Amphibian" (1872): "What if a certain soul / Which early slipped its sheath, / And has for its home the whole / Of heaven, thus look beneath, / Thus watch one who, in the world, / Both lives and likes life's way" (ll. 33-8; this edition. Vol. 11). Both instances, and others in B's later poems, look back to Dante's earth-bound yearning for contact with Beatrice in the *Divine Comedy*.

10]   *perfect*   Both the sense and the dactylic rhythm require this to be taken as a transitive verb (= make perfect), with the stress on the second syllable.

DONALD

Composition and Source]   DeVane's assertion that "Donald" was written in August of 1882 while the poet was in the French Alps (*Hbk.*, 462) has commonly been accepted, but better evidence establishes that it was drafted more than a year earlier, in London, by December 1881. On 1 January 1882, B wrote to Katharine deKay Bronson: "I wrote,—about a story I heard more than forty years ago and never dreamed of trying to repeat,—a poem of some two hundred lines a month ago" (Meredith and Patteson, 8). Mrs. Bronson quoted—in fact, misquoted—this letter in her reminiscence, "Browning in Venice" (*Century Magazine*, 63 [1902]: 574-5), and identified the poem as "Donald." (DeVane apparently presumed from Mrs. Bronson's article that this letter had been written in September 1882, during the poet's planned visit to Mrs. Bronson' Venetian palazzo, but that visit never occurred; see Bronson, op. cit., 576 and Peterson, 60.)

As to the source of "Donald," D. S. Curtis reported a conversation with the poet shortly after *Jocoseria* was published: "Asked if the Poem of the Man and the Stag was founded on fact?" B replied: "Exactly, the man told me his story forty years ago" (see Meredith and Patteson, App. c., 170). However, he had probably not "heard" but read the story in Sir Walter Scott's "A Highland Anecdote," published in the *Keepsake* for 1832 (283-6). Scott claimed to have "heard" the anecdote in his "early youth," and to have actually "known" its dubious hero ("Duncan, for so I shall call him") as an old "disabled cripple, scarce able to limp along the streets." He disapproved of Duncan's "conduct towards the deer in a moral point of view," as breaking the "implicit compact which certainly might have been inferred from the circumstances of the situation."

Scott put the blame on "the devil, or the untameable love of sport, peculiar to his country," and admitted the strength of the "temptation." B made no such allowances. Taught by his mother in childhood to love animals, he had recently published "Tray" (see this edition, 14.249 and nn.) in support of the anti-vivisectionist Victoria Street Society for the Protection of Animals, of which he was Vice-President. Taught as a teenager by Shelley to hate "the brutal pleasures of the chase . . . [or] delight in the death-pangs and last convulsions of dying animals" (Shelley's Notes to *Queen Mab*, 8.211-12), he deeply disapproved of Pen's passion for field-sports. From Loch Luichart in Scotland he wrote to Isa Blagden in 1869: "Pen (for whose sake I came) . . . has got what he wanted—shooting and deer:-stalking: he began operations the day before yesterday &, much to his credit as a hunter, shot a splendid stag—'royal': the head of which will glorify his rooms at Ch. Ch. [= Christ Church, Oxford]" (McAleer, *DI*, 322). Two years later he wrote from Pitlochry: "Pen enjoys the shooting much: shot, by himself, today 14 1/2 brace of grouse, 4 hares & a plover—on the eighth day of shooting,—that is, when the birds have been, two thirds of them, shot, and the rest effectually frightened. A poor business, & one I could wish him to hate as much as I do: but 'who can control his fate?' Jowett is close by, with a reading-party . . . to a certain degree, I am relieved about Pen by knowing the very worst of the poor boy, to-wit that he won't work, or perhaps can't" (McAleer, *DI*, 363-64).

By emphasizing the unrepentant Donald's later life and importuate story-telling (ll. 209-24), B creates an ironic version of another cautionary ballad, Coleridge's *Rime of the Ancient Mariner* (1797).

3-4] *The boys were a band from Oxford / The oldest of whom was twenty.* Pen Browning was twenty in 1869 when he shot the "splendid stag" mentioned in the preceding note.

5] *Bothy* Small hut or cottage (Scottish). The use of the word suggests B was thinking of A. H. Clough's *The Bothie of Tober-na-Vuolich* (1848), in which Oxford undergraduates spend the Long Vacation in a reading-party in Scotland (like the one conducted by Jowett "close by"; see above). And the mention of "Donald the Innkeeper" (*Bothie*, 1.46) may have helped to turn Scott's Duncan into Donald.

8] *Whereof Sport turned the handle* I. e., all on the subject of sport. The metaphor is drawn from an early form of the fairground carousel, powered not by steam (introduced in the 1860s), but by the showman himself turning a crank.

9] *turf-smoke* From the peat used as fuel.

10] *trivet* The iron bracket attached to the fire-grate for the kettle to stand on.

12] *Glenlivet* A Scotch malt whisky, named for the district where it is distilled. Whisky mixed with hot water and sugar is known as "hot toddy."

13] *loyal* I. e., to the truth, honest: a rhyme-dictated extension of the normal meaning, possibly encouraged by B's knowing that the word was derived from Latin *legalis* (= legal).

16] *Royal* "A stag having a head of twelve points or more"(*OED*); see *Composition and Source* above.

22] *Havanna* Cigar; Cuban cigars were famous for their high quality by the early 19th century.

26] *Would a man fulfil* If a man wants to fulfil.

33-4] *Good sportsman . . . the centre* Cf. B's comment on Pen's character: "He is clever & in the main very good & very conscientious: everybody likes him" (McAleer, *DI*, 364).

39] *Oh no, Sir, no!* The narrator has shown signs of offence at being called a mealy-mouthed mild milksop.

42] *A Double-First* The rare university student who gains First-Class Honours in two separate subjects is called a "Double First."

what, the jigger   A mild substitute for stronger language, such as "what the hell."

54]   *all on a level*   An implicit answer to the suggestion that everything is different for those who achieve Double Firsts: at that time, the narrator and his friends were exactly like the present "band from Oxford."

55]   *gone to the Bench*   Become a judge.

60]   *No need of our playing Inquisitor!*   We didn't have to drag the story out of him (an allusion to the use of torture for such a purpose by the Inquisition).

61]   *Ross-shire*   An ancient county in the Scottish highlands, NW of Inverness, consolidated in 1889 with Cromarty. In Ross lay Loch Luichart and its Lodge, home to Lady Louis Ashburton, whom B and his son visited in 1869 and 1871. Lady Ashburton's involvement with the poet is detailed in Irvine and Honan, 444ff.

62]   *Ben*   from Gaelic (= peak, horn, conical point), used in names of numerous Scottish mountains.

64]   *rags and tatters*   The phrase hints that the "ghastly visitor" will prove to be a beggar, but may here refer modestly to the speaker's narrative technique, or perhaps the fragmentary nature of his own recollections.

75]   *He has to*   That he has to.

76]   *burnie*   Tiny stream (diminuitive of *burn*).

79]   *bluff*   With a vertical cliff, precipitous.

an end in ich   Though the reference is deliberately imprecise here, *ich* is a common ending in Scottish place names.

91]   *if heart and brain be proof*   If he's brave and clever enough.

103]   *callant*   Lad; youth (Scottish)

107]   *brig*   Bridge (Scottish).

107-8]   *'twixt mount / And moor*   I. e., between the two possible routes to his rendezvous, the short cut over the mountain or the long tramp over the moor.

120]   *scouted ignoble pacing*   Scorned the lower and easier route.

122]   *dear*   Perhaps used with a double meaning: the danger that he loved, and that he would pay a high price for.

126]   *magnific*   Magnificent.

128]   *pacific*   Here, to strengthen his moral point, B slightly modifies Scott's version of the story: "if Duncan had turned his back to go down, he knew enough of the creature's habits to be certain that he would rush upon him while engaged in the difficulties of the retreat . . . . At length the deer, which was of the largest size, began to lower his formidable antlers, as they do when they are brought to bay, and are preparing to rush upon hound and huntsmen. Duncan saw the danger of a conflict in which he must probably come by the worst, and as a last resource, stretched himself on the little ledge of rock, which he occupied, and thus awaited the resolution which the deer should take, not making the least motion for fear of alarming the wild and suspicious animal" (Scott, op. cit., 284-5).

129] *a red deer is no fallow deer* The red deer (*Cervus elaphus*) of N. Europe, the largest mammal native to Britain, stands 5 ft. at the shoulder, while the fallow deer (*Cervus Dama dama*) has a shoulder-height of only 3 ft. The fallow deer is semi-domesticated in British parks.

133] *volte-face* Used unusually in its literal sense of turning to face in the opposite direction.

134] *valour advised discretion* Adapting Falstaff's "The better part of valour is discretion," in Shakespeare's *1 Henry IV*, 5.4.120.

136] *Blondin* Charles Blondin (1824-97), French aerialist who first crossed Niagara Falls on a tightrope (1859). He performed to great acclaim in London and elsewhere in Britain in the 1860s and 70s.

140] *admiring* Probably used less in its modern sense of regarding with respect, approval, or satisfaction than in its original Latin sense of wondering at.

144] *grovel!* The exclamation mark suggests a playing with the fact that *grovelling* at first had a literal (physical) meaning only: "having the face or belly towards or on the ground; prone" (*OED*). In this case, of course, it had to mean supine (see l. 150).

148] *inch and inch declension* A gradual leaning back, lowering. The noun seems to be used in the Latin sense of the verb *declino* (= turn aside, bend down, lower), or in the early sense of English *declension*, "sinking into a lower position" (*OED*).

152] *If he cross me!* If only he will step across me.

153] *Minutes were an eternity* The author's imaginative substitute for Scott's barely credible statement: "They remained in this posture for three or four hours" (Scott, op. cit., 285).

157-62] *Feelingly he extends a foot . . . no less finely* A brilliantly concise and graphic description of the whole infinitely delicate process, *tastes the way* precisely expressing the calculated movement of the foot through the air, and *Nor hold of the same unclutches* the cautious clinging to the first tiny foothold until the second is reached.

163] *So a mother removes a fly* The simile derives from Homer's *Iliad* (4.131), where the goddess Athena diverts an arrow from the flesh of Menelaus "as a mother brushes off a fly from her sleeping child."

171] *lightened* Flashed like lightning—though another meaning of the verb (= reduce) is also relevant here, since he became less cautious.

176]   *down and dead and trampled*   The three metaphorical words for the defeat of other sportsmen have literal meanings very apt in the context: both man and animal will fall *down*, the animal will be *dead*, and the man might well have been *trampled*, but had not been, thanks to the animal.

177]   *tenderly*   The maternal implications of the quasi-Iliadic simile in ll. 163-64 are significantly stressed.

179]   *now is the time!*   Scott's Duncan had the stag from the front, when its formidably armed and still potentially hostile head was bent down at him: "At length the buck seemed to take the resolution of passing over the obstacle which lay in his path, and with this purpose approached towards Duncan very slowly, and with extreme caution. When he came close to the Highlander he stooped his head down as if to examine him more closely, when the devil, or the untameable love of sport, peculiar to his country, began to overcome Duncan's fears . . . . With one hand he seized the deer's horn, while with the other he drew his dirk" (Scott, op. cit., 285). B's Donald waits until the immediate danger is almost past, until no doubt remains of the animal's intentions, before attacking it without warning in the most underhand way possible.

181]   *the stomach's soft*   The phrase underlines Donald's ingratitude by inviting comparison with l. 159, where the stag had taken special care not to tread on *man's soft*.

182]   *pastern*   The part of the stag's foot immediately above the hoof.

184]   *this turn's the last turn!*   The rhyme with *pastern* involves a complicated pun. The *last turn* is the denouement or *catastrophe* of the drama (καταστροφή = down-turn—in this case literal: the fall over the cliff). Hitherto the two characters in the drama have taken turns to act: the stag decided to climb carefully past the man, who in his turn responded with his dirk. And behind the pun is the proverb conspicuously contravened by Donald: "One good turn deserves another."

192]   *At following game no laggard*   Always quick to follow up and locate animals he had shot: a sarcastic tribute to Donald's usual "sportsmanship," since on this occasion he "followed" involuntarily.

195]   *stayed*   I. e., broken.

199-200]   *a toast . . . soaken*   It was once customary to float a piece of toasted bread in wine or punch, particularly if served warm; as B's simile points out, the toast would soon distingrate.

   soaken   Soaked (a form of the past participle still current in 1898 [*OED*]).

206]   *clouted*   Mended with a patch.

   cobbled   Roughly repaired (like an old shoe).

207-8]   *Goliath*   The giant killed by the boy David in 1 Sam. 17:42-50.

210]   *for a bracket*   I. e., to display on a bracket (just as Pen Browning would have displayed the head of the stag he had shot, "to glorify his rooms" in Christ Church college (see *Composition and Source* above).

211]   *twelve tines*   Twelve points (of its antlers) which made it a "Royal" (see l. 16n. above).

214]   *His win-penny*   His way of gaining a little money.

218]   *harvest was sure*   He was sure of making plenty of money.

226]   *By Jingo*   A polite substitute for "By Jesus" or "By God." The phrase was famously used in a belligerent music-hall song in 1878: "We dont want to fight / But, by Jingo, if we do / We've got the ships, / We've got the men, / We've got the money, too." *OED* notably adds: "In Scotland *by jing* (or *jings*) has long been in common use."

228]   *tug*   Evidently used like *pull* to mean "a long or deep draught of liquor" (*OED*).

232]   *trump*   An admirable person, a good fellow.

   Tory   The poet's Liberal sympathies (see his sonnet, "Why I am a Liberal," published in 1885; this edition, Vol. 17) may largely explain why the drunk "sportsman" is sardonically labelled a Tory.

233]   *I hope I gave twice as much as the rest*   Presumably because he was the oldest and richest person present; also out of natural humanity; and to compensate for his deep disapproval of the man's behavior.

234]   *as Homer would say*   An allusion to a common Homeric formula for protesting against something that someone has said: ποῖόν σε ἔπος φύγεν ἕρκος ὀδόντων (=What a word has escaped the fence of your teeth! Homer, *Iliad* 4.350, and elsewhere in both *Iliad* and *Odyssey*). The implication is that some things may be all right to think, but should not be said: they should be firmly imprisoned inside the fence of the teeth. Needing a rhyme to his climactic: *Ingrate!*, B seems to have concentrated on the notion of imprisonment implied by the formula, and thought of something like a "dungeon-grate," sensationally used by Coleridge in "The Rime of The Ancient Mariner": "And straight the Sun was flecked with bars, / . . . / As if through a dungeon-grate he peered / With broad and burning face" (ll. 177-80). He may also have assumed an etymological connection among ἕρκος (= fence), Latin *cratis* (= hurdle) and English *grate*. Some editors emend *grate* to *gate*, without textual support; but this spoils the rhyme to the most important word in the poem (since ingratitude is its central theme). Furthermore, the *gr* sound is an essential component of B's inward *growl* (l. 1235). Cf. the beginning and end of "Soliloquy of the Spanish Cloister": "Gr-r-r—you swine!" (this edition, 3.211, 213).

SOLOMON AND BALKIS

Sources]   One version of the story of Solomon and the Queen of Sheba is narrated in 1 Kings 10:1-13 and 2 Chron. 9:1-12; in Islamic legend and in the Talmud, the Queen of Sheba, identified as Balkis, becomes one of Solomon's wives. Exactly where and when the poet encountered these materials is unknown, but he and EBB certainly read Hebrew adequately. Mrs. Orr attests to his "power of reading Hebrew in its most difficult printed forms" (Orr, *Life*, 384), and he declared to Mrs. FitzGerald, "I get more and more attached to that grand language" (McAleer, *LL*, 162). Interestingly, B inscribed two books in Hebrew with the phrase "My Wife's Book and mine" on 17 April 1883 just after *Jocoseria* was published; a week later he signed and dated his copy of *The Jewish Family Bible* (see *Reconstruction*, A209, A215, and A229). For a full discussion of B's familiarity with Hebrew scriptures and Rabbinical lore, see Judith Berlin-Lieberman, *Robert Browning and Hebraism* (Jerusalem, 1934). To this valuable study the editors are especially indebted for information about the poet's knowledge of Hebrew and Judaism.

It is possible that B read the following brief account of Solomon and Balkis in Edward Fitzgerald's translation of the Persian poet Jami's *Salámán and Absál*, published anonymously in 1856 and reprinted in the 4th edition of FitzGerald's *Rubáiyát of Omar Khayyám* (1879; see also *Ferishtah's Fancies, Sources and Backgrounds* below):

> Once upon the Throne together
> Telling one another Secrets,
> Sate Sulayman and Balkís;
> The Hearts of both were turn'd to Truth,
> Unsullied by Deception.
> First the King of Faith Sulayman
> Spoke—"However just and wise
> Reported, none of all the many
> Suitors to my palace thronging
> But afar I scrutinize;
> And He who comes not empty-handed
> Grows to Honour in mine Eyes."
> After this, Balkís a Secret
> From her hidden bosom utter'd,
> Saying—"Never night or morning
> Comely Youth before me passes
> Whom I look not after, longing"—
>   (1.147-63)

1] *Balkis* "The name Balkis is derived from an Arabic source. In the Bible she is known as the Queen of Sheba. Balkis is an Arabic word and is akin to the [Hebrew] word . . . meaning concubine. For according to Arabic tradition the relation . . . between the Hebrew king and the Abyssinian queen was of a sensual nature. This idea was taken over by the Rabbis," according to whom Solomon "had intimate relations with the Queen of Sheba, the offspring of which was Nebuchadnezzar, the same king who destroyed the Temple" (*Hebraism*, 80; see also L. Ginzberg, *The Legends of the Jews* [Philadelphia, 1914-28], 1.65; 4.142-49, 300; 5.87-88; 6.290-92, 389-90).

2] *the ivory throne* 1 Kings 10:18, 2 Chron. 9:17: "Moreover the king made a great throne of ivory, and overlaid it with the best gold."

3] *why else has she sought Mount Zion* The question was possibly ironical, since according to Talmudic legend she was actually responding to the threat made in diplomatic language by Solomon to his immediate neighbours: accept my authority, or I shall compel you by force to do so. The Queen of Sheba (modern Yemen) had so far failed to accept it (E. Berdoe, *The Browning Cyclopaedia* [2nd ed., 1892], 475-6).

Mount Zion In Jerusalem, where Solomon's palace stood.

4] *six golden steps . . . lion and lion* 1 Kings 10:19, 2 Chron. 9:18.

5] *She proves him with hard questions* 1 Kings 10:1, 2 Chron. 9:1.

7] *there is left no spirit in her* 1 Kings 10:5, 2 Chron. 9:4.

9] *monster* Used in on the non-pejorative sense of Latin *monstrum* (= a wonder, a prodigy), though the potenially pejorative word suits her flirtatiously antagonistic tone.

10] *construe or* vulgo *conster* The verse requires the stress of *construe* to be put on the second syllable (as normal since the end of the nineteenth century) and that of *conster* on the first (as usual in earlier times). The commonest meaning (especially in schools) was to analyse the grammatical structure of a sentence in Greek or Latin, with a word for word translation; hence to interpret, explain. Balkis means to say "answer this riddle," but implies by her verb that she is a schoolmaster examining a pupil.

vulgo Latin (= by the multitude, so, commonly, generally). The tinge of contempt for the "vulgar" suits Balkis's pedagogical pose.

12] *spheteron do* σφέτερον δῶ (= his house). Though the two Homeric words do not appear together in Homer, similar phrases are to be found in the *Iliad* and *Odyssey*, e. g. ἐμὸν δῶ (= my house), ἡμέτερον δῶ (= our house), ὑμέτερον δῶ (= your house).

his dome The second Homeric word, δῶ is a shortened form of δῶμα (= house) which B habitually translated "dome" (even in contexts where there was no reference to a dome in the ordinary sense), presumably to indicate the etymological connection between the Greek and English words. He had developed the habit in *Aristophanes' Apology* and *The Agamemnon of Aeschylus* (this edition, 12.166, 295, 378; 14.38, 311), and now, to get his rhyme, infects Balkis with his own eccentricity. Since the meter used in this poem often sounds like a Homeric hexameter, the quasi-Homeric phrase fits in well enough.

16] *kingly in craft* I. e., in intellectual power. The neatly alliterative phrase was possibly suggested by Plato's notion of the philosopher-king (*Republic*, 5.473).

18] *the partition* I. e., the *weak walls* (l. 14) dividing kings from their intellectual *peers*.

24] *mate* Not the happiest synonym for *fellow* or *peer*, but required for the ingenious rhyme.

25] *upbridled* A coinage for *bridled up* (= took offence), presumably at the idea that she could be anything but virtuous in her choice of dependants.

26] *or in travel my eyes have idled* Or the travel which should have sharpened my insight has been a waste of time. She protests a little too much, in view of the sexual motives which she is going to confess.

28] *Permit me to drop my wimple* The removal of her veil (associated with nuns) is both a flirtatious ploy to show off the attractiveness of her face, and an excuse for the movement that contrives to turn round the ring on Solomon's finger.

29] *peace* Hold thy peace, i. e., don't make the satirical comment that you were going to.

32] *The Ring* According to Arabic legends, King Solomon had a magic ring that allowed him to converse with animals.

    the Name i. e., of God.

33] *The truth-compelling Name!* the name that compels one to speak the truth. The phrase "suggests the Jewish notion of the 'Extraordinary Name' . . . and the 'distinguished Name' . . . . By these names the Rabbis and particularly the Cabbalists refer to the real name of Deity" (*Hebraism*, 78).

38] *hest* an old form of *behest* (= command), used by Carlyle as late as 1858; here the command to tell the truth.

39] *proper* Used in its old sense of "handsome, good-looking."

44] *the earthly mansion* the body. Cf. 2 Cor. 5:1: "if our earthly house of this tabernacle were dissolved, we have a building of God, a house not made with hands, eternal in the heavens." The use of the phrase suggests that the apostrophe to *Soul* (l. 41) alludes to Shakespeare's Sonnet 146: "Poor soul, the centre of my sinful earth, . . . Why so large cost, having so short a lease, / Dost thou upon thy fading mansion spend? / Shall worms, inheritors of this excess, / Eat up thy charge? Is this thy body's end?"

47-48]   *cedar . . . hyssop*   Cedars from Lebanon often symbolize strength in the OT; both cedar and the herb hyssop were used in purification rituals. Solomon connects the two in 1 Kings 4:33: "And he spake of trees, from the cedar tree that is in Lebanon even unto the hyssop that springeth out of the wall."

50]   *aether*   The upper air.

52]   *praise . . . Vanity*   Perhaps echoing the analysis of folly in Eccles. 7:5-6: "It is better to hear the rebuke of the wise, than for a man to hear the song of fools . . . the laughter of fools . . .   is vanity."

60]   *one fool's small kiss!*   Give this fool a little kiss. The last two rhymes in the poem exemplify one typical source of jocosity in *Jocoseria*. B's current interest in such rhymes was shown in a letter of 16 August 1882 to Mrs. Thomas Fitzgerald, completing her quotation from a mediaeval Latin drinking song: "Mysterious truths and rites divine / I never could unfold 'em / Without a flaggon of good wine / And a slice of cold ham" (McAleer, *LL*, 148).

CRISTINA AND MONALDESCHI

Composition and Sources]   Probably written in the late summer or autumn of 1882 at St. Pierre de Chartreuse (see *Jocoseria, Composition*). In connection with the subject-matter of this poem, Furnivall recalled his oft-repeated wish that B would put an explanatory "Argument" before each of his poems. The poet refused, as Furnivall recalls: "No, he wouldn't. He didn't make us buy his poems, we could let 'em alone if we liked; but if we did buy 'em, we must take 'em as he chose to print 'em; and if he'd taken the trouble to write 'em—'Cristina and Monaldeschi', for instance,—we surely might take the trouble to look up the historical facts he alluded to. He didn't believe in feeding his readers with spoon-meat" (Peterson, 196). One reader who did take that trouble, C. N. Wenger, was shocked to discover how roughly those "historical facts" had been handled by the poet ("Clio's Rights in Poetry: Browning's Cristina and Monaldeschi," *PMLA* 60 [1945]:231-70). His chief distortion of history was to assume that Christina and Monaldeschi had been lovers, and that she murdered him in revenge for his sexual infidelity. There is no such suggestion in the either of the poet's two most probable sources: his old friend Anna Brownell Jameson's *Memoirs of Celebrated Female Sovereigns* (London, 1831); and *Queen Christina of Sweden*, a Lothian Prize Essay (Oxford and London, 1880) by A. H. Hardinge, a member of Balliol College, Oxford, of which B had been an Honorary Fellow since 1867. The monologue is spoken by Cristina, i. e., Queen Christina (1626-1689), who has abdicated the throne of Sweden and is now (1657) staying in the royal palace at Fontainebleau, as a guest of King Louis XIV of France. She has summoned the Marquis Monaldeschi, her Grand Equerry, to the Galerie des Cerfs (= gallery of deer), having detected him in a secret correspondence prejudicial to her interests. What the correspondence was about is unknown; but B interprets it as an exchange of love-letters, and makes Cristina lead her victim through the Galerie de Diane on their way to the historical site of the execution or murder, the "Gallery of the Deer" (l. 112).

1] *how each loved each, Marquis* Cristina's showing a picture of François I and Diane de Poitiers is evidently B's invention, since historically Diane was the mistress, not of François I, but of Henri II.

4] *lend your rod* She borrows the chamberlain's official wand to point out the Latin motto of the picture.

5-6] *Quis / separabit?* Who shall separate (them)? (Latin)

13] *her Crescent* I. e., Diane's symbol, since Diana was the goddess of the moon.

14] *his Salamander-sign* François used the salamander as his heraldic emblem.

15] *Flame-fed creature* The salamander was once thought able to live in fire.

24-25] *the Crescent . . . Diane* Pressing the parallel between the two love-affairs, Cristina equates Monaldeschi with Diane, not only as the non-royal partner in the affair, but also as a lover whose moon-like changeability might well earn him Diane's very name.

27-32] *Woman-like . . . I do not* Cristina's claim to male constancy is in line with the masculine tendencies of the historical Christina. After her abdication she once "cut her hair short, and disguised herself as a man, with a plumed hat and a sword, in order to travel more freely" (Hardinge, op. cit., 47).

33] *my habit* B was probably thinking of how the historical Christina behaved, not merely of how she dressed. According to Madame de Motteville,

> "She was utterly unlike a woman . . . she was even without a woman's modesty . . . . She would roar with laughter when anything tickled her, particularly at the Italian comedy, if the buffoonery was good. She would often sing in company, or appear to wander in her mind . . . . She was rough and free in all that she

said, both in talking about religion, and also about subjects respecting which the decency due to her sex should have made her more reserved. She used to swear by God; and in the presence of the king, the queen, and the whole court, she would put up her legs on to chairs quite as high as the one on which she herself was sitting, and exhibit them very much too freely. She professed to despise all women for their ignorance, and talked with men on subjects of every kind, both good and bad."

(Hardinge, op. cit., 57)

34] *my people* My household staff (since her abdication, she had no subjects to refer to).

36] *Quis separabit?* See ll. 5-6n. above.

60] *as* As if.

74] *be sage!* Used in the sense of the French phrase addressed to a child: *sois sage* = Be good!

79] *unmeet* Unsuitable, i. e., unnecessary.

94-5] *waif . . . estray* Both words mean a stray, ownerless animal; but *waif* has the extra meaning, relevant here, of something cast up on shore by the sea.

99] *our sculpture* I. e., the *statues* of l. 86

105] *Juno strikes Ixion* Ixion of Thessaly tried to seduce Juno the queen of the gods. He was punished (not by her but by her husband Jupiter) in the underworld by being tied on a perpetually revolving wheel. See "Ixion" below.

106] *Primatice* French spelling of the Italian painter, sculptor and architect Francesco Primaticcio (1504-70), who painted murals with mythological subjects at Fontainebleau for François I.

107] *Florentine Le Roux* French name of the Italian painter Giovanni Battista Rosso Fiorentino (1494-1540), who worked with Primaticcio at Fontainebleau.

108] *I've lost head for who is who* B resourcefully attributes to Cristina's real or pretended mental confusion the ignorance of art historians: "The exact shares of Rosso and Primaticcio in the designing and decoration of Fontainebleau are not known" (*Oxford Companion to Art* [Oxford, 1970], 1016).

116] *Avon* A village near Fontainebleau.

129] *my four! You, Priest* Historically, the priest (named in the sources as Père Le Bel, the Mathurine Prior) was present from the beginning of the interview, and had produced the sealed packet of letters which had been entrusted to his keeping.

Sending for him [Monaldeschi] on the 15th of November, to the
Galerie des Cerfs at Fontainebleau, she confronted him with Père
Le Bel, who at her request then handed back to her the sealed
packet confided to him. It contained the clearest evidence in his
own handwriting of Monaldeschi's guilt. He at first tried to deny
it; but on his letters being read, and his own signature shewn him,
his courage completely gave way. Throwing himself at her feet, he
clung to the queen, and implored her to allow him to clear him-
self. She heard his defence, which was nothing but a tissue of ex-
cuses and appeals for mercy, patiently and without emotion. The
scene lasted more than an hour. At last Christina turned to the
prior: "I leave this man," she said, "in your hands. Prepare him for
death. And do what you for can for the salvation of his soul." In
vain the good priest endeavoured to intercede for him: Christina
was not to be moved: once more recommending Monaldeschi to
prepare for death, she passed out of the gallery, leaving him
alone with the prior, and with three men with drawn swords, who
had been stationed there to execute him.

(Hardinge, op. cit., 59)

131-2]   *Care / For no mail such cowards wear!*   B credits Cristina with
prior knowledge of what came as a surprise to the historical killers.
After hacking off half of his fingers, they "hewed at his head and neck
until he fell to the ground, where they struck repeated blows at him as
he lay. These were, however, without effect, for he wore under his
clothes a suit of armour, the interposition of which prolonged his
agony . . . he lay more than a quarter-of-an-hour gasping on the
ground, and slowly bleeding to death"(Hardinge, op. cit., 60).
135]   *Dead at last?*   Unlike her historical original, B's Cristina has
been present throughout the whole killing process.

MARY WOLLESTONECRAFT AND FUSELI

Source]   The probable source was John Knowles's *Life and Writings of
Henry Fuseli* (London, 1831), a copy of which the poet owned (*Recon-
struction*, A1004). Knowles told the story of Mary Wollstonecraft's ob-
sessive passion for the Swiss painter, Johann Heinrich Fuesli (1741-
1825). B appears to class the episode in the "grave and gay" category
for its mixture of pathos and comic paradox: that Wollstonecraft

(1759-1797), founder of feminism and famous for her *Vindication of the Rights of Woman* (1792), should have fallen so heavily for such a man. According to Knowles, Fuseli was "not very ready to make new acquaintances, and was not only a shy man, but had rather a repulsive manner to those he did not know" (1.161-162). He was also "already married to a woman whom he loved" (1.164). As for his attitude to Mary, "he admired her chiefly for her talents" (1.165). Otherwise, he "found in her (what he most disliked in woman) a philosophical sloven: her usual dress being a habit of coarse cloth, such as is now worn by milk-women, black worsted stockings, and a beaver hat, with her hair hanging lank about her shoulders" (1.164). She made valiant efforts to please him: "moulded herself upon what she thought would be most agreeable to him. Change of manners, of dress, and of habitation were the consequences; for she now paid more than ordinary attention to her person, dressed fashionably, and introduced furniture somewhat elegant into commodious apartments, which she took for that purpose" (1.166). When this had no effect, in desperation "she had the temerity to go to Mrs. Fuseli, and to tell her, that she wished to become an inmate in her family; and she added, as I am above deceit, it is right to say that this proposal 'arises from the sincere affection which I have for your husband, for I find that I cannot live without the satisfaction of seeing and conversing with him daily.' This frank avowal immediately opened the eyes of Mrs. Fuseli, who . . . instantly forbade her the house"(1.167).

Such details of the historical relationship, however, may be apocryphal. In *William Godwin, His friends and Contemporaries* (London, 1876), Charles Kegan Paul found Knowles' account of Mary Wollstonecraft "extremely inaccurate," and judged that "his testimony may be wholly set aside" (1.207). But B seems to have written his poem as a generalized instance of female unrequited love, without bothering to make it fit the facts of Mary's life. The supposed transformations from timidity to courage (ll. 1-10) and from dim-wittedness to brilliance (ll. 11-20), as well as the final indifference of Fuseli, are unflattering to both parties.

1] *Oh, but is it not hard, Dear?* Mary is (in thought) addressing Fuseli.

9] *dare and do* A version of the poet's favored phrase "dared and done," used throughout his life and work to express triumph. See *La Saisiaz*, l. 1 and n., this edition 14.99 and 401.

29-30] *love's labour's due / Utterly lost* The wording is adapted from the title of Shakespeare's *Love's Labour's Lost*.

ADAM, LILITH AND EVE

Title]   The proposition that Lilith was Adam's first wife and Eve his second first appears in the medieval *Alphabet of Ben-Sira*; it was circulated more widely by J. Buxtorf's *Lexicon Talmudicum* (1640). However much B knew of the legend, he seems to be using the three names quite non-specifically, to suggest any triangular relationship between a man and two women. He disavowed any direct reference to the legend in a letter to Mrs. FitzGerald:

> the story is simply that a man once knew a woman who, while she loved him, pretended that she did not—which pretence, like a man and a fool, he believed, so of course was not married to her—but to a woman who did *not* love him but another though she said she did love him—which, like a man and a fool—he believed: one day as they sat together, each, on a sudden impulse, told him the truth—which, like a man and a fool, he disbelieved. Surely there is nothing so difficult here . . . .
>
> (McAleer, *LL*, 156)

7]   *mind*   Remember.

IXION

Title]   Ixion was a king of Thessaly, whose crime and punishment were thus summarized by the mythographer Apollodorus: "Ixion fell in love with Hera and attempted to rape her. When Zeus [her husband] wanted to know if it was really so, and she confirmed it, he made a cloud look like Hera, and let Ixion go to bed with that; and when he boasted that he had slept with Hera, Zeus tied him on to a wheel, which carried him on the winds through the air, and that is his punishment. And the cloud gave birth by Ixion to Centaurs" (Apollodorus, *Epitome,* ed. R. Wagner [Leipsig, 1926], 1.20). For Pindar, Ixion's crime was aggravated by gross ingratitude, since Zeus had kindly taken him up to Olympus to purify him of the murder of his father-in-law: "and they say that Ixion is commanded by the gods to keep saying this to mortals, as he spins round and round on the winged wheel: 'repay a benefactor with gentle recompense.' And he learned this clearly, for having got a sweet life alongside the kindly children of Cronos, he did not long enjoy his good fortune, after he madly fell in love with Hera, who belonged to Zeus's happy bed . . . and soon meeting his deserts he got a special torment. Thus he suffered for two offences: he was the very first to shed a kinsman's blood . . . and he made an attempt on the wife of Zeus" (Pindar, *Pythian Odes*, 2.21-35).

B owned two editions and three translations of Pindar (*Reconstruction*, A1850-A1854). He also possessed, among other editions of Sophocles, L. Campbell and E. Abbot's edition of the *Philoctetes* (Oxford, 1879; *Reconstruction* A2170), presented to him by the editors, so he may have recalled what Sophocles had said about Ixion in that play (ll. 676-686). There the Chorus leader said he could think of nobody but Ixion who had suffered more cruelly than "this man," i. e., Philoctetes, and went on, "who, having done no harm to anyone or stolen from anyone . . . was perishing so undeservedly." Perhaps, in a rapid rereading of the passage, B mistook the antecedent of the relative "who" for Ixion (which the word-order makes easy enough to do) and so started the train of thought of Ixion's unfair treatment. At any rate his poem contradicts both Pindar and Sophocles in minimizing Ixion's crime, and maximizing the unfairness of his punishment. Of course, in representing Zeus as a cruel tyrant, B was following both the *Prometheus Bound* of Aeschylus, and especially the *Prometheus Unbound* of his old hero, Shelley; echoes of the latter work can be detected in his poem. He was also clearly registering a religious protest of his own against the Christian doctrine of Eternal Punishment (see C. R. Tracy, "Browning's Heresies," *SP* 33 [1936], 624). He had made a similar protest in the *Inn Album* (1875), 4.358-408 (this edition, 13.76-78), and would do so again in "A Camel-Driver" (*Ferishtah's Fancies* below), where it was associated with a protest against cruelty to animals, as in "Donald."

"Ixion" is written in an imitation of classical elegiacs. One can only guess why B chose that metre, which was mostly used for epigrams and epitaphs in the Greek Anthology, for flippant satire such as Ovid's *Ars Amatoria*, and for laments like the *Tristia*. None of these associations seems relevant to B's theme; but he knew that Ovid's appealing love-letters in the *Heroides* are, in form, predecessors of his own developed dramatic monologue form; and he may have felt that the recurrent moral comparison between Ixion and Zeus, first expressed in l. 2, demanded the use of a couplet, of which elegiacs were the obvious classical example.

1]   *triumph*   Used with a hint of the word's meaning in Roman history: an ostentatious procession, in which a victorious general had prisoners of war dragged along behind his chariot.

    Us]   Ixion and Zeus.

2]   *Here . . . revenge . . . God . . . there . . . amends . . . Man*   The pentameter which forms the second line of an elegiac couplet consists of two rhythmically identical halves, well suited to express, as here, the neatly balanced antithesis which epitomizes the theme of the poem.

6]   *Doles*   The word seems to be used in two senses: the modern one, "deals out," and an archaic one suggesting pain or suffering (from Latin *doleo* = feel pain, and *dolor* = pain).

7]   *rainbow*   In Rev. 4:3 there is a "rainbow round about the throne" of God. Here it arches over the sufferings of a man.

8]   *Tears, sweat, blood*   There may be an implicit allusion to Jesus, when "being in an agony he prayed more earnestly: and his sweat was as it were great drops of blood falling down to the ground" (Luke 22:44; cf. *Book of Common Prayer*, "Litany": "By thy agony and bloody sweat").

11]   *Bestowment of Zeus*   I. e., the body bestowed by Zeus

19]   *Beguiled and betrayed*   I. e., by sexual desire, and by optical illusion.

20]   *Made things false seem true*   Zeus made him mistake a cloud for a goddess.

21]   *reported*   By the physical organs of perception, *eye* and *ear*.

23]   *the only apparent*   The only thing that would then appear to the soul.

24]   *Was I Ixion or Zeus?*   The end of the pentameter verse runs more smoothly than it may seem, because B gives Ixion the correct Greek accent on the second syllable, not the first, i. e., Ixíon.

26]   *This proves shine, that — shade?*   This turns out to be white, that black. B repeats the neatly alliterative antithesis that he had invented in the *Ring and the Book* (1.1359-65; this edition, 7.56):

> Man, like a glass ball with a spark a-top . . .
> Shifted a hair's breadth shoots you dark for bright,
> Suffuses bright with dark, and baffles so
> Your sentence absolute for shine or shade.

28]   *Sisuphos . . . Tantalos*   The correct Greek spellings of the names more familiar in their Latin forms of Sisyphus and Tantalus. For B's justification of his revolutionary "conservatism" in this matter, see his foreword to his translation of Aeschylus' *Agamemnon* (this edition, 14.7-11, 272-75). Sisyphus, the founder of Corinth, was punished eternally in Hades by having to roll up a steep hill a great rock which, whenever it got to the top, rolled down again (Homer, *Odyssey*, 11.593-98). What he was punished for, is variously explained: either for imprisoning Death, when it came to fetch him, or for otherwise cheating the gods of the Underworld, or for informing a father that Zeus had seduced his daughter (*Oxford Companion to Classical Literature* [Oxford, 1989], 525). Tantalus' punishment was to suffer perpetual hunger and thirst while standing in water that dried up whenever he stooped to drink it, under a tree laden with fruit that was blown out of reach whenever he tried to eat it (*Odyssey*, 11.582-92).

31]   *scouts*   Scornfully rejects.

to Tantalos treason   What Tantalus was punished for is uncertain: "either he invited the gods to dinner and served them his son's flesh . . . or he stole nectar and ambrosia from the gods' table, where he had been invited, and gave them to his friends, or he told his friends the gods' secrets" (*Oxford Companion to Classical Literature*, 549). The last comes nearest to *treason*, but the word was perhaps chosen chiefly for its alliteration with *Tantalos*.

33]   *What is the sin*   The question is purely rhetorical, implying that *no* sin can ever be proved to be a sin by the infliction of pain.

35]   *thought . . . deed*   B echoes the Anglican *Book of Common Prayer*: "We acknowledge and bewail our manifold sins and wickedness, which we, from time to time, most grievously have committed, by thought, word, and deed, against thy divine majesty" ("General Confession").

conceited me   Imagined myself to be.

36]   *my friend . . . my love*   Imagining Zeus to be my friend, and Hera my love; *Heré* is the correct Greek spelling of Zeus' wife, Hera.

38]   *Film-work — eye's and ear's*   The result of a film on eye and ear. The word *film* is used almost in *OED*'s Sense 4: "A morbid growth upon the eye", then extended metaphorically to the ear.

40]   *thought . . . deed*   See l. 35n. above.

71]   *Ixion the cherished*   With the correct Greek accent on the second syllable of *Ixion*, the hexameter verse ends smoothly; see l. 24n. above.

75]   *Man among men . . . must regard me*   Apparently a confusion of two constructions: "I behaved so well that the gods, as I imagined, must surely think highly of me," and "I went on behaving well until I imagined the gods must surely think highly of me."

77]   *how other*   How else (the hexameter needed a disyllable to end with).

79]   *Heré*   See l. 36n. above.

82]   *my heart for thy heart*   I. e., let us exchange hearts in mutual love. B contradicts all classical sources of the myth in making Ixion's offence against Hera hardly more than a brash speech and a social kiss.

85]   *Olumpos . . . Erebos*   For B's use of the original Greek spellings, see l. 28n. above.

Erebos   The nether darkness of the Underworld.

91]   *Man made you*   The proposition that human beings imagine the gods in their own image shaped B's earlier "Caliban upon Setebos" (in *Dramatis Personæ*, this edition, 6.259).

273

95] *iris* Used in the sense of the original Greek word ἶϱις = rainbow (see l. 7); but perhaps also with a reminder that Iris in Homer was the messenger of the gods. So here it seems to imply a message from *the Potency o'er* Zeus (l. 121), promising more merciful treatment of humanity in future, like the rainbow in the Bible: "I do set my bow in the cloud, and it shall be for a token of a covenant between me and the earth . . . and the waters shall no more become a flood to destroy all flesh" (Gen. 9:13-15).

96] *Cold white—jewelry quenched* I. e., pure white instead of brightly colored, to represent the overriding *Potency.* B was doubtless remembering Shelley's elegy "Adonais": "Life, like a dome of many-coloured glass, / Stains the white radiance of eternity" (52.3-4; ll.462-63).

102-3] *the entity Thou . . . Not-Thou* The contrast recalls Matthew Arnold's famous definition of God, in *Literature and Dogma* (1873), as "the Eternal Power, not ourselves," (*The Complete Prose Works of Matthew Arnold*, ed. R. H. Super [Ann Arbor, 1960-77], 6.181-86; 409).

112] *Tartaros* See l. 28n. above.

124] *and sink* The picture and wording of Zeus's fall echo that of Jupiter in Shelley's *Prometheus Unbound*: "I sink / Dizzily down, ever, for ever, down" (3.1.80-81).

JOCHANAN HAKKADOSH

Sources] The Judaic and Talmudic backgrounds and contexts of *Jochanan Hakkadosh* are described at length in *Hebraism*, 54-77, which establishes that B drew upon the lives and characters of three Rabbis: Judah Hannasi (called "Hakkadosh," Hebrew for "holy"), Jochanan Nappcha, and Jochanan ben Sakkai. Their stories are narrated in the Talmud. B probably consulted the 12th-century *Travels* of Rabbi Benjamin of Tudela, which mentions places alluded to in the poem and contains the anecdote about Rabbi Perida employed in ll. 215-43. B's copy of a translation of Benjamin's *Travels* was inscribed by him in Feb. 1882, but he had owned the book for many years (*Reconstruction*, A194; see Curle, 42).

The poem's situation, though not its argument, is similar to that in "A Death in the Desert" in *Dramatis Personæ* (1864; this edition, 6.235). Unlike that poem, however, the chronoligical setting of *Jochanan Hakkadosh* is left deliberately vague, in the manner of many Rabbinical stories (though a reference to maize [l. 324] places the events of the poem later than the 15th century).

Title] In MS and P1883, B entitled the poem "Hakkadosh Jochanan" (Holy Jochanan), applying the epithet as an honorific title. According to P-C (11.345-46), someone informed him that this was not correct usage; he transposed the words on the proofs.

2]   *Mishna*   An early written compilation of Jewish oral tradition, the basis of the Talmud.

5]   *Schiphaz*   Old name for Shiraz, the capital city of Fars province in Iran (see also l. 801 n. below).

12]   *Eximious*   Excellent

Jochanan Ben Sabbathai   An invented name, which follows the pattern of "Jochanan ben Sakkai" (see *Sources* above), but does not refer to him; B was at pains to explain that "Ben Sabbathai" was "expressly added to prevent *that* mistake" (McAleer, *LL*, 156)

18]   *wool-plant*   *OED* speculates ("wool," 2. d, citing this usage as the sole example) that B means a plant of the mullein family—a plausible guess, since many mulleins (sp. *Verbascum*) have leaves with soft, downy hairs.

32]   *Partest . . . in peace*   Echoing part of Luke 2:29, the scriptural basis of the *nunc dimittis* in Christian liturgy.

37-39]   *Eden's tree . . . sapience]*   The tree of knowledge of good and evil in the garden of Eden appears in Gen. 2:9, 17; 3:1-6.

49-55]   *David . . . wield*   David's battle with the giant Goliath is narrated in 1 Sam. 17; David refuses Saul's armor and weapons in 1 Sam. 17:38-40.

60-61]   *Moses' stick / A serpent*   For the rod that changes into a snake, see Exod. 4:2-4.

71-72]   *pearl-gift . . . hogs*   See Matt. 7:6; an emblem of waste.

89]   *Khubbezleh*   An invented name, with a cross-lingual pun. *Khubbaza* is an Arabic name for the Mallow plant (*Malva silvestris*), which bears rose-colored flowers.

120]   *Targums*   Aramaic interpretations of Hebrew scriptures, containing religious instructions.

122]   *The Nine Points of Perfection*   An allusion to the Kabbala of Jewish mysticism, which lists nine human virtues that manifest the existence of God.

127-36]   *If haply folk . . . time recorded*   In regard to this folk belief, B wrote to Furnivall, "the old Rabbins fancied that *earnest wishing* might add to a valued life" (Peterson, 69).

143]   *The way of all flesh*   A traditional figure of speech for the path to inevitable death, based on an expression used by dying patriarchs in Josh. 23:14 and 1 Kings 2:2, "I go the way of all the earth."

144]   *Olive-branch Tsaddik*   The name of Jochanan's persistent student means "righteous one" in Hebrew; the olive symbolizes virtue and piety.

147-54]   *constellation . . . 'The Bear' . . . Banoth*   Biblical astronomy is a murky subject which B fails to clarify. Tsaddik's rhetorical aim is to compare the possibility of lending Jochanan fresh life with the revolution of the stars around Polaris, the North Star. His depiction of the Great Bear (Hebrew *dob* = bear) constellation focuses on the seven bright stars within it, known in North America as the Big Dipper. Arab astronomers called the four stars forming the bowl of the dipper *Na'sh*, "the bier," and the three stars *Banat Na'sh*, "daughters of the bier." Exploiting both the English pun and the competing astronomies, B enables Tsaddik to interpret an everyday natural phenomenon to his specific purpose. The Hebrew names *Ayish* (*Ash, Aish, Aisch*) and *Banoth* appear in Job 9:9, Job 38:31-32, and Amos 5:8; the former is taken to refer to the Great Bear, and the latter means "daughters."

   Satam   Apparently an invented name.

154]   *list . . . unfold*   The diction may echo the Ghost in *Hamlet* 1.5.15 and 22.

156]   *East-cone*   Clearly the pole-star, around which the stars appear to revolve, but no source for this curious term has been identified.

160]   *Salem*   Hebrew for "peace"; by extension, a place of peace.

166]   *The Chosen*   For the concept of the Jews as the chosen of God, see Exod. 19:5, Deut. 7:7-8, and Amos 3:2.

168-71]   *Old Just Ones . . . the Ten . . . our Race*   During the reign of the emperor Hadrian (AD 117-38), ten Rabbis were executed in Rome for teaching the Jewish Law. Their suffering and courage became a powerful part of Rabbinical tradition. B's use of the term *volunteered* in l. 170 needlessly mitigates the cruel cleverness by which the Romans turned the Law against the Rabbis.

175]   *Akiba*   The third of the ten martyrs to die, in the fashion B describes.

176]   *'Hear . . . One'*   English translation of the Hebrew prayer "Shema" (Deut. 6:4).

177]   *Jischab*   I. e., Yeshebab, another of the martyrs, whose manner of death is not described in the sources; B provides the circumstances of another martyr, Hananiah, who was burned along with a Torah.

186]   *no Selah, 'twixt two psalms*   Selah (Hebrew = lift up) is a cryptic word of exultation found within and at the conclusion of numerous psalms (e. g., Ps. 3, 4, 24, 39, 46, etc.).

187]   *quirist*   I. e., *choirist*, singer. B's spelling variant, which does not appear in *OED*, may look back to Shakespeare's music of the spheres, "Still quiring to the young-ey'd cherubins" (*Merchant of Venice* 5.1.62).

188-89]   *lion-flag . . . Zion's mount*   The lion is an emblem of the tribe of Judah (Gen. 49:8-9; Rev. 5:5); the reclaiming of Mt. Zion (in

Jerusalem) symbolizes the restoration of Israel to its ancestral home-land.

196] *Shah* No particular Persian king seems to be intended.

210] *appointed Fourscore* With sufficient strength, a human life may be extended to 80 years, according to Ps. 90:10.

211-12] *worm . . . butterfly* The metamorphosis of caterpillar into butterfly has since ancient times symbolized the release of the soul from the dying body.

215-43] *Perida . . . patience . . .* In Rabinnical lore, Rabbi Perida re-peats a lesson for a slow pupil 400 times; when the pupil was distracted, Perida repeated the lesson 400 more times. A voice from heaven then asks Perida to choose a reward for his extraordinary patience, but here (as in the matter of the number of repetitions) B departs from his source. In the Talmudic version, God offers a choice between 400 more years of earthly life for himself or the entrance of Perida's whole generation into the afterlife. When Perida takes the second option, God says "Give him both"; B makes the choice of futures apply only to Perida. Almost twenty years earlier, B had recounted to Julia Wedge-wood the story of Rabbi Perida from Benjamin of Tudela's *Travels*, re-taining the original numbers and the offer of "eternal life for thee *and thy posterity*" (Curle, 41-42; emphasis added).

221] *Uzzean* I. e., Job, the man of Uz (Job 1:1), and the Biblical pat-tern of patience.

256] *Rudesby* An insolent or disobedient person (archaic).

264] *vine and figtree* These emblems of peace and comfort appear in Mic. 4:4 and Zech. 3:10.

266] *turtle* Turtle-dove (archaic).

274] *usury* Interest paid on a borrowed sum (in this archaic sense, without the implication of exorbitance).

284] *Like earth-smoke . . . crevice* In volcanically active regions such as the Mediterranean basin, vapors and gasses are emitted from cracks and fissures in the earth.

294] *custom the accloyer* A fusion of *accloy* (= fill to satiety) and *cloyer* (= that which cloys); the diction may recall Shakespeare's "Age cannot wither her, nor custom stale / Her infinite variety. Other women cloy / The appetites they feed" (*Antony and Cleopatra*, 2.2.234-35).

319] *the horned band* A Homer-like epithet (though not in Homer), with *hornéd* pronounced in two syllables for the meter.

324] *maize and cummin* Corn and cumin, alluring luxury grains for the steer (l. 314); cumin has been cultivated in Europe and Asia since ancient times, but maize became known outside of the Americas only in the 15th century.

337]   *the victor's palm*   The palm frond, symbolic of victory in many civilizations, was carried in triumphal parades.

340]   *excellence of Judah*   The tribal name *Judah* (see l. 188-89n. above) is used as a synecdoche for all of Israel.

354]   *sycamine*   A Biblical name for the mulberry tree (Luke 17:6); taken here to mean a producer of figs. The fig tree fruits on old wood in the spring and new growth in the autumn.

386]   *fares*   Some editions prefer the MS reading *fires*, and the metaphor of sudden incandescence would support an emendation to *flares*. But elsewhere B combines *fares* and *forth* in association with flame ("Numpholeptos," ll. 67, 75, and 149-50; this edition, 13.193, 197), and the copy-text reading emphasizes the motion of the meteor in addition to its flammability.

396]   *Djinn*   In Arabian mythology and Islam, a djinn is a spirit-creature made of fire.

413]   *Edom's children*   The Rabbis referred to Rome as "Edom," identifying the city with the ancient of Edom, which was enimical to the Israelites (Num. 20:14-21); thus "Edom's children" here means "Christians."

413-14]   *turn / Cheek to the smiter*   Jesus offers this principle in Matt. 5:39 and Luke 6:29.

      Sic Jesus vult   "So Jesus wishes" (from Latin *volo* = to will, to ordain).

428]   *sycamine*   See l. 354n. above.

472]   *dubitation*   Doubt (archaic).

474-77]   *Joshua-like . . . assistance*   See Josh. 10:12-13.

521-22]   *Day's . . . owls and bats*   An allusion to the poet's own "Pippa Passes," 4.86-98, seems inescapable (see this edition, 3.81-82).

534-35]   *fool cicada . . . Spring*   This embellishes Æsop's fable, "The Grasshopper and the Ant," substituting *cicada* for the grasshopper (and the poet).

539-40]   *Sampsons . . . valour*   A catalogue of legendary Jewish men of action. The heroic feats of *Samson* are narrated in Judg. 13-16; *Abner*, the successful captain of Saul's troops, was murdered by the crafty *Joab*, commander of David's army (1 Sam. 14:50, 2 Sam. 2, 3); *Judas* Maccabeus rebelled against Syrian rulers in Palestine and captured Jerusalem (see 1 Macc. in the Apocrypha).

560-63]   *shrewd Ahithophel . . . Chosen*   Both King David and his rebellious son Absalom consulted the wise Ahithophel (2 Sam. 16:23); the advisor whom Jochanan cannot recall is presumably Hushai, whose counsel to Absalom is given in 2 Sam. 17:5-16.

566]   *sagacious ant*   See ll. 534-35n. above.

578]   *sons of Shimei*   During Absalom's rebellion, Saul's kinsman Shimei cursed and threatened the fleeing David (2 Sam. 16:5-13); when David returned to power after the death of Absalom, Shimei begged forgiveness (2 Sam. 19:18-23).

579]   *rape*   A rhyme-driven use of an archaic sense of the word, "to sieze or take by force."

585-88]   *alkahest . . . gold miss*   The alchemist Paracelsus, whose works B knew well (see *Parcelsus,* this edition, 1.69-277), posited the existence of the *alkahest,* or universal solvent; this substance would have dissolved not only lacquer, but brass and gold as well. B may be recalling the various acid-tests for the purity of gold.

593]   *life's wood*   The image recalls the opening of Dante's *Divine Comedy,* Canto 1.

600]   *hinds*   Farmhands.

601]   *legislate*   See l. 619n. below.

612-13]   *Mizraim . . . Goshen*   The Hebrew name for Egypt is *Mizraim;* Goshen, which Joseph offered to the Israelites as a home (Gen. 45:10), is thought to be a fertile valley in NE Egypt. Jochanan attributes *cold* and *murk* to the place because of events in the book of Exodus. While the Israelites were enslaved in Goshen by the Pharaoh, God and Moses inflicted ten plagues on Egypt; the seventh of these was a hail-storm (Exod. 9:18-33) and the ninth three days of darkness (Exod. 10:21-23).

619]   *legislate . . . poet*   The characterization of a poet's influence as "legislation" looks back to Shelley ("Poets are the unacknowledged legislators of the world" [*A Defense of Poetry*]) and Dr. Johnson ("He must write as the interpreter of nature, and the legislator of mankind" [*Rasselas,* Ch. 10]).

625]   *Princes of Night*   Since the passage is about the time of Jochanan's death, Tsaddik may be referring to the position of the stars.

   acquist   That which was acquired (archaic).

626-7]   *corners . . . Aisch*   See ll. 147-54n. above.

628]   *Mishna's lore*   See l. 2n. above.

632]   *the Bier*   See ll. 147-54n. above.

665]   *fattening lees*   During the first fermentation of red wines, the grape juice is left in contact with the skins as yeast converts sugars to alcohol; the skins and yeast settle as the *lees* in the fermentation vessel; up to a point, the longer the wine is left on the lees, the stronger its flavors and color.

669]   *verjuice*   Sour juice from unripe fruit.

670]   *Shushan's flower*   The Hebrew word for "lily" is *shushan.*

696-97]   *why kick . . . pricks*   Odd as it may be for Jochanan to quote the NT, this phrase appears in Acts 9:5 and 26:14.

out-wormed   If we can presume that B alludes here to his earlier metamorphosis-figure (see ll. 211-12), as the reference to *wings* in l. 700 suggests, the participle means "entirely transformed from body to soul."

707]   *My way . . . rejoicing*   Echoing Acts 8:39.

710-11]   *Vanity of vanities*   From Eccles. 1:2-3; used memorably by B's dying Bishop in "The Bishop Orders His Tomb at St. Praxed's Church" (1845; this edition, 4.189).

718]   *He the Operant*   I. e., God the creator and life-giver.

720]   *thaumaturgic*   Miraculous.

721]   *tohu-bohu*   Hebrew for "empty void" or "chaos"; used in Gen. 1:2, "the earth was without form and void."

747]   *Oppugnant*   Contrary; opposed.

759-61]   *a rape / Like . . . flesh*   As in the story of Ixion, in Greek mythology and B's poem of the same name, above.

777]   *Halaphta*   The name of several Rabbis in the Talmud; one was a pupil of Akiba (l. 175n. above).

780-84]   *the Ruach . . . victim*   In Judaism the *Ruach* is the breath of life, i. e., the incarnated soul (Gen. 2:7). The belief described here is found in the Talmud.

801]   *Schiphaz . . . Farzistan*   In earlier European transliterations, the name of the ancient city of Shiraz was given as *Shiphaz*; the river Bandimir runs near the ruins of Persepolis, NE of Shiraz; both are in the province of Fars, sometimes called Farzistan by European geographers. B may have borrowed *Bendimir* from a song in Thomas Moore's popular oriental romance *Lalla Rookh* (1817): "There's a bower of roses by BENDEMEER's stream, / And the nightingale sings round it all the day long; / In the time of my childhood 'twas like a sweet dream, / To sit in the roses and hear the bird's song." Moore glosses "Bendemeer" as "a river which flows near the ruins of Chilminar," (another name for Persepolis); this lyric was set to music numerous times in the Victorian era.

CONCLUDING NOTE AND SONNETS

Sources]   The three sonnets appended to "Jochanan Hakkadosh" continue to draw on the Talmud and the Bible; J. Berlin-Lieberman traces the substance of each sonnet to its Hebraic source, demonstrating the range of B's reading in Talmudic legends (*Hebraism*, 72-75). In the Bible, Moses led the Israelites in defeating King Og, the last of the race of giants (Deut. 3:1-11).

In a letter to George Barnett Smith accompanying the Pforzheimer proofs (see *Jocoseria, Text and Publication*), B explained the Hebrew phrases that appear in his note: "The two Hebrew quotations (put in to give a grave look to what is mere fun & invention) being translated amount to—1ˢᵗ—'A collection of many lies'—and the 2ⁿᵈ is an old saying 'From Moses to Moses arose none like Moses.'" Though the grammar of the first phrase is faulty, J. Berlin-Lieberman exonerates B by finding its source in a translation of Tudela's *Travels* (*Hebraism*, 75-76).

From Moses to Moses   That is, between the Biblical Moses and Rabbi Moses Maimonides (1138-1204), the most influential Jewish philosopher of the middle ages. The saying quoted by B became Maimonides' epitaph, frequently appearing as an epigraph to his *Guide for the Perplexed.*

l. 1]   *Moses the Meek*   "Moses was very meek, above all the men which were upon the face of the earth" (Num. 12:3).

l. 13-14]   *a frog . . . an ox*   An allusion to Æsop's fable about the frog that burst while trying to make himself as large as an ox.

NEVER THE TIME AND THE PLACE

Composition]   Unorthodox Christian though B may have been, this strikingly personal lyric expresses one of his strongest religious convictions: he will be reunited with EBB after death.

7]   *the house is narrow*   A figurative expressions for the grave—see "The Statue and the Bust," l. 215 (this edition, 5.270).

12]   *enemy*   The "serpentine" enemy is perhaps doubt, which figures repeatedly in the poems of *Jocoseria*. A similar figure appears in Coleridge's "Dejection: An Ode": "Hence, viper thoughts, that coil around my mind, / Reality's dark dream!" (ll. 94-95).

PAMBO

Sources]   The story of Pambo (a 4ᵗʰ-century saint and disciple of St. Anthony) is taken from one of the poet's favorite sources, *The Wonders of the Little World* (1667), by Nathaniel Wanley (for B's copy, see *Reconstruction*, A2412). In Chapter 4 of Book III he found the following account:

> Pambo came to a Learned Man, and desired him to teach him
> some Psalm; he began to read to him theThirty-ninth, and the

first Verse, which is: "I said, I will look to my ways, that I offend not with my tongue." Pambo shut the Book, and took his leave, saying, "he would go learn that point." And having absented himself for some months, he was demanded by his teacher, "when he would go forward?" He answered, "That he had not yet learned his old lesson, to speak in such a manner as not to offend with his tongue"

2] *crambo*   Doggerel, from a rhyming game of the same name. Used comically by Burns, one of B's favorite poets, in "Epistle to J. Lapraik, An Old Scottish Bard" (ll. 44-45) and "On a Scotch Bard, Gone to the West Indies," where poets are addressed as "A' ye wha live by crambo-clink" (l. 2).

15] *Pellucid streams*   In picturing the gaining of wisdom as drinking from a stream, the Professor is perhaps recalling Pope: "A little learning is a dangerous thing; / Drink deep, or taste not the Pierian spring:" (*An Essay on Criticism*, 2.15-16).

16-18] *the Nine-and-thirtieth . . . not*   In the AV, Ps. 39 begins "I said, I will take heed to my ways, that I sin not with my tongue: I will keep my mouth with a bridle"; B uses Wanley's wording.

26] *restive*   Obstinate or difficult to control; here the word applies to horses, as indicated by *driven* (l. 27) and *collar* (l. 28).

27] *I had*   I would have.

   I wis   I know.

50] *Arcades sumus ambo!*   Latin for "We are both Arcadians"; from Virgil, *Eclogues* 7.4. Virgil potrayed the land of Arcadia as a pastoral paradise.

52] *critic's flambeau*   A *flambeau* is a torch; metaphorically, then, the *critic's flambeau* is the light, or intelligence, provided by the critic.

FERISHTAH'S FANCIES

§The basic research for this edition of *Ferishtah's Fancies* was begun by the late Jack W. Herring. Professor Herring's work has been incorporated into the Editorial Notes and textual apparatus.§

Emendations to the Text

The following emendations have been made to the 1889a copy-text:

The Melon-Seller, ll. 39-40: Diacritical marks in the Hebrew, present in MS-1885a, are missing in the copy-text; they are restored.

Shah Abbas, l. 139: In 1889a, this line ends with a single closing quotation mark where a double quotation mark is required. The MS-1885a reading is restored.

The Sun, ll. 17-18: A line-space marking a new paragraph, present in MS-1885a, is missing from the copy-text; the paragraph is restored.

Two Camels, l. 21: The copy-text prints a two-point ellipsis here, while all previous texts have the conventional three points. The MS-1885a reading is restored.

Two Camels, l. 65: In MS-1885a, this line ends with an exclamation mark; the copy text has no punctuation here, garbling the grammar of the following lines. The MS-1885a reading is restored.

Two Camels, l. 86: MS-1885a end this line with an exclamation mark, but 1889a has no punctuation here. Clearly some sentence-ending punctuation is required; the earlier reading is restored.

Two Camels, l. 89: Diacritical marks in the Hebrew, present in MS-1885a, are missing in the copy-text; they are restored.

Two Camels, l. 110: The copy-text ends this line with a period, but the colon found in the earlier printed texts is clearly preferable. The lack of any punctuation at this point in the MS indicates that B's sentence runs from l. 109 to the full stop in l. 111. The P1884-1885a reading is restored.

Cherries, l. 58: A comma at the end of this line, present in MS-1885a, is missing in 1889a. Some punctuation is required by the syntax, so the MS-1885a reading is restored.

Cherries, l. 74: In all texts, the question mark is within the quotation marks, though the syntax (*What if he boasted*, l. 73) clearly requires that the punctuation be reversed. The reading *be'*? is supplied.

A Bean-Stripe: Also, Apple-Eating, l. 304: The copy-text prints a question mark after *strength*, where all previous texts have a dash. Though the syntax is obscure, this part of the passage does not seem to be an interrogative. Furthermore, B is generally quite scrupulous in treating a question mark as terminal punctuation and thus capitalizing the next word (see ll. 278, 283, 292, and 297). The dash of MS-1885a is restored.

A Bean-Stripe: Also, Apple-Eating, l. 423: The disappearance of the question mark at the end of this line in 1889a is surely a compositor's error. The first two words of the next line (*Dead worthies!*) are the answer to the question *How come they short* in this line. The MS-1885a reading is restored.

A Bean-Stripe: Also, Apple-Eating, ll. 478-79: In the MS, B placed a rule between the narrative poem and its appended lyric, as he had done in every parallel instance. However, none of the printed texts prints the rule; the MS reading is restored.

Composition

The composition of *Ferishtah's Fancies* appears to have been relatively swift—it took no more than six months—but not linear. Throughout the autumn and winter of 1883-84, B went back and forth over his collection of poems, composing, revising, adding, and rearranging even after the volume was in proofs. With his sister Sarianna, B left London on 13 August 1883 and arrived in Gressoney St. Jean in the Italian Alps on 22 August; it is possible he had some of the poems for *Ferishtah's Fancies* with him, especially if he had been prompted to consider Persian themes by the publication of Helen Zimmern's *The Epic of Kings* in 1882 and by the death of Edward FitzGerald, translator of the *Rubáiyát of Omar Khayyám*, in June 1883 (see *Sources* below).

By 9 September, B characterized himself as "writing some poetry" (Peterson, 76), and only three days later he composed and dated his "Prologue." The conceit of the "Prologue" depends on B's having already composed a number of poems, and they must have struck him as quite diverse—so varied as to raise the question of how he would string them together. But his metaphor for diversity in mode and content—the skewered ortolans, sage leaves, and toasted bread—could not at the given date of 12 September have included his clever formal "spitting" of monologues, conversations, and lyrics. The interspersed lyrics, B claimed, were written last. In the presentation copy of *Ferishtah's Fancies* B gave him, Frederick Furnivall recorded the poet's remark about the lyrics: "All the Songs or Interludes written in one week, after the rest of the Poem, to lighten it. R. B. 23 Nov. 1884" (Peterson, 99; but see "Plot-Culture," *Composition* below).

Writing to Furnivall on 29 September, B had characterized what he had in hand: "a continuous set of—shall I call them, Studies?—in which, at least, you will find 'plenty of myself'. . . . Don't say anything about what is all in the rough, and may continue so" (Peterson, 78). Just two days later, the Brownings left Gressoney for Venice, arriving on 4 October at Katharine deKay Bronson's palazzo, where they stayed for over two months. There he composed his "Epilogue" for *Ferishtah's Fancies* and dated it 1 December 1883. Evidence is plentiful, however, that B continued writing and revising—even beyond adding all the lyrics—after returning to London in mid-December. In the Balliol MS, line 111 of "A Camel-Driver" is followed by the date "Sept. 23. 1883," suggesting that half the volume was drafted by late September; B cancelled that date and appended the lyric later, extending the poem onto the verso of the last leaf. Another cancelled date—"Sept. '83-Jan. 15. '84"—appears part way through "Two Camels" (after l. 65); and just before the lyric in "Cherries" B wrote "Jan. 15. L. D. I. E." (for the Latin *Laus Deo in Excelcis*, "Praise God in the highest"). "Plot-Culture," which in the MS lacks its lyric but does bear B's note, "Leave room for a small poem's insertion here," ends with the date "L. D. I. E. Jan. 17. 84." A month later, on 14 February 1884, the MS was complete enough that B could consider an American publication: "what would Messrs. Harper give for twelve consecutive poems in blank verse, preceded by a lyrical prologue and epilogue, forming one poem on a variety of exceedingly serious subjects, connected one with the other, and making together a volume of some 1500 or 2000 lines . . . ?" (Peterson, 92). Yet still he was not finished: he wrote the lyric appended to "Plot-Culture" in early September of 1884, and added the "Apple-Eating" section that concludes "A Bean-Stripe" when *Ferishtah's Fancies* was in proof (see *Text and Publication* below).

Sources and Background

The main source for the Persian names and references in *Ferishtah's Fancies* was the quasi-historical collection called the *Shah-Nameh* (The Book of Kings), by the tenth-century Persian poet Firdausi (or Ferdowsi). B knew this book through the translation of his friend Helen Zimmern; in the first edition of her *Epic of Kings, Stories Retold from Firdusi* (1882), Zimmern thanked B for his encouragement of her work. Other friends of B were also involved in the project: Edmund Gosse contributed an introductory poem, and the Orientalist painter Lawrence Alma-Tadema provided two illustrations. (For B's copy, see *Reconstruction*, A964; he acknowledged receipt of the book in a letter dated 22 November 1882 [Browning Database, ABL, 82:180].) The *Shah-Nemeh*, considered by many to be a masterpiece of Persian literature, unified numerous legends and oral traditions into one comprehensive epic; parts of the work were translated into English by 1785, and many more translations followed in the Victorian era. A large portion of the *Shah-Nameh* features the adventures of the warrior-king Rustem, the father who unknowingly kills his son in Matthew Arnold's "Sohrab and Rustum" (1853); B knew Arnold's poems well, and some of the heroes and places he takes from *The Epic of Kings* also appear in "Sohrab and Rustum."

Most of *Ferishtah's Fancies* is, as B asserted, the product of the poet's own inventiveness, but the volume grew from a literary origin. In the explanatory notes he added to Mrs. Orr's copy of *Ferishtah's Fancies* (see *Text and Publication* below), B says he took the incident in *The Eagle* from the fables of Pilpay (or Bidpai): "This is from Pilpay's Fables: I read it when a boy and lately put it into verse: then it occurred to me to make the Dervish one Ferishtah, and the poem the beginning of a series" (*1884O*, 7; for Pilpay, see notes to "The Eagle" below). Of the remaining poems in the collection, only "The Melon-Seller" has a specific source—a newspaper report from 1846 (see "The Melon-Seller," *Source*, below). Ultimately, the substance of the fourteen poems in *Ferishtah's Fancies* has little to do with Persian or other Arabic sources. B himself characterized the Oriental aspect of the volume as "a thin disguise of a few Persian names and allusions" (B to G. B. Smith, 19 October 1884 [Browning Database, ABL, 84:221]), acknowledging to Furnivall that there was "plenty of myself" in the book (see above).

The surprising popularity of *Ferishtah's Fancies* was due in part to the book's resonance with contemporary interests, particularly the phase in the history of taste now termed Victorian Orientalism. English interest in Middle Eastern literature, art and culture grew as the empire grew; as early as 1772, Sir William Jones—scholar, jurist, and friend of Samuel Johnson—broke new ground by translating a collection of Persian poetry. Following Jones's example, Walter Savage Landor published a volume of *Poems from the Arabic and Persian* (1800). (Decades later, Landor became fast friends with B, who received many books from the elder poet, including several copies of this one [*Reconstruction*, A1405-10]). In 1817, Thomas Moore captured the public taste with his "oriental romance" *Lalla Rookh*, and subsequent English popular literature from Byron to Wilde incorporated exotic Eastern elements. In the 1850s appeared not only Arnold's "Sohrab and Rustum," and B's own "Epistle of Karshish, the Arab Physician" (1855; see this edition, 5.219), but also the vastly more popular *Pilgrimage to Al-Medinah and Mecca* (1855) by Richard Burton. The publication of Burton's celebrated translation of the *Arabian Nights* commenced in the same year as *Ferishtah's Fancies.*

Perhaps the most famous piece of English literary Orientalism, the *Rubáiyát of Omar Khayyám*, translated by Edward FitzGerald, appeared in an obscure pamphlet edition in 1859. Shortly thereafter, D. G. Rossetti came across this collection of Persian quatrains and sent copies to friends, including B., Ruskin, and Swinburne. FitzGerald's second, expanded edition of the *Rubáiyát* in 1868 proved successful, and the much-reprinted fourth edition of 1879 established the work as a classic (this edition also included FitzGerald's translation of *Salámán and Absál* by the Sufi poet Jami, which B seems to have known). FitzGerald's death in June 1883 may have stirred favorable thoughts about Persian poetry in B's mind; his infamous rage at FitzGerald did not arise until 1889. It cannot be said that FitzGerald's *Rubáiyát* was a direct source for *Ferishtah's Fancies*, but some of the names and places B mentions do appear in FitzGerald, and in the MS, l. 133 of "Mihrab Shah" contains the word "Rhuibayat" (replaced with "poetry").

In realms beyond literature, B had further contact with Orientalism. The Great Exhibition of 1851 brought vast quantities of Middle Eastern and Asian goods and artifacts for display in London; it is not certain that the Bs attended the Exhibition, but they were in London that summer, and EBB mentioned the Crystal Palace in a letter (21 October 1851; *Letters of EBB*, 2.24). Furthermore, the Bs were acquainted with several artists associated with Orientalism. They met Frederic Leighton in Florence in 1852, and became life-long friends; Leighton's "The Music Lesson," from 1877, is Orientalist in its details of decoration and architectural setting. In 1877-79, Leighton had a Moorish-style "Arab Hall" built in his house in Holland Park, (now known as Leighton House). B surely saw that room, if not at the invitation of the painter, then at that of his sister, Alexandra Leighton Orr, B's friend and biographer. James Whistler, who like B was a regular guest at Katharine deKay Bronson's house in Venice, produced one of the pinnacles of Orientalist design in his Peacock Room, completed in 1877. This spectacular dining room in F. R. Leyland's London mansion was made available for public viewing and became a popular sensation. (The Peacock Room is now housed in the Freer Gallery of the Smithsonian Institution in Washington, D. C.) Among other Orientalist works B would have seen were the very popular paintings of Lawrence Alma-Tadema, who not only produced a series of Egyptian scenes in the 1860s and 70s, but contributed illustrations to Zimmern's *Epic of Kings* (see above). B knew Alma-Tadema well by 1880 and met him frequently at London social occasions.

Orientalism as a style had begun to wane by the mid-1880s, but another intellectual movement of the day, one related to Orientalism in several ways, also contributed indirectly to the writing of *Ferishtah's Fancies* and its critical reception. The pervasive optimism of the volume—surely a cause of its immediate popularity—has often been deprecated since its first appearance for its sometimes facile or disingenuous treatment of human suffering. In taking this view, B was quite deliberately out of step with the times. As DeVane puts it, "in the last fifteen years of his life . . . [he] began to dustrust knowledge when the tide of historical and scientific fact went directly against most of the doctrines he held dear" (*Hbk.*, 487-88). The 1870s had seen a distinct darkening in the philosophical outlook of Europe, and the pessimism inherent in the writings of Schopenhauer, Hartmann, Heine, Leopardi, and James Thomson provoked occasional outcries in the British press (see, for example, J. Tulloch, "Pessimism," *Edinburgh Review* 149 [1879], 500-33; and Richard Garnett's essay, "Leopardi," in the 9th edition of the *Encyclopaedia Britannica* [1881]). But if B intended *Ferishtah's Fancies* to be a serious contribution to the discussion, he failed egregiously in some eyes. In an important review in *The Athenaeum*, Theodore Watts-Dunton, long a loyal appreciator of B's poetry, dismissed his philosophy: "If the pessimism of the present day is to be confronted and answered, it is not by such optimism as this" (6 Dec. 1884, 725-27).

Text and Publication

There are six surviving texts of *Ferishtah's Fancies* which were under B's control: a printers'-copy manuscript, a set of proofs of the first edition, the published first edition, which exists in three impressions, and the collected edition of 1888-1889. The collation of these texts is recorded in the variant lists.

The Balliol Manuscript (MS)   The manuscript of *Ferishtah's Fancies* preserved in the Balliol College Library (*Reconstruction*, E127) consists of seventy-four full leaves and three inserted part-leaves, irregularly numbered by B and renumbered by the printers. That this MS, which contains numerous revisions and additions, was used as printers' copy is evidenced by "take" marks and the names of the compositors to whom they were assigned. Parts of the MS are clearly fair copy, while other parts show the familiar pattern of revision typical of B's compositional MSS. In the fair-copied portions, the lyric that ends each section is continuous with the main body of the poem, though sometimes concluded on the verso of a leaf. In the more heavily revised parts of the MS, some lyrics are inserted on part-leaves, and the one for "Plot-Culture" is missing. B's remark to Furnivall about writing all the lyrics in a week after the rest of *Ferishtah's Fancies* was finished (see *Composition* above) probably marks the assembly of the printers' copy in February 1884. The six fair-copied leaves containing the "Apple-Eating" section of "A Bean-Stripe: Also, Apple-Eating," and its concluding lyric were submitted after the volume was in proof; these sheets must have been added to the earlier printers' copy when it was returned to the poet. Four poems in the MS—"Two Camels," "Cherries," "Plot-Culture," and "A Bean-Stripe" are surely original drafts; they are the most heavily reworked, and their dates (each crossed out when he resumed composition) are all accompanied by B's celebratory "L. D. I. E." (for the Latin *Laus Deo in Excelcis*, "Praise God in the highest"). For further discussion of the MSS of individual poems, see *Composition* above and the Editorial Notes below.

The Widener Proofs (P1884)   The only documentary source of information about the typesetting and proofing of *Ferishtah's Fancies* is a set of page proofs housed in the Widener Library at Harvard University.   These proofs were provided by B himself to George Barnett Smith, who was writing a review of the book for the *Times*. The Widener proofs contain several kinds of material beyond their printed readings. B has added thirteen explanatory comments (included in our Editorial Notes) and made ten textual corrections (recorded in the variant lists). Also, someone at Spottiswoode & Co., Smith, Elder's printers, has marked ten instances of mechanical problems with the types, such as high spaces or damaged letters. The importance of the Widener proofs, which represent a late stage of compositing, is established by their origin and history.

According to B himself, the proofing of *Ferishtah's Fancies* took just over a month in the late summer of 1884. In a letter to Furnivall B announced that he was "correcting the proofs" of *Ferishtah* on 22 August, while he was in Switzerland (Peterson, 98). These were probably not first proofs but early revises, because a note near the end of the MS alludes to the pagination of the book (see "A Bean-Stripe: Also,

Apple-Eating," *Composition* below). B acknowledged the receipt of another set of proofs on 2 September, and wrote to Mrs. FitzGerald that he had sent back these "final proofs" on 8 September (B. Miller, *Robert Browning: A Portrait* [New York, 1953], 288; McAleer, *LL*, 183). But the sheets sent from Switzerland were not the final press-proofs; the date stamps on the Widener proofs show them to be still further revises. Clean page-proofs, they were sent out in batches by Spottiswoode beginning on 3 September. The new revises of sheets B-E (pages 1-64) could have reached B abroad, but when he wrote on 28 September from St. Moritz that "the last corrected proofs are at the Printer's," he was not actually done with his task (Peterson, 100). He must have found the sheets of at least gatherings F-K (pp. 65-143, dated 27 and 29 September) waiting for him in London upon his return on 3 October. The title-page and other preliminaries in the Widener proofs bear the Spottiswoode date stamp for 6 October 1884. It is equally possible that the entire set of revises had accumulated at his London home, and that he made his few last-minute changes there. In either case, he finished his work on 6 October, as he announced to G. B. Smith in a letter that suggests the status of the Widener proofs:

> With this, will also go to the Printer's the last revises of the Poem,—including a request that I may have at once a clean copy of the whole: when this arrives, you shall have it immediately . . . . [T]here are a few Persian names, and allusions which you might like explained, and I will make a note of these . . . .
>
> (DeVane and Knickerbocker, 310)

But what Browning sent to Smith was not a further revise or a press proof; it is not a "clean copy of the whole." The Widener proofs are either (a) the same set of proofs B sent back to Spottiswoode on 6 October, bearing his final corrections; or (b) a duplicate set of what B sent to the printers that day. If these are the very proofs used to instruct Spottiswoode's compositors, then B retrieved them from the printers and added his explanatory notes before he sent them to Smith on 19 October. If the Widener proofs were originally duplicates, then B copied his corrections onto them and added his notes. B's letter to Smith accompanying the proofs favors the second explanation: "as the copy of the poem, promised for you, has not yet arrived . . . I send by this post the only proofs I retained—which will serve your purpose, I hope, as well as a cleaner copy."

The thirteen marginal notes B provided are nearly identical with those he made in Mrs. Orr's copy of the first edition, but there are fewer of them. Of the ten textual corrections B entered on the Widener proofs, eight were made in the first edition.

The First Edition (1884)   The publication of *Ferishtah's Fancies* was deliberately delayed for marketing reasons; B explained to G. B. Smith on 19 October 1884: "the publication of my Poem might possibly be postponed for some three or four weeks, in consequence of an arrangement with America" (Browning Database, ABL, 84:221). The first edition was announced for 21 November, but B signed his presentation copy to Furnivall on 18 November and inscribed more copies, including one to Helen Zimmern, on the 20th (*Reconstruction*, C315, C327). Given the success of *Jocoseria* the year before, this first impression may have comprised 2000 or more copies. The book immediately sold very well; the latest date on a presentation copy was 9 December (C319), just two weeks before B signed a copy of the 2nd "edition" (C328).

The copy of the first edition that B presented to Alexandra Leighton Orr, his friend and future biographer, has special significance. Preserved in the Balliol College Library, the volume (*Reconstruction*, C321) contains twenty marginal notes and one textual correction in B's hand. The contents of these annotations are recorded in the Editorial Notes below, where the Orr copy is referred to as *1884O*.

The First Edition, Second Impression (1885)   The first impression of *Ferishtah's Fancies* sold so quickly that a new press-run was soon needed. Following normal Victorian publishing practice, the new copies bore on their title-pages the proud designation, "Second Edition," when in fact the sheets were produced from the existing typesetting and are more correctly called a second impression. The only parts of the volume that were reset were the lines where B's thirty-eight corrections were made. The most substantial change B made was the addition of two and a half lines (ll. 40-42) to "The Melon-Seller."

The earliest reference to the new impression is 13 December 1884, when C. J. Lyall sent B a list of corrections for "the new edition of *Ferishtah's Fancies* which I see is now passing through the press." Lyall, a noted scholar of Arabic, suggested five changes in the spelling of Persian names, and one change in scansion. His list arrived too late for the second impression, but B followed Lyall's advice about spelling in the third impression. Lyall's letter is reproduced in *Intimate Glimpses From Browning's Letter File*, Baylor Browning Interests, Series 8 (Waco, TX, 1934, 100-101 [also in Browning Database, ABL, 84:286]). The same publication preserved David Masson's observation on 15 December that "the second Edition is announced" (101), and B signed a presentation copy of the second impression on 24 December. Copies of the second impression—it is not clear how many were printed—are dated 1885, but were available to the public for Christmas, 1884 (the editor's own copy is so inscribed).

The Third Impression (1885a)   Collation shows that the so-called third edition of *Ferishtah's Fancies* was in fact a third corrected impression from the same types as its two predecessors. Exactly when it was produced during 1885 is unknown, but the bound-in advertisements announced the first segment of the *Dictionary of National Biography*, which began publication in January of that year. B makes no allusion to this reprinting in his published correspondence. He did, however, make ten corrections in the new impression, most of them in response to C. J. Lyall's suggestions, which had arrived too late for the second impression (see above). Two corrections which had been called for on the Widener proofs were finally made in the third impression. How many copies of *1885a* were printed is not known, though his publisher's practice seems to have been to order a minimum of 500 copies when reprinting.

Collected Edition (1889a)   In the 1888-1889 *Poetical Works*, *Ferishtah's Fancies* occupies pages 1-92 of the sixteenth volume. B's care with his final text is well-illustrated by the presence of ninety-three changes originating in *1889a*. Some of these are routine or trivial, but a substantial number sort out confusions in the punctuation of quotations. Other changes clarify pronoun references, and a few errors introduced in *1885a* are corrected.

Title

Though the MS used as printers' copy is entitled *Ferishtah's Fancies*, B apparently considered the title *Seriora* for the volume. An undated leaf in B's hand (*Reconstruction*, E129), now at the Armstrong Browning Library, is headed "Seriora—being divers fancies of the Dervish Ferishtah." Below this are the two quotations B used as epigraphs. The first is identified as being from "Jeremy Collier's Dictionary Article Shakespeare," though the lines from *King Lear*, slightly misquoted, bear no source information. Beneath the Shakespeare quotation is a description of the collection: "Introductory Lyric, Twelve Fancies, Concluding Lyric." The approximate date of this draft of preliminary materials for the volume can be deduced from its parallels with the enumeration B offered to Furnivall in a letter of 14 February 1884 (see *Composition* above).

Seriora, Latin for "the more serious things," suggests that B considered *Ferishtah's Fancies* to be the serious counterpart to his more lighthearted preceding volume, *Jocoseria* (1883). The tentative Latin title of the new collection derived from Otto Melander's book of anecdotes, *Jocorum atque Seriorum*, as had its predecessor (see *Jocoseria, Title* n., above).

Epigraphs

The proof-correction of the date of Jeremy Collier's *Great Historical, Geographical, Geneaological and Poetical Dictionary*, 2nd ed. (London, 1701) was prompted by Frederick Furnivall; in thanking him, B explained, "I have the work, 2 vols folio, and read it right through when I was a boy,—my Father gave it me many years after" (Peterson, 101). The brevity of Collier's entry on Shakespeare—B quotes about one sixth of it—suggests the low state of his reputation in the late seventeenth century. Given the personal element in *Ferishtah's Fancies*, the quotation may have been intended by B as self-description.

In the passage quoted from *King Lear*, 3.6.78-81, Lear is attempting to enlist the loyalty of Gloucester's son Edgar, who is disguised as a madman and wearing only a blanket (see 3.4.65). Because Persian costume was considered elaborate and exotic, Lear's comment constitutes absurd comedy. This, and indeed much of the third act of *King Lear*, illustrates rather the reverse of the comment quoted from Collier: the seriously disturbing disintegration of Lear's mind is punctuated by flashes of manic wit. But the occurrence of the word *Persian* was perhaps sufficient reason for B to choose the lines.

The use of these epigraphs may have resulted from B's having seen *King Lear* about the time he was completing the MS of *Ferishtah's Fancies*. On Saturday, 1 March 1884, he saw the eminent Italian tragedian Tommaso Salvini play Lear in London, in a performance he called "magnificent." B knew Salvini personally, and attended more of his Shakespeare productions that season, including *Othello* and *Hamlet* (see DeVane and Knickerbocker, 298-301 and nn.; McAleer, *LL*, 13; Hood, *Ltrs.*, 228).

PROLOGUE

Date] The MS of the "Prologue" is dated 12 September 1883; it was probably written after some of the other poems in the volume. See *Composition* above.

1] *ortolans* The Ortolan bunting (*Emberiza hortulana*) is a small (6.5 in.) seed-eating bird of eastern and southern Europe. Ortolans migrate in large flocks in autumn; though protected today, huge numbers of them were once netted, force-fed, and fattened for human consumption. Considered a delicacy, they were plucked, roasted, and eaten whole, bones and all.

38] *Gressoney* The village of Gressoney St. Jean, where B sojourned in 1883 and 1885, lies high in the Val d'Aosta in the Italian Alps, 18 mi. S of the Matterhorn. He described it as "the most beautiful little cluster of cottages nested in a valley" and "a paradise of coolness and quiet, shut in by the Alps" (DeVane and Knickerbocker, 288; Peterson, 74). A substantial portion of *Ferishtah's Fancies* was written during the five weeks B spent in Gressoney (see *Composition* above).

THE EAGLE

Composition] In the MS, the lyric (ll. 36-47) is continuous with the body of the poem, on the same leaf. After the rule following l. 35, B has instructed in the margin, "(Print in smaller type)" referring to the 12 lines that follow. He refers back to this instruction throughout the rest of the MS with the phrase "(Print as before)."

Source] In Mrs. Orr's copy of *Ferishtah's Fancies*, B wrote at the end of "The Eagle": "This is from Pilpay's Fables: I read it when a boy and lately put it into verse: then it occurred to me to make the Dervish one Ferishtah, and the poem the beginning of a series" (*1884O*, 7). DeVane (*Hbk.*, 478-79) speculates that B read an 1818 collection of *Fables of Pilpay*, but it is equally possible that the poet or his father owned an earlier copy of the popular *Instructive and Entertaining Fables of Pilpay*, translated by Joseph Harris, which went through six editions between 1699 and 1789. *The Fables of Pilpay* and *The Fables of Bidpai* are titles given by Europeans to a diverse collection of beast-fables, folk-tales, and proverbs that originated in India in the fourth century A. D. and spread throughout the ancient world. It was translated into Arabic (as *Kalila wa Dimna*) in the eighth century, and into Persian (with the title *Anwari Suhaili*) four centuries later. By the seventeenth century the

Fables were among the most popular books in Europe, having been translated into Greek, Latin, German, Italian, and French. One of the French versions was the basis for Harris's English edition. The tale B remembered appears as the third story in the second of the fifteen sections of the *Fables*; he changed a few details, but retained the essentials. Taking the feeding of the raven chick by the eagle (a hawk in the original) as proof that God will provide for the faithful, the Dervish fasts for three days. He starves himself to the point of inanition, at which point God offers him not food but correction: " if thou canst be the means of imparting advantage to another, it is better than to be obliged to be succoured by others. Be like the hawk—the quarry chase, and food to others give."

1] *Dervish* A member of one of the mystical Sufi sects of Islam. Though B must have known that Dervishes seek direct contact with and revelation from Allah, in Ferishtah he emphasizes their sublunary attributes, such as asceticism, calmness, indifference to material things, and a taste for witty parables. To become a Dervish involves a long process of training, education, and prayer.

5] *Ferishtah* In his annotations for Mrs. Orr and G. B. Smith, B defined his speaker's name as "Fairy" (*P1884, 1884O,* 5). In classical Persian the word *firishta* means "angel," "messenger," or "apostle" (F. J. Steingass, *A Comprehensive Persian-English Dictionary*). B may also have known of the Muslim historian named Ferishtah (c.1560–c.1620), whose four-volume *History of the Rise of the Mohamedan Power in India* was translated into English in 1829. But B thought of his Ferishtah as fictional: "There was no such a person as Ferishtah, the stories are all inventions," he wrote to G. B. Smith (19 October 1884; Browning Database, ABL, 84:221). Sources aside, B's Ferishtah is widely recognized as a spokesman for the poet himself (see *Sources and Background* above).

A few weeks before the volume was published, B happily forwarded to F. J. Furnivall an epigram by J. D. Williams which observed that the transliteration of "Ferishtah" into Greek yielded a meaning of "the best" (Peterson, 103-104).

35] *Ispahan* Today called Isfahan (or Esfahan), capital city of Esfahan province in central Iran. Shah Abbas I (see "Shah Abbas" below) made Isfahan his capital city in the 16th century and built grand palaces, mosques, and gardens there. The city became, and continues to be, a center for the weaving of fine carpets. B may have remembered the name from the popular romance *The Adventures of Hajji Baba of Ispahan* (1824) by J. J. Morier.

THE MELON-SELLER

Source]   B explained to Mrs. Orr: "This incident I read of in a letter from the 'Times' correspondent many years ago" (*18840*, 9). His remarkable memory was at work here, since he first mentioned the tale of the disgraced high official in a letter to EBB dated 6 August 1846. B tells her of an unrelated incident reported in the *Times* and adds:

> How strange—and a few weeks ago I read, in the same paper, a letter from Constantinople—wherein the writer mentioned that he had seen (I think, that morning) Pacha somebody, whose malpractices had just drawn down on him the Sultan's vengeance, and who had been left with barely his life,—having lost his immense treasures, palaces and gardens &c along with his dignity,—the writer saw this old man selling slices of melon on a bridge in the city,— and on stopping in wonderment to praise such constancy, the Turk asked him with at least equal astonishment, whether it was not fitter to praise Allah who had lent him such wealth for forty years, than to repine that he had judged right to recall it now?
>
> (*Correspondence*, 13.232)

The original report, in the *Times* or elsewhere, has proved elusive; but nearly forty years later, B found the right poetic occasion for this bit of inspiration. An interesting parallel instance of the "long and obscure process" of B's "mental digestion" involves the source-story for "Donald," in *Jocoseria*.

1]   *Ispahan*   See "The Eagle," l. 35n. above.

2]   *Dervishhood*   See "The Eagle," l. 1n. above.

11]   *Shah*   The Persian word for *king*.

21]   *hell from heaven*   Recalling the fall of Lucifer (Isa. 14:12, Lk. 10:18) and other angels, rendered memorably in the first two books of Milton's *Paradise Lost* (1667).

34-35]   *Nishapur. . . Elburz . . . turquoise*   The ancient city of Nishapur (modern Neyshabur) in NE Iran was an important trading center on the Silk Road. It was the home of the poet Omar Khayyâm (1048-1122), whose *Rubáiyát* became immensely popular in the translation of Edward FitzGerald (see *Sources and Background* above). Near Nishapur is the vast Elburz mountain range, where turquoise is still mined.

39-42]   האלהים . . . *receive?"*   In his notes for Mrs. Orr, B provided the A.V. translation of these words from Job 2:10: "Shall we receive good at the hand of God and shall we not receive evil?" (*18840*,12). To G. B. Smith he sent a different version of what he added in the second edition of *Ferishtah's Fancies* (1885): "Shall we receive good from the hand of the Lord, and not receive evil?" (*P1884*, 12). The melon-seller's message of acceptance accords well with both the book of Job and the anecdote in B's letter of 1846 (see *Source* above).

SHAH ABBAS

Composition]   In the Balliol MS, the poem is entitled "Belief"; the MS appears to have been fair-copied and then revised further. Though B indicated to Mrs. Orr that his Shah Abbas was invented (*1884O*, 14), at least three Persian kings (or Shahs) bore this name. Shah Abbas I (1557–1629) ruled all of Persia from Isfahan, a city mentioned elsewhere in *Ferishtah's Fancies*. The incident of the spider appears to be B's creation.

1]   *full Dervish*   See "The Eagle," l. 1n. above.

3]   *Nishapur*   See "The Melon-Seller," ll. 34-35n. above.

6]   *Lord Ali*   Ali ibn Abi Talib (c. 599-661 A. D.), cousin and son-in-law of the Prophet Muhammad. B would have remembered that Ali is affectionately praised by Carlyle in the second lecture of *On Heroes and Hero-Worship and the Heroic in History*, which B had heard delivered in 1840 (Irvine and Honan, 84).

8-10]   *'It is . . . beauty'*   Transformations of Keats's "Beauty is truth, truth beauty" ("Ode on a Grecian Urn," 49).

47]   *Yakub . . . Yusuf . . . Zal*   The names of Feristah's interlocutor and his father are common enough, but in *The Epic of Kings* the great knight Zal is the father of the hero Rustem (chap. 3-5; Zimmern, 39-84, passim).

63]   *twelve dinars*   A small fine; the copper dinar of Persia was the lowest denomination coin in circulation. (The word *dinar* was also used in ancient times for an Arabian gold coin of much greater value, but B seems to mean a small amount of money, both here and in "A Pillar at Sebzevar," below.)

81]   *Tahmasp*   B stated that the story of Tahmasp, Zurah, and the snake was his own invention (*1884O*, 19), but his spelling of the name as *Thamasp* (in MS-1885) suggests that he took the name from *The Epic of Kings*, where it appears in passing (chap. 5; Zimmern, 73). The change in spelling to *Tahmasp* was recommended by C. J. Lyall (see *Text and Publication* above). Historically, Tahmasp I (1514-76) was an important Shah of Persia.

84]   *Zurah*   More commonly spelled *Zuhrah*; the Arabic name for the planet Venus, as B knew (see "A Bean-Stripe," ll. 438n., below, and *1884O*, 136).

86] *nine heads* The serpentine Hydra of Greek mythology, slain by Hercules as his second labor, had nine heads, but no Persian equivalent has been traced.

89] *Day of Judgment* The eschatological concept of a final judgment by God, after which all souls are placed eternally in heaven or hell, is a fundamental tenet of both Christianity (see Matt. 25: 31-34, 41, 46) and Islam (in which it is known as Qiyâmah).

99] *Ishak son of Absal* Again, B states that the names and incident are invented (*1884O*, 20), but he probably took the name *Absal* from the Persian allegory *Salámán and Absál* by the Sufi poet Jami (1414-92). It was translated into English by Edward FitzGerald and published several times between 1856 and 1883; from 1879 onward it was included with his *Rubáiyát of Omar Khayyám* (see *Sources and Background* above).

102] *Yezdt* The ancient Persian city of Yezd (or Yazd) is located in central Iran; though the area of Yazd was fought over many times, B does not apparently allude to any particular battle or war.

107] *Mubid* A Zoroastrian priest; in *The Epic of Kings* they figure as counsellors, magicians, astrologers, and seers.

THE FAMILY

Title] In the Balliol MS, the poem bears the title "The Father's Family."

4] *Gudarz* The name of an aged ally of Rustem's in the *Epic of Kings* (chap. 8; Zimmern, 143).

22] *a tale* B noted in Mrs. Orr's copy that this story is his invention (*1884O*, 26).

23] *Shiraz* A grand and ancient city in SW Iran.

26] *leech* Physician (the term derives from the old practice of using leeches for bloodletting).

51, 57] *Hakim* In Persian and Arabic, the word for physician is *Hakim*. C. J. Lyall (see *Text and Publication* above) objected that B's scansion produced an erroneous emphasis on the first syllable, but B did not choose to revise in this case.

THE SUN

Title] In the Balliol MS, B entitled this poem "Incarnation."

18-20] *During . . . Yon orb* The benign god in Zoroastrianism, the religion of Persia before Islam, was Ormuzd (Ahura Mazda), a sun-god.

43-48] *Go up . . . prime giver* An iteration of B's heirarchical view of the universe, deriving as much from the Great Chain of Being as from 19th-century evolutionary thought.

59] *Sheikh, Shah* As a *sheikh* was the senior official of a village or extended family, he was subservient to a *Shah*, or king, who ruled a much larger territory.

70] *tomans* The toman was a Persian coin worth ten thousand dinars (see "Shah Abbas," l. 63n. above).

91] *Prime cause this fire shall be* In Western thought, the elevation of fire as primal substance is associated with the Greek philosopher Heraclitus (fl. c. 500 B.C.); but B may have made the common error of believing that Zoroastrians were fire-worshippers.

113, 115] *A stone . . . curing drouth* It is a common folk belief that certain stones, particularly agates, cure thirst if placed in the mouth.

MIHRAB SHAH

Title] In the Balliol MS, this poem is entitled "Pain." The MS is heavily reworked throughout; the added lyric concludes on the verso of the last leaf. In this part of the MS, B changed his page numbering, indicating rearrangement, deletion, or addition. Though B stated to Mrs. Orr that Mihrab was his invention (*1884O*, 56), King Mihrab of Cabul (Kabul, Afghanistan) appears in *The Epic of Kings* (chap. 4; Zimmern, 41ff.).

17] *pure of evil . . . deed* Ferishtah's enquirer echoes the wording of the "General Confession" in the Anglican *Book of Common Prayer*, which acknowledges sins committed in "thought, word, and deed."

27] *Firdausi's tale* There are hundreds of beheadings in Firdausi's *Epic of Kings* (see *Sources and Background* above), but none in which a head falls off unchopped. Presumably the "inquirer" (l. 1) intends "Firdausi's tale" to be figurative of the incredible. In MS-1885, B spelled the name *Firdusi*; the change was suggested by C. J. Lyall (see *Text and Publication* above).

64] *pipe-stick* The small wooden tube used as the stem of a clay tobacco pipe (*OED*, s.v. "pipe" 11.b).

80] *belled* The hood and jesses worn by a trained hunting falcon are often decorated with small bells.

81] *Simorgh* In Persian mythology, the Simurgh (Simurg, Simorgh) is a huge immortal bird with magical powers; in *The Epic of Kings* it rescues and nurtures Zal, the father of the hero Rustem (chap. 3, 17; Zimmern, 33ff., 314ff.). B described it to Mrs. Orr and G. B. Smith as a "fabulous creature" (*1884O* & *P1884*, 52).

91-92] *leech . . . Tebriz* For *leech,* see "The Family," l. 26n. above; Tebriz is an ancient city in Azerbaijan, near the border with Iran.
130] *Mihrab Shah* See *Title* above.

A CAMEL-DRIVER

1] *Pilgrims* Presumably Muslims on their holy pilgrimage to Mecca; B indicated to Mrs. Orr that he invented the story (*1884O,* 59)
6] *sawn asunder* This was the grisly manner of death for the legendary Persian king Jemshid (*The Epic of Kings,* chap. 1; Zimmern, 6).
13] *fled to Syria* I.e., far away to the W, across several borders.
29] *Rakhsh* As B explained to Mrs Orr and G. B. Smith, this is the name of a horse in the *Shah Nemeh* (*1884O & P1884,* 61). In *The Epic of Kings* (chap. 5; Zimmern, 75-76), the hero Rustem acquires the remarkable horse Rakush (Raks, Reksh, Rakhsh; the name means "lightning"), which is not only obedient to his hand, but shows considerable intelligence. In MS-1885, B spelled the horse's name *Ruksh*; the change to *Rakhsh* was suggested by C. J. Lyall (see *Text and Publication* above).
51] *twy-prong* A two-tined fork (*OED,* s.v. "twi-" e., with B providing the only examples).
53] *noddle* A disparaging term for the head, with the imputation of foolishness.
55] *as voluble as Rakhsh* In *The Epic of Kings,* Rustem's horse repeatedly awakens the hero when danger threatens; Rustem learns to trust such warnings ("The March into Mazinderan," ch. 6; Zimmern, 94-99).
60] *playsomeness* Playfulness.
81] *snatch-grace* One who seizes an opportunity to elude punishment; *OED* cites this line as the sole instance.

TWO CAMELS

Composition] The extensive revision and the cancelled date at l. 64 in the MS indicate two stages of composition. Besides renumbering the MS leaves, B added ll. 82-96 on a verso and ll. 97-108 on an inserted part-leaf.
27] *Nishapur to Sebzevar* A westward journey of about 50 mi. For Nishapur, see "The Melon-Seller," ll. 34-35n.; *Sebzevar,* modern Sabzevar, is a city in NE Iran, and the trade center of a region noted for weaving and rug-making. In MS-1885, B spelled the name *Sebzevah*; the

change here and elsewhere was recommended by C. J. Lyall (see *Text and Publication* above).

35] *Grass, purslane, lupines* Like the *chervil* of l. 46, plants not suitable for the gramnivorous camel.

43] *simooms* Hot, dry, sand-laden desert winds (in Arabic *simoom* means "poison wind).

58] *good-and-faithful-servant* In recounting the praise of the camel, Ferishtah, perhaps unexpectedly, quotes from Jesus's parable of the talents (Matt. 25:21, 23).

64] *Lilith* In Talmudic legend, Lilith is the name of Adam's first wife, but here B seems to use it simply as an exotic female name. He had used the name in a similarly unspecific way in "Adam, Lilith, and Eve," in *Jocoseria*.

88-90] *The Adversary said . . . naught?'* In the Bible, "The Adversary" is a name for Satan, and also the literal meaning of *satan* in Hebrew. The Hebrew of l. 89 is from Job 9:1, which B translates in l. 90. B provided English pronunciation and the translation in his notes for Mrs. Orr and G. B. Smith (*1884O & P1884*, 75). He explained to Mary Gladstone in a letter of 19 May 1885: "The putting in of a bit of Hebrew was a mere piece of fun: I have heard so often, these fifty years, that all I wrote was absolutely unintelligible, that I meant to submit to my critics that one form of speech must be as easily understood by their intelligence as another."

95] *A proper . . .* מאלהים The Hebrew means "from God," and "proper" is used with ironic scorn as Ferishtah invents an indifferent deity. The god of the Book of Job makes it apparent that he and Job are anything but equal in knowledge or power (Job 38-41). B gave the English translation in his notes for Mrs. Orr and G. B. Smith (*1884O & P1884*, 75).

105-8] *Wherefore did I . . . me play?* As one of the earliest Western instruments, the lyre is emblematic of music itself. B often represented music—both the appreciation and the creation of it—as a divine gift, and the assertion that human beings are meant to enjoy life's pleasures is commonplace in his poetry.

seven-stringed instrument Ancient lyres from around the Mediterranean basin were often seven-stringed instruments (though the earliest ones had only four strings); B may have seen ancient lyres and harps in the British Museum or in Paris or Rome.

CHERRIES

Composition] In the Balliol MS, this poem bears the title "Gratitude." The numerous revisions and additions indicate that this is the compositional MS. A date (15 January 1885) at l. 101 was cancelled and replaced by B's instruction, "(Print as before)."

9] *great and small* Perhaps recalling Coleridge, *The Rime of the Ancient Mariner*, "He prayeth best who loveth best / All things both great and small" (pt. 7, st. 23).

19] *Star-King Mushtari* The Arabic and Persian name for the planet Jupiter is *Mushtarie*, known in Babylonian, Roman, and Chinese astronomy as the king of stars. Mushtari is also mentioned in the *Rubáiyát*, st. 75 (see *Sources and Background* above). B identified the reference in his notes for Mrs. Orr and G. B. Smith (*1884O & P1884*, 79).

24] *Ispahan palace-gate* See "The Eagle," l. 35n. above.

75] *Mushtari . . . seven times seven* For *Mushtari*, see l. 19n. above. "Seven times seven" is formulaic for a large quantity, and is particularly appropriate here because Jupiter is one of the seven "stars" recognized by the ancients (Saturn, Jupiter, Mars, the Sun, the Moon,Venus, and Mercury).

80] *twinks* Twinkles; not a B coinage, though he provides a citation in the *OED*.

88-89] *Dust thou art, / Dust shalt be* See the Anglican *Book of Common Prayer*, "Burial of the Dead": "Earth to earth, ashes to ashes, dust to dust."

101] *Mushtari* Jupiter; see l. 19n. above.

PLOT-CULTURE

Composition] The MS is heavily revised; B appears to have composed through l. 58 by 17 January 1884. He later added ll. 59-60, cancelled the date, and instructed the printer to "(Leave room for a small poem's insertion here)." There remained enough room on the leaf for the lyric ("Not with my Soul, Love"), but it was added considerably later, when *Ferishtah's Fancies* was in proof. There is no MS of these sixteen lines, which are taken by B's biographers as a response to Mrs. Bloomfield-Moore's profession of her "soul love" for the poet while he was her guest in Switzerland. Since her declaration occurred before she left St. Moritz on 2 or 3 September 1884, and since B sent what he took to be his "final proofs" to London on 8 September, the concluding lyric of "Plot-Culture" must have been composed in that week and included with the proofs. (See DeVane, *Hbk.*, 487; Irvine and Honan, 493; DeVane and Knickerbocker, 307-8; McAleer, *LL*, 181-83; B. Miller, *Robert Browning: A Portrait* [New York, 1953], 286-88).

2] *twinks* See "Cherries," l. 80n. above.

3] *arrides* Pleases or amuses.

23] *deed, word, thought* The disciple reverses the phrasing of the "General Confession" of the *Book of Common Prayer* (see "Mihrab Shah," l. 17n. above).

A PILLAR AT SEBSEVAR

Title] In the Balliol MS, the poem is entitled "A Pillar at Khorasan," referring to the large province in NE Iran where Sebzevar is located; see "Two Camels," l. 27n. above.

76] *a certain pillar* The pillar sun-dial appears to be B's invention.

86] *Hudhud* The name of the hoopoe (*Upupa epops*; the Arabic name for the bird is *hudhud*) that carries messages between King Solomon and the Queen of Sheba. Hudhud appears in Jewish, Arabian, and Persian folklore. Identified as the "fabulous bird of Solomon" in B's notes for Mrs. Orr and G. B. Smith (*1884O & P1884*, 99).

91] *Mushtari* Jupiter; see "Cherries," l. 19n. above.

124] *visible . . . invisible* Echoing Col. 1:16, "by him were all things created, that are in heaven, and that are in earth, visible and invisible."

146] *dinar* See "Shah Abbas," l. 63n. above.

147] *Sitara* The Persian word for "star," as explained by B in his notes for Mrs. Orr and G. B. Smith (*1884O & P1884*, 103).

A BEAN-STRIPE; ALSO APPLE-EATING

Composition] The Balliol MS of this poem appears to be the original draft, and though it is extensively revised in many places, it is also illustrative of B's facility in versification at this stage of his career. The first 77 lines are almost as clear as fair copy, with only occasional revisions, suggesting that the opening of the poem was written at a single sitting. The next nearly 200 lines, representing a second round of composition, are more heavily altered, and the revisions give the sense of having been done quickly, as the writing proceeded. Lines 264-70 appear on a half-leaf, the lower portion of which seems to have been torn off. The next 100 lines of the poem are extensively revised, except for the last twelve lines (353-64), which at this stage concluded the poem. Later, B added the *Apple-Eating* section, comprising 113 lines on five separately-numbered and fair-copied leaves. His instruction to the printer at the top of the first leaf, "Insert this, page 126, after 'In fancy, if it take a flight so far,'" signifies that the additional MS was submitted separately, after B had a set of page-proofs of the volume before him. The early proofs lacked some of the lyrics appended to other poems: in the later Harvard proofs, the "Apple-Eating" insertion would begin on p. 130, not 126. Though the last leaf of the inserted section ends with the instruction "Go on to Epilogue page 127," it is in fact followed in the MS by the lyric, "'Why from the world,'" on its own unnumbered leaf. This too must have been submitted to the compositors separately and gathered back into the Balliol MS after publication.

17] *the Indian Sage* I. e., the Buddha (Siddhartha Gautama, ca. 623-543 B. C.), viewed by many Victorians as a voice of philosophical pessimism (see *Sources and Background* above).

38] *bolder critics of the Primal Cause* Ferishtah's interlocutor (the scholar of l. 2) modestly distinguishes himself from pessimistic philosophers and skeptical intellectuals engaged in the Higher Criticism. (See *Sources and Background* above. For additional background on B's theology, see "Christmas-Eve and Easter-Day," this edition, 5.49-133, 340-49.)

91] *was and is . . . evermore* Echoing the Anglican *Book of Common Prayer*, "Gloria Patri": "As it was in the beginning, is now, and ever shall be, world without end."

150] *palm-aphis* B gives an accurate description of the restricted life of the palm aphid (*Cerataphis palmae*), a tiny insect native to SW Asia.

202] *disintensify* To make less intense (*OED*, with this usage as the only example).

239] *over-mounts* Beyond the mountains (*OED*, with B providing the only examples).

251-52] *sourly-Sage, / The Indian witness* The Buddha (see l. 17n. above).

270] *Liked . . . his dinner* Chinese and Indian representations of the Laughing Buddha emphasize his corpulence.

297-98] *Ahriman . . . Ormuzd* Supernatural beings in Zoroastrianism, the religion of Persia until the 7th century A. D. Zoroastrianism posits a dualism in all existence: all things beneficial to humanity are created by Ahura Mazda (or Ormuzd), and all things detrimental to humanity are the creations of Ahriman.

329-33] *"How reconcile . . . intelligence?"* In the MS and 1884, these lines are spoken by Ferishtah.

336] *Ispahan* See "The Eagle," l. 35n. above.

391, 421] *Shalim-Shah . . . Shahan-Shah* B explained to Mrs. Orr and G. B. Smith that the epithet means "King of Kings" (*18840 & P1884*, 132); both spellings are acceptable transliterations from the Persian. No reference to the familiar Biblical use of the phrase "king of kings"

(1 Tim. 6:15 and Rev. 19:16) seems intended. In the MS and the first edition, B. uses the spelling "Shalim-Shah" in both instances, though in Mrs Orr's copy of the first edition he altered the reading in l. 391 to"Shahin-Shah" (*1884O*, 132); no such change was made in the second edition. C. J. Lyall recommended that B change the spelling in l. 421 to "Shahan-Shah," but made no mention of the parallel instance in l. 391. When correcting for the third edition, B altered l. 421 as suggested by Lyall, and left an inconsistency by ignoring l. 391.

422, 425-26]   *Rustem and Gew, Gudarz . . . Sindokht . . . Sulayman . . . Kawah*   As B noted for Mrs. Orr and G. B. Smith, most of these are heroes in Firdausi's *Shah Nameh*, the *Epic of Kings* (*1884O* & *P1884*, 135). The gifts of Queen Sindokht (chap. 3) are moral and intellectual; Kawah is valiant in defying the evil Shah Zohak (chap. 1). Though King Solomon (*Sulayman*) is not mentioned in the *Epic of Kings*, his sagacity is attested to in both Biblical and Persian tradition.

438]   *Seven Thrones, Zurah's beauty, wierd Parwin*   Persian astronomers termed the constellation Ursa Major (in English, the Great Bear, Big Dipper, or Charles's Wain) "the Seven Thrones." The collection of seven epic poems by Jami which contained *Salámán and Absál* (see "Shah Abbas," l. 20n. above) was entitled *Haft Aurang* (*The Seven Thrones, or Ursa Major*). As in European tradition, Persian astronomy associated Venus (*Zuhrah*; see "Shah Abbas," l. 84n. above) with female beauty.

Parwin is the Persian name for the Pleiades, a group of stars in the constellation Taurus; the Persian name appears in the *Rubáiyát*, st. 75. How Parwin is *weird* is not obvious, but the Pleiades are also known as the Seven Sisters, and B may have produced the adjective from a recollection of Shakespeare's Weird Sisters (*Macbeth* 3.1.32). B provides the English names for the three heavenly bodies in his notes for Mrs. Orr and G. B. Smith (*1884O* & *P1884*, 136).

440]   *Mubid*   See "Shah Abbas," l. 107n. above.

452-54]   *let the stars . . . both were blank*   Ferishtah imputes to his interlocutor the solipsism associated with British empiricist philosophers such as George Berkeley and David Hume.

462]   *Fomalhaut . . . fen-fire*   The brightest star in the constellation Piscis Austrinus is named Fomalhaut; B terms it simply "a great star" in a note to G. B. Smith (*P1884*, 137). *Fen-fire* is another name for *ignis fatuus* (Latin for "foolish fire") or "will-o'-the-wisp," a faint glow sometimes seen over marshes and bogs.

472]   *Zerdusht*   The name used in Firdausi's *Epic of Kings* for Zoroaster, founder of the old religion of Persia (see ll. 297-98n. above); identified in B's notes for Mrs. Orr and G. B. Smith (*1884O* & *P1884*, 138)

477] *gall-nuts* The quite inedible swellings produced on trees by certain parasitic insects.

EPILOGUE

Date] In the Balliol MS the "Epilogue" is a fair copy dated "Venice, Dec. 1. '83"; it was not, however, the last part of *Ferishtah's Fancies* to be written. See above, *Composition*; "Plot-Culture"; and "A Bean-Stripe: Also, Apple-Eating."

27] *late enchantment* B may have recalled the well-known evocation of Oxford University in the Preface of Matthew Arnold's *Essays in Criticism* (1865): "steeped in sentiment as she lies, spreading her gardens to the moonlight, and whispering from her towers the last enchantments of the Middle Age" (*The Complete Prose Works of Matthew Arnold*, ed. R. H. Super [Ann Arbor, 1960-77], 3.290).